Speaking with the Dead
in Early America

EARLY AMERICAN STUDIES

Series editors:
Daniel K. Richter, Kathleen M. Brown,
Max Cavitch, and David Waldstreicher

Exploring neglected aspects of our colonial,
revolutionary, and early national history and culture,
Early American Studies reinterprets familiar themes
and events in fresh ways. Interdisciplinary in character,
and with a special emphasis on the period from about
1600 to 1850, the series is published in partnership with
the McNeil Center for Early American Studies.

A complete list of books in the series
is available from the publisher.

SPEAKING
with the
DEAD
in
EARLY
AMERICA

Erik R. Seeman

PENN

UNIVERSITY OF PENNSYLVANIA PRESS

PHILADELPHIA

Published by
University of Pennsylvania Press
Philadelphia, Pennsylvania 19104-4112
www.upenn.edu/pennpress

Printed in the United States of America on acid-free paper
1 3 5 7 9 10 8 6 4 2

Library of Congress Cataloging-in-Publication Data
ISBN 978-0-8122-5153-1

In memory of
Ernest Barany (1925–2016)
The Ghost

CONTENTS

ILLUSTRATIONS

Speaking with the Dead

Woodbridge, New Jersey, September 2016. The First Presbyterian Church is straight out of Central Casting: white brick, Greek Revival pediment, soaring steeple piercing the steel-gray sky. At the front of the sanctuary my grandfather, Ernest Barany, is sealed inside a gunmetal casket, its color recalling the U.S.S. *Becuna* he served on in World War II. Because my grandfather was active in this church for decades the place is full, and because he lived well for ninety-one years the eulogists adopt a tone of fond reminiscence rather than unspeakable loss. One man shares stories from the days when Ernie was the star running back on the high school team, known to everyone as "The Ghost" for the way he floated across the field, eluding all tacklers. The youngest eulogist, my twenty-something cousin Katie Rose Barany, rises to speak. "I didn't really plan anything, but I want to share something with you. I'm a millennial, so it's on my phone." She explains that when she used to go to Bible camp every summer, Ernie never forgot to call on her birthday. One time he left a voice mail, and she has kept it over the years, transferring it from phone to phone. She swipes a few times. "Let's see if this works." She holds the phone up to the mic. "Hi, Katie, this is Grandpa." The audience gasps. "We want to wish you a very, very happy birthday. And we hope to see you when you get back, I'm sorry we missed you now, okay?"[1] Dozens of tissues rustle. We weren't expecting to hear Ernie speak today.

　　Watervliet, New York, spring 1843. The young Shaker woman lies peacefully on a bier. Family members and friends gaze upon the corpse, praying and singing as they say their final farewells. The service, held in the family's house and marked by religion, sentiment, and attention to the dead body, could be the funeral of any white Protestant in antebellum America. Until, that is, one of the female Shakers standing next to the corpse suddenly becomes "as it were *entranced*, and announce[s] herself to be the *Spirit of the departed one*," in the words of a sympathetic outside observer. Adopting "a voice sweetly modulated," the visionist comforts the gathered mourners. The deceased woman tells her loved ones that they too can expect to go to heaven when they die. "When the time comes for you to cast off the perishable clay," she says, "your freed spirit will fly to realms of bliss." She also brings a more startling message: "I am not dead." She elaborates that "though my spirit is released from the cold and inanimate clay which lies there, and which it lately inhabited, I am still in your midst." Her spirit, to everyone's delight, will remain a presence among the living.[2]

Dorchester, Massachusetts, January 1668. Mourners stand in the grave-yard, near the simple meetinghouse that dominates the town's public life, and gather around Lydia Minot's closed coffin. The thirty-seven-year-old woman has recently died delivering her sixth child. Minot's husband, children, min-ister, and many others prepare to watch the sexton lower the coffin into the hole he has prepared. But first, someone unfolds a sheet of paper and reads an elegy. Puritans worry that a funeral sermon might seem too much like a Cath-olic Mass for the dead, but they consider a poem an appropriate way to pay tribute to the deceased and inculcate piety among the bereaved. Standing in close proximity to the corpse, the speaker offers eighteen lines of Minot's imagined words from heaven, which reveal tantalizing details about the af-terlife: "New Robes I have, new Company, new Skill / To sing th'new Song."[3] She is wearing new garments, among new friends, singing the song to the Lord that Psalm 96 describes. The mourners' Calvinist faith tells them they can't be sure Minot is in heaven, but on this day they choose to overlook that, reas-sured by Minot's imagined voice.

Three funerals across more than three centuries, among three religious groups that trace their lineage back to the Protestant Reformation. The dead speak in all three. But wasn't the Reformation supposed to end communica-tion between the living and dead?

It turns out the answer to that question is more complicated than histo-rians have realized. Yes, the Protestant Reformation dramatically reconceived the relationship between the living and dead. In late medieval Catholicism, mourners employed an array of practices to maintain connections with the deceased. Crucial to this was belief in purgatory, a middle place between heaven and hell, where the vast majority of souls went to experience purgation—cleansing by fire—before ascending to heaven. While in purgatory, souls could be helped by the actions of the living: saying prayers, paying for Masses, endowing chantries where priests did the praying. The living could also maintain relationships with saints—the "very special dead," in one historian's phrase—by praying to them, sometimes aided by proximity to the saints' bodily remains, and asking the dead to intercede with Christ on the petitioner's behalf.[4]

In the early sixteenth century, the Reformation abolished purgatory and the veneration of saints. Protestants could no longer help their loved ones' souls in the afterlife and they could no longer enlist the aid of the very special dead. As one recent, comprehensive history of the Reformation puts it, "Protestantism stripped religion of mediation and intimacy with the dead."[5]

At least in theory. In practice, Protestants proved not quite so willing to abandon the relationships with the dead to which they had long been accustomed. The dead, for example, continued to return as ghosts: not just right after the Reformation but in all three centuries this book covers. The theology of ghosts changed—for Protestants, they could no longer be souls returned from purgatory—but ghosts remained a way that laypeople and ministers continued to imagine interacting with the dead. But whereas some people believed their ghost sightings were real, other ways of thinking about the dead were understood to be in the realm of imagination. When people wrote poems that portrayed the dead speaking, or sang songs addressed to the dead, or spoke to portraits of their deceased loved ones, they did not think they were actually communicating with the dead. Nonetheless, Protestants eagerly interacted with the dead through imaginative literature and material culture because doing so fulfilled their desires to continue thinking about their loved ones. This was how the living maintained some aspects of the relationships they had shared with people now dead.[6]

Thus it is important to pay attention to the differences among the three funerals that open this book. All three involved the speaking dead, but only in the Shaker funeral did participants think the deceased was actually communicating with them. When Lydia Minot's family members listened to the poet ventriloquize her, they did not think the elegist was privy to some divine communication. Nor were my family members confused by the source of my grandfather's voice; we didn't think he was actually talking to us. But my experience of that moment's power—the sobs it elicited from me and others—leads me, in an act of historical empathy, to infer that the puritans who gathered around Minot's coffin felt a connection with her when the poet spoke in her voice. You don't need to take my word for it, though. My informants will repeatedly attest, through their actions and writings, that communication with the dead was deeply meaningful, even when it was understood to be imagined.

I discovered this neglected aspect of Protestant belief and practice—this desire for continuing relations with the dead—when I tried to answer what I thought was a straightforward question: Where did séance Spiritualism come from? Or more precisely, How did Spiritualism gain so many adherents so quickly? I had long been struck by how both historians and contemporaries portray Spiritualism as exploding like a supernova in the 1850s, seemingly without warning. After the Fox Sisters of Hydesville, New York, began to interpret the rappings of a spirit in 1848, and especially after they demonstrated their supernatural talents on stage in New York City two years later, legions of Americans tried to communicate with deceased loved ones. As the New York lawyer George Templeton Strong wrote in 1855, "What would I have said six years ago to anybody who predicted that before the enlightened nineteenth century was ended hundreds of thousands of people in this country would believe themselves able to communicate with the ghosts of their grandfathers?"[7] While largely avoiding Strong's condescension, scholars have echoed his astonishment, portraying Spiritualism as a dramatic and surprising break with the past. It was a movement, according to one historian's estimate, that had millions of followers within a decade of its founding.[8]

Even if Spiritualists exaggerated about "millions" of adherents, this seemed a question worthy of investigation. How does a new religion go from zero to many hundreds of thousands of participants in less than a decade? So I began this book as a "prehistory" of Spiritualism, looking for its roots in American culture. I soon became dissatisfied with the answers that historians have offered. Confining themselves largely to the two or three decades before 1848, most scholars point to a short list of antecedents: Emanuel Swedenborg, the Swedish mystic who spoke with angels; the Shakers and their practice of spirit communication; the American incarnation of Mesmerism, which emerged in the late 1830s; and the trance healer Andrew Jackson Davis, the "Poughkeepsie Seer," who gained widespread notoriety in the late 1840s.[9]

These sources all undoubtedly helped pave the way for Spiritualism; they all promoted communication between this world and heaven; all will receive their due in *Speaking with the Dead*. But could such marginal sources really explain Spiritualism's broad appeal? As late as 1840, the Swedenborgian New Church in America claimed only 850 members. There were a few thousand Shakers, a handful of Mesmerist magazines, and (to the relief of many) only one Poughkeepsie Seer. In fact, for Shakers and other new denominations the influence actually ran in the opposite direction: rather than teaching main-stream Protestants how to speak with the dead, Shakers and Mormons and Swedenborgians built on the preexisting interest in maintaining relationships with the dead.

The more I looked, the more I found that communication with the dead appeared in virtually every genre of source I examined. For the nineteenth century, I found the practice represented in parlor songs, funeral hymns, letters, diaries, and sentimental poems. I turned to earlier sources and found speaking with the dead in elegies and epitaphs, newspapers and witchcraft narratives, sermons and ghost stories and plays. I found writers spanning the full social and educational spectrum, from minister-scientists such as Cotton Mather and Joseph Glanvill to the humble women and men whose heavenly visions filled broadsides on both sides of the Atlantic.

By the time I traced the phenomenon back to the English Reformation, I realized I was no longer writing a prehistory of Spiritualism. Speaking with the dead was so various in its manifestations, so diverse in its goals and audiences, that I could no longer say that all of its expressions were "leading to" Spiritualism. Such teleology did a disservice to the sources and the women and men who wrote them. At that point the book assumed its current form: a history of Protestant communication with the dead before the advent of Spiritualism.[10]

This intellectual trajectory helps explain the book's thematic and geographical limits. The title claims *Speaking with the Dead* will cover "America," but that exaggerates. The book focuses on people of European descent. African Americans and Amerindians had their own traditions of spirit communication, but they deserve separate treatment. And in researching two previous books, I did not find significant Amerindian or African influences on Euro-American communication with the dead.[11] Moreover, Euro-American postmortem communication is the more surprising story, given how historians have long written about Protestantism as a religion that does not allow interaction with the dead. Finally, to provide coherence and allow for an in-depth examination of sources, the book starts within the relatively narrow compass of New England and then broadens to include the northern colonies and states.

Speaking with the Dead begins with ghost belief in the sixteenth century. Protestant ministers and laypeople alike believed in apparitions of the dead, though ministers—actively involved in a campaign against purgatory, the source of Catholic ghosts—insisted that most ghosts were demonic delusions:

apparitions sent by Satanic minions to tempt the unwary into sin. Most lay-people were not so deeply invested in the exact ontological status of a given apparition. If it looked like someone they knew, they assumed it was that person's soul returned from heaven. Starting in the late seventeenth century and gaining speed in the eighteenth, ghost belief gradually diminished, especially among ministers and educated laypeople. Most members of the literati continued to assert that God had the power to send souls back to earth, but they believed God rarely did so. Almost all ghost sightings, elites increasingly insisted, were the result of credulous people being fooled by a shadow, or a dream, or a guilty conscience. For their part, laypeople in the eighteenth and early nineteenth centuries held a wide range of views, from belief to skepticism and every point in between. To be clear, this is not a linear narrative of the "disenchantment" of the West, to use the German sociologist Max Weber's highly contested term. Instead, ghost belief persisted, transformed, and even gained key elite adherents, all against a background of gradual decline.[12] Indeed, one of my key findings is the surprising persistence of serious, unironic ghost reports in American newspapers through the first half of the nineteenth century.

This story of decreasing ghost belief among the educated is familiar to historians. My narrative breaks new ground, however, in weaving the history of ghost belief together with much broader, previously unexplored ways of portraying communication with the dead in imaginative literature and material culture. Some elegies spoke, like Lydia Minot's, in the deceased's voice; others directly addressed the dead. After 1750, many American gravestone epitaphs likewise represented the dead as speaking or being spoken to. The mid-eighteenth-century "Graveyard School" of English authors explored the connection between the living and dead in verse and prose; later Gothic fiction only intensified the literary focus on corpses and the returned dead. Nineteenth-century sentimental literature—a mainstay of American magazines, especially those marketed to women—depicted dead children speaking from heaven and showed cemeteries as places where the living could make contact with departed spirits. Parlor songs invited middle-class women and men to voice the words of departed spirits. Portraits and photographs of the dead beckoned mourners to imagine conversations with their loved ones in heaven.

All these forms of imaginative literature and material culture responded to and stoked widespread interest in the relationship between the living and dead, what the English clergyman Isaac Watts referred to as people's "Curiosity" about "the Circumstances of our pious Friends departed."[13] Do the dead take an interest in what we're doing? Can they protect us from evil? Do they ever return to earth? Imaginative literature and material culture never claimed to answer such questions definitively but rather served as a forum for people to explore those issues on their own or with a like-minded community of readers, singers, writers, and graveyard visitors.

By the start of the nineteenth century, as ghost belief faded among educated Americans, a new complex of religious ideas emerged about the relationship between the living and the deceased. I call these beliefs a "cult of the dead," using the religious studies definition of a "cult" as a form of veneration focused on a specific figure, such as the early Christian cult of saints or the early modern cult of the Virgin Mary.[14] Ghosts no longer were the main way most people thought about interacting with the dead. Rather, participants in the cult of the dead imagined they were able to maintain postmortem relationships with their deceased loved ones. They held, in tension with three hundred years of Protestant teachings, five distinctive beliefs: bodily remains deserved adoration; the souls of the dead became angels in heaven; those souls could return to earth as guardian angels and hover around the living; cemeteries were locations especially well-suited to communing with the dead; and it was legitimate to pray to the dead, addressing them in diaries using forms almost identical to prayers to God. Participants in the cult of the dead built on key Protestant tenets, including belief in an afterlife populated by the souls of the dead. But they also drew on the imaginative literature and material culture of previous centuries, pushed the ideas found therein even further, expressed their ideas in published poems and short stories and mourning embroideries, and helped expand the circle of believers. A reciprocal relationship thus existed between lived religion and imaginative forms of expression.

The cult of the dead began to emerge, it is important to note, well before the Fox Sisters received their first supernatural message. When reports of the "Rochester Rappings" began to circulate, participants in the cult of the dead most likely responded with knowing nods. They did not need Swedenborg, or Mesmer, or A. J. Davis, or even the Fox Sisters to tell them that communication with the dead was possible. They already acted on that belief in their diaries, prayers, and graveyard visits.

It is also important to point out that the large majority of participants in the cult of the dead were women. A vast, intertwined array of changes in culture and society began in the second half of the eighteenth century and continued in the nineteenth century among the urban and town-dwelling middle classes, altering women's lives in ways that would slowly filter down the social ladder and outward to rural areas. Families became smaller, and in those

smaller families companionship and affection replaced patriarchal domina-
tion as the ideal of interpersonal relations. As more men worked outside the
home, women increasingly took charge of inculcating their children with
Christian piety. Even though Second Great Awakening revivalists such as
Charles Finney tried to increase the number of male members in churches,
women continued to make up a disproportionate share of churchgoers and
full members. Mortality rates remained high, and women, as they had for centuries, continued to perform the physical labor of caring for the dying and
dead; with the rise of sentimental culture, women increasingly bore a disproportionate share of the emotional labor of grieving and memorialization. This
largely female culture of mourning gained widespread representation in popular sentimental literature.[15]

Scholars have long been aware of women's deep involvement in grief work
and consolation literature in the nineteenth century. A previous generation
was quite critical of the mourning poems and short stories that women so eagerly wrote and read. These scholars insisted that consolation literature, with
its implication that all deceased loved ones reached heaven, lacked the "rigor"
of earlier Calvinist beliefs. Such literature was, in this view, merely "therapeu-
tic self-indulgence" and "determinedly nonintellectual."[16] My interpretation,
by contrast, emphasizes how female authors and readers carved out a cultural
space for the sincere expression of grief; even for those not actively grieving,
such literature created communities of readers bound by a shared culture of
sentimentality.[17] Female and male participants in the cult of the dead thereby
constructed a new intellectual system, expressed in literature, material culture,
and lived religion, that focused on maintaining postmortem relationships.

In uncovering these relationships, *Speaking with the Dead* makes its most
significant contribution by reconceiving Protestantism as a religion in which
the dead are important figures. A concept formulated by the religious studies
scholar Robert Orsi is pertinent here. According to Orsi, one should think of
religion not as a set of abstract beliefs but rather as "a network of relationships
between heaven and earth involving humans of all ages and many different
sacred figures together."[18] Orsi's main area of expertise is twentieth-century
Catholicism; one can readily see how a religion with Marian apparitions and
prayers to St. Jude is indeed a network of relationships between heaven and
earth. But Orsi contends that his definition of religion is broadly applicable
beyond Catholicism, though he mostly leaves it to others to substantiate that
claim. This is the challenge that *Speaking with the Dead* takes up: showing
that in the three centuries after the Reformation, Protestantism was a religion

that allowed room for relationships between heaven and earth beyond the ties that connected humans with God.

To use another of Orsi's concepts, this book maintains that Protestantism was not a religion of "absence," as it is sometimes caricatured to be. Orsi shows that since the Reformation, many people (not least Protestant propagandists) have insisted on a simple equation: "Catholics = presence, Protestants = absence," where "presence" refers to "all the special suprahuman beings with whom humans have been in relationship in different times and places."[19] In other words, many people have maintained that Protestantism does not include the "special suprahuman beings" that are so central to Catholicism. But as the evidence in *Speaking with the Dead* demonstrates, that is a false and polemical understanding of lived Protestantism.

I am not the first historian to claim that Protestantism was a religion of presence (though I am among the first to use that term). Books on providentialism, miracles, ghosts, and heavenly visions in early modern England have demonstrated that the supernatural was an active force in Protestant lived religion.[20] Classic and recent works on the religion of lay New Englanders have shown how witchcraft, faith healing, dreams, and the influx of the Holy Spirit were all part of a Protestant world rich with supernatural activity.[21] Moreover, histories of religion have paid attention to the ways that *death* shaped early modern Protestantism.[22] What scholars have mostly overlooked, however, is the important role of *the dead*.[23]

Focusing on the relationship between the living and dead nuances our understanding of early American religion in several ways. Most fundamentally, Protestantism was a religion of presence. The dead remained a part of the imaginative landscape after the Reformation, and suprahuman beings would only increase in religious significance with the cult of the dead's development. Other implications emerge from this most basic one. First, Protestantism was also a religion of materiality and not just the internal acceptance of a set of creeds. Broadside elegies, gravestones, mourning embroidery, locks of hair, and posthumous portraits were all religious objects: when people viewed or handled them, they were better able to maintain relationships with suprahuman beings.[24] Second, although it has been a long time since historians have claimed that puritans practiced unadulterated Calvinism, attention to the dead's presence in elegies, dreams, and ghost narratives offers evidence that people almost never imagined their loved ones in hell, despite Calvin's estimate that only one in a hundred would reach heaven.[25] Third, the history of heaven acquires a new timeline in my telling. Ministers and laypeople were interested in heavenly reunions with loved ones a full century earlier than scholars have previously known.[26] And finally, with the cult of the dead's emergence, lay men and especially women initiated important religious changes. In formulating new ideas about the deceased as suprahuman beings who maintained relationships with the living, participants in the cult of the dead made innovative contributions to antebellum Protestant belief and practice.

But phrasing it that way is far too abstract, as if women and men were chiefly concerned with shaping Protestantism. They were not. Mourners simply hoped to maintain some sort of connection with the departed. Sometimes they spoke to the dead, addressing a portrait of a deceased husband or praying to a dead child. Other times they imagined the dead talking, either in a dream or in a poem. They experienced, as I did at my grandfather's funeral, the power of speaking with the dead.

CHAPTER I

The Transatlantic Science of the Dead

In 1691, the eminent New England minister Increase Mather was in London when he heard about an intriguing ghost sighting. Although his mission in the city was of grave political importance—he was Massachusetts Bay's envoy to England, trying to procure a new charter after the revocation of the colony's previous one—he found time to investigate the apparition. Mather wanted to "satisfy my self, by enquiring into the Truth of what was reported." So on February 23, 1691, he and his brother Nathaniel, a minister at London's Lime Street Church, "Discoursed the Gentlewoman" who claimed that her dead son had appeared to her. This might be valuable evidence of the supernatural world, and if so, it couldn't be left to hearsay.

The woman was happy to tell the Mathers of her extraordinary experience. In life her son had been "a very civil young Man," but still he had given cause for worry, being "more airy in his Temper than was pleasing to his serious Mother." Because of this "she was much concerned in her Thoughts about his Condition in the other World." Was he in heaven or hell? How could she know? Two weeks after the young man's death, the mother received an answer from the invisible world. His ghost appeared, saying, "Mother, you are solicitous about my Spiritual Welfare. Trouble your self no more, for I am happy." Errand completed, the spirit vanished.

Increase Mather was convinced. Soon he would use this case in his famous tract, *Cases of Conscience* (1693), as evidence that "the Great God" occasionally allows "Persons after their Death to appear unto the Living." This was not a common occurrence, Mather cautioned. "It would breed Confusion" if there were "a continual Intercourse between the Visible and the Invisible World." But the reader should understand that "the Great Ruler of the Universe" had the power to do so.[1]

This example neatly encapsulates many of the themes concerning Protestant communication with the dead in the seventeenth century. Lay women and men longed for information about the afterlife. So did their ministers. Both groups were eager to learn whether their loved ones were saved or damned and to gain information about heaven and hell. Laypeople on both sides of the Atlantic turned to vision narratives, ballads, orally transmitted ghost accounts, and printed tracts to learn about the dead. They wanted to know whether it was possible to maintain relationships between heaven and earth. Some ministers likewise investigated the invisible world, using cutting-edge scientific methodologies and setting up correspondence networks to share the latest findings.

The unnamed London woman's story conformed to the main features of Anglo-Atlantic ghost belief. While some ghosts were anonymous spirits, most were known to the witnesses. They almost always spoke: sometimes their words were frightening, but in many cases they brought comforting news of a loved one's state in the afterlife. Mather did not say, but the woman must have been relieved to learn that her son was "happy," meaning in heaven. She also must have told her story to family members and neighbors, and these people passed along the narrative in an oral chain of transmission. As Mather attested, there was "much Discourse in London" about this ghost sighting.

Mather's written account similarly partook of cultural conventions, specifically the standards for how minister-scientists were supposed to explore the supernatural world. The science of the dead demanded that investigators speak directly to eyewitnesses, rather than relying on secondhand accounts. With its emphasis on empiricism, the new Baconian methodology of natural philosophy demanded credible informants, so Mather needed to note that his witness was a "Gentlewoman." For similar reasons Mather provided the exact date of his interview with the woman, to bolster his account's veracity. Finally, the narrative is directly linked to the most dramatic outbreak of supernatural activity in the seventeenth-century Anglo-Atlantic. Though best known as an effort to rein in the Salem witchcraft trials, Mather's *Cases of Conscience* was mostly a compendium of supernatural incidents, meant to demonstrate the reality of witches, ghosts, and demons. Mather's point was that the Devil had the power to deceive, and therefore people should be careful about information gathered from supernatural sources. The invisible world was real. It deserved close scrutiny.

The End of Purgatory

Increase Mather and other late seventeenth-century minister-scientists inherited ghost beliefs shaped by a century and a half of polemics over purgatory, even as Mather and others departed from earlier Protestant theologians on key issues. Since the thirteenth century, purgatory had been one of those rare concepts developed by theologians that was extremely popular with lay women and men. Although Christian thinkers going back at least to Augustine had conceived of a "third place" between heaven and hell, it was not until the late twelfth century that the concept of purgatory became fully articulated. In this newer theology, the souls of the vast majority of Christians—all who were not absolutely evil and not absolutely good—went to purgatory for an undetermined length of time, where in the fires of that region their sins were "burnt and purged away." When that process was complete, the soul triumphantly ascended to heaven.[2]

This idea proved so popular with laypeople because of the active role it prescribed for the living. People could shorten their loved ones' time in purgatory by praying for their souls, paying for Masses, and performing acts of charity. The souls of the dead would then return the favor, helping those who helped them with prayers of their own. The result was that in late medieval and early modern Catholic Europe, the living and dead were bound together in a powerful reciprocal relationship. This sounds like a comforting doctrine, and it was. But purgatory also caused anxiety, not least because it served as the source of most Catholic ghosts. The returned dead could be unpredictable, even violent. Still, numerous late medieval ghost narratives demonstrate the connections that persisted between the living and the dead.[3]

In 1517, when Martin Luther started the chain of events that historians would eventually dub the Protestant Reformation, he was thinking a lot about purgatory, but not its abolition. Indeed, Luther continued to believe in purgatory until 1530, when he finally abandoned the idea. In 1517 it wasn't purgatory itself that upset Luther but rather abuses of the indulgences that Catholics had long been able to purchase to shorten their time in purgatory. In his 95 Theses, Luther protested many Catholic practices, including indulgences, which contravened his newly formulated ideas about justification by faith (that divine grace comes from God alone, not from human actions). The disputations that followed inspired more radical reformers to insist that purgatory was a figment of the Catholic imagination. With their rallying cry of *sola Scriptura*, "only the Bible," these early Protestants contended that no evidence for purgatory could be found in either the Old or New Testament. Even before he abandoned his belief in purgatory, Luther "absolutely denied" the Catholic doctrine that the prayers of the living could help the souls of the dead, because this too contradicted justification by faith. For Protestant theologians, these innovations ended the interactions between the living and dead that had been so crucial in Catholic Europe.[4]

To symbolize this new, bright line between the living and dead, many German towns adopted extramural burials: interments outside the city walls. This process began before the Reformation in response to plague epidemics, as an effort to prevent the living from breathing the "poisonous vapors" thought to emanate from cemeteries. These public health efforts got a boost from the Reformation, which provided a theological justification for separating the dead and the living, now that prayers could not help souls get to heaven and burial near saints' relics in churches was irrelevant.[5] For reasons that historians have not adequately explained, this movement never took hold in England. A handful of zealous puritans wanted to move burial grounds away from churches, but their ideas did not resonate with either Church of England officials or the vast majority of laypeople.

However, the boundary between the living and dead was indeed sharpened in the Church of England's Order for the Burial of the Dead as outlined in the new Reformation Prayer Books. The Church of England's first Protestant Prayer Book was published in 1549 and maintained many continuities with earlier Catholic practices. As directed by the Prayer Book, the priest met the corpse and funeral procession at the entrance to the churchyard and said, quoting the Gospel of John, "I am the resurreccion and the life (sayth the Lord): he that beleveth in me, yea though he were dead, yet shall he live." He then led the procession to the graveside. The priest, casting earth upon the body, directly addressed the corpse: "I commende thy soule to God the father almighty, and thy body to the grounde, earth to earth, asshes to asshes, dust to dust, in sure and certayne hope of resurreccion to eternall lyfe."[6]

It was a powerful moment, but it bore too much resemblance to the discredited Catholic belief in continued relations with the dead, at least in the opinion of reformers such as Archbishop of Canterbury Thomas Cranmer. As a result, when the Prayer Book was revised just three years later, it removed any hint of conversation between the priest and the deceased. Now when the priest cast earth upon the corpse, he spoke to the assembled mourners: "Forasmuche as it hathe pleased almightie God of his great mercy to take unto himselfe the soule of our dere brother here departed: we therefore commit his body to the ground, earth to earth, asshes to asshes, dust to dust."[7]

Owing to the changes in the burial rite and the denial of purgatory, the living and dead in Reformation England were no longer supposed to be able to communicate. This transformation led, in theory at least, to a dramatic narrowing of the conditions under which individuals could witness apparitions of the dead. Without purgatory, Protestants could not countenance the idea that wandering souls had returned from the "third place" between heaven and hell. In the new theology, apparitions of the dead could be only angels or demons. Either God sent angels to deliver an important message (which he did only rarely), or Satan used his wiles to convince people that they were seeing and communicating with the dead—often loved ones—as a way to lead them into sin and temptation. These demonic apparitions often tried to get people to believe in the forbidden concept of purgatory.

This theological revolution in the relations between living and dead led to a number of confident pronouncements in sixteenth-century England that ghosts were a thing of the past, a Catholic fallacy thankfully no longer credited. As early as the reign of Henry VIII some reformers were taking credit for ending ghost belief. In 1543 Robert Wisdom proclaimed that "sowles departed do not come again and play boo peape with us."[8] The Elizabethan bishop Edwin Sandys flatly asserted that "the gospel hath chased away walking spirits."[9]

But Protestantism's sharp theoretical boundary between the living and dead was blurred in practice. This was not merely a bottom-up story of cultural persistence, with lay women and men clinging to older beliefs in the face of dizzying theological changes. Rather, both ministers and laypeople remained interested in communication with the dead, if sometimes for different reasons. Take the issue of the beatific vision, the direct and unmediated viewing of God's splendor that both Catholics and early Protestants believed was the main activity of souls in heaven. Despite the efforts of John Calvin and other reformers to say that in heaven the souls of the dead have relations with none beside God and Christ—that is, to emphasize the beatific vision above all other heavenly activities—most ministers found their parishioners keenly interested in the question of whether they would meet their loved ones in heaven. Pastorally it was simply not helpful for ministers to ignore these concerns, so some shaped their messages to reflect their parishioners' interests. The strong emphasis of Protestant preaching about heaven remained on the beatific vision, but ministers also tried to comfort their parishioners with occasional discussions of heavenly reunions.[10]

While preaching about heaven sometimes reflected a negotiation between ministers and laypeople, other practices seem more like the survival of cherished lay practices that no longer fit the new Protestant theology. This was the case for ringing bells on All Saints Day, November 1, a Catholic holiday to remember those in heaven and ask their prayers to aid souls in purgatory. Before the English Reformation, church bells pealed from the end of the All Saints service until midnight to comfort those enduring purgatory's torments. Evidently the All Saints tolling greatly appealed to laypeople, because when Edwardian and Elizabethan reformers banned the bells, now that purgatory had been declared nonexistent, the new regulations were met in some locales with reactions ranging from feigned ignorance to outright defiance. As late as 1587, a group of men in Hickling, East Anglia, "used violence against the parson at that time to maintain their ringing."[11] It is hard to know what the bell-ringers of Hickling were trying to preserve with their intimidation tactics. Did they still believe in purgatory, forty years after it was officially abolished by the Church of England? Or did they ring the bells for their loved ones in heaven rather than in purgatory? Whatever the case, they resisted a change that might alter relations between the living and the dead.

An even more dramatic transformation implied by the Reformation's denial of purgatory was its redefinition of ghosts. In 1569 Ludwig Lavater penned what one historian calls the "definitive statement" of the new Protestant theology of ghosts.[12] Lavater's tract, *De spectris* (On Specters), sheds light on the orthodox English understanding of ghosts, even though Lavater was a minister in Zurich. Only three years after the book's first printing, it was published in England with the title *Of Ghostes and Spirites, Walking by Night.* There it became highly influential, cited or simply appropriated by virtually every Protestant who wrote on the topic for the next century.

Lavater's argument was straightforward. First, he wrote that "there are visions and spirits, and that they appear unto men sometimes, and that many and marvellous things happen besides the ordinarie course of nature." Here Lavater simply stated the continued Protestant belief in supernatural occurrences in the natural world. Second was the explanation for these visions and spirits, and the crux of Lavater's polemic against Catholicism: such apparitions are "not the souls of dead men, as some men have thought, but either good or evill Angels." Apparitions were not souls returned from purgatory but either angels or, "for the most part," demons. Technically, the spirits people saw were not "ghosts"—the returned dead—but rather angelic or demonic apparitions.[13]

Lavater was careful to point out that not everything that seemed like a supernatural occurrence was actually the work of angels or demons. Many weak-minded people imagined seeing things that just weren't there. "Melancholike persons, and madde men" often falsely persuaded themselves that they had seen spirits. Importantly, there was a gendered component to Lavater's scheme. "Fearefull men" (meaning "fearful persons") were more likely to convince themselves that something natural was actually an apparition, and Lavater felt that women were especially likely to imagine seeing spirits: "Women, which for the most part are naturally given to feare more than men . . . do more often suppose they see or heare this or that thing, than men do."[14] With this Lavater helped initiate a three-century Protestant tradition of seeing women as prone to imagining ghosts and later, starting in the eighteenth century, scaring children in their care with ghost stories.[15] But overall, Lavater's key theological point was that apparitions were not the souls of the dead returned to earth. Protestant reformers through the first half of the seventeenth century were unanimous in their agreement.[16]

Protestant theologians and ministers thus presented a united front, insisting that the souls of the dead could not return. But in practice, this unanimity sometimes broke down. When ministers were not acting as polemicists but simply living their lives, they occasionally behaved like the laypeople who believed that ghosts were the returned dead. For example, the puritan minister William Twisse had a conversion experience soon after seeing a ghost. Twisse's son reported that when the elder Twisse was a schoolboy in the 1590s, he "saw the Phantome of a School-fellow of his[,] deceased." The dead child had been a "very wicked Boy" and the ghost's message for Twisse was brief and terrifying: "I am damned." If his classmate could burn in hell, perhaps he too might be destined for damnation. This realization was "the occasion of Dr. Twiss[e] (the Fathers) Conversion."[17] Evidently the elder Twisse did not interpret the apparition as a demonic delusion, or else he would not have responded so strongly to its message.

In other cases, ministers disagreed among themselves, as in 1627 when Thomas Crosfield, a clergyman and Fellow at Oxford, made this notation in his diary: "Upon a relation of Dr. Lambes execution, the question disputed whether spirits really and substantially appeare, i.e. the ghosts of the deceased. See Plinies Epistles."[18] The learned men at Oxford did not know for sure one way or another about the reality of ghosts, so in good scholarly fashion, they debated. Crosfield referred to the first-century Roman magistrate Pliny the Younger, who described several ghost sightings in his letters, which were well known among educated Englishmen.[19] Like Pliny, Crosfield approached such stories with caution but not outright dismissal.

Such disagreements among ministers left space for laypeople to interpret apparitions according to their own reasoning. In 1603, a ghost appeared in the Cornwall home of a Protestant layman, Sir Thomas Wise. One night Wise was awakened by the shrieks of his maids, who told him that "they were frighted with a walking spirit," a woman who appeared in their bedchamber. At first, Wise was dismissive, believing it merely the "vaine fancy of womanly feare." But the next night he saw the ghost at the foot of his own bed, and suddenly their claim seemed a lot more plausible. The ghostly woman remained there for about a half hour before disappearing. This apparition resulted in numerous interpretations. Wise sought out the local archdeacon, who insisted Wise had seen "an angellical apparition and not a diabolicall illusion." Another minister begged to differ. Because it had no heavenly message, and because it assumed the form of a woman, the apparition must have been "an evill spirit": the work of Satan. Wise's confusion is demonstrated by his pursuit of multiple opinions; his maids, though, likely held the older belief that the ghost was the returned soul of the dead.[20]

For ghost narratives from individuals such as Wise's maids and other non-elites, however, the sixteenth century remains almost a complete mystery. Virtually all that survive are ministerial complaints that humble women and men were the ones most likely to say they had seen apparitions. A greater number of accounts survive from the first half of the seventeenth century. Most of these sightings involved the recognizable dead and demonstrate the widespread belief in a permeable boundary between this world and the next. Despite the abolition of purgatory, many laypeople believed that communication with the dead was sometimes possible. Two cases from West Somerset featured the returned dead; both involved guilt over crimes committed. In 1613, a man confessed that he had killed a rich widow after experiencing a series of hauntings: "the ghost of the woman he had slain was continually before him, so as his very life was burdensome to him." Nine years later and a dozen miles away, another ghost made a mark on the historical record. A man told neighbors that his daughter had witnessed the ghost of Christian Godfrey, a local woman recently deceased. Godfrey described how she was in hell and knew the names of others in the neighborhood who would soon join her there.[21]

But ghosts who offered details about heaven and hell were less common than those that hoped to right a wrong, especially if that unfinished business involved a bad death or burial. In 1635 the Scottish gentleman David Person related a story about the supernatural ramifications of a bad burial. As a "Gentlewoman" with the surname of Lawder lay dying, she made the common request of burial in the churchyard. After she died, however, her husband ignored her request because there was an epidemic of the plague at that time. If he buried her publicly he feared that people would suspect he was contagious, so he buried her in his garden. This did not please the woman's spirit. "Thereafter, this womans ghost," Person wrote, "did so incessantly both haunt and affright, both him, his children, and family, that there was no resting for them at any time." The husband sought the advice of a minister, who urged him to disinter her and bury her in the churchyard. The haunting ceased.[22]

The accounts about Godfrey, Lawder, and others demonstrate three significant themes in seventeenth-century English ghost narratives. First, ghosts were associated with specific places: the Lawder garden, Godfrey's home, and the like. Second, ghosts retained a connection to the corporeal remains of the dead, where the person had either died or been buried. This led to the idea that graveyards often held the spirits of the dead, a belief that would later be incorporated into the cult of the dead. Third, the dead returned to attend to a problem or injustice left unresolved. The theological interpretation of apparitions had changed dramatically after the Reformation—these could no longer be souls returned from purgatory—but that did not stop people from interpreting what they saw as souls of the recognizable dead. None of these informants even hinted that the sightings might be demonic delusion.

This points to a disjuncture between the Protestant theology of ghosts and the interpretations of lay men and women who encountered apparitions. The Lawder family, for example, presumed the ghost was the soul of their deceased wife and mother, returned to fix the injustice of a bad burial. Now that purgatory no longer existed, where that soul returned from—heaven? hell?—was a theological knot the Lawders and others faced with recognizable ghosts did not try to untie. They left that task to minister-scientists who, in the second half of the seventeenth century, would show a greater openness to the idea that ghosts were the returned souls of the deceased.

The Thanatologists

Thanatology is the scientific study of everything related to death: dying, corpse disposal, memorial rituals, ideas about the afterlife, and more. In the seventeenth century, Protestant minister-scientists on both sides of the Atlantic focused on one specific aspect of thanatology: the science of the dead. They tried to answer questions of vital importance, including, What happens to the soul when a person dies? What is the soul made of, and how does it separate from the earthly body upon death? Can spirits of the dead return to earth? Can they influence the actions of the living?

To many readers today, such questions sound more like theology than science, but no such neat distinction existed in the seventeenth century. Even the most au courant practitioners of the "new science," exemplified in the Anglophone world by Francis Bacon, felt that the methodology of natural philosophy (the contemporary term for what we call "science") could and indeed should be used to gain a clearer understanding of religion. To do so, self-styled "moderns" advocated procedures built around a key concept: empiricism. Bacon and like-minded natural philosophers insisted that investigators use their senses to learn about the world around them. According to Bacon, the "ancients" and their Scholastic disciples in the Renaissance relied on the authority of written texts even when those sources contradicted what investigators observed in the natural world. By contrast, Bacon proposed an inductive method: start with facts based on direct observation and use those to fashion general principles and laws of nature.[23]

But the ambition for pure empiricism was difficult to implement in practice. Not every natural philosopher could repeat every experiment and witness the results for himself; moderns had to rely on the authority of written reports. So the problem became which secondhand accounts to credit. For Bacon and his followers, Aristotle and other classical writers were no longer credible sources about the natural world. When judging more recent informants, natural philosophers relied on a gentlemanly code of honor that was rarely articulated. One just *knew* who was trustworthy. Unsurprisingly, this led to highly gendered and class-based assumptions about authority. As Bacon wrote in 1605, using the new methodology to gain a deeper understanding of Christianity exposed the "old wives' fables" and the "ignorance of the people" that led to the "superstitious" beliefs of the masses.[24]

What was therefore needed, some mid-seventeenth-century ministers concluded, was an impartial investigation of the supernatural world to help separate the "old wives' fables" from the truly creditable evidence of God's sovereign power. This became a pressing issue in midcentury England because of the seeming rise of what ministers sometimes described as "atheism" but more frequently dubbed "sadducism." The Sadducees were a Jewish sect that did not believe in resurrection; they appear in the Gospels quarreling with Jesus about the afterlife (e.g., Mark 12:18–27). "Sadducism" thus came to denote any belief that seemed to deny the immortality of the soul or the existence of the afterlife.

Midcentury ministers rang the alarm bell of sadducism in response to the publication of Thomas Hobbes's *Leviathan* (1651) and other works by materialists, who argued that there were no incorporeal substances such as the soul, only matter. In *Leviathan*'s chapter "Of Daemonology," Hobbes offered a materialist explanation for the appearance of ghosts, likening them to the impression one gets by pressing hard on one's eyes: "there appears to him a light without, and before him, which no man perceiveth but himselfe; because there is indeed no such thing without him, but onely a motion in the interiour organs." Ghosts and spirits were thus "phantasms" of the imagination.[25] Such skeptical ideas were even more widespread than they appeared in print, being more often expressed orally among the educated "wits" of Restoration London's court and coffee houses.[26] Most ministers took materialism and sadducism as grave threats to the very foundations of Christian religion. If there are no incorporeal substances, there is no soul, no afterlife—no God? So some ministers decided to use the new Baconian methodology to prove the existence of the soul and, by extension, the existence of God. The seventeenth-century ministers who hunted for credible eyewitness accounts of ghosts and apparitions were therefore not throwbacks to the Middle Ages but rather on the modern vanguard of natural philosophers.[27]

Early in the century, Bacon argued that the new science's capstone project was to compile everything that could be observed in nature. In 1656, the English Presbyterian Matthew Poole launched the first effort to create a compilation of *super*natural occurrences observed by credible eyewitnesses. Poole attempted to set up a network of learned investigators for the "registring of Providences."[28] For Protestants in seventeenth-century England and New England, "providences" were examples of God's active hand in the world: lightning that struck down the sinful, drought that betokened an angry deity, ghosts that allowed the living to learn about the afterlife.[29] Poole's registry was an effort to systematize knowledge about such events so as to combat sadducism and convince skeptics of God's sovereignty.

To that end, Poole followed the reigning Baconian methodology. When his hoped-for correspondents in England, Scotland, and the American colonies learned of an example of God's providence, they would "draw a short, yet full narrative of the Case, & get it subscribed by the Witnesses (naming the place of their abode & (where it is convenient) the Quality of the Person witnessing it) & that they will be ready to sweare it."[30] Then they would send the affidavit to Poole in London, where he would compile the examples and eventually publish them. As with Bacon, so with Poole: the "Quality" of the

eyewitnesses mattered enormously, because without evidence that the informants were "judicious" and "credible," it would be impossible to separate their
supernatural observations from "old wives' fables."

Poole was ultimately unable to realize his registry of providences. But the
dream of a supernatural compilation lived on and was brought to fruition by
two prominent Anglicans: Henry More and Joseph Glanvill. They eagerly
sought out examples of the supernatural—especially stories of the returned
dead—both to counter sadducism and to appeal to ordinary parishioners. Here
the interests of the learned and unlearned intersected, with ghost stories form-
ing a common language that addressed the widespread curiosity about the
dead and the afterlife.[31]

Henry More conceived of his audience primarily as theologians, ministers, and other learned readers. A wide-ranging and idiosyncratic thinker, More
attempted to use Cartesian philosophy to prove the reality of the immaterial
substances whose existence Hobbes and other materialists denied. Book III
of his *Antidote Against Atheism* (1655) was full of supernatural stories meant to
demonstrate the reality of spirits and, therefore, God. In two crucial chapters, More explored the natural history of guardian angels, or genii (sing.
"genius"). He focused on the well-known account of the sixteenth-century
French legal theorist Jean Bodin, who had a long series of interactions with a
kindly spirit.[32] Aside from the fact that the story demonstrated the reality of
the spirit world, More did not have a firm interpretation of Bodin's experiences but rather a series of questions the account raised. Foremost among them,
he wondered whether such guardian spirits were "Angels uncapable of incor-
poration into humane Bodies" or "the Souls of the deceased."[33] The latter
seemed likelier to More. For the science of the dead, this was a key issue,
whether the souls of the deceased could return to earth and associate with
the living. In the sixteenth century, Protestants such as Lavater had said that
was not possible, arguing that returned souls were a discredited Catholic idea.
Seventeenth-century thanatologists, farther removed from the struggle against
Catholicism, weren't so sure. Many were open to the idea that ghosts could
be the souls of the dead. If ghosts were not merely demonic delusions, then
they could bring back useful information about the afterlife.

Henry More built on the foundation of his *Antidote* with a tome of more
than five hundred pages, *The Immortality of the Soul* (1659). This book, with
its tales of witches, ghosts, and apparitions, was cited for decades by all who
investigated the supernatural world. More's accounts of spirits were so detailed
that he only half-jokingly anticipated some readers objecting "that I have taken

upon me to describe the state of the other World so punctually and particularly, as if I had been lately in it."[34] At this point More still relied mostly on historical rather than contemporary accounts, as he had not yet joined with Glanvill in attempting to create a compendium of supernatural events.

More's work was, in effect, a lengthy response to Hobbes. Several chapters addressed Hobbes's arguments directly, with More making the case both for an "Immateriall Substance" or spirit in humans and for the existence of a range of "Immateriall Beings" including angels and the souls of the deceased. Because they were immaterial, these substances and beings possessed qualities that explained many supernatural occurrences. Spirits kept their form and didn't get broken up into "an infinite number of shreds and rags of Souls and Spirits." This meant that the souls of the deceased remained whole in the afterlife and, if they returned to earth, were recognizable as the departed.[35]

These properties of souls were on display in the "appearing of the Ghosts of men after death." Indeed, More admitted, such stories are "so numerous and frequent in all mens mouths, that it may seem superfluous to particularize in any." Significantly, More attributed ghost stories to *all* people, not merely the vulgar masses. In Restoration England, interest in ghosts was a cross-class phenomenon. All agreed that among the places most likely to harbor ghosts were "publick Buriall-places." According to More, sadducists asserted that such ghosts were "nothing but the reek or vapour of the Bodies of the dead, which they fancy will fall into the like stature and shape with the man it comes from."[36] Absurd, More retorted. These were clearly the souls of the deceased. A century after the English Reformation, More didn't even feel the need to say that the ghosts in burial grounds were not returned from purgatory. Like other Restoration-era thanatologists, More had moved away from the sixteenth-century insistence that ghosts were either angels or demons, not souls.

More's theories about the agency of souls also led him to support the feasibility of postmortem pacts, in which living friends promise that the first to die will return to the living partner to reveal details of the afterlife. Such pacts were popular in medieval Europe, but Catholic antecedents did not prevent More from marshaling this practice as further evidence for the reality of souls.[37] Later, Increase and Cotton Mather would denounce such agreements when they learned of them in New England. But More did not criticize the practice, instead relating the "noble" example of the pact made by the fifteenth-century Italian Neoplatonists Marsilio Ficino and Michael Mercatus.[38]

Henry More's first two books on the supernatural straddled newer and older scientific methodologies. On the one hand More was conversant with the cutting-edge arguments of Hobbes and Descartes. On the other hand, with some references to poorly attested stories from centuries past, More did not always adhere to the Baconian imperative of relying only on contemporary eyewitnesses. Perhaps to remedy this shortcoming, More worked with the Anglican minister Joseph Glanvill to collect first-person accounts of supernatural events.

In this project, one of More's most important correspondents was Lady Anne Conway, an innovative philosopher. Conway was also deeply interested in the supernatural. Pursuing this interest, she helped More and Glanvill find well-attested examples of ghost sightings. In 1663 she wrote to More describing the accounts of "two simple Country-people" who had recently been vexed by the ghosts of "two several Persons who have died lately." Their narratives, Conway insisted, were "certainly liable to as little Exception as any one shall meet with" because the men were disinterested observers: they stood to gain nothing from their story, unlike some who reported ghosts with suspiciously remunerative messages. Thus the highborn Conway departed from one aspect of the Baconian model of authority, as she (and by extension Glanvill, who published several of her narratives) was willing to accept "simple Country-people" as credible informants. At the same time, she applied Baconian rigor in analyzing whether the men had anything to gain from their tale.[39]

The accounts that More, Conway, and other correspondents gathered were eventually published in several volumes by Glanvill, and these books reached a wider audience than did More's. Glanvill's publications had a powerful transatlantic impact, cited by the Mathers, invoked in the Salem witchcraft trials, and referred to—frequently, perhaps, without knowledge of the original source—by countless colonists conversant with the poltergeist known as the Drummer of Tedworth and other supernatural figures.[40] With account after account of ghosts, witches, and haunted houses, the compilations had something for every reader, though Glanvill himself insisted that "I have no humour nor delight in telling Stories."[41] His books suggest otherwise.

Glanvill's most enduring contribution was *Saducismus Triumphatus*, "sadducism triumphed over," published with More's help in 1681, a year after Glanvill died, and reprinted as late as 1726. Among the dozens of supernatural accounts are thirteen stories of the returned dead. One way to understand the compilation's significance is to consider the thirteen accounts as a group. All are from the seventeenth century: none are based on ancient testimony, or biblical authority, or even narratives from Catholic Europe. All are based on eyewitness testimony, rather than the second- or thirdhand accounts that frequently made their way into broadside ballads. Glanvill provided the name and social position of each informant to demonstrate his or her credibility. In these ways the relations conformed closely to modern scientific methodologies.[42]

In 1664 Glanvill had been elected a Fellow of London's newly established Royal Society for Improving Natural Knowledge, a locus of Baconian science. Glanvill's thirteen accounts of the returned dead thus foregrounded his informants' reliability and judiciousness, and as a result, his witnesses included significantly more men (nine) than women (four). Still, the four female informants demonstrate that the Royal Society's ghost hunters listened to women, or at least those of a certain station. Glanvill relied on Lady Anne Conway for at least two relations. He also credited accounts from Mrs. Taylor, evidently Joanna, the wife of the Anglican divine Jeremy Taylor, and Elizabeth Foxcroft, wife of a prominent merchant. Perhaps connected to the disproportionate maleness of the witnesses, the ghosts themselves are mostly men (ten of thirteen).

Suggesting that most ghost sightings resulted from survivors' desires to maintain relationships with the departed, the majority of the sightings involved people who had been dead for less than six months. Four had been dead less than a month and three had been dead from one to six months. Only five were spirits of those dead longer than a year (and one was unspecified). All of the ghosts appeared at night, and all but one were recognized by the witnesses, because they were with the one exception all family members or close friends, and because they often wore their regular clothes rather than the winding sheet of broadside woodcuts. Mrs. Bretton's ghost was "in a Morning-Gown" like the one she ordinarily wore; Edward Avon's spirit had on "the same Cloths . . . he did usually wear when he was living"; George Villiers returned in his homey "Morning Chamber Gown."[43] (Notably, the two ghosts in morning gowns would have looked not unlike spirits in winding sheets.)

Because they were so well attested, Glanvill's relations are exceptionally valuable for understanding how seventeenth-century English men and women thought about the dead. Gathered as the crowning achievement of learned thanatology, the narratives shed just as much light on popular beliefs. They demonstrate that everyday ghosts reflected relatively humble aspects of interpersonal relations, such as the ghost who complained to his living friend that he wasn't keeping the dead man's sword clean enough.[44] Concerns like this were in sharp contrast to the legendary ghosts of ballads, who were more often connected with gory murders or sensational revelations about buried treasure.[45] As an example of a more ordinary ghost, take the one that appeared to Mary Toppam of York. Toppam's father and her husband did not get along, so she saw her father much less often than she would have liked. Once, upon bidding farewell to her father after a rare visit, she said she was worried she might never see him again. He responded that, "if he should dye, if ever God did permit the dead to see the living, he would see her again." This promise was a variation on the classic postmortem pact, and it reflected a popular faith that God allowed the souls of the dead to return, or at least the hope that such was the case.

Sadly, Toppam's premonition was correct; her beloved father died before she could see him again. Six months after his death, Toppam lay in bed in the middle of the night, sleepless. Suddenly she heard music, the chamber brightened; she was "broad awake" and "saw her Father stand at her Bedside." Not "her Father's ghost," just "her Father." Clearly Glanvill and his informant meant that this was the returned spirit of the dead man, but the locution demonstrates how closely such figures were associated with the actual living people they represented. Amid the music and light the ghost spoke: "Moll, did I not tell thee, that I would see thee once again?" Their conversation was pretty prosaic in light of the supernatural circumstances. He told her to obey her mother. He said this was his last visit to earth, the last time she would see him until she died and went to heaven. He was right: not only did she never see his ghost again, she never even dreamed of him after his visit. Evidently his appearance soothed her longing for him and convinced her that he was happy in the afterlife.[46] If Glanvill's narratives are at all representative, postmortem pacts were more common in seventeenth-century England than historians have realized, appearing in three of his thirteen relations.[47]

Glanvill's compilation was extremely popular and influential, but it did not go uncontested among thanatologists. On the Continent, Balthasar Bekker, a German Protestant preacher based in Amsterdam, took aim at the antisadducists in general and Glanvill in particular in his four-volume *De Betoverde Weereld* (*The World Bewitch'd*), published in the early 1690s.[48] More influential in the English-language conversation was John Webster's *The Displaying of Supposed Witchcraft* (1677), which responded not to *Saducismus* but rather Glanvill's earlier writings. Webster framed his arguments in classic Baconian terms. He asked rhetorically, "We must know of Mr. Glanvil, how he comes to know that the Devils sucking of the Witches bodies is a truth, or ever was proved to be a matter of fact, who were by and present that were ear or eyewitnesses of it?" Here Webster insisted that Glanvill, for all his supposed methodological rigor, actually relied on traditional beliefs rather than eyewitnesses to document some key claims about demons. Whereas almost all of Glanvill's information about *ghosts* came from eyewitnesses, other parts of his supernatural compendium were of necessity less well attested. But even for Webster, it was Glanvill's methodology that was at issue, not the possibility that spirits could make appearances in this world.[49]

Indeed, in the late seventeenth century, Webster and others who were skeptical about many of Glanvill's claims did not deny the supernatural, and they certainly were not "atheists" as sometimes charged. Webster himself acknowledged some "unquestionable testimonies" that "there are effects that exceed the ordinary power of natural causes," offering examples of murdered people who had returned to earth to demand justice. Where Webster did disagree with the anti-sadducists was in his explanation for such apparitions. Whereas Glanvill believed that ghosts were the returned souls of the deceased, Webster saw this as an unconscionably "Popish" view. Instead, Webster posited that every human had an "astral spirit," consisting of the elements fire and air, and distinct from the incorporeal soul that resided in heaven. Sometimes after a person died this astral spirit "wanders in the air," which explained at least some apparition reports. This distinction between returned souls and astral spirits was almost certainly of no interest to lay men and women. If the dead returned, did the scientific explanation for their appearance matter?[50]

New England's Science of the Dead

Across the Atlantic, New England ministers joined the thanatological efforts of their English counterparts. Even though Increase and Cotton Mather have gotten most of the credit (and no small amount of ridicule) for such investigations in the colonial setting, they were merely the ones who published the results of what were, in fact, cooperative efforts among many. In 1681 Increase Mather learned about Matthew Poole's unsuccessful 1656 attempt to establish a network of correspondents to record examples of God's providence. Intrigued by the possibility of such a network, Mather suggested a colonial version at a meeting of Massachusetts Bay ministers in May 1681. They would gather relations of earthquakes, witchcraft, demonic possessions, and "strange Apparitions": in short, anything supernatural. The assembled ministers chose Mather to compile the narratives, but he made it clear in the resulting volume, his famous *Essay for the Recording of Illustrious Providences* (1684), that he was "Engaged [i.e., obliged] to many for the Materials."[51]

The science of the dead represented only one aspect of this colony-wide investigation of natural philosophy, and in fact Mather's correspondents did not produce any examples of the returned dead. They did send him accounts of poltergeists, demons, and witches, but the chapter "Concerning Apparitions" included no fresh New England examples to contribute to the transatlantic thanatological conversation. Mather had learned of some appearances of dead people, but "upon enquiry, I cannot find that there was any thing therein, more than Phansie, and frightful Apprehensions without sufficient ground."[52] The ghost stories Mather investigated did not meet his Baconian standards for inclusion in his compilation.

Indeed, Mather even declined to include a case from his father's church. After reading Increase's supernatural collection, his brother Nathaniel asked him, "Why did you not put in the story of . . . H[enry] Lake's wife, of Dorchester?" Nathaniel referred to Alice Lake, "whom, as I have heard, the devill drew in by appearing to her in the likenes, & acting the part of a child of hers then lately dead, on whom her heart was much set."[53] In other words, Alice Lake, who would later be hanged for witchcraft, was first attracted to Satan by his appearance as the ghost of her beloved child. Evidently Increase did not think the story sufficiently well attested. Thus faced with a lack of ghost narratives for his compendium, Mather drew heavily on Glanvill's *Saducismus*.

Still, the dearth of New England ghosts did not prevent Increase Mather from trying to contribute to the transatlantic science of the dead with some metaphysical speculations. Mather started with a simple assertion: the appearance of spirits in this world is "amongst sober Men beyond controversie." Whether such spirits were the returned dead or mere demonic delusion was harder to discern. One way to get a hint was to examine the circumstances around the appearance. If the spirit revealed "some sin not discoverable in any other way," such as a murder, this was a strong indication that it was actually the soul of the deceased because a demon would not do something so useful. Or sometimes God allowed the soul of a dead person to return to earth so that "Atheists might thereby be astonished and affrighted out of their Infidelity." In publishing such accounts, Mather hoped to expand upon God's efforts to combat sadducism. For this reason he reproduced Glanvill's accounts of the postmortem pacts that Mary Toppam and others made. Even though these examples were powerful evidence for the afterlife, Mather proclaimed his disapproval of such pacts, which Glanvill never did. Mather worried that "after Men have made such agreements, Devils may appear to them, pretending to be their Deceased Friends, and thereby their Souls may be drawn into woful Snares."[54]

Illustrious Providences did not contain any new accounts of the returned dead, but only three years after its publication New England's thanatologists finally had a certifiable ghost sighting that met their Baconian standards. This was the encounter that Joseph Beacon narrated in 1687, which Increase's son Cotton Mather collected, circulated, and interpreted for the public. For the next forty years, until the younger Mather's death in 1728, Beacon's ghost remained Exhibit A in Mather's decades-long prosecution of the case that the dead could return to this world.

We know nothing about Joseph Beacon beyond what Mather relates, that he was "a most ingenious, accomplished and well-disposed young Gentleman" and, elsewhere, a "Religious Young Gentleman."[55] That this resident of Boston deserved the honorific "Gentleman" was crucial to establishing Beacon's bona fides as a credible eyewitness, an especially important point in light of the extraordinary tale he told. On May 2, 1687, Beacon lay in his bed in Boston at about five o'clock in the morning: perhaps sleeping, perhaps awake, he wasn't sure. Suddenly he "had a View of his Brother then at London." Much was familiar about the figure, "having on him a Bengale Gown, which he usually wore," though in two ways the apparition was dreadfully changed from his brother's ordinary appearance: "his Countenance was very Pale, Ghastly, Deadly, and he had a Bloody Wound on one Side of his Forehead!"[56]

Beacon spoke to the dead man, crying out, "Brother!" The ghost spoke as well, offering a few details about how he had received his mortal injury. A "Debauch'd, Drunken Fellow" completely unknown to the brother had "most Barbarously and Injuriously Butchered" him. The reason the brother's spirit had crossed the Atlantic was to tell Beacon that the murderer was seeking to escape to New England aboard a ship and that Beacon should alert the authorities to apprehend the evildoer when he disembarked. Why would magistrates believe Beacon's supernatural story? Simple, the ghost answered. "I'le Stand by you, and prove the Indictment." With that the apparition vanished. For a week Beacon was exceedingly depressed and, crucially for the later attestation of the case, told some members of his household why he was troubled.[57]

Six or seven weeks later Beacon learned "by the common ways of communication" that his brother had, indeed, died at precisely five in the morning on May 2 in London. In late April the brother had run into a "fellow then in drink" and his "Doxy" (mistress or prostitute) and somehow offended the inebriated rogue. The drunkard stumbled into a nearby tavern, grabbed a "Fire-fork," and returned to crack the brother's skull. The wounded man hung on for a few days until he died on the second of May. The ghost was right that the killer tried to escape, but as it happened there was no need to apprehend him in Boston; the brother's friends had seized him in time and he was being prosecuted for murder.[58]

Beacon's account offers some of the earliest evidence about popular ghost beliefs in New England. Beacon was "Affrighted" when he saw his brother's ghost, but not so terrified that he did not try to engage the spirit. This was because the figure was familiar, a recognizable loved one, not an anonymous haunting spirit. Beacon therefore had the courage to speak first to the dead man. Indeed, the conversation between the living and the dead is the point of the story; the spirit has returned to earth to impart crucial information, otherwise unknowable. The one piece of evidence about the story's popular reception comes from England. A reader wrote to the ministerial editor of a London newspaper in 1693, "Pray give your Answer to the following Questions, occasioned by a Story in Mather's Witch-book, about a Man that appeared to his Brother at Boston." The querist went on to pose six questions, including, "Whether Ghosts be the very Persons of those men departed this Life, whom they resemble when they appear? or the Similitude only of the departed be assumed by some other Spirit?"[59] Beacon's account of conversation with the departed generated interest among lay women and men on both sides of the Atlantic.

It is also apparent why this story so appealed to Cotton Mather and learned thanatologists in England and New England. The eyewitness met all the Baconian criteria: he was a young gentleman, not addled by drink or dementia, pious and of good standing in the community. He produced a written narrative that could be examined by disinterested observers. That Beacon wrote the story just before his own death was a crucial detail: as Mather later wrote, "at the Time of his giving me this Relation . . . he had his own Death so much in View, that his own Testimony must be very credible."[60] With Beacon's day of reckoning near at hand, Mather implied, Beacon certainly would not have lied, fearing that he would wind up in hell for it. Belief in this tenet ran so deeply in Anglo-American culture that under the common law, "a dying man is ever presumed to speak the truth," as it was phrased in the 1603 trial of Sir Walter Ralegh.[61]

Just as important for establishing the truth of this narrative was the signed attestation of two "Gentlewomen of the House" where Beacon lived. Mather transcribed the document: "In the Beginning of May, 1687, Mr Joseph Beacon told us, of an Apparition of his Brother Benjamin, as murdered; and seemed for a Week following much disordered with the Thoughts of it. And about the Latter End of June, he had his Letters of his Brothers Death. This we attest. Elizabeth Sharp. Elizabeth Thompson." Like More and Glanvill, New England's learned thanatologists did not discount the words of "Gentlewomen."[62]

The lessons the Mathers drew from Beacon's narrative were the same as those of other anti-sadducists: the supernatural world is real and God sometimes allows the spirits of the dead to return to earth. This was the message about Beacon's spirit that the Mathers expounded for public consumption in Cotton Mather's *Wonders of the Invisible World* (1693) and *Magnalia Christi Americana* (1702), Increase Mather's *Disquisition Concerning the State of the Souls of Men* (1707), and Cotton Mather's unfinished "Triparadisus" (1726–27), as well as an unknowable number of times in conversation and from the pulpit.[63] English authors read and repeated the story, making it an important part of the transatlantic conversation about ghosts.[64]

Cotton Mather also used Beacon's apparition to delve into the mysteries of the soul and afterlife. Because Mather expected pious laypeople to read *Wonders of the Invisible World* and other books in which he described the case, he kept his abstruse philosophizing to a minimum. But among learned thanatologists, Mather explored the issue of how exactly the apparition was able to appear in Boston. In November 1712 Mather sent the Royal Society thirteen long letters on the natural history of the colonies, gathering the missives under the heading "Curiosa Americana." One focused on ghost sightings in New England.[65] The Royal Society warmly received the letters and, in response, elected Mather a Fellow in July 1713.

An issue Mather treated with scientific nuance was the ghost's supposed appearance to Beacon at the exact moment his brother died in London, at five in the morning. In his public writings, Mather never mentioned that 5:00 A.M. London time is not the same as 5:00 A.M. Boston time. That would have deflated the story's drama. With his scientific colleagues, however, Mather hypothesized that "the spectre, it seems, took the same time, that the Sun takes, to pass over the Degrees of Longitude, into America." Mather did not speculate about why ghosts might travel at the same speed as the earth's rotation.

He also made a scientific distinction between the "internal" apparition of spirits, which was generated by the imagination, and "external" apparitions, "wherein the Spirits do really present themselves unto the Ocular View of those to whom they make their Visit." Whereas in published venues Mather insisted that Beacon's was an external apparition, to his colleagues at the Royal Society he admitted that "we seem to be left at a loss, which of those, was Beacons Apparition."[66]

Even more privately, in his diary, Mather hinted at why he might have found Beacon's story so compelling in 1687. The previous year Mather had undergone his own intense experience of speaking with the dead, in this case in a dream. In September 1686 Cotton Mather was a young man in the midst of dramatic life changes. He had married a few months earlier and had just moved with his new wife into the house in Boston where he had lived as an adolescent from 1677 to 1678. One night in September 1686 a dream shook him to his core. As Mather recorded, "I dreamt that in a Room with other Gentlemen there was my friend Mr. Shepard of Charlstown, whom yett in my sleep, I knew to bee dead." This was the son of the famous Rev. Thomas Shepard of Cambridge, also named Thomas, who had died of smallpox in 1677—at the very time nine years prior that Mather had lived in the house into which he had just moved. Perhaps the association with that time and place brought his dear friend back to him. That Shepard was dead discomfited Mather in the dream: "I dreamt that being somewhat shye of him, on that account, I was contriving to slip out of the Room; whereupon Hee nimbly coming up with mee, took mee by the Hand, and said, 'Syr, you need not bee so shie of mee, for you shall quickly bee as I am, and where I am.'"[67]

As a memento mori, Shepard's words were entirely conventional, but they had a powerful effect on Mather. "I was presently taken," he wrote, "with a Fit of my Ephialtes which almost killed mee." In the seventeenth century, "ephialtes," like "incubus," could refer to a nightmare or to the demon thought to cause a nightmare.[68] The supernatural encounter with Shepard gave Mather a cold so violent he feared that he was experiencing a "mortal Feavour." While Mather was battling his illness, God allowed him to overcome "the Fears of Death" that the dream had provoked. Less than nine months later Mather learned of Beacon's ghost sighting; perhaps Mather's earlier encounter with the speaking dead shaped his sympathetic reaction to Beacon's story and helped him frame his distinction between "internal" and "external" apparitions.[69]

Eight years after Beacon saw his brother's specter, Boston once again was home to a ghost sighting that generated both popular and learned interest.

This one, like several in Glanvill's collection, took the form of a postmortem pact. A pair of twenty-year-old friends, Mehetabel Warner and Mary Johnson, talked often about death and the afterlife, because Johnson was "sickly." Like virtually all Anglo-Americans, they wondered about "the State of our Spirits after Death" and whether such spirits "have any knowledge of what is done in this World." Was it possible to maintain relationships between heaven and earth? Johnson suspected that the answer was "yes," so she urged her friend to enter into a postmortem pact with her: whoever died first would return to the survivor and let her know about the afterlife. Warner was reluctant, perhaps knowing that ministers such as the Mathers objected to such promises. So they never formally ratified the pact, though as Johnson was leaving she portentously added, "Well, If I Dye first, you shall hear of me."[70]

Not long after this Mehetabel Warner heard a voice calling to her, "Hitty come here!" Warner had not yet learned of Johnson's death, but she suspected that her friend was the source of the voice and concluded that it "came from none but the Invisible World" and was "the Departed Spirit of that Young Woman." For several nights more the spirit visited Warner, now knocking rather than speaking. Word started to get around about the case, with neighbors investigating to ensure that Warner and her family weren't making up the story. Finally Warner mustered the courage to address the ghost. Using the formula for addressing a ghost that went back to medieval Catholic Europe, Warner cried out, "In the Name of the Lord, what is it that you come for?" Invoking God's name was supposed to protect one if the spirit was not the soul of a loved one but rather a demon.[71] The ghost responded, "Hitty, Come hither! Hitty, Come hither! Hitty, Come hither!" a trinity of commands that did not answer Warner's question, though they were also heard by her mother, "a vertuous and credible Woman," which was crucial for corroborating the account.[72] With two trustworthy ear-witnesses, the supernatural voice provided clear evidence, to Warner and Boston's ministers, that the spirit world was real. Perhaps that knowledge comforted Warner in the story's sad postscript: a few days after speaking with the dead she herself took sick, "fell into some odd extatic circumstances," and died.[73]

The story of Mary Johnson's ghost was less uplifting than Beacon's narrative. Warner was more frightened of the ghost than was Joseph Beacon, finding the knocking "troublesome" and speaking to the dead only with a "sweating terror upon her." Moreover, the conversation between the living and the dead was not as satisfying in the second case. Johnson's ghost brought no detailed information about the afterlife, though her voice did demonstrate that it existed and that spirits of the dead were interested in the lives of the living. And though Beacon also died not long after his supernatural encounter, there was no suggestion that there was a causal link between his death and the ghost sighting. By contrast, Increase Mather hard-heartedly commented on Warner's death by writing about "the folly of those that promise to appear to their Friends on Earth after they are Dead."[74] The fact that Mather castigated "those" who made postmortem pacts indicates that Johnson and Warner were not alone in their pursuit of knowledge about the afterlife.

Still, despite the evident interest of neighbors and minister-scientists in the Beacon and Johnson ghosts, historians have nothing for New England like the abundance of English source material on ghost belief.[75] Did colonists simply not believe in ghosts to the extent that their English counterparts did? Were ghosts—like maypoles and holy wells—something left behind when puritans crossed the Atlantic?

The answer is no: at least some colonial New Englanders experienced the presence of the dead via visits from their loved ones' ghosts, and this almost certainly happened more frequently than we can know.[76] Indeed, Rev. John Hale of Beverly, Massachusetts, wrote in 1697 that he had "spoken with very credible persons of discretion and piety that have told me they have seen such Apparitions when in their perfect health and senses." Tantalizingly he added, "but I spare to enlarge."[77] Likewise, Cotton Mather insisted that "Apparitions after Death . . . have been often seen in this Land." In particular, "Persons that have died abroad at Sea, have within a day after their death been seen by their Friends in their Houses at home." And these were not demonic delusions, as Lavater would have insisted, but the *actual souls* of the deceased individuals. "A Good Spirit," Mather explained, "would not Ly, and assert himself to be a Person, which he is not: Then, it must be the Soul of the Deceased." Understandably enough, such cases "have occasion'd much Notice and much Discourse at the very time of them."[78]

Then why don't we have full accounts of them, as we do with Beacon's and Johnson's ghosts? Mather blamed a lack of assiduous record-keeping: "Neighbours have not been careful enough to Record and Attest the prodigious Occurrences of this Importance, which have been among us." As a result, "many True and Strange Occurrences from the invisible World, in these parts of the World, are faultily buried in Oblivion."[79] As a natural philosopher, Mather was frustrated that so much thanatological data vanished into the ether.

But in 1692 the supernatural world burst forth onto New England with unprecedented, malignant force. Historians and thanatologists have been arguing about the resulting data ever since.

The Ghosts of Salem

The supernatural figures for which the 1692 Salem witchcraft trials are best known are "specters": the spirits that witches sent to perform their evil tasks. Sometimes the specter appeared in the form of the witch, other times in the shape of a "familiar" such as a bird or moth. Young female accusers crying out as they claim to be pinched and pricked by specters are some of the most dramatic figures in everything from the trial transcripts to Arthur Miller's *The Crucible*. But although in other seventeenth-century contexts "specter" and "ghost" were used interchangeably, in the trials "specters" were not "ghosts"; they were not the returned dead.

But if specters overshadow ghosts in popular and scholarly accounts of Salem, for participants the returned dead played a crucial role. Sometimes called "apparitions" in the trial transcripts, they were more often described by the way they looked: "Two women in winding sheats" or "a yong man in a winding sheet."[80] These were ghosts: the returned dead, the *speaking* dead, and their presence upended the proceedings in Salem.

Before any girls showed signs of supernatural affliction in 1692, before Salem became synonymous with witchcraft, transatlantic thanatologists continued their investigations into the secrets of the invisible world. Cotton Mather generated a great deal of interest with his 1689 account of the demonic possession that bedeviled the family of John Goodwin, a pious stoneworker in Boston. Four of Goodwin's children, and one daughter in particular, seemed possessed by evil spirits in 1688. Although a couple of women were suspected of witchcraft, no formal accusations were lodged and the incident resolved itself without trials or hangings. But Mather's vivid descriptions of the children's supernatural afflictions caught the attention of a broad audience. The four New England ministers who wrote a preface for Mather's book placed the work squarely in the ongoing campaign against sadducism.[81] The English puritan minister and ghost-hunter Richard Baxter likewise praised the Mathers for their hard work in demonstrating, as the title of Baxter's book put it, "the certainty of the worlds of spirits": "They that will read Mr. Increase Mathers

Book, and especially his Sons, Mr. Cotton Mathers Book of the Witchcrafts in New-England, may see enough to Silence any Incredulity [i.e., skepticism about spirits] that pretendeth to be Rational."[82]

The Goodwin children were not tormented by the returned dead, but their supernatural experiences resonated with people who were interested in ghosts. Baxter's influential 1691 book had several chapters devoted to ghost sightings, many from Glanvill, some from the Mathers and other writers. One was a story about a habitually drunk London gentleman who was hounded by an evidently good spirit that tried to get the man to lay off the alcohol. This led Baxter to muse, "Do good Spirits dwell so near us? Or are they sent on such Messages? Or is it his Guardian Angel? Or is it the Soul of some dead Friend, that suffereth, and yet, retaining Love to him . . . would have him saved?"[83] By the late seventeenth century learned thanatologists had moved away from the previous century's view that a ghost could not be the soul of the deceased and instead embraced that as a possibility.

At the same time, popular interest in ghosts peaked in England. The *Athenian Mercury*, a London newspaper that in 1691 pioneered the "Dear Abby" format of answering readers' questions—and the *Mercury* consisted of nothing else—demonstrated that English men and women could not sate their curiosity about the returned dead.[84] The newspaper's editors received so many questions about ghosts that they devoted a special issue to the topic, appropriately on All Hallows' Eve, October 31, 1691. Because Rev. Samuel Wesley, John Wesley's father, was the editor who answered theological questions, he probably wrote this issue. As the editor put it, a wide-ranging discussion of ghosts was not only useful for "reducing the many Proselytes of Sadducism and Hobbism amongst us, but also of great satisfaction to all our Querists in general."[85] In this issue readers asked whether ghost sightings proved that there is life after death; in other issues they posed the classic question of lay curiosity about the dead: "Sirs, Please to resolve me, what Knowledge and Concern the Dead have for their surviving Friends and Relations, whom they loved passionately when alive, and if it be in their power to appear to them again?"[86]

Thus the writings of Baxter, the Mathers, Glanvill, and other learned thanatologists—along with the popular interest in ghosts and the dead documented in the *Athenian Mercury* and elsewhere—formed the backdrop for the Salem trials. When the returned dead appeared in Salem, they did so at a pivotal moment in the trials. Several girls had showed signs of illness in February 1692, and their symptoms had quickly been diagnosed as having supernatural causes. The girls had leveled witchcraft accusations later that month, with the first examinations taking place in March. For several months the trials had proceeded according to a process that drew on precedents from England and elsewhere in New England. It had been serious business but it had not differed appreciably in scale or scope from earlier witchcraft trials on both sides of the Atlantic.[87]

That all changed on April 20 with Ann Putnam Jr.'s accusations against a minister, George Burroughs. Putnam insisted she had been visited by Burroughs's specter—not the returned dead, for the former Salem Village minister was very much alive in Maine—and the specter had tried to get Putnam to sign her name to the Devil's book. Putnam testified that she was shocked that Burroughs was in league with Satan: at the time she had asked aloud, "oh dreadfull, dreadfull here is a minister com[e]: what are Minsters witches to[o]?"[88] Now that a minister had been accused of witchcraft, anyone was fair game. Before April 20, the afflicted girls had accused fourteen people of witchcraft. This was a large number but, again, not without precedent. Seventeenth-century England had witnessed a handful of similar outbreaks, with sixteen people tried in Pendle (1612), fifteen accused in Leicester (1616), and thirty in Chelmsford (1645). Similarly, Hartford, Connecticut, was home to a witch panic that swept up roughly a dozen suspects in 1662–63.[89] By contrast, within six weeks of Burroughs being named in Salem, the number of accused skyrocketed from fourteen to sixty-eight.[90]

As the accusations began to snowball, the returned dead made their first appearance. On May 8, George Burroughs's specter again visited Ann Putnam Jr. to torment her, but this time he was accompanied—to his chagrin—by ghosts: "two women in winding sheets and napkins about their heads." These were the spirits of his first two wives; both had died under mysterious circumstances (he was currently married to a third woman). Residents of Salem had long gossiped about their former minister's maltreatment of his wives, but even in that context the ghosts brought shocking news: Burroughs had murdered them. First, the ghosts "turned their faces towards Mr Burroughs and looked very red and angury and tould him that he had been a cruell man to them, and that their blood did crie for vengance against him." Their vengeance they would exact by informing the living of his deeds. So the ghosts turned and addressed Ann Putnam. "One tould me," the girl testified, "that she was his first wife and he stabed hir under the left Arme and put a peace of sealing wax on the wound and she pulled aside the winding sheat and shewed me the place."[91]

Putnam's testimony drew deeply on popular ideas about the returned dead, demonstrating that New Englanders shared England's vibrant culture of ghost belief. If learned thanatologists loved nothing more than to debate how ghosts were visible to the living—was it the "astral spirit," or the "plastic" part of the imagination?—for ordinary men and women the answer was much simpler. A ghost was the dead person's soul, clothed in a winding sheet because that was how the person left this world (though some sightings reported the ghost dressed in the deceased's regular clothes). In popular literature such as broadside ballads, ghosts were usually represented as wearing a winding sheet and carrying a taper to help light their way through the darkness in which they customarily traveled.[92]

In addition to their appearance, the spirits' actions also fit with how ghosts were ordinarily represented. Most obviously, they spoke; ghosts usually returned because they had a message for the living. The returned dead could convey a wide range of information from the other side, but most frequently they brought news of murder. Even skeptical thanatologists such as John Webster agreed with this motivation, finding it plausible that God would send the murdered back to earth to bring the killer to justice, in cases when the sole eyewitness perished with the crime.[93] In addition, the ghosts appeared "at evening," for the returned dead were rarely seen during the day, and their faces "looked as pail as a white wall."[94] In contrast to these conventional ghostly characteristics, Putnam added one vividly idiosyncratic detail to her description: that Burroughs had stabbed his first wife under the arm and then plugged the wound with sealing wax. Was the implication that the wax prevented those who prepared the woman's corpse for burial from knowing the true cause of death? It is impossible to say. In any case, several other girls also reported nearly identical interactions with the "murdered" women's ghosts, which contemporaries took as corroboration, while modern commentators tend to suspect collusion or mass hysteria.[95]

After the May 8 appearance of Burroughs's wives, the ghosts kept coming, and the court continued to find their messages convincing. The next day, eighteen-year-old Susannah Shelden testified that she saw four ghosts, all clearly recognizable, and they all accused John Willard of murdering them. Like Burroughs's wives, these four ghosts "turned As Red As blood" when they looked at the person who murdered them, or as another observer memorably put it, "as if the Blood would fly out of their Faces."[96] The four ghosts then "turned As pale As death" when they faced Shelden. Ten days later, Ann Putnam Jr. had a supernatural encounter that added to the evidence against

Willard. The ghost of her "little sister Sarah," who had died at only six weeks old, appeared to Putnam. Sarah's spirit was "crieing out for vengeance against John Willard," who had murdered her. Likewise, a "woman in a winding sheat" who was Salem Village resident John Wilkins's first wife returned from the dead with an accusation that Willard "had a hand in hir death."[97] In the face of all this supernatural testimony, it is unsurprising that Willard, like Burroughs, found himself at the end of a noose only three months later.

More ghosts appeared. On June 2 Ann Putnam Sr., the thirty-year-old mother of Ann Jr., testified to the arrival of the returned dead. Samuel Fuller and Lydia Wilkins appeared in winding sheets and told Putnam Sr. that "if I did not Goe & tell [Judge] Hathorne that John Willard had Murdered them, they would tare Me to pieces." Putnam Sr. was certain of the ghosts' identities: "I knew them when they were living & it was Exactly thier resemblance & Shape." Five days later Mary Walcott and two other accusers saw eight ghosts, all crying for vengeance. Three months after that, Walcott testified to seeing another spirit of the dead.[98] For those who experienced them, these were terrifying encounters with the supernatural. As Cotton Mather wrote, the ghosts of these murder victims "do always affright the Beholders, more than all the other spectral Representations."[99]

The returned dead could be frightening, but the girls and women who saw them gained a great deal of power through these supernatural interactions. Because their descriptions of the returned dead conformed to conventional ghost beliefs, many local residents and magistrates were convinced of the veracity of their claims. Communication with the dead, long an important aspect of Anglo-Protestant belief, simply did not seem far-fetched to most observers. The accusers presented themselves as having privileged information from the other side, and they parlayed this knowledge into playing key roles in the trials.[100]

In light of the power the girls wielded based on their interactions with the dead, some of the accused confessed to the lesser crime of white magic, which includes divination, magical healing, and other practices that neither harm others nor require a pact with the Devil. A forty-year-old widow named Rebecca Johnson denied accusations of witchcraft but admitted "the turneing of the sieve, in her house by her daughter, whom she desyred to try if her brother Moses Haggat was alive or dead." At a time of high mortality and poor communication networks, family members often wondered whether their loved ones were still alive or just out of touch. Evidently Johnson feared for her brother-in-law's life, so she asked her daughter to perform coscinomancy, popularly known as turning the sieve, a form of magic with roots back to ancient Greece. According to a nineteenth-century guide to magic, this form of divination is performed "by suspending the sieve by a thread, or fixing it to the points of a pair of scissors, giving it room to turn."[101] As Johnson phrased it on the witness stand, "If the sieve turned he was dead, and so the sieve did turn."[102] Even if Salem was not the hotbed of witchcraft that magistrates originally believed it was, some of its residents did engage in magical practices that sought to gain hidden information about death and the afterlife.

It is thus appropriate that only a supernatural counterargument prevented the trials from spiraling completely out of control. It slowly dawned on ministers and magistrates that the supernatural evidence in the trials could be the result of demonic delusions. In the sixteenth century, Protestant polemicists had argued that apparitions of the dead were usually demonic delusions. Seventeenth-century Anglo-Atlantic thanatologists, further removed from the battle over purgatory's existence, allowed that at least some ghosts were actually the returned dead. But this still meant that an unknown percentage of ghost sightings were the result of Satan's deceptions.

Following this logic, two Boston ministers, Increase Mather and Samuel Willard, cast doubt on the validity of using ghostly evidence to prove witchcraft. In the fall of 1692 each published a book that criticized testimony purporting to reveal the words of the dead. They argued that Satan undeniably has the power to impersonate returned spirits. How then, Mather and Willard asked, can a court of law trust what the dead allegedly have told the living, when there are no eyewitnesses to such communication? And as Mather famously concluded his argument, "it were better that Ten Suspected Witches should escape, than that one Innocent Person should be Condemned."[103] Magistrates and lay observers eventually accepted this view, and the proceedings petered out in the first months of 1693. Thus, what ended the trials was not proto-Enlightenment skepticism about the spirit world but rather its opposite: the insistence that Satan was an active force in the world, able to delude people into thinking they spoke with the returned dead.

But not before one final ghost appeared. The last spirit arrived in November 1692, and its message shows how much had changed in the months since the accusers were at the peak of their supernatural powers. Mary Easty was a fifty-eight-year-old woman known for her piety; the accusation that she was a witch was one of the trial's most surprising. Nonetheless, the court found her guilty and sentenced her to death, largely on the basis of supernatural evidence. While in jail awaiting her execution, instead of pleading her own case, she wrote to the judges on behalf of those who still might be saved: "I petition your honours not for my own life, for I know I must die, and my appointed time is set; but . . . if it be possible, that no more innocent blood be shed, which undoubtedly cannot be avoided in the way and course you go in."[104] Easty was right that her death was nigh. She was hanged on September 22.

Less than two months later, a seventeen-year-old girl named Mary Herrick, whose aunt and uncle had testified against a woman executed for witchcraft, insisted that Mary Easty's ghost had returned. As always, the ghost had a message for the living. Easty "came to tell her She had been put to Death wrongfully and was Innocent of Witchcraft, & she Came to Vindicate her Cause & she Cryed Vengeance, Vengeance." The dead woman's spirit told Herrick that if she brought this information to two ministers who had turned against the trials, her ghost "would rise no more."[105] Consonant with Anglo-American ghost belief, once the spirit had accomplished its errand it no longer haunted the living. As it turned out, there would be no vengeance for Mary Easty, if that is even what the pious goodwife would have wanted, but there was a measure of vindication. Easty's jailhouse wish came true; no more innocent blood was spilled in Salem; the hangings were over.

* * *

Historians sometimes portray Salem as the dividing line between a seventeenth century in thrall to the invisible world and an eighteenth century of enlightened reason, but reality proved more complicated.[106] Although some participants in the Salem trials—most famously Samuel Sewall—later regretted their role in sending twenty people to their deaths, these same individuals believed no less fervently in the power of supernatural beings after 1692. They still lived in a world of frequent and capricious mortality, they still believed in a religion in which one's final estate was indiscernible, and they still longed for relationships between heaven and earth.

Indeed, seventeenth-century New Englanders sought other ways to maintain imaginative connections with the dead. In addition to engaging with ghost narratives, many read and wrote funeral poems that represented the dead as speaking or being spoken to. In elegy, the living could maintain at least the idea—and maybe more than just the idea—of continued interactions with the dead.

CHAPTER 2

Elegy in Puritan New England

In April 1682, Elizabeth Stetson suffered the fate that all women in seventeenth-century New England feared. Having given birth to living twins, she died eight days later. Stetson was likely in her early to mid-thirties, in light of her husband's age of thirty-seven. Given that her natal and marital families left little mark on the historical record of Scituate, her hometown twenty-five miles south of Boston, she was probably of solid middling status. Had she lived in England, her life and untimely death would almost certainly not have been marked by a published elegy. But in New England, where a large pool of pious subscribers made elegies a good financial venture for printers, her minister penned a poetic tribute to this "Virtuous and Truly Religious Young Woman" and had it published as a broadside, adorned only with a thick, black, funereal border (Figure 1).

The minister's poem was characteristic of New England elegies in its close attention to the deceased's corpse. Unlike most funeral poems published in England, the elegy for Elizabeth Stetson bears evidence that it was read at the graveside during the funeral. One can imagine the minister, William Witherel, gesturing toward the disturbed earth that covered Stetson's corpse while he read the poem's first line: "Here lies Inter'd a little weary Wight." Because of the proximity of the speaker and listeners to the dead person's body, it required only a small leap of imagination to render the first-person voice of the dead a convincing rhetorical device. And because Witherel wrote about a member of his congregation, he felt comfortable putting words into Stetson's mouth, imagining her speaking from heaven. The words he had her speak were not self-deprecating or tremulous; the woman's imagined soul confidently offers her townspeople pointed advice about reaching heaven: "A place worth all your pains, but you must fight / The fight of faith, else never see its Light."[1]

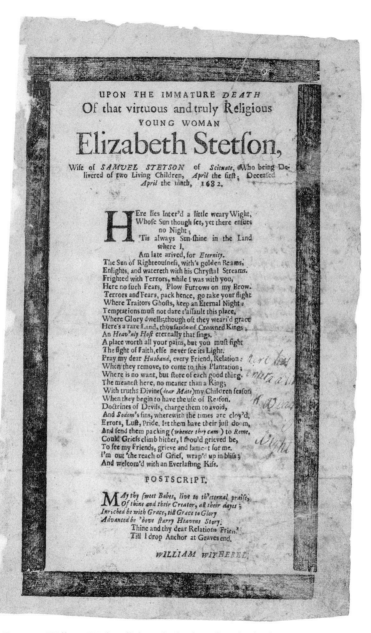

Figure 1. William Witherel's broadside elegy for Elizabeth Stetson (1682).
The thick, black border makes its subject immediately apparent to viewers.
Courtesy of the American Antiquarian Society.

Funeral poetry was, at least in the extant sources, the primary way that seventeenth-century New Englanders imagined the dead speaking and being spoken to. Only a handful of ghost narratives from the period survive, but elegies frequently represented communication with the dead. Such imagined interaction thus formed an important—and neglected—part of puritan death-ways. In particular, elegies offered mourners a way to think about the net-work of relationships between heaven and earth. Moreover, New England's women were sometimes the authors and often the subjects of elegies. As por-trayed in elegies these women were comfortable speaking their minds, and they seem to have been associated more closely than men with crossing the bound-ary between this world and the next.

But speaking with the dead was hardly confined to elegies by and about women. In a religious culture that defined itself in sharp opposition to Ca-tholicism, and in a region where belief in purgatory never held sway, women and men turned to funeral poetry to express their desires to maintain a con-nection with the dead, a desire that in the nineteenth century would blossom into the cult of the dead. The leading historians of heaven argue that Protes-tants did not become deeply interested in reunions with their loved ones in the afterlife until the second half of the eighteenth century, largely as a result of the Swedish mystic Emanuel Swedenborg's influence.[2] But the evidence in elegies suggests that a deep interest in maintaining relations with the dead ex-isted more than a century earlier. As the deceased Rev. Ralph Partridge of Duxbury, Massachusetts, was imagined in 1658 to call out from heaven to those gathered around his grave, the "Mansions in Heaven" are "Where we that Death doth for a time now sever, / Shall meet, embrace, and shall not part for ever." Despite living in a society of strict Calvinists, the "true Admirer" of Partridge who "presented these [lines] at his Funerall" could imagine no other destination for his beloved pastor, and the pastor's companions, than heaven.[3] New England's speaking dead warmly called to their loved ones, an-ticipating a blissful reunion among the cherubs and celestial choirs.

Poetic Voices in England

Protestant funeral poetry in Tudor-Stuart England was likewise marked by frequent communication with the dead. Such poems illuminate the origins of American practices, even as they demonstrate some important differences between the two locales. In particular, whereas English elegists were as comfortable as New Englanders in addressing the dead, they represented the deceased speaking in the first person much less often than did their American counterparts.

When English men and women wrote funeral poetry that spoke to or for the dead, they partook of a Western rhetorical tradition with roots in ancient Greece and Rome. Two millennia of writers and their audiences understood that the dead were not actually speaking or being spoken to, that these were rhetorical devices. Yet the devices' power derived from the grieving individuals' strong desire to communicate with the dead and learn about the afterlife. These desires were broadly shared, creating a community of like-minded authors, readers, and listeners.

Quintilian, the first-century Roman rhetorician, was the ancient writer who most clearly defined the figures of speech authors could use to represent communication with the dead. His twelve-volume *Institutio Oratoria* (*The Orator's Education*) described a wide range of rhetorical devices, including the one Quintilian called "prosopopoeia."[4] Simply put, by this device an author represents an absent speaker. The speaker may be dead, or fictional, or an inanimate collective such as a city. According to Quintilian, this device gives the author a great deal of power: "We are even allowed in this form of speech to bring down the gods from heaven or raise the dead."[5] Here Quintilian indulged a telling locution: the author who uses prosopopoeia does not literally "raise the dead," of course. It only seems that way.

Using prosopopoeia has two important ramifications. First, as Quintilian noted, this figure of speech is "credible only if we imagine them [the speakers] saying what it is not absurd for them to have thought." When elegists in Tudor-Stuart England and colonial America conjured voices of the dead, they did so constrained by what readers understood to be the plausible sentiments of the departed. New England puritans occasionally wrote didactic elegies, in which the author harnessed the supposed words of the dead to teach a lesson. These are some of the least powerful prosopopoetic elegies. Second, Quintilian asserted that "great powers of eloquence are needed" to use prosopopoeia because things that are "in their nature unbelievable must either strike the hearer with special force, because they surpass the truth, or else be taken as empty nothings, because they are not true."[6] Elegists who invoke the voice of the dead must do so within a community of readers who find that invocation plausible. Readers must agree with the elegist that the deceased has passed to the afterlife and that in the afterlife the deceased's soul retains consciousness. Otherwise the rhetorical device falls flat, or worse, seems ridiculous.

Complementing prosopopoeia is apostrophe: directly addressing the dead or other absent figure. This rhetorical device was more common than prosopopoeia in English and American elegies but is arguably less powerful—or at least less striking—than the first-person words of the dead. As Quintilian stated, apostrophe can be "remarkably effective," but its "effect can be achieved by many different Figures."[7] In other words, some uses of apostrophe can be expressed differently without much change in meaning; "Caesar thou art great" differs little from "Caesar is great." Still, when used to address the dead, apostrophe creates a more intimate connection across the boundary between this world and the afterlife than indirect expressions. "Mary, I will always miss you" is undoubtedly more powerful than "I will always miss Mary"; the former suggests a continuing connection between the living and the dead.

Among seventeenth-century Protestants, the most self-conscious users of these two rhetorical devices lived in the German-speaking states of central Europe. Addressing the dead, however, had not always been sanctioned there. Early in the Reformation, German leaders opposed anything that resembled communication between the living and the dead. As Luther wrote in 1521, "the living asking the dead . . . is like a man taking advice from a piece of wood."[8] But by the early seventeenth century, a great deal of orthodox Lutheran funeral poetry and music featured communication with the dead. Numerous writers championed the effectiveness of these devices. The Calvinist musical composer Heinrich Alsted, for example, wrote in 1625 that prosopopoeia "in serious matters, for instance in admonitions and vehement reproaches, is a remarkable figure."[9]

Literate Lutherans used both rhetorical devices with abandon. When the musician Johann Heermann's first wife died in 1617, he gained comfort by writing a chorale that imagined a reunion with her in heaven. "You don't return to me / In this troubled life. / But I'll come up to you / In the utmost joy, bliss, and passion." Heermann sees this as helping him in future dark times. "Whenever sadness overtakes me, / I'll take this to heart." Likewise, the choir master Johann Hermann Schein used apostrophe in the funeral songs he wrote in memory of his dead children. Schein lost no fewer than seven children between 1619 and 1630, and when one son died in 1628 the father wrote a sweetly intimate passage to the little boy. "Now I turn this heart of mine / To you at last / Oh dearest little son, / in whom I delighted."[10]

English elegy writers likewise employed prosopopoeia and especially apostrophe. These devices drew on the tradition, predating the English Reformation, of first-person epitaphs. Examples of Protestant prosopopoetic epitaphs from Tudor-Stuart England include the following. In 1571, Thomas Tyndall was buried in the chancel of the church at Thornbury, Gloucestershire, with this inscription on his monument, addressed to passersby:

Ye se how deathe dothe spare no age no kynd
How I am lapt in claye and dedd you fynde
My wyfe and Childeren lye here with me
No gould no Frende no Strenthe could ransome bie.

Margaret Hill, the wife of a Church of England clergyman, likewise spoke to those who viewed her monument in London after she died in 1615:

Now I rest my soule, where rest is found,
My body here, in a small piece of ground,
And from my Hill, that Hill I have ascended,
From whence (for me) my Saviour once descended.

The epitaphs of Tyndall and Hill grab the viewer's attention with first-person address to deliver conventional sentiments about death as the great leveler and the desirability of life everlasting.[11]

Elegy drew from the epitaphic tradition, with some continuities and some important distinctions. On the most basic level, both emerged from the context of mourners' grief. Historians used to argue that early modern Europeans, in the face of extremely high mortality rates, did not mourn deeply for deceased children and spouses. Now the scholarly consensus is that death was accompanied by grief that could be powerful and profound. Seventeenth-century diaries abound with expressions of deep sadness at the loss of loved ones. It was even possible to die of sadness: the 1665 London bill of mortality listed forty-six people whose deaths were caused by "grief."[12]

In addition, the Reformation shaped elegies and epitaphs, with both expressing almost uniformly orthodox Protestant views by the seventeenth century. But whereas there was no great surge in the number of epitaphs with the start of the English Reformation, some scholars maintain that the advent of Protestantism helped increase the popularity of elegies. In particular, the denial of purgatory, abandonment of prayers for the dead, and removal of the priest's address to the corpse in the burial liturgy had the "direct consequence" of the funeral elegy's emergence as a distinctive genre.[13] Such scholars, however, do not consider the role of prosopopoeia and apostrophe in representing the exchange between the living and dead.

Whereas Tudor-Stuart elegies regularly employ apostrophe, they use prosopopoeia less frequently than do epitaphs in the same period, and less frequently than seventeenth-century New England elegies. Out of many dozens of English elegies published before 1640, only a few feature the first-person voice of the dead. This may be because most subjects of published English elegies were nationally prominent figures.[14] Evidently, few English elegists felt comfortable ventriloquizing such renowned subjects as Queen Elizabeth or Henry, Prince of Wales. In New England, by contrast, most people commemorated in published elegies were known only within their town or their church, so having them speak in the first person seemed merely like an extension of the close relations the poet and deceased shared.

But a handful of English elegies did feature the first-person voice of the dead, as in this example from among the many poems that poured from English pens after the death of the great poet Philip Sidney. When Sidney died in 1586, he was mourned as a Protestant hero in more than two hundred published elegies.[15] John Phillips, for example, presents the renowned poet as not only speaking from the grave but also addressing readers directly: "You noble Brutes bedeckt with rich renowne, / That in this world have worldly wealth at will: / Muse not at me, though death have cut me downe, / For from my grave, I speake unto you still." The grave cannot silence Sidney. Phillips has Sidney go on to describe his own heraldic funeral in great detail, ending with a statement that reads like an epitaph: "Thus from my grave I bid you all adew. / Your Sidneis wordes remember rich and poore, / Though dead, my life doth daily call to you. / Thinke yee how death knocks daily at lifes doore."[16] To create an intimate exchange with the reader, Phillips relies on the fiction that Sidney was still able to communicate from his grave. This is an obvious metaphor for Sidney's poetry, which lives on after his death and continues to speak to readers, but it is significant that Phillips infuses that hackneyed trope with greater power by delivering it in Sidney's first-person voice.

Apostrophe, by contrast, was as common as prosopopoeia was rare. Direct address of the dead appears in at least one poem in virtually all of the elegy collections that toward the end of the sixteenth century became fashionable to produce when notables died. The collections of funerary verse gathered for Sir William Butts (1583), Philip Sidney (1587), Queen Elizabeth (1603), Prince Henry (1612), Sir Anthony Alexander (1638), and Edward King (1638) all included at least one elegy that speaks to the dead.[17] When the deceased was of extremely high station, poets clearly felt greater liberty to speak *to* the dead person than to speak in his or her voice. And so it is no surprise that individual elegies composed for ordinary men and women likewise used the device to show the intimate relationship the living had with the dead.

One of the most powerful demonstrations of a continuing postmortem relationship appears in an unpublished elegy by the English puritan William Tipping, whose young wife died in the late 1620s. Foreshadowing a key practice of the nineteenth-century cult of the dead, Tipping eagerly made physical contact with his wife's remains: "How oft Times I did kiss my deere / when dead I lovd thee soe." In addition to kissing the corpse, Tipping performed the traditionally female act of washing the dead body, as he explains in a poem addressed to his wife:

> I covetted to die
> And to bee buried with thee
> that I by Thee might Lie.
> With waters well perfumd I washt
> thy hands and face my deere
> fower mornings after thou wast dead.[18]

Tipping's tender attention to his wife's corpse and his elegy's use of apostrophe both served the same end: to signal that death did not end the couple's connection.

Given that the relationship between the living and dead was also at the center of Tudor-Stuart ghost narratives, elegies of the period sometimes expressed interest in the deceased's "ghost." This term can be read as standing for the person's spirit or soul, but it also might be read simply as "ghost": the returned dead. In Henry Gosnold's contribution to the elegy collection honoring Sir William Butts of Norfolk, the poem's speaker wishes he could get the dead man's ghost to return:

> If Countrie teares might call thy ghost from the grave,
> Or friends could force thy carcase to retire,
> Both countrie should (as earst) thy succour have,
> And friends againe possesse a saged syre.[19]

Gosnold means this metaphorically; the speaker does not plan to pay a local conjuror to raise the dead man's ghost. But the choice of imaginative device is telling. Gosnold and other poets used ghosts to signify the permeability between this world and the next that people wished for, imagined, and perhaps believed in. Other elegists had their poems' speakers directly address the spirit of the deceased: William Alexander has his speaker converse with the "happie Ghost" of Prince Henry; Patrick Mackgueir, in a poem styled as a letter from himself to the dead man, cries out to the "Blest Ghost" of his patron.[20]

And in the prefatory poems to John Donne's renowned *Anniversaries*, the speaker likewise plays with the boundary between this world and the next. The *First Anniversarie* was published in 1611, the *Second* the following year. They commemorate the death of a girl Donne had never met: Elizabeth Drury, the fourteen-year-old daughter of his patron, Sir Robert Drury. Each elegy was published with an anonymous introductory poem of between forty and fifty lines: "To the Praise of the Dead, and the Anatomy" introduces the *First Anniversarie*, and "The Harbinger to the Progresse" precedes the *Second*. These were written by Joseph Hall, an Anglican priest who knew Elizabeth Drury well.[21]

Donne's *Anniversaries* have been the subject of wildly divergent interpretations, with Elizabeth Drury seen as standing in for figures ranging from Jesus Christ to Queen Elizabeth. Most scholars simply ignore Hall's introductory poems. Of the few who pay them any attention, none mention that both poems are written almost entirely as apostrophe, addressing first Elizabeth Drury's soul and then Donne himself. One critic dismisses Hall's first introductory poem as "rather conventional," but that's the point: in their closer adherence to the norms of Tudor-Stuart elegy, Hall's poems demonstrate mainstream attitudes about the relation between the living and the dead better than Donne's brilliantly unorthodox *Anniversaries*.[22]

Donne held an unusual theory about the relation between the soul and body. He believed that the soul was formed inside the body rather than the more orthodox position that God created both the body and soul and joined them together at birth. Donne's view led him to portray the soul as having difficulty leaving its body behind at death.[23] By contrast, Hall's "Harbinger" is far more typical in portraying the soul enjoying heaven's delights. Moreover, Hall's use of apostrophe to address Drury's soul creates a paradox: the poem asserts an unbridgeable gulf between the living and dead, while its guiding conceit—that it is a conversation between a living speaker and a dead person's soul—undermines that very idea.

In "The Harbinger," Hall's speaker describes the "lively bliss" that Drury's soul savors in heaven. But we the living, the speaker asserts, can have no understanding of the supernatural process that brought the soul there:

No soule (whiles with the luggage of this clay
It clogged is) can follow thee halfe way;
Or see thy flight; which doth our thoughts outgoe
So fast, that now the lightning moves but slow.[24]

We do not have the sensory ability to witness the soul's flight to heaven; we cannot accompany our loved one's soul there; we are bogged down by our earthly (read: sinful) bodies. Hall's lines thus emphasize the gulf between the living and the dead, while at the same time overcoming that distance by speaking to Drury's soul. We can't see the flight of souls, we can't understand heaven—but we *can* communicate with the dead, even if only imaginatively. For countless readers and authors of elegies in Tudor-Stuart England, when purgatory had been abolished in the not-so-distant past, that was a powerfully appealing poetic conceit.

A Cultural Biography of New England Elegy

It was a rhetorical practice that also appealed to New Englanders, as revealed by the analytical method of "cultural biography," a framework for understanding the role of an object in a society. Just as a historian does when writing the "life and times" of an individual, a scholar taking a biographical approach to things asks questions such as, "Where does the thing come from and who made it? What has been its career so far, and what do people consider to be an ideal career for such things? What are the recognized 'ages' or periods in the thing's 'life,' and what are the cultural markers for them?"[25] These questions open fresh perspectives on the importance of elegy in colonial New England. They orient us toward the many ways in which elegy was deeply embedded in New England's death rituals. And because so many elegies spoke to the dead or represented the voice of the deceased, they made supernatural communication a frequent topic of contemplation for mourners. This section traces the life course of elegy, including birth, life, death, and afterlife. A cultural biography of elegy, in short, provides a thick description of the centrality of poetry—and communication with the dead—to New England's death culture.[26]

　　Elegy was born in death. Without death, of course, there would be no need for elegy. Though an obvious point, it is worth lingering on for a moment, for it highlights the motivations and desires that animate elegy. If poetry is a universal human art, elegy is a particular expression of that universal form, responding to the rent in societal fabric caused by death and shaped by the mortuary culture of a specific society.

As with any newborn, one can trace elegy's genealogy. For mourning poetry the lineage is long and distinguished. Perhaps the first elegy in the Western canon is the biblical King David's lament for Jonathan and Saul (2 Sam. 1:27). Funeral poetry was common in ancient Greece and Rome; verses frequently praised the deceased and lamented the person's death. Renaissance interest in the classical world brought forth a revival of elegy in Continental Europe and England. Although generalized poetic laments had long been a part of England's literary culture, the personal elegy—written to mark the death of an individual rather than to confront mortality or loss more generally—first appeared with this Renaissance rehabilitation of the form. After the Protestant Reformation, the tradition of English elegy only grew in the variety of its styles and the diversity of its sources.[27]

The puritan migration to New England narrowed elegy's gene pool both stylistically and in terms of subject matter. Elegies for monarchs or nobles did not wear down the pens of pious New Englanders. Nor did pastoral elegy—lamenting death while also idealizing country life—find many practitioners in a place where most saw themselves carving a society out of a "howling wilderness."[28] In fact, the puritan disdain for pastoral elegy and the insistence on writing personal elegy were important factors in shaping the early twentieth-century critical dismissal of much New England elegy as simplistic and unoriginal.[29]

But such negative views overlook the purposes of elegy, which in colonial New England had both individual and collective dimensions. For the person composing an elegy, the process of writing helped channel grief; simply put, it was something one could *do* after a death.[30] When confronted with human helplessness in the hands of an angry God, when faced with the inevitability of death for even the most beloved, writing an elegy could restore a sense of agency. As one scholar puts it, elegies were "material prayers," concrete markers of the mourner's hopes and wishes.[31]

For society the ramifications were just as important. Puritan elegies, according to one literary scholar, helped create an "ideal collective self" in which the deceased's virtues stand as a model for the living. Elegies presented the deceased person's positive qualities in general terms so the characteristics were widely applicable to hearers and readers. Whereas the deceased is the poem's ostensible subject, the audience is, in fact, its true subject. The audience was supposed to submerge its selfhood in the virtues of the collective self.[32]

Not every death birthed an elegy, however. Most obviously, elegies were typically reserved for those who stood as models of saintly behavior. Rare is the surviving elegy, such as the broadside *On the Death of Beulah Worfield* (1776), whose subject is an unrepentant sinner.[33] But even beyond that, elegy was a function of unequally distributed cultural capital. The beloved mother or father of an illiterate family could not be memorialized in written poetry by loved ones. Ministers were frequently elegized, because they had highly educated colleagues and literate parishioners who could take up the task. New England's Amerindians and African Americans generally stood outside the elegy tradition, at least until the transatlantic success of Phillis Wheatley in the second half of the eighteenth century, but Wheatley was the exception that proved the rule. Still, those elegized in New England were far humbler as a group than the renowned public figures whose deaths generated funeral poetry in England.

Once born, elegy lived a life at the very center of New England's mortuary culture. Elegy was an important part of what one scholar calls New England's "theater of burial," but a substantial portion of the death drama had already played out by the time elegy strode onto the stage.[34] The actors knew their roles. Female family members or servants had washed and shrouded the body and placed it in a coffin. Watchers had spent the night beside the coffined corpse, praying and listening for signs of life. Bearers had carried the coffin, accompanied by a procession of family members and neighbors, from the home to the burial ground. The sexton had dug a grave, the gash in the earth a warning to passersby of their own inevitable end. Mourners had assembled next to the hole with their box of mortal remains. The scene prepared, elegy made its entry.[35]

Frequently a member of the funeral party stepped forward and read a poem. In almost all cases, the elegy had been prepared for the occasion; New Englanders did not recycle elegies for great men and women at the funerals of their loved ones. Sometimes the elegy's reader was a minister, sometimes it was a family member who had penned the lines. Given the frequency with which New England elegies either spoke to or in the voice of the deceased, reading the poem aloud made the communication with the dead all the more realistic. Many times the elegy's words were geared specifically toward being read at the funeral. When Rev. Samuel Danforth of Taunton, Massachusetts, wrote an elegy for Thomas Leonard in 1713, his opening lines made sense only in the context of the theater of burial: "We do assemble that a Funeral / With grief and sorrow we may solemnize."[36] Even at the end of the century the convention persisted. John Warren's 1796 elegy for Thomas Russell of Boston likewise begins by acknowledging the graveside setting: "Shade of departed worth! we come / To pour our sorrows oe'r thy hallow'd bier."[37] Apostrophizing the dead man's "shade" or ghost, Warren uses the gathering around the grave to intensify the impact of his words. The churchyard was a space where one might encounter—or at least imagine encountering—the spirits of the recently dead.

At the start of the colonial period, when puritans remained highly sensitive to any suggestion that they were indulging in "popish" mortuary practices, reading an elegy offered a way for New Englanders to have a graveside ritual that was not a funeral sermon.[38] Although the strictures against funeral sermons would relax toward the end of the seventeenth century, in their settlement's early decades puritans still feared that a sermon next to the corpse implied the derided Catholic belief that prayers for the dead could help the deceased's soul. As phrased in the 1645 Westminster Directory, published when puritans controlled Parliament during the English Civil War, the corpse was to be brought to the burial ground "and there immediately interred, without any Ceremony." The minister, "*if* he be present," should not deliver a sermon, but he "may put [the mourners] in remembrance of their Dutie" with suitable words about mortality and the deceased's virtuous qualities.[39] Puritans brought these views with them to New England, and as a result elegy grew in stature as a sanctioned alternative to the funeral sermon.

When read beside the grave, the elegy was inclusive, gathering the mourners and the deceased into a community of believers. Many elegy authors employed prosopopoeia, with the dead addressing the assembled mourners.[40] In some formulations it was easy to imagine the dead present at the funeral, and not just as the mortal remains in the wooden box that stood before the crowd. When an anonymous author sought to remember Rev. Ralph Partridge in 1658, the elegist, adopting the voice that had recently rung from the pulpit, has Partridge address the mourners: "Oh Brethren, Sisters, Neighbours, Country, Friends, / I'me now above you: Hark to them God sends."[41] As Partridge urges the mourners to listen to him, they could easily imagine their departed friend and minister speaking to them from heaven. The "textualized dead," in one scholar's apt phrase, were thereby able to remain a part of the community.[42]

Such an effect was not fleeting, disappearing as the spoken words faded away, because the elegy continued its life in material form. Mourners brought to the funeral copies of their elegies written on paper. After the 1710 funeral for his five-year-old daughter Rebecca, Samuel Sewall Jr. noted that Rev. Benjamin Tompson had "made 2 coppies of verses on her."[43] This refers to the two separate elegies Tompson crafted, one twenty-eight lines long and the other forty-six. Tompson must have handed the poems to Sewall to keep as a memorial, because the bereaved father soon commissioned a printed version that drew on both.[44] Many funerals likewise featured ministers or other literate mourners bearing handwritten poems.

And in one of the most arresting material uses of the elegy, paper copies of the verses were sometimes pinned to the hearse or pall during the funeral.[45] A hearse was "a light framework of wood used to support the pall over the body at funerals."[46] Because so many New England elegies communicated with the dead, the presence of poems so close to the deceased's mortal remains would have heightened the sense of interaction between these "material prayers" and the dead.

Several elegies refer to the practice, including Cotton Mather's poem on the death of Rev. Urian Oakes in 1681, which offers a genealogy of elegy in seventeenth-century New England: "[John] Cotton Embalms great Hooker; Norton Him; / And Norton's Herse do's Poet-Wilson trim / With Verses."[47] In other words, John Wilson trims John Norton's hearse with his elegy. Likewise, in Samuel Danforth's poem for Thomas Leonard, the elegist alludes to the importance of this material expression of grief:

> Tho' I pretend no skill in Poetry,
> Yet will adventure once to Mourn in Verse
> Rather than such a Worthy, dead should ly
> Without a due Encomium on his Hearse.[48]

Although it was unpleasant for Danforth to imagine Leonard's hearse without at least one elegy pinned to it, other poems take note of hearses without verses, suggesting that the custom was sometimes observed in the breach. Cotton Mather points to just such a situation in his elegy for the "Never-To-Be-Forgotten" Rev. Nathanael Collins: "The Death of Collins tis. He dead without / A Paper winding sheet to lay him out! / A shame."[49] Mather's syntax makes it unclear whether it *would* be a shame if Collins did not have a "Paper winding sheet," that is, a hearse or pall with elegies pinned to it, or that it *is* a shame that he did not. But in an example offered by Samuel Sewall, the meaning is clearer. At the funeral for Rev. Thomas Shepard in 1685, according to

Sewall, "there were some Verses; but none pinned on the Herse."[50] Whether
Sewall considered this "a shame" is not known; he did not editorialize. But
he did consider it noteworthy in a funeral description of only fifty words.
This was probably because pinning elegies to hearses was all about visibility.
The wooden framework hearse was originally associated with heraldic funerals; it was a device that allowed bystanders to more easily view the pall, decorated with escutcheons and coats of arms.[51] Rather than communicating
rank like escutcheons, elegies pinned to the hearse were material evidence—
even to the illiterate—of testimony to the deceased's virtues.

   While the life span of the elegy is often imagined to be confined to the
seventeenth century, the genre remained hale and hearty through the eighteenth century and into the nineteenth.[52] Yes, Benjamin Franklin famously
satirized the elegy in 1722 in one of his Silence Dogood letters, offering a "receipt" or recipe showing just how formulaic the genre had become: "Having
chose the Person, take all his Virtues, Excellencies, &c. and if he have not
enough, you may borrow some to make up a sufficient Quantity: To these add
his last Words, dying Expressions, &c. if they are to be had; mix all these together, and be sure you *strain* them well."[53] Nonetheless, a great amount of evidence attests to elegy's continuing appeal. A writer for Boston's *New-England
Courant* mocked elegy as appealing to a provincial audience, but in so doing
he demonstrated the widespread embrace of the genre. "Nor is there one Country House in Fifty," the author sniffed, "which has not its Walls garnished
with half a Score of these Sort of Poems (if they may be so call'd,) which *praise
the Dead to the Life*, and enumerate all their Excellencies, Gifts, and Graces."[54]
Maybe in the city sophisticates admired Pope and Dryden, but in a "Country
House" the elegy still was worthy of display on the walls. As late as 1790, Philip
Freneau, perhaps America's most prominent poet at the time, remarked that
"no species of poetry is more frequently attempted" than elegy.[55]

   If elegy as a genre lived a lengthy life, an individual elegy written on a
piece of paper generally did not survive as long. Indeed, several scholars assert
that elegies pinned to the hearse or pall were buried with the corpse, hastening the end of the material poem's life through decomposition in the soil.[56]
One offers a detailed analysis of the alleged "ritual sacrifice" of puritan elegies, writing that in this "grave-good ritual" the object "descends below ground
in appeasement to a deity." The image is beguiling, but it seems to be a mis-
conception; the evidence does not withstand close scrutiny. According to this
argument, "the ritual of burying the text with the coffin is glimpsed in the
subtitle to the Collins elegy ('Funeral-Tears At the Grave of the much Desired

and Lamented Mr. Nathanael Collins') and in a rhyme from Mather's Oakes elegy: 'Oh! but a Verse to wait upon thy Grave, / A Verse our Custome, and thy Friends will have.'"[57] The first example, from Cotton Mather's elegy for Nathanael Collins, confuses tears shed "at" or beside the grave with tears or verses placed *in* the grave. And the second hinges on the phrase "to wait upon," which has multiple meanings, the most relevant of which is "to accompany; to be associated with; to attend as a concomitant or consequence."[58] Mather writes that the elegy accompanies or attends the *grave*, not the corpse or coffin. No other evidence for the practice exists from New England. In light of Reformed Protestants' long-standing antipathy toward grave goods, and their disdain for Catholic rosaries and Indian shell beads buried with the dead, stronger evidence is needed to sustain the argument that puritans buried their elegies.[59]

It seems that most material elegies, handwritten on paper, met less extravagant ends. Although "hundreds" are extant in manuscript form, surely this means that thousands do not survive.[60] Many, mirroring the subjects of their verses, succumbed to the passing of time. Humidity and insects took their toll on these keepsakes made of organic, perishable material. Others were simply lost or forgotten, as the memory of their subjects faded and keeping track of them seemed ever less urgent.

But, after death, many elegies entered a glorious afterlife. Publication was the most common way for handwritten elegies to achieve this state. At first the number of the elect—the handwritten poems that managed to get published—was small. By 1729, thirty-three elegies had been published in New England as broadsides.[61] But the chosen only grew in number over time. No complete census exists for the rest of the eighteenth century, but the total must be an order of magnitude higher than the 1729 figure. The Early American Imprints database lists 333 elegies published before 1800, and this records only surviving titles (though it does include a small number from outside New England). Once published, elegies could be much more widely distributed than they ever could in manuscript.

Some published elegies appeared as appendices to funeral sermons, but the large majority were printed as broadsides. Given that broadsides were designed to be posted, it is important to consider their visuality. For those poems that spoke to or in the voice of the dead, the broadsides engaged both visual and aural responses, which amplified the effect of keeping the deceased among the community of the living. The most common visual idiom of broadside elegy was to be printed in the form of a gravestone, so the poem appeared

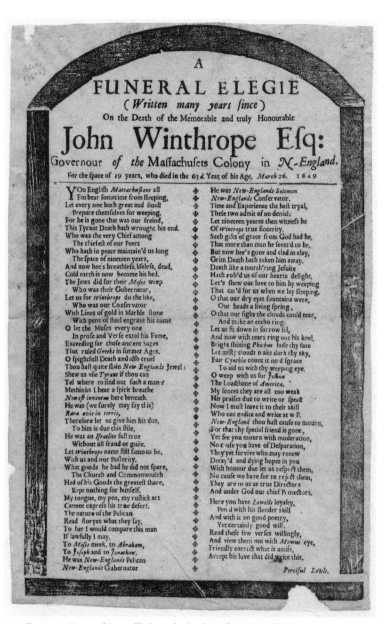

Figure 2. Percival Lowell's broadside elegy for John Winthrop. With a
simple curved border, the printer rendered the poem as a gravestone
inscription. Percival Lowell, *A Funeral Elegie (Written Many Years Since)
on the Death of the Memorable and Truly Honourable John Winthrope Esq*
(Boston, 1676). Collection of the Massachusetts Historical Society.

as an inscription on a burial marker. Even from a distance, such poems were instantly recognizable as elegies. Some of these designs were restrained, such as the 1676 elegy published several decades after John Winthrop's death. With only a graceful curve at the top of the poem's border, the printer elegantly suggested a gravestone's tympanum (Figure 2).

Most printers, however, opted for a more baroque visual effect, with a jumble of mortuary symbols leaving no doubt about the poem's subject. When Samuel Sewall Jr. had Tompson's elegy for his young daughter printed, he likely paid extra for an elaborate woodcut rendering the poem's title as a gravestone inscription (Figure 3).

In similar fashion, the Boston printer Samuel Green published an elegy in 1668 for Lydia Minot beneath a banner featuring two skull-and-crossbones designs, two winged hourglasses, a pick and shovel, a funeral procession, and a tomb. Most eye-catching is a skeleton wielding a sharp scythe, with word bubbles coming out of its mouth saying "Memento Mori" and "Remember

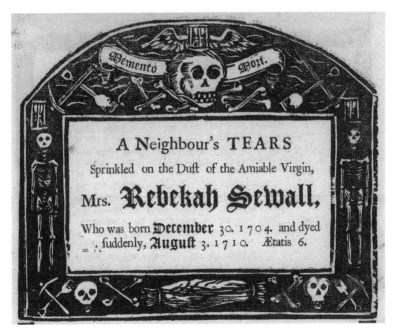

Figure 3. Detail of Benjamin Tompson, *A Neighbour's Tears Sprinkled on the Dust of the Amiable Virgin, Mrs. Rebekah Sewall* (Boston, 1710). The elegy's title is surrounded by a dense field of mortuary symbols derived from gravestone iconography. Collection of the Massachusetts Historical Society.

Figure 4. Detail of an anonymous broadside elegy, *Upon the Death of the Virtuous and Religious Mrs. Lydia Minot* (Cambridge, Mass., 1668). The lively woodcut adorned New England elegies for over a century. Collection of the Massachusetts Historical Society.

DEATH" (Figure 4). Remarkably, this exact design would be used at least another dozen times over the next 102 years.[62] These gravestone-broadsides highlighted the connections between the living and the dead in churchyards. The skeletal figure of Death is positioned between the funeral procession and the tomb, telling those in the burial ground to remember their mortality. The effect of supernatural communication is heightened by Lydia Minot's own voice. Minot, who died in childbirth, is represented as speaking directly to the gravestone-broadside's reader: "In leaving your dark World, I left all Night; / Ascended where, nor Sun, nor Moon, we crave."[63] Minot's words from heaven were thus able to enjoy a lengthy afterlife in published form: posted, gifted, and presumably treasured.

Yet even a poem that was not published could have a long and meaningful afterlife. Nothing demonstrates this more clearly than the manuscript journal of the layman Joseph Tompson of Billerica, Massachusetts, brother of the poet Benjamin Tompson. Between 1712 and 1723, Joseph Tompson copied into his journal eleven elegies, seven of which had never been published. All of them were occasioned by the deaths of Tompson's family members, so they had powerful meanings for him. One was written by his sister, Anna (Tompson) Hayden, others by leading ministers such as Samuel Danforth and John Wilson. Tompson's labor in transcribing the poems was a sacred calling: he found a "soule satisfiing delight" in reading the elegies and in "pondering & writeing and remembring afresh my Dear father and his Contemporaries with him." Several of the poems speak to the dead ("Ah, my dear brother, tho your gone" by Anna Hayden) or in the voice of the dead ("The blessed news I send to the[e] is this: / That I am goon [gone] from the[e] unto all bliss," by John Wilson).[64] This must have increased the intensity of Tompson's communion with the poems as he filled his journal with their verses. The elegies offered a connection to the afterlife, even as the poems themselves enjoyed an afterlife in Tompson's journal.[65]

Elegies lived on in other ways. When Samuel Sewall "accidentally lit upon" the verses on a boy named John Eyre who had died four years earlier in an ice skating accident, he "nail'd up" the poem on the wall. Visitors and Sewall's family could now view the elegiac lines and remember young John more readily. Elegies also retained their life in New England's gift economy. When Sewall wrote a letter in 1677 to Daniel Quincy, he included "a copy of verses made on Mr. Reynor."[66] This was Joshua Moodey's elegy for Rev. John Reiner of Dover, New Hampshire. It is possible that Sewall sent Quincy the printed version of the poem, but the "copy" he referred to may have instead been a handwritten transcription, as this is one of the many elegies Sewall copied into his notebook. If so, the effort that Sewall put into transcribing the poem—it was 114 lines long—would have increased its "value" in the exchange. And given that the elegy directly addresses the deceased, it would have been especially powerful for Reiner's brother-in-law Quincy, who was living in London and far from family.[67] The poet wrote, "My Brother *John*, I am distress'd for thee, / Thou very lovely, pleasant wert to me."[68] Quincy likely read those lines with a stab of memory.

Finally, if Samuel Sewall is any guide, elegies circulated in their afterlife among friends and loved ones. For example, Sewall's friend James Bayley was very ill in the fall of 1706. When Sewall visited Bayley the sick man had a "Paroxism" and cried out, "My Head, my Head; Cutting, Cutting, Cutting all to pieces," evidently in response to someone loudly chopping wood right outside his door. Hoping to help his distressed friend, Sewall gave Bayley some of Nicholas Noyes's elegies. Today many would consider it a breach of etiquette to visit a sick friend and offer him poems about death. But when Sewall called on Bayley again three weeks later, the sick man offered "much Thanks for his verses which had been a great Comfort to him."[69] Bayley was evidently solaced by the frank engagement with his own mortality that the elegies offered, and probably also by having Sewall as a friend with whom he could discuss such weighty topics. It is possible that Sewall is an outlier in making elegies part of a gift economy, but it is more likely that Sewall was unusual only in documenting such social interactions so thoroughly. Given the vigorous market for published elegies, Sewall cannot have been the only pious New Englander buying and gifting these material prayers. Rather they lived on, passed hand to hand, read by candlelight and nailed to walls. Like the gravestones they physically resembled, elegies placed communication with the dead at the center of New England's mortuary culture.

Elegiac Souls of the Dead

Recent work on puritan sympathy makes a powerful case that "fellow feeling" was central to colonial New England culture.[70] Such scholarship does not examine mortuary poetry, but seventeenth-century elegies are among the best sources for discovering puritan fellow feeling. Using apostrophe and prosopopoeia with abandon, puritan elegists posited a powerful connection with the dead. Deceased women and girls were disproportionately represented among those who spoke from the dead or were spoken to in heaven, suggesting that sympathy for the dead was gendered. And one female poet wrote some of the period's most powerful elegies, all of which speak to the dead.

The seventeenth-century New England elegist who has received the most attention is, of course, Anne Bradstreet. Not that Bradstreet wrote only or even primarily elegies, but her three elegies for deceased grandchildren are among her best-known poems, at least in part because they voice a tenderness toward the dead that upends the popular—and historiographically outdated—image of puritans responding coolly to the deaths of young children.[71]

Many readers admire the "carefully controlled" tone of Bradstreet's elegies, a tone that epitomizes the "willed resignation" that most puritans hoped to achieve in response to the death of loved ones.[72] Such a balance was hard to pull off, a tightrope walk between love of the deceased and love of God, between excessive grief on the one side with its implied questioning of God's will and callousness toward the dead on the other.[73] Scholars have not, however, noted that all three elegies directly address the dead. Bradstreet wrote the first of these poems, "In memory of my dear grand-child Elizabeth Bradstreet, who deceased August, 1665, being a year and half old," for the eldest child of her eldest child, Samuel. The poem begins at once by apostrophizing the dead:

Farewel dear babe, my hearts too much content,
Farewel sweet babe, the pleasure of mine eye,
Farewel fair flower that for a space was lent,
Then ta'en away unto Eternity.
Blest babe why should I once bewail thy fate,
Or sigh the dayes so soon were terminate;
Sith thou art setled in an Everlasting state.[74]

With gentle endearments—"dear babe," "sweet babe," "fair flower"—the poet addresses her deceased granddaughter. The child is dead but Bradstreet wants to maintain a connection by speaking directly to her. The lines are fairly conventional except for Bradstreet's twist on an idiom: "my heart's content" becomes "my hearts too much content." Shakespeare had published the first known usages of the more common phrase only a half century earlier, in *Merchant of Venice* and *Henry VI, Pt. 2*.[75] Bradstreet's update suggests that she may have worried that she took "too much" pleasure in her granddaughter's life, perhaps even forgetting the infectious diseases and other dangers that stalked toddlers in the early modern world. Did she fear that she provoked God's wrath by loving the little girl too intensely?

The following, three-line sentence is just as surprising. Bradstreet takes a question that was utterly conventional—why should I cry when the deceased is happy in heaven?—and changes its valence by addressing it to the deceased child. "Blest babe," she asks, "why should I once bewail thy fate." The question scholars have not posed is, why does Bradstreet address this question to the child? Shouldn't she direct the question to God, or her minister, or herself? What kind of answer could she hope for from eighteen-month-old Elizabeth? None directly, but the convention of direct address in elegies allows Bradstreet to formulate the question in a way that brings her the greatest comfort. God, her minister, or she herself might answer that question more sternly—"you're weeping because you don't trust God"—than would the child's soul, which is what she conjures with the line. This is what enables her to reach the resignation of the final line, that it is "His hand alone that guides nature and fate." Apostrophizing the dead allows Bradstreet to find that balance between love of God and love of her granddaughter.

Bradstreet's other two elegies for grandchildren also speak to the dead, but in these cases the purpose is to assert the reality of loved ones meeting in heaven, more than a century before the period when such reunions are supposed to have become commonplace in Protestantism. Bradstreet had cause to write such poems twice in a span of only five months in 1669. First, her three-year-old granddaughter and namesake Anne died in June. The poem's speaker says, "Farewell dear child, thou ne'er shall come to me, / But yet a little while, and I shall go to thee; / Mean time my throbbing heart's cheered up with this: / Thou with thy Saviour art in endless bliss."[76] When grandson Simon died in November, Bradstreet directed these words to the soul of the month-old child: "Go pretty babe, go rest with Sisters twain / Among the blest in endless joyes remain."[77]

Again, commentators have ignored Bradstreet's direct address of the dead, as if it were entirely unexceptional, but just because it was conventional does not mean it is unworthy of attention. In the first Bradstreet asserts a reunion between herself and the child in a realm of "endless bliss." Despite being a good Calvinist, Bradstreet allows no doubt about the child's or her own future estate to cloud the elegy. Likewise with the poem for Simon, though here Bradstreet insists that the soul of the dead boy will rest with his sisters in heaven. Direct address of the dead may have increased the likelihood that a poet would express certainty that the deceased was a member of the elect. It seems that it would be harder for the speaker to say that she is not certain about the deceased's future estate when speaking directly to his soul.

Many seventeenth-century elegies exhibit characteristics similar to Bradstreet's: she drew on the poetic conventions of her time and place rather than boldly overturning them. A great number of elegies similarly speak to the dead and assert that the deceased's soul is certainly in heaven. This is true even for elegies written by ministers. When John Cotton's daughter Sara died of smallpox at age fourteen in 1650, he wrote a poem so moving that Cotton Mather included it in his *Magnalia Christi Americana* more than a half century later:

> Farewel, Dear Daughter Sara; Now Thou'rt gone,
> (Whither thou much desiredst) to thine Home:
> "Pray, my Dear Father, Let me now go Home!"
> Were the Last Words thou Spak'st to me Alone.
> Go then, Sweet Sara, take thy Sabbath Rest,
> With thy Great Lord, and all in Heaven Blest.[78]

As in two of Bradstreet's elegies, Cotton bids his daughter "Farewel" and tells her to rest in heaven. He does not worry—in the poem at least—that she might not be saved. Or as Rev. Ichabod Wiswell of Duxbury, Massachusetts, spoke to the soul of a ministerial colleague in a broadside elegy, "thou shalt surely rise again."[79]

Also like the Bradstreet poems, other seventeenth-century elegies made the leap from being convinced that the deceased's soul was in heaven to the expectation that the living would meet the dead in the hereafter. How exactly the living imagined heavenly geography remains a mystery. Were all the saints gathered in one room? Would it be hard to find one's friends and relatives? Such musings were relegated to theologians; pastors and laypeople simply expected to be reunited with their loved ones after death. To cite just one example among many, in the elegy written by "P. B." after the death of Rev. Thomas Hooker of Hartford, the speaker confidently voices an expectation for a heavenly reunion:

> Sense of our loss would call thee back again,
> But out of love, we bid thee there remain,
> Till we yet left behinde our course fulfil,
> To meet thee on the top of Zion hill;
> When thou and we shall both rejoyce together,
> So fast united as no death shall sever.[80]

An unusual aspect of this elegy is that the speaker addresses the dead in the first-person plural: *we* will meet you in heaven, *we* will rejoice together. The effect is to draw the reader into the conversation with the dead even more powerfully than is typical. The reader does not merely listen in on the speaker's colloquy with the deceased but rather takes an active part in the conversation. The point is not that readers thought they were having an actual conversation with the dead. Still, the convention is significant. More than a century after the Protestant Reformation, a bright line between living and dead still did not exist.[81]

An elegiac convention new to the seventeenth century was to address the "blest shade" of the dead. A "shade" is simply a ghost, or, as the *Oxford English Dictionary* more ponderously phrases it, the "visible but impalpable form of a dead person."[82] Unsurprisingly, given his sense of the narrow separation between the living and dead, Cotton Mather was the puritan poet who most frequently used this term. The earliest English example I have found of a poet addressing the deceased's shade is Thomas Beedome's "Epigram 20: To the memory of his honoured friend Master John Donne," published in 1641. The poem's speaker implores, "Burst ope thy Cell, blest Shade, and rise, that we /

May doe some homage to thy excellency."[83] Thus, even though the title states that the poem is addressed to Donne's "memory," it is in fact addressed to his "blest Shade." A few earlier elegies address the deceased's "ghost"—"happie Ghost" or "Blest Ghost"—but the poem for Donne appears to be the first to speak to the more poetic "blest shade."[84]

The Early English Books Online database reveals eight other usages of "blest shade" before Mather's first appropriation of the phrase in his 1682 elegy for the recently deceased president of Harvard College, Urian Oakes. Mather speaks to Oakes's ghost:

> Blest Shade! an Universal Tax of Sorrow
> Thy Country ow[e]s thee! Ah! we need not borrow
> The Praefica's: Say, Oakes is dead! and there!
> There is enough to squeeze a briny Tear
> From the most flinty Flint.[85]

Mather tells the shade that the ghost's countrymen do not need to rely on praeficas (or praeficae), women hired to lament at a funeral.[86] No, professional mourners are not needed; merely say the words "Oakes is dead!" and the tears will begin to flow. "Dear Saint!" Mather continues, creating an equivalency between "shade" and "saint," "I Rue / Thy Death!"[87] The shade is a saint; Oakes's soul is surely in heaven.

Twice more does Mather use "blest shade" in his elegies, and both times the phrase signals that communication with the dead will soon commence. In the latter two examples, however, it is the dead rather than the poet who speaks. In his elegy for Rev. Nathanael Collins (1685), many pages of encomiums build toward an expression of overwhelming grief. The poet shudders with "Incohaerent Throbs," the deceased man's parents weep, his widow sighs, his "Orphans" cry out. Then, suddenly, a change in the atmosphere signals a supernatural occurrence:

> In this Distraction mixing once again
> A Consolation-cup; Thick Mists amain
> About us gathering; a Murmur there
> Of the blest Shade himself we then might hear.

Thick mists indicate that we "might hear" the speech of the dead man's ghost. Mather is careful to maintain the fiction that this is a poetic ghost we are encountering, but the effect is dramatic nonetheless. The ghost commands the mourners, "wipe your eyes." He continues, "To weep / For my Sake, is but to Ignore my Bliss." The sentiment is conventional—don't cry for me, I'm happy in heaven—but the delivery gives it more force than it would otherwise have. Collins continues to speak from heaven for nine more stanzas, telling the reader, among other details about heaven, that "I'm got within the Vail, and there I see / The ever-glorious Face of the GOD-MAN."[88]

Likewise, when Mather eulogized the Boston schoolmaster Nathaniel Cheever in 1708, his use of "Blest Shade" also indicates that the dead person is about to speak: "But in his Paridisian Rest above, / To Us does the Blest Shade retain his Love."[89] Building upon his belief that the living should engage in "Conversation with the Departed," Mather assures readers that Cheever's spirit continues to love us.[90] The dead man is still concerned for us, so Mather ventriloquizes Cheever. In this case, the message is even more mundane than that of Collins: "'Tutors, Be Strict; But yet be Gentle too: / Don't by fierce Cruelties fair Hopes undo.'"[91] The dead remain so connected with us, Mather implies, that they offer instructions about quotidian matters such as how to do our jobs.

Mather's use of prosopopoeia dovetailed nicely with his campaign to convince New Englanders to incorporate the deceased into their daily practice of piety. But Mather was hardly alone in employing this rhetorical device. Many other elegists represented the dead as speaking, and they did so disproportionately for dead women. From 1650 to 1800, seventy-three published elegies represent the dead as speaking or being spoken to. These poems eulogize men more than twice as often as they do women (50 to 23, or 2.2:1). But of the twenty-three deceased women, 48 percent speak, compared with only 32 percent of the dead men. Women thus gained notice in published elegies less often than men, but when they did get such attention, nearly half of them spoke from beyond the grave. Given that most such elegies were authored by men (8/11), was this a case of male writers finding it easier to appropriate the presumed words of deceased women? Or did the male elegists believe that women more easily breached the boundary between this world and the next?

To begin answering these questions, it is worth lingering over the first published New England elegy written to honor a woman. This broadside poem, or rather series of poems, did not identify the author, but the high quality of the verse and the use of multiple anagrams and an acrostic suggest an educated, ministerial hand: perhaps Richard Mather, pastor of the deceased woman's church. Lydia Butler was born in England in 1628 and was likely brought to Massachusetts Bay by her parents. When she was nineteen she married John Minot, who was two years her senior, in Dorchester, near Boston. She bore five children but while delivering the sixth in January 1668 she and the child died. As the elegy's author memorably phrases it, "She first to it was Life; Then to't became a Grave." The two, "Fruit and Tree together," were interred in one coffin in the Dorchester North Burying Ground.[92] This sad story provided the author an irresistibly didactic opportunity: "The Life and Death of both, his Sov'raignty Makes known, / Who gives and takes at will, and no Controll can own."[93]

The broadside contains three anagram poems, all in Lydia Minot's voice, and an introductory poem in the third person. The first anagram poem, "I di to Al myn," features Minot's words from her deathbed (whether fictionalized or not is impossible to know), where she is not just resigned to death but eager for it: "happy Death, my welcome I'le thee give." Women's deathbed speeches typically received more attention than their everyday words; certainly their dying utterances were far more likely to be immortalized in print.[94] The next anagram poem, "I di, not my Al," features eighteen lines of Minot's imagined words from heaven. Her body is "dust" but her soul lives on. "Life hath my Better part; which soon did post / By Angels Conduct, to the Heav'nly Host." The couplet reflects the belief that the souls of the dead were whisked to heaven by angels, and Minot is now in a position to testify to the reality of that process. As discussed in the opening to this book, Minot offers listeners details about the afterlife. "New Robes I have, new Company, new Skill / To sing th'new Song." She is wearing new garments and singing the new song the Bible mentions several times. In their emphasis on newness, elegies that feature the speaking dead drew on the conventions of the conversion narrative: both are delivered in the style of first-person testimony, and both attest to the speaker's dramatic spiritual transformation.[95]

Although Minot describes her new "Company" in heaven, she does not refer to a reunion with loved ones. In this her voice differs from that in Bradstreet's elegies for her grandchildren. Whereas Bradstreet eagerly anticipates heavenly reunions, the author of Minot's elegy is content to describe the beatific vision as heaven's main attraction:

In leaving your dark World, I left all Night;
Ascended where, nor Sun, nor Moon, we crave:
My God, & th'Lamb's the light that here we have.

Protestant ministers considered the beatific vision—the face-to-face viewing of God—to be the soul's primary activity in heaven. It would be joyful beyond description, and although theologians tried out various metaphors to describe the ecstasy of the beatific vision, they ultimately agreed that language fell far short of the actual experience.[96] Later, in the eighteenth century, laypeople and ministers would begin to focus more on the reunions of loved ones as heaven's chief attraction.

Reunion was likewise downplayed in another elegy written for a young woman who died in childbirth. In this case the poem memorializes Elizabeth Stetson, whose story of dying eight days after she delivered twins opens this chapter. The poem's author was the deceased woman's pastor, William Witherel of Scituate in Plymouth County. The broadside elegy begins with some ambiguity as to who is speaking:

> Here lies Inter'd a little weary Wight,
> Whose Sun though set, yet there ensues no Night;
> 'Tis always Sun-shine in the Land where I,
> Am late arived, for Eternity.[97]

From lines 3 through 30 (that is, to the end of the elegy), Stetson is the speaker. But does she speak the first two lines? They seem more like the words of the minister at the graveside, but they are separated from the first-person line 3 only by a semicolon. Either way the words connect the gravesite to the speaking dead. Once again the graveyard is represented as a place where one readily hears the voices of the dead.

Although Stetson's voice does not emphasize the potential for reunion with her loved ones, she does maintain a connection with her husband by directly addressing him. She offers child-rearing advice: "With truths Divine (dear Mate) my Children season / When they begin to have the use of Reason." Perhaps he would have preferred her to call them "our" children instead of "my" children, but the words nonetheless seek to maintain a bond between the living and the dead. In the poem's culmination she urges her loved ones to moderate their grief, telling them, "Could Griefs climb hither, I should grieved be, / To see my Friends, grieve and lament for me." Stetson finds herself in an unusual situation: she *would* be sad that her friends are grieving for her, but sadness is not possible in heaven, so she discusses her own grief only in theoretical fashion. Even though the sentiment—moderate your grief—fits a widespread ministerial campaign of the seventeenth and eighteenth centuries, the lines come off as less didactic than they do in other genres, softened as they are by the first-person delivery from a beloved friend.[98]

Perhaps most noteworthy about the elegies for Minot and Stetson is the lack of explicitly feminized language. Aside from each one mentioning her husband, there is nothing in the elegies that identifies the deceased as female. If their names were removed and the references to "husband" omitted, the reader would have no reason to suspect that the speakers are female. To the contrary, their words are crisp, concrete, and full of unequivocating descriptions of heaven and the extraordinary spiritual transformation they have undergone in death. "Here's a rare Land, thousands of Crowned Kings, / An Heav'nly Host eternally that sings," Stetson tells the reader (or listener when it was read at her funeral). Minot offers her readers and listeners a vivid picture of the moment of death: "When Breath expir'd, my Life came flowing in; / My Soul reviv'd, made free from th'death of Sin." These voices are confident and knowing—perhaps because they were written by ministers (certainly in Stetson's case, highly likely in Minot's). But the point is that the ministers did not feel the need to write female voices that were weak and trembling. They believed that if a woman spoke from the dead, she would speak with all the force and authority that her heavenly position granted her.

In elegies in which deceased men spoke from heaven, one sees how little male voices differed from female. Take Josiah Winslow's elegy for William Bradford, written in 1657. If any elegy should swell with the manly language of politics and public life it is this, composed in honor of Plymouth Colony's former governor by a man who would himself become governor in sixteen years. But the acrostic on Bradford's first and last names, written entirely in the first-person voice of the dead, is perhaps even more tender than Minot's and Stetson's. The poem begins with the conventional statement that mourners shouldn't grieve because the dead man is happy in heaven: "Why mourns the People thus for me, since I / In Heavens dwell shall to Eternity?" This might sound a little stern, but the lines are immediately followed by five emotional lines full of the language of tears, affections, and bosoms:

> Let not so many Tears fall from my Friends;
> Live holy, happy, God will recompense
> Into your bosomes all your love again,
> And your affections whiles I did remain
> Mongst you, but now you must refrain.

The speaker urges readers and listeners not to be sad, but at the same time he recognizes that they *are* sad. Live in a holy fashion, he tells them, and God's love will substitute for the love that we shared while I was alive.

The next stanza positively gushes with emotion as Bradford begs his "Dear friends"—"dear hearts" he also calls them—to imagine when he can at last embrace them in heaven:

> Bear up your hearts, dear hearts, when thoughts of me
> Run in your mindes, with this, The time will be,
> And every hower brings it on apace,
> Dear friends, when we for ever shall imbrace.[99]

Scholars have long known that puritan men's devotional poetry could be very passionate and sensual, with references to embracing Christ, shedding tears, and swooning with love for God.[100] But there has been less recognition of similar emotionalism in puritan elegies. As Winslow's elegy demonstrates, poems for the dead expressed not only intense grief at the departure of loved ones but also eager anticipation for future reunions and excitement about the glories of heaven. Speaking with the dead was an effective device for conveying all these sentiments.

*   *   *

Death evokes powerful emotions. This was no less true for the supposedly dour and self-abnegating puritans than for members of any society. Given its public nature, funeral poetry cannot offer insight into every recess of the bereaved heart in seventeenth-century New England. But it does illuminate conventional expressions of grief and longing, and those societally sanctioned articulations included frequent imaginative interactions with the dead. Godly puritans considered necromancy—raising the spirit of the dead to learn hidden secrets—to be a grievous sin. But no one in early New England, as far as the sources reveal, looked askance at imagining the dead speaking from heaven, or hoping for a joyful embrace in the afterlife, or speaking to the deceased's soul in an elegy. As Rev. Benjamin Tompson put it in his elegy for young Rebecca Sewall, "Pleasant Rebecka, heres to thee a Tear / Hugg my sweet Mary if you chance to see her."[101] Mary was Tompson's seven-year-old daughter who had died a decade earlier; the poet imagined Sewall's soul as an emissary, bringing love to the dead child with whom he still maintained a connection.

In practice such ideas moderated Calvinism's harshest aspects, as laypeople and ministers alike imagined the dead in heaven, almost never in hell. In their celestial abode the dead were happy beyond description and eager for their loved ones to join them. Moreover, the dead remained interested in the living, offering imagined advice and succor from heaven. These were indeed comforting thoughts.

Another material object that generated thoughts about continuing relationships with the dead appeared in New England's graveyards. "Talking gravestones," like elegies, represented the dead speaking and being spoken to. The same desires that led New England's mourners to read and write so much funeral poetry also led them to local burial grounds, where stone markers continued the conversations with the dead.

CHAPTER 3

Talking Gravestones and Visions
of Heaven

Standing in the center of every New England town is an archive exposed to the elements day after day after day. Wind and acid rain have slowly eroded markers made of slate and limestone, yet these seemingly silent sentinels remain valuable sources for understanding how a broad cross-section of the population thought about death, the afterlife, and the possibility of maintaining relationships between heaven and earth. The vast majority of scholarship on early New England religion is based on traditional paper sources—sermons, diaries, letters, conversion narratives—in which the voices of ministers and elite laypeople are overrepresented. By contrast, gravestones, and in particular their largely ignored epitaphs, shed light on ideas across the social spectrum, including beliefs about communication with the dead. It is no coincidence that in the early modern Anglo-Atlantic world graveyards were considered the most likely location for ghost sightings and that gravestone iconography frequently represented supernatural beings in transit from this world to the next. Burial grounds were the locus for belief in communication with the deceased, the spatial setting for ideas that in the nineteenth century would become incorporated into the cult of the dead.

To understand this physical archive, insights from scholars of religion and material culture are valuable. As the editors of the journal *Material Religion* put it, objects "are not something *added* to a religion, but rather inextricable from it."[1] Historians who want to understand religion need to place objects at the center rather than the margins of their analyses. Following that logic, this chapter examines objects I call "talking gravestones," markers whose epitaphs speak to the viewer, to the deceased, or to others. Those markers in the center of New England towns aren't so silent after all. They use the same techniques of apostrophe and prosopopoeia employed by elegists on both sides of the Atlantic. Viewing talking gravestones played an important role in the material expression of religious beliefs. This chapter argues that all gravestones, talking or otherwise, were "religious objects." While this might seem like a humble claim, it goes beyond the existing literature's emphasis on puritan iconoclasm.[2]

Considering gravestones as "religious objects" does not imply that they were "devotional objects." Protestant gravestones were not analogous to the bleeding Eucharists and weeping statues of medieval Catholic devotion.[3] Rather, according to one helpful definition, religious objects are not "worshipped as such" but are "focal material nodes in private Protestant prayer and worship through which believers experience the presence of God."[4] With talking gravestones, the objects have less the presence of *God* than the presence of the *deceased*. They are further evidence of Protestantism as a religion of presence.

Talking gravestones have a long history, but in New England they appear in large numbers only after 1750, with popularity peaking in the decades around 1800. This chronology is connected to a shift in Protestant ideas about heaven, from the sixteenth- and seventeenth-century focus on the beatific vision to the eighteenth- and nineteenth-century interest in heavenly reunions. "Conversation with the Departed," in Cotton Mather's phrase, became more imaginable as people believed their loved ones awaited them in heaven.[5] New Englanders expressed this interest materially, on gravestones, which were perhaps the region's most frequently encountered religious objects. The result was both a religious object and a literary genre, heretofore unexamined by scholars, that reveals lay men and women's deepest desires for connection with the dead.

Conversation with the Departed

To understand how Anglo–New Englanders experienced epitaphs requires an exploration of graveyards' social and intellectual history. Did laypeople visit burial grounds? If so, did they read epitaphs and think about the dead? The evidence before the nineteenth century is not as abundant as one would hope, but that which exists points toward a culture of graveyard visitations and engagement with gravestones. This supports the contention of material religion scholars that viewing objects is an important component of belief, even for

Protestants.[6] This chapter extends that idea to the act of reading epitaphs and hearing the voice of the dead. The common denominator is that these experiences occurred in the interaction between humans and objects.

Some seventeenth-century Protestant writers in England and America, both ministers and godly laypeople, urged readers to visit graveyards to be reminded of their mortality. In 1591 the Anglican clergyman Bartholomew Chamberlayne delivered a funeral sermon praising those who "to remember death do go every morning into the churchyeard and behold the graves."[7] It is impossible to know how many people—other than the sexton—actually went to the burial ground "every morning," but presumably Chamberlayne's statement contains at least a grain of truth. Likewise, in 1618 the barrister George Strode described graveyards as "places to which we may resort to be put in minde of our mortallitie and future mutability."[8]

Others advised readers to visit graveyards while acknowledging that this might have Catholic overtones. One such writer was John Weever, an English antiquarian with a keen interest in tombstones. In 1631 Weever published *Ancient Funerall Monuments*, the first book dedicated to collecting epitaphs from English gravestones and church tombs. Summarizing the conventional wisdom regarding gravestones' didactic function, Weever asserted that "the frequent visiting, and advised reviewing of the Tombes and monuments of the dead (but without all touch of superstition) with the often reading, serious perusall, and diligent meditation of wise and religious Epitaphs or inscriptions . . . is a great motive to bring us to repentance." Given that concerns about Catholicism still troubled many English Protestants, it is no wonder Weever insisted that his readers visit the dead "without all touch of superstition." He was also trying to inoculate himself against accusations that his project smacked of popery in its seeming veneration of the dead. Elsewhere in the book he wrote that it was beneficial to view graves, "provided alwayes that we do not intermixe our devotions with superstitious adoration."[9] Protestants were expected to visit burial grounds and think about their own mortality, but they were not supposed to pray to the dead or for the souls of the deceased, actions forbidden by the Reformation.

In subsequent decades, though, perhaps because concerns about Catholicism eased among Protestants in England and New England, some authors of devotional manuals suggested visiting burial grounds without feeling the need to warn readers away from "superstitious" Catholic practices. In 1671, just as gravestones were coming into wider usage in England and America, the English puritan minister Edward Pearse wrote, "'The meditation of Death' (saith one [church patriarch]) 'is Life': it is that which greatly promotes our Spiritual Life; therefore walk much among the Tombs, and converse much and frequently with the thoughts of a Dying-hour."[10] Here Pearse uses the term "converse" in the seventeenth-century sense; "conversation" referred not only to spoken exchange but also to "the action of consorting or having dealings with others; living together; commerce, intercourse, society, intimacy." "Converse" could also mean "spiritual or mental intercourse; communion."[11] Pearse thus expected readers to commune with their thoughts of mortality "among the Tombs," demonstrating that Protestants considered gravestones to be religious objects.

First-person accounts of lay New Englanders visiting graveyards are rare before the nineteenth century. Therefore it is difficult to know how frequently laypeople heeded the suggestions of ministers such as Pearse and what they thought when they did so. The two accounts that survive from colonial America involve individuals who left unusually detailed diaries. It is unsurprising, in light of Pearse's terminology, that one of these writers would "converse" with the dead. This was Samuel Sewall, the Boston merchant, judge, and diarist. In 1696 Sewall buried his "little daughter" Sarah, only two years old, in the family tomb. Because "twas wholly dry," he took the opportunity to examine the nine coffins that remained in the tomb. "There I was entertain'd with a view of, *and converse with*, the Coffins of my dear Father Hull, Mother Hull, Cousin Quinsey, and my Six Children."[12]

It is likely that Sewall's "converse" with the coffins consisted of "mental intercourse" rather than spoken words. Nonetheless, his feelings of interaction and communion were strikingly similar to those that spoken dialogue would have produced. The very arrangement of the coffins demonstrated that relationships continued even among the dead: "My Mother ly's on a lower bench, at the end, with head to her Husband's head: and I order'd little Sarah to be set on her Grandmother's feet." Grandparents head to head, with a darling granddaughter at their feet: a tableau reminiscent of a fireside gathering for stories and cider, except in a tomb. If relationships continued among the dead, they also persisted between the dead and the living, as Sewall's leisurely viewing demonstrates. Fittingly for a time period in which people were comfortable with death and human remains, Sewall was not at all disturbed by the sight of his decomposing family members. Quite the opposite: "'Twas an awfull yet pleasing Treat."[13]

The other extant account of a layperson visiting a burial ground to commune with the dead takes place outside New England and does not use the word "conversation," but the incident is nevertheless best described as an attempted dialogue. In 1710 the Virginia planter William Byrd II was troubled about his dead parents. Byrd's father, a distant figure in life, had been dead for six years. After a horse and coach got loose in the cemetery and damaged his mother's tombstone, Byrd wondered whether he should build a fence in the churchyard to protect his parents' graves. Seeking an answer from the dead, he "tried to consult his father," as Byrd's biographer puts it. According to Byrd's account, "I had my father's grave opened to see him but he was so wasted there was not anything to be distinguished."[14] Disappointed that his father's face was too decomposed to offer an answer, he had the remains reburied. This was a conversation that remained frustratingly one-sided.

The multiple senses of "conversation" create ambiguity in the writings of the puritan minister who most enthusiastically encouraged laypeople to interact with the dead: Cotton Mather. In 1723 Mather entered his sixties and witnessed the death of his larger-than-life father, Increase. The confluence of these two events—but especially Increase's death—spurred Cotton Mather to develop novel arguments about the relationship between the living and the dead.[15]

When Cotton Mather published *Cœlestinus: A Conversation in Heaven* (1723), his father was still alive but the deathwatch was on. In that context, *Cœlestinus* made the case that souls in heaven were supernatural beings with whom the living could maintain a relationship. Mather stated that an occasion "for our Conversation with the Departed Spirits of the Faithful in the Heavenly World" is "when we are in the midst of our Lamentations for their Departure from us."[16] Thus, as mourners wept for their recently departed loved ones, they should engage in "Conversation" with those spirits. Mather's exact meaning remains ambiguous. Should the bereaved speak with the dead?

Most of Mather's suggestions involve mental communication—praying and meditation—rather than verbalization.[17] In addition, laudable communion with the dead could involve imagining what they would say to the living, which is just how Mather represented his father. As he informed those who heard or read his funeral sermon honoring Increase, "I will now put you in mind, of what I am well assured our Departed Father and Pastor would speak unto us, if he might from the Paradise where he is now Comforted, speak unto us, or, if we might Converse with him."[18] Mather then offered six paragraphs describing an imagined colloquy with his father.

But on occasion Mather went beyond the realm of imagination and "mental intercourse" and suggested something that seems more like speaking with the dead. "When we become Dull in our Approaches unto God," Mather advised, "call down the Spirits that are Above, to be swift Witnesses against our Lukewarmness in what we have before us." A mourner could "call down" spirits from heaven by opening her mouth and crying out to her beloved spouse or child. But even if the bereaved were to "call down" the deceased mentally, this required—indeed is the very definition of—communication with the dead. Likewise with Mather's advice to "Rejoyce in the Views of the Joys, which our Departed Friends are flown unto: and Hear them from their Cælestial and Superiour Joys calling to us, 'Weep not for us, but weep for yourselves.'"[19] Writing these words as he watched his father die, Mather imagined the dead calling to mourners. It is not a stretch to think that Mather hoped he would soon hear his father calling to him from heaven.

Other contemporary ministers in England and New England asserted the benefits of conversing with the dead. Several English nonconformists, for example, prescribed to their readers that they should maintain relationships with their loved ones in heaven. In 1692 John Shower wrote of the dead, "Let us therefore . . . resolve to have Communion with them, though they are Departed." Shower's recommendations for doing so consisted of mental rather than spoken intercourse: contemplating what they were doing in heaven and striving to imitate them. Three decades later, Isaac Watts, perhaps the most popular eighteenth-century devotional writer on both sides of the Atlantic, insisted that there was no "sweeter Employment" than to "trace the Souls of our departed Friends into those upper and brighter Regions" of heaven. Doing so "puts us in mind of the Communion that we have with those blessed Spirits in Heaven, while we belong to the Church on Earth."[20]

Still, of all the dissenting and puritan ministers in England and New England, Cotton Mather most forcefully asserted the benefits of communing with the dead. Given that he offered the strongest such statements, it is unsurprising that he anticipated potential objections: "There is a 'Communion with the Departed Saints'; which is indeed so far from its being Unlawful to be ask'd for and sought for, that our Sanctity, and a Conversation in Heaven, lies very much in the Study of it."[21] Mather suspected that some of his readers might wonder whether such communion with the dead was "Unlawful." Or as he put it in a later, unpublished work, this "Intercourse with Paradise, and Communion with the Departed Spirits of the Faithful there . . . will be no Criminal Necromancy!"[22]

As long as people did not wish for apparitions of the dead, their behavior remained orthodox, in Mather's opinion.[23] But when an apparition did appear, it could bring information about the heavenly world, including the message that communication with the dead was not only possible but also desirable. In the unpublished "Triparadisus" (1726–27), a lengthy description of the invisible world, Cotton Mather recounted the example of a man who saw his dead brother's ghost. Mather does not identify the man the ghost visited other than to assert that he is someone "whom I know!" When the apparition appeared, the living man said, "Well, I shall be with you Anon; It won't be long!" To which his brother's ghost replied, "In the mean time, keep up a Good Intercourse with our World; It may be done!"[24] Thus, according to Mather, one should not wish for an apparition, but if one does appear, it might bring news about the value of maintaining relationships between heaven and earth.

If Cotton Mather was especially strident in his insistence that conversation with departed saints was a laudable devotional aid, he was not unusual among colonial ministers in imagining what the dead might say to the living. As we have seen, this was a common technique among elegists. Clergymen also liberally used the technique in funeral sermons. The Boston minister William Cooper, for example, appealed to readers by imagining the voice of the dead. Cooper did so in a 1720 sermon urging his parishioners to mourn the dead moderately, one of many such tracts that New England ministers wrote. Ministers expected the bereaved to be sad and shed tears, but they should not carry on too dramatically nor grieve too long, both of which seemed to question God's sovereignty.[25]

Offering comfort to the bereaved, Cooper asserted that survivors could reasonably hope that their loved ones were in heaven if they "fell asleep in Jesus." And if the deceased were in heaven, it stood to reason they might want to communicate with the living. "Could our deceas'd godly Friends speak to us from the Regions of the Blessed," Cooper wrote, "it would be as our Saviour once spake to the People that bewailed and lamented him, as He was carried to His Cross; 'Weep not for me.'"[26] Cooper asked his readers to imagine the voice of the departed, with the dead saying, in effect, that survivors should be happy their loved ones were in heaven.

Isaac Watts similarly anticipated his readers' interest in hearing from their deceased loved ones. He recognized that "our Curiosity, or our Love, has a mind to know what are the Circumstances of our pious Friends departed," so he tried to satisfy those desires with imagined words from heaven. Like Cooper, Watts described the dead speaking in reassuring tones: "Could the Voice of those Blessed Spirits made perfect reach our Ears, we should hear them speak in the Language of their Lord, 'Weep not for us, but for yourselves; you are still incompassed with Temptations and Difficulties, we have surmounted them all.'"[27] Comforting passages such as this help explain why the English Watts was perhaps the most popular devotional writer in eighteenth-century New England: Boston printers published no fewer than eighty editions of his works before 1800.[28]

Several decades after Watts wrote, Rev. Samuel Buell of East Hampton, Long Island, penned a much more detailed account of what he imagined a dead woman might say to her surviving friends. In 1763 and 1764, Buell was a major figure in the Seacoast Revival that swept from East Hampton to the north shore of Massachusetts.[29] But even prior to that awakening, Buell preached with the passion that served him well during the revival. This is evident in the funeral sermon Buell published in 1760 in memory of Catharine Davis, who died at age thirty-nine.

The centerpiece of Buell's sermon was a rendering of what he imagined the dead would say to their loved ones from heaven. "I have attempted to talk the Language of Immortality," Buell explained, "supposing after what manner our departed pious Friends and Relatives would address us, could they speak to us, from the World of Glory." Buell then offered more than three pages of first-person-plural messages from the collectivity of saints in heaven. Their words, as Buell imagined them, fit comfortably within two centuries of Protestant preaching about the glories of heaven, the inferiority of the earthly world, and the imminence of bodily resurrection. And yet despite the familiar themes, the presentation of these ideas as the words of deceased friends brought them home with extra force. "Ye Friends below," the saints implored, "put of[f] your Garments of Heaviness, and cease to mourn for us in these blissful Realms above." Heavenly existence was so delightful that the living should not be sad that their loved ones were dead; life in heaven was "infinitely preferable" to life on earth. Best of all was the beatific vision, the viewing of God in all his glory.[30]

Emerging from this lengthy reverie, Buell reminded his readers—now in his own voice—that the words of the saints were only from his imagination: "In some such Language as this, I imagine the departed Spirit of Mrs. Davis, whose bodily Remains we last Week attended to the Grave, would address us, could she now speak to us."[31] The sermon was a work of imagination, but Buell deliberately adopted the rhetorical strategy of ventriloquizing the dead because he knew it would effectively convey his message to his readers. It was an unmatched method for grabbing an audience's attention.

But there was one thing the "Spirit of Mrs. Davis" did not say that her surviving husband may have longed to hear: that she eagerly awaited seeing him again in heaven. In this Buell's sermon was slightly out of step with its time, for by the middle of the eighteenth century most ministerial discussions of the afterlife included comforting words about how people would meet their loved ones in heaven. This had not always been the case. In the early decades of the Protestant Reformation, ministers preached much more about the torments of hell than the glories of heaven. When they did get around to talking about heaven, ministers focused almost entirely on the contemplation of the divine. The beatific vision was to be the primary activity in heaven.

Most early Protestant reformers also agreed that there was a social aspect to heaven, that the souls of the saved would meet and recognize the souls of their loved ones who were among the saints. Only John Calvin, in characteristically stern fashion, denied that reunions were part of heaven's joys. Martin Luther and others believed that saints would come together in heaven, but this was never the center of their ministry. In their writings and sermons they always focused on the beatific vision.[32]

The emphasis on the beatific vision persisted in seventeenth-century England and New England. For example, the 1648 Westminster Confession of Faith, the outline of Protestant beliefs formulated when puritans controlled Parliament during the Interregnum, included a chapter on "the state of men after death, and of the Resurrection of the dead." The picture of heaven offered there was solely focused on the beatific vision, without a word about meeting loved ones in the afterlife.[33]

A similar emphasis appeared in seventeenth-century tracts about heaven. In these books, published in both England and New England, ministers rarely discussed reunions of loved ones. This was not because strict Calvinist beliefs kept ministers from encouraging their parishioners to imagine themselves going to heaven. *A Glance of Heaven* (1638) by the English Anglican Richard Sibbes, for example, was optimistic about the possibility of believers entering heaven but did not mention reunions at all.[34] Even when seventeenth-century writers did discuss how loved ones would be reunited in heaven, they did so with seeming reluctance. Richard Baxter's widely popular *The Saints Everlasting Rest* (1650) was over a thousand pages long but spent only five pages on heaven's social aspect. Similarly, in 1673 the English puritan William Gearing wrote *A Prospect of Heaven*, which included nearly four hundred pages about what the afterlife entailed for believers. Only one chapter out of thirty-five examined heavenly reunions.[35]

In the eighteenth century, however, ministers slowly became more willing to appeal to people's desires for heavenly reunions. In New England, Increase and Cotton Mather led the ministerial turn toward greater attention
to heavenly reunions. In 1707 Increase assured readers that "in Heaven Believers gain the sight of and a blessed conversation with their Friends that are
gone thither before them; their Godly Parents, their Children, and other dear
Friends."[36] Again one of the Mathers focused on the importance of "conversation," in this case among the dead rather than between the living and dead.
It was an image well designed to appeal to readers, who wanted to see their
friends and family members in the afterlife.

Later in the eighteenth century, ministers devoted increasing attention
to these desires. In a sermon preached in London in 1755, the English minister John Gill asserted simply that "the saints will see and know one another
in this perfect state" of heavenly bliss.[37] Peter Powers, the minister at New-
bury and Haverhill, Massachusetts, preached a funeral sermon in 1772 for a
twenty-four-year-old woman who died while giving birth. Her husband and
friends could rest assured that in heaven "the saints in that eternal house enjoy one another and the holy Angels in sweet society, union and communion,
in all the comforts and blessings of the kingdom of God."[38] This woman's good
death, recounted in great detail in the sermon, gave her family members strong
hopes that she had gone to heaven. They could thus anticipate "union and
communion" with her before too long.

It is, of course, much easier to know what ministers wrote than to discern how strongly laypeople desired to meet their loved ones in heaven. As we
have seen, seventeenth-century elegies by laypeople sometimes voiced a desire
to see the deceased in heaven. In the eighteenth century, pious women and
men occasionally expressed interest in heavenly reunions in their diaries and
letters, but this was not a topic about which they wrote frequently. One as-
sumes that the documentary record understates lay interest in heavenly meetings; this suspicion is bolstered by gravestone epitaphs, examined below.
Nonetheless, lay writings do contain enough references to meeting in the
afterlife to demonstrate a broad interest in the topic—at least a half century
before the leading historians of heaven say it emerged.[39]

Take, for example, the spiritual journal of John Paine, a deacon in the
Congregational Church of Eastham on Cape Cod. In 1716 the death of Paine's
beloved wife of twenty-seven years demanded something of a eulogy. In
his brief memorial, Paine wrote that he had "good reason to hope" that his
wife's soul was in heaven, where she could "Sing Eternal praises to our Glori-

ous & blessed redeemer." Just as important to Paine, heaven was a place "where I hope through the riches of free grace to meet her and till then adieu my dearest mate."[40] Not only did Paine attempt to assuage his grief by thinking about meeting his wife in heaven, but he also addressed the dead woman directly, bidding her a touching "adieu." This direct address of the deceased in diaries would become much more common in the nineteenth-century cult of the dead.

Unlike Paine, Sarah Pierpont did not try to talk with her grandmother after the elderly woman died in 1735—or at least no record exists of such an attempted conversation. But Pierpont did take comfort from imagining her grandmother meeting loved ones in heaven. "Her dying agonies," Pierpont wrote, "led me to think . . . what a joyful Meeting she wou'd have with her Child (my Mother) as also with her Fri[e]nds & Acquaintances, but above all with her Jesus."[41] Such reunions were so important to pious laypeople that it was painful to even think about what it would be like to be denied such a fate. This is evident in the diary of the Medford, Massachusetts, housewright and lumber merchant Jonathan Willis. A devotee of lively preaching, Willis frequently made the five-mile journey from his home to Boston's Brattle Street Church to hear William Cooper's sermons. A year after Cooper's 1743 death, Willis still mourned the great preacher. He imagined his minister in the afterlife, which triggered this terrible thought: What if, because of his own sins, he never got a chance to see Cooper in heaven? "O God forbid," Willis pleaded, "that this should be my amazing fate & aggravated condemnation, O must I be eternaly shut out from Christ from all thy dear saints that ever I knew on Earth."[42] Never again to see the "dear saints" he loved was nearly too much for Willis and other pious laypeople to contemplate.

By contrast, it was much more comforting to imagine speaking with the dead in heaven. Daniel King, a math instrument maker who lived in Salem, was sixty-three years old when his wife died. Upon her death, he wrote a poem expressing his grief, part of which directly addresses her:

tis come at last oh mournful time
when thou no longer must be mine
Why did I live this time to see
to have all comfort rent from me[43]

Presumably King did not use the archaic "thou" when he spoke to his living wife; he was not a Quaker. Rather, a poem marking the death of his beloved demanded the stately language of the King James Bible. As Chapter 8 argues, such direct address of the dead deserves to be called a "prayer," and in the nineteenth century it would become a central practice of the cult of the dead.

Because of the widespread desire for reunion and postmortem conversation, some laypeople experienced visions in which they imagined interacting with the dead. This was most common during the Great Awakening, when many converts went into trances and had visions of heaven. One young boy in Ipswich, Massachusetts, was entranced for several hours in January 1742. When he awoke, he said that angels had carried his spirit to heaven, where he had seen Jesus surrounded by departed saints, including his deceased grandfather.[44] Also during the revival, Rev. Joseph Fish of Stonington, Connecticut, complained that ecstatic converts in his town claimed to have visions of "such and such persons" in "heaven or hell."[45]

These Great Awakening visionaries seem only to have *seen* the dead in heaven rather than communicating with them. By contrast, the dead sometimes spoke in ordinary nighttime dreams, bringing comforting words from beyond. This had a long history in the Anglo-Atlantic world. In sixteenth-century England, *Dreams of Daniel* (1566?) was a widely used dream dictionary. This book asserted that dreaming of the dead augured good tidings. "He that dreameth that he speaketh with a deade body," the anonymous author wrote, "betokeneth goodnes that is to come. . . . To se[e] a dead body, and therwith to speke, betokeneth joye, & gladnes."[46] Not something to be feared, speaking with the dead in a dream was a good omen and something to look forward to.[47]

In seventeenth-century New England, Samuel Sewall recorded several dreams where he saw deceased individuals and two in which he spoke with the dead. In 1688 Sewall dreamed he discussed "military matters" with Daniel Gookin, who had died the previous year, and in 1695 Sewall dreamed he spoke about church affairs with his friend William Adams, who had been dead for ten years. After the latter dream, Sewall calmly noted, "Thus I was conversing among the dead." In addition, the dream about Adams put Sewall in mind of "Mr. [Urian] Oakes's dream about [the deceased] Mr. [Thomas] Shepard," which demonstrates that friends sometimes discussed their dreams of the dead with one another.[48]

In the eighteenth century, Martha Brewster of Lebanon, Connecticut, recorded a dramatic encounter with the dead in her published collection of poems. In 1744, soon after her father died, Brewster dreamed that he was standing in her room. He was not a decomposing corpse but rather "in good Habit, with a healthful and pleasant Countenance." Seeing his face as it was in life filled her with joy; father and daughter then began a lengthy discussion of the afterlife. Brewster's first question concerned heavenly conversation: "I asked him if he had Conversed with the most ancient and primitive Saints?" He answered yes, all saints in heaven are able to do so. Reflecting her concerns about what her father experienced while dying, she "asked him what the Pains of Death were?" Her father answered reassuringly, "it was little or nothing, I was immediately Transmitted into Glory." And so the dialogue continued for some time, until Brewster woke up "Refreshed, . . . without any fear, or uncomfortable awe of Ghostly Death, but as tho' I had had a real Visit from a dear deceased Father."[49] Brewster was careful to distinguish between a dream and what she considered a more problematic ghost visitation. Nonetheless, like many other laypeople, Brewster's desire to communicate with those in heaven led her to imagine a conversation with a departed loved one. Dreams were yet another way to maintain relationships between heaven and earth.

Talking Gravestones

Thus there was a long Anglo-Atlantic tradition of interacting with the dead in visions, dreams, elegies, diaries, and conversations with the departed. Lay and ministerial ideas about the possibility for communication with the dead shaped gravestone iconography, epitaphs, and even the location of burial grounds. For the first half century of English settlement in New England, colonists shared the Continental Protestant discomfort with the traditional placement of the burial ground adjacent to the church.

This was an attitude with roots in the Reformation. In Europe's German-speaking states, as we have seen, the Reformation spurred dramatic changes in cemetery placement. Protestant reformers insisted that the living could not influence the postmortem state of the deceased's soul, and they denied the power of relics. These two new beliefs undercut the logic behind Catholic burial *ad sanctos*, "near the saints." For medieval and early modern Catholics, the most desirable burial spot was within the church because proximity to saints' relics could help the deceased's soul get to heaven.[50] Next best was burial in the adjacent churchyard. German Protestant leaders, by contrast, argued that churchyard burial was of no use to the dead; Martin Luther famously said his body could be buried in a forest or stream for all he cared. This attitude led to the rise of burials outside the city walls in the Protestant-controlled portions of present-day Germany and Switzerland.[51]

Some sixteenth-century English Protestants with strong puritan inclinations shared this disdain toward churchyard burials. Henry Barrow, a separatist executed for his religious beliefs, wrote in the late 1580s that churchyard burial was "a thing never used until popery began . . . neither comly, convenient, nor wholsome."[52] But only a tiny minority of English men and women shared Barrow's views. Most saw nothing popish about burying the dead next to the church, where the living could see the graves as they went about their daily business. So England did not witness a move away from churchyard burial.

Some puritans who migrated to New England, however, shared Barrow's suspicion about churchyards. This is revealed by burial patterns in Middlesex County, Massachusetts, located to the west and northwest of Boston. In the seventeenth century, residents of Middlesex County established eighteen burial grounds. Only six were adjacent to churches. The other twelve were located anywhere from four hundred feet to one-half mile away from the town's meetinghouse. The use of separate burial grounds was a striking departure from English practice, inspired by the reforming impulse of New England colonists eager to purge their religion of any "popish" elements, including the connection with *ad sanctos* burial.[53]

Another important break with English practice involved burial ground consecration—or lack thereof. In England the churchyard was consecrated ground, ritually purified by a diocesan bishop and regulated by the Church of England. In New England, by contrast, the burial ground, whether separate from or adjacent to the meetinghouse, was owned and operated by the town and no formal rituals blessed the space.[54]

In their unconsecrated, sometimes non-adjacent burial grounds, New England puritan funeral rituals—at least in the first few decades of colonization—were stripped down to their essentials. In this they reflected the ideals that English puritans attempted to legislate when they briefly held power during the Civil War. As the puritan Westminster Assembly decreed in 1645, interments should take place "without any Ceremony." Indeed, because "praying, reading, and singing both in going to, and at the Grave, have been grossly abused" and are "no way beneficial to the dead," the Westminster Assembly forbade such practices.[55]

Connected to this reasoning, and contrary to the popular image today, New England's first puritan churchyards were not filled with slate markers inscribed with glowering death's heads. Many burials remained unmarked, at least partly owing to puritan iconoclasm or at least image-wariness. Indeed, churchyard crosses had been among the leading targets of iconoclasts during the early years of the English Reformation.[56]

As concerns about images eased after the first decade of puritan migration to Massachusetts, and some families became interested in memorializing the dead, the first markers were wooden rather than stone. Typically, wooden posts were driven into the ground at the head and foot of the coffin; sometimes the posts were connected by one or two rails.[57] The use of wood partly reflected the relative poverty of colonial residents in the first half of the seventeenth century. But early New Englanders may also have chosen this material because of its ephemerality. Stone markers could seem to display an unbecoming vanity, and they might call to mind proscribed monuments such as churchyard crosses. By contrast, wooden posts and rails—cheap to produce, simple to carve—bespoke an admirable humility, especially as they decomposed back into earth along with the corpse buried beneath.

New Englanders began using stone markers in the 1670s as part of a broader trend away from the stark simplicity of the region's earliest funerals and as images no longer seemed as threatening as they did during the English Reformation. New England's first published funeral sermon, for example, appeared in 1679, as puritans began to lose their fear that a minister's graveside words might be interpreted as a Catholic attempt to help the deceased's soul into heaven.[58] The increasingly elaborate mortuary practices of the late seventeenth and early eighteenth centuries—what became known as the "large funeral"—included long processions, painted coffins with brass hardware, and a gifting culture centered on gloves, scarves, and rings.[59] These funerals increasingly took place in burial grounds that were adjacent to churches. Of the burial grounds established in eighteenth-century Worcester County, immediately west of Middlesex, 64 percent (29 of 45) were adjacent to a meetinghouse, as opposed to only 33 percent in seventeenth-century Middlesex.[60] In both new and well-established burial grounds, stone markers began to appear in the last decades of the seventeenth century.

It is these stone markers, with death's heads and other folk icons of mortality and everlasting life, that historians and the general public have found so compelling. Indeed, the carving on these stones is so visually appealing that historians have almost entirely neglected the inscriptions and epitaphs that accompany the images. The abundant literature on New England stonecarving has taught us a great deal about gravestone iconography, chronological changes in carvings, the geographical distribution of specific images, and the regional influence of particular carvers.[61] Only a few scholars pay equal attention to epitaphs.[62] This has led to an incomplete narrative about gravestones in New England from the seventeenth to the early nineteenth century.

Here is the story that historians have told about the evolution of gravestone iconography in New England. Starting in the 1670s, churchyards were dominated by the death's head: the winged, grimacing skull that instantly conjures "puritans" for American readers. The death's head, for most gravestone historians, encapsulates all that was terrifying about puritanism, including the "anxieties" about one's future estate, the lack of assurance, the "desperate introspective fear" of death, and the "ideological dualism that divided mankind into good and evil, saved and damned."[63] In the middle of the eighteenth century, as puritanism lost strength in New England, and as itinerant preachers stoked the Great Awakening, death's heads were replaced by chubby, smiling cherubs. These happy icons, in this narrative, represent the revivalists' allegedly more "optimistic" faith.[64] By the end of the eighteenth century, cherubs were falling out of fashion, quickly replaced by the restrained willow-and-urn motif. Along with other neoclassical icons such as columns and arches, the willow-and-urn image demonstrates, in this interpretation, how gravestones had become less about religious belief and "more a secular symbol of an increasingly settled and prosperous society."[65] Such stones were evidence of a society "engulfed by the secular sentiments of the Enlightenment" where "an individual's search for salvation" was now "less critical" than when death's heads dominated the landscape.[66]

This narrative contains elements of truth. Most obviously, gravestone iconography did change from death's heads to cherubs to willows and urns, though more unevenly than the narrative allows. Moreover, the standard history points toward important changes in religion and society. The older work also includes an argument that has been ignored more recently: that early iconography portrayed connections between the living and the dead. According to one scholar, death's heads represented spirits separated from their bodies: either souls on their way to the afterlife or spirits waiting rejoin their bodies on Judgment Day. If the latter, "the winged skull may have been a 'ghost' in the real sense of the word."[67]

But the literature's overarching narrative of secularization is sustainable only if one ignores the epitaphs that deepen the meaning of the stones on which they were carved. Epitaphs, in fact, are key to understanding gravestones as religious objects. The epitaphs on talking gravestones may be divided into three categories:

1. Stones where the deceased speaks to passersby. This is the most common type of talking gravestone, the classic version of which begins, "Stranger, stop and cast an eye, / As you are now, so once was I."[68]

2. Stones on which the deceased speaks to someone other than passersby, usually a surviving loved one, sometimes Christ, rarely Death itself. This is the least common of the three categories and includes examples such as "Farewell my loving friend, farewell!" from a woman to her husband, and "O death thou'st conquered me by thy dart I'm slain."[69]

3. Epitaphs in which the stone speaks to the deceased, often in the voice of one or more mourners. A typical example of this category is an 1808 marker for an unnamed infant: "Sleep on dear babe and take thy rest / No mortal cares can seize thy breast."[70]

Non-talking gravestones fall into one of two additional categories:

4. Stones with epitaphs that do not speak. Most of these are brief aphorisms about death and mortality such as "tempus fugit" (time flies), "memento mori" (remember that you will die), or Anglicized versions thereof, such as "Remember sudden death" on a 1763 stone.[71] Some in this category are third-person tributes to the deceased, including simple statements such as "This stone is erected by her mourning Husband" and more elaborate encomiums.[72]

5. Stones with no epitaph, only an inscription. These became increasingly rare after 1750.[73]

Talking gravestones appear throughout the Anglo-Atlantic world in the eighteenth and nineteenth centuries, in England, New England, New Jersey, Pennsylvania, the Carolinas, and elsewhere.[74] But to better assess their meaning, this analysis focuses on a limited geographical area, applying the five categories to 810 markers from 1700 to 1849 found on the website Cape Cod Gravestones.[75] The 810 stones are from burial grounds from one end of the Cape to the other, so the epitaphs were not the work of one idiosyncratic carver or minister (Figure 5).

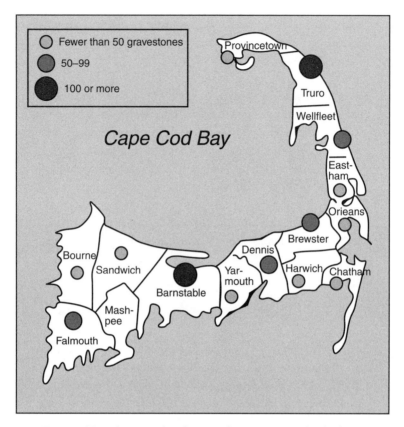

Figure 5. Town-by-town distribution of gravestones in the database.

Information from the 810 stones forms a database: name, sex, age at death, year of death, cemetery name and town, and epitaph category. The database reveals which variables were disproportionately represented. For example, females were slightly more likely than males to have talking gravestones. The overall distribution of stones was nearly equal by sex: 50.7 percent of the stones (411) were for males, 49.3 percent (399) were for females. But 52.5 percent (137/261) of the talking gravestones were for females, while only 47.5 percent (124/261) marked the graves of males (Figure 6). Or, put another way, 34.3 percent (137/399) of females had talking gravestones compared with only 30.2 percent (124/411) of males.[76]

Age proved an even stronger predictor of what kind of talking gravestone memorialized an individual. The deceased fall into five age groups: 0–2 years, 3–18, 19–40, 41–60, and 61+. Several interesting patterns emerge. First, infants

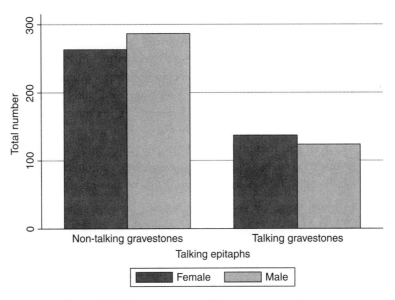

Figure 6. Talking versus non-talking gravestones, by sex.

and toddlers up to two years old represent 12 percent of the total sample (95/810) but 36 percent (18/50) of epitaph type 3, in which the stone speaks to the deceased. Many of these markers use variations of the "Sleep on dear babe and take thy rest" formulation. It makes sense that infants and toddlers were three times likelier than a random sample to have these kinds of stones, given that such children would have been too young to speak or would have spoken in simple baby talk that would not seem appropriate on a gravestone. Children in this age group made up only 3.3 percent (7/211) of gravestones that spoke either to passersby or to someone else (types 1 and 2). The effect of these stones—with infants represented as speaking in mature voices—can be quite jarring. Take the 1796 stone of Samuel Chapman, who lived only seven months and sixteen days. He addresses the reader in a confident voice:

> When alive with joy was I then carefree
> Now dead mourn'd for while taking my rest
> Here I lie till ye lofty trumpet gives alarm
> Then with joy I leap to my Saviour's arms.[77]

Samuel Chapman's parents sought to comfort themselves with an epitaph that speaks of resurrection and eternal life, but they were unusual in commissioning a stone that represents their baby's voice. Only six other sets of parents made the same choice in the 150 years of the sample.[78]

Likewise, those who died in the prime of their lives (19–40 and 41–60) were especially likely to have talking gravestones, while the elderly (61+) were almost never memorialized with stones that spoke to them. Specifically, 38 percent (110/290) of those aged 19–40 and 41 percent (49/119) of those aged 41–60 had talking gravestones. For the elderly, only 3 of the 220 stones (1.4 percent) erected in their honor purport to speak to the deceased.

Finally, New England's talking gravestone phenomenon had a strong chronological dimension. As discussed in Chapter 2, some talking gravestones appeared in late medieval and early Reformation England. But on Cape Cod, such stones were essentially unused before 1750. In Figure 7 the sole outlier—a 1733 footstone for twenty-year-old Abigail Davis in Barnstable—is represented by the bar standing alone to the left. This conforms with other evidence from New England.[79] After 1755 on the Cape, talking gravestones accounted for 20–30 percent of the total number of stones in each five-year period. This figure jumped in the 1790s, reaching 48 percent in 1795–99, stayed high in the first decade of the nineteenth century (43 percent, 42 percent), before settling back into the 20–30 percent range for the rest of the period, except for a brief spike to 38 percent in 1840–44.

The emergence of talking gravestones is linked to changing beliefs about heaven. Historians have long tried to connect changes in gravestone *iconography* to the Great Awakening, but that argument does not hold up under close scrutiny.[80] Nor does it work for the rise of talking gravestones. If they were related to the Awakening, they should appear in the 1740s rather than 1750s, and they should be found more frequently in evangelical cemeteries, which they are not.[81] Instead, evolving ideas about heaven provide a more persuasive explanation.

As Protestant interpretations of heaven shifted during the eighteenth century from focusing on the beatific vision to reunions with loved ones, ministers and laypeople became more interested in imagining the afterlife. Women and men wrote and read poems, short stories, and news accounts that imagined or claimed to describe aspects of the afterlife. The image of heaven that emerges from these sources focuses on departed loved ones; it is a mourning vision rather than a beatific vision. In this context, talking gravestones helped represent a connection with an afterlife that seemed more approachable and imaginable than before.

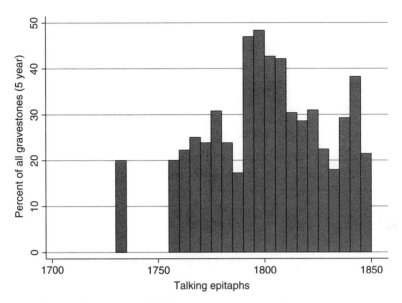

Figure 7. Percentage of talking gravestones among all gravestones per five-year period.

The way epitaphs on talking gravestones functioned was related to the materiality of the objects themselves. Stone markers presented a material profile that was solid and weighty, seemingly immovable. But from the beginning, iconographic traditions emphasized upward flight. The winged skull of the puritan death's head represented hope for bodily resurrection, while the winged cherub of the eighteenth century also pointed upward, symbolizing the soul's ascent at the moment of death.[82] Some stones even showed the soul fluttering above the tomb, presumably on its way to heaven, perhaps offering an opportunity for communication with the dead in the graveyard (Figure 8).

Epitaphs mediated between these two materialities—the heaviness of stone and the upward flight of the soul—by offering an opportunity for conversation between residents of this world (heavy, solid) and residents of heaven (light, ethereal). This was the case with markers that promised a reunion in heaven, a message especially well-suited to talking gravestones. In a dialogue between the living and the dead, the possibility of a heavenly reunion offered hope where otherwise there might be only grief.

The oldest talking gravestone that survives on the Cape is the footstone of Abigail Davis, the teenaged wife of Barnstable's John Davis (Figure 9). It is

Figure 8. Betsy Shaw gravestone (1795), Burial Hill Cemetery, Plymouth, Massachusetts (detail). Shaw's soul hovers above her tomb, offering the possibility of communication between the living and dead. Farber Gravestone Collection. Courtesy of the American Antiquarian Society.

not merely the blank-eyed death's head that connects this 1733 stone with puritan sensibilities. In addition, the epitaph revels in the details of bodily decomposition in a manner that recalls the seventeenth century: "Though worms & putrefaction shall consume / This mortal body in the silent tomb / I shall revive & from the grave arise / & see my God with these corporeal eyes." The words echo in verse Job's stirring affirmation (19:26–27) of his belief in bodily resurrection. The first-person rendition on Davis's stone increases the epitaph's immediacy. Instead of being just a biblical quotation, the words become the witness of a specific individual—Abigail Davis, friend and loved one—to God's power to triumph over death and bodily decay.

Another theme that resonates with older puritan concerns is avoiding excessive mourning. Even as mourning conventions in New England and elsewhere in the Anglo-Atlantic world were beginning to mandate longer and deeper expressions of grief in the second half of the eighteenth century, some

Figure 9. Abigail Davis gravestone (1733), Cobb's Hill Cemetery,
Barnstable, Massachusetts. Davis speaks from the dead to affirm her
triumph over bodily decay. Farber Gravestone Collection.
Courtesy of the American Antiquarian Society.

talking gravestones continued to voice older views that excessive mourning
demonstrated a problematic questioning of God's will. This was often expressed simply, as when the appropriately named Patience Hall urges readers,
"Go home my friends, dry up your tears / For you must heed till Christ appears."[83] For mourners and passersby alike, the message is the same: don't cry,
don't question God's will.

A subject that is less specifically puritan and more broadly early modern is death as relief from pain. In an era before effective analgesics, dying could be agonizing and death could be a welcome end to suffering.[84] This category of epitaph is especially compelling on a talking gravestone; "He suffered and is now with God" is less affecting than "I suffered and am now with God." Take, for example, Abigail Baker's 1804 stone. Baker evidently lived with pain for an extended period of time: "Long has my life most irksome been / Opprest with care & pain / . . . Better to die than live / For death to mind worn out with care / Glad peace & rest will give."[85] Similar sentiments found their way onto a number of gravestones for infants. Even children who were too young to speak were represented as offering their parents soothing words.[86]

Such sentiments comforted the living, which was likewise the goal of markers that promise a reunion in heaven, a message that talking gravestones express powerfully. In a dialogue between the living and the dead, the possibility of a heavenly reunion consoled the afflicted. As the eighteenth century progressed, and heavenly reunions became an increasingly central part of Protestant belief, talking gravestones more frequently promised fellowship in the afterlife.

This was the case on the numerous stones testifying to the dangers of the nautical life practiced by so many of the Cape's men. Lewis Parker of Falmouth "unfortunately perished at sea" at age thirty-two, and his wife either composed or commissioned a verse that begins with the terror she felt when she feared for his life and ends with her hope that they would meet in death: "The raging Sea proclaim'd thy fearful doom / And fill'd thy anxious wife with wild alarms / Ah! hast thou found[,] my friend[,] a wat'ry tomb / Farewell! O may we meet in Jesus arms."[87] Here the widow's anguish—and desire for reassurance that she would see her husband again—was probably compounded by the fact that she had not, apparently, been able to view his corpse. Nevertheless, the gravestone offers the opportunity for conversation between the earthbound wife and her heavenly husband, who awaits her in Jesus' arms.

Men, too, spoke passionately to their deceased spouses on the gravestones they erected. John Collins III, for example, apostrophizes his deceased wife on her gravestone, imagining a heavenly reunion of his whole family. The stone he purchased memorializes not only his wife, Mary, who died at age twenty-three in 1817 but also their six-month-old son Caleb—"Love's darling pledge"—who died a month before his mother. On the stone, Collins speaks to his wife: "Thy spotless soul has flown to Realms on high, / To reembrace Love's pledge, thy cherub boy; / When God Shall bid thy husband's spirit fly, / May thy fond souls unite in endless joy."[88] Mary and her son are already embracing in heaven; John Collins hopes to join them in "endless joy." The phrase "fond souls" is telling. In previous centuries, when the beatific vision was heaven's central activity, souls were seen as glorifying God. With the advent of the cult of the dead, fond familial souls re-created this world's domestic bonds in heaven.

Talking gravestones were also especially well-suited to have the deceased request that the living visit their graves. None of the burial grounds in this sample are "rural" cemeteries in the Mount Auburn mold, and thus none have the parklike landscaping that starting in the 1830s would encourage picnicking and promenading. Still, numerous talking gravestones voice the deceased's expectation of postmortem visits. To an extent this is seen in the very common formulations addressing the reader, "Pray think of me as you pass by" or "All you that pass by pray cast an eye." But such stones imply that the person reading the epitaph merely happens to "pass by" the marker. Others, however, more explicitly address those who have come to visit the dead. Ruth Crowell's 1799 marker is one such example: "Stranger as this spot you tread / And meditate upon the dead" it begins.[89] The implied reader does not know Crowell; he is a "Stranger." Nonetheless, he is imagined to be thinking about death, not just going about his business. The gravestone thus becomes a religious object, a focal node for prayer and thoughts about the afterlife.

Some talking gravestones make the activity of visiting burial grounds even more intimate by narrating the activity in the first person. An early example of this is Hannah Dunster's 1766 marker, which declares, "I once the Graves of others viewed / as now to others I am Shew'd."[90] Here the use of prosopopoeia creates an odd effect: "I" once visited graves, and now "I" am shown to others. But it is not Dunster herself that "others" are viewing, as they might at a funeral, but Dunster's stone. This makes the marker—complete with voice—even more of a stand-in for the deceased's body than usual. Here the presence of the dead signals that the gravestone is a religious object in the eyes of those who read the epitaph. Half a century later, Azubah Handy's stone is especially insistent that her loved ones visit her grave. It begins by speaking to her husband: "My bosom friend come here and see / Where lays the last remains of me." Handy's bodily remains are to be the focus of her husband's visit. She wants him and also her children to think often about her death: "Husband and children here I lay / Stamp on your minds my dying day / Come often here and take a view / Where lays the one that loved you."[91] Not only are her dying moments supposed to be stamped upon the minds of her survivors, but she also expects them to visit her grave "often." By 1819 the cult of the dead was fully fledged, so such a request from the deceased was not a surprise.

Talking gravestones reserved some of their most demonstrative epitaphs for infants, toddlers, and young children. As the eighteenth century turned into the nineteenth, children became ever more exalted in American culture and Protestant theology. The idea that children might burn in hell—already restricted to ministerial sermons and largely ignored by laypeople in the eighteenth century—virtually disappeared from Protestant theology in the nineteenth.[92] Infants and children came to be seen as possessing the purest of all souls, which virtually guaranteed that those souls would ascend to heaven upon death.

Talking gravestones address children with a variety of intimate terms: "darling," "sweet babe," "pretty youth," and "dear child" are the most common. All these endearments imply the innocence of youth, a fact sometimes made explicit on stones, even ones with an epitaph as arresting as that composed for one-year-old Francis Jones in 1811: "Stop traveler as you pass by / To see an infant slain / Who lived & died in innocence / And turned to dust again."[93] Here young Francis is "slain" by Death while still in a state of innocence. His entry into heaven is thus guaranteed and does not even need to be mentioned in the epitaph.

Increasingly common were epitaphs that likened death to sleep. For five-week-old Caroline Huckins: "Sleep on dear babe & take thy rest / God called thee home & tho't it best."[94] For the unnamed boy who died the same day he was born in 1803: "Sleep on Dear babe and take thy rest / No mortal cares ne'er reached thy breast / Thy eyes ne'er opet to view the light / Nor give the fond parents' heart delight."[95] Parents found it comforting to think of death as sleep: it connoted peaceful continuation of life on earth. The conventionality of these epitaphs attests to the widespread acceptance of their ideas.

The trope of death as sleep was also a staple of the romanticized death imagery that began to appear in mid-eighteenth-century England with the Graveyard School of poetry and prose; such language came to dominate American death discourse by the nineteenth century. In this century the word "cemetery," from the Greek meaning "sleeping chamber," surpassed usage of the older "burying ground" and "churchyard."[96] In the Age of the Beautiful Death, as one historian calls the nineteenth century, Europeans and Americans increasingly imagined the deceased sleeping peacefully rather than moldering beneath the soil.[97] This Romantic context made talking gravestones seem especially appropriate, as the bereaved were increasingly likely to visit cemeteries and commune with loved ones. Such burial ground communion would become a central practice in the nineteenth-century cult of the dead. As the novelist Washington Irving urged his readers in 1819, "go to the grave of buried love and meditate."[98] Those who visited cemeteries sought out the religious objects associated with their "buried love," and there they prayed, meditated, and maintained relationships between heaven and earth.

Language of death as sleep is found frequently on Cape Cod's talking gravestones. An original and insistent use of the metaphor occurs on the marker of Barbary Weekes, who died in 1798 at age fifty-one. The epitaph divides her life into four phases: the first twenty years, a "pleasing life"; the next eleven "married with now my left hand dust"; three years of a "sorrowfull widows life"; and, finally, seventeen years again "a married Wife." The "left hand dust" refers to Weekes's first husband; evidently he is buried to her left. The rest of her epitaph has Weekes speaking to him and other denizens of the burial ground: "O my friends I beg a place in your cold bed / That I may rest my limbs and akeing head."[99] The "bed" of the cemetery is cold, yet it is also a place of rest and comfort. When nineteenth-century Americans used sleep imagery to describe death, they were not pretending that the deceased was alive. Still, the language on Weekes's stone was a long way from the puritan-inflected Cape Cod epitaphs such as Seth Hall's "Worms devour my waisting flesh."[100] Yet it is important to note that Hall's and Weekes's epitaphs, different as they are, were essentially contemporaneous: only five years separated them.

This blurring of chronological distinctions is demonstrated in the earliest Cape Cod stone that shows the direct influence of English Graveyard School literature: that of Phebe Gorham in 1775 (Figure 10). Beneath a round-faced but unsmiling cherub, the epitaph recounts Gorham's conventional female roles as "dutiful Child," "Virtuous Wife," and "tender Parent." It then quotes four lines from Edward Young's *Night Thoughts*, the ten-thousand-line poem from the early 1740s that was one of the best-loved exemplars of the Graveyard School, published in forty-eight authorized editions before the author's death in 1765.[101] In the poem, the narrator meditates on death and loss during nine "nights"; each night is a separate poem. Gorham's epitaph draws from the ninth, "Consolation":

"Henceforth my Soul in sweetest Union join
The two supports of human Happiness,
Which some erroneous think can never meet:
True Taste of Life, and constant thought of Death."[102]

Readers familiar with the poem would have been reminded of the joyous tone of this stanza, which begins triumphantly, "Then, farewel Night! Of Darkness, now, no more: / Joy breaks, shines, triumphs; 'tis eternal Day."[103] These lines, combined with the four chosen for Gorham's epitaph, look backward to puritan ideas about death and forward to Romantic sensibilities. Seeing the "constant thought of Death" as a central aspect of "human Happiness" is a sentiment that could have been drawn directly from a seventeenth-century puritan sermon. At the same time, the poem's exclamation points and the epitaph's desire for a "True Taste of Life" point forward to the emotional, life-embracing poetry of the Romantics, who later drew upon the Graveyard School.

Yet carving the lines on a talking gravestone also changed their meaning. In the poem, the living narrator addresses his soul. He tells his soul to keep death in mind while also enjoying life and God's creation. "Hope, be thy joy," the narrator states a few lines later; "thy" refers to his soul. Given that the narrator is still alive, this is a joyful message. But on Gorham's talking gravestone, the lines take on a more ambivalent cast. She is dead, so what does it mean to join a "True Taste of Life" with "constant thought of Death"? Perhaps the line is meant to suggest how she lived, but in light of the talking gravestone tradition, it seems more like Gorham is speaking to her departed soul, which will not be able to taste life, except of the eternal variety.

Poetry about mortality also appears on several Cape Cod talking gravestones that address the deceased's "shade" in the first person. This was likewise a convention of English verse. A "shade" is simply a ghost, as we have seen. The use of the word "shade," however, with its poetic connotations, was more acceptable in epitaphs than "ghost," which to some nineteenth-century consumers bespoke folk beliefs and superstition. Nonetheless, in these epitaphs, and in much verse from the period, the speaker apostrophizes the deceased person's shade.

One 1826 example honors Maria Otis, who married into the Cape's most prominent family. Otis was well educated for a woman born in the first half of the eighteenth century, and her epitaph lauds her "superior excellence of mind and character." It may be that she selected the poem that graces her gravestone. Whatever the case, her family's wealth allowed the carver to fit twenty-four of the poem's twenty-eight lines on the large monument. The verse was written by one of England's most prominent female poets, Anna Letitia Barbauld, whose *Poems* of 1773 was popular on both sides of the Atlantic,

Figure 10. Phebe Gorham gravestone (1775), Lothrop Hill Cemetery,
Barnstable, Massachusetts. The marker quotes four lines from Edward
Young's *Night Thoughts*, demonstrating Graveyard School poetry's
far-reaching influence. Farber Gravestone Collection.
Courtesy of the American Antiquarian Society.

reaching five editions by 1777.[104] Chosen for the epitaph was an elegy that Barbauld wrote for her grandmother.[105] The poem and epitaph begin with the
same two lines: "'Tis past, dear venerable shade farewell / Thy blameless life,
thy peaceful death shall tell."[106] The gravestone thus says, "Goodbye, dear ghost
of Maria, your peaceful death resulted from your blameless life." Otis's soul

straddles this world and the next: it is somehow present, able to be addressed in the graveyard, but it is also on its way to the afterlife. This is suggested by the prose portion of the epitaph, which states that Otis died "in the joyful hope of rising in the likeness of her Glorious Redeemer." Yet this third-person statement, so conventional in its formulation, lacks the power of the first-person lines that the gravestone directs to her ghost.

* * *

Cape Cod markers are part of a broader Anglo-Atlantic memorial tradition in which talking gravestones occasionally appeared even before there was a single Protestant marker in New England. In London, for example, William Lambe's monument (c. 1600) speaks in the first person about his love for his three wives: "With wives three / I joyned wedlocke band, / Which (all alive) / True lovers were to me: / Joane, Alice and Joane, / For so they came to hand."[107] Such stones were relatively rare, however, and in New England it was only after 1750 that they became popular in both senses of the word: frequently used and reflecting values farther down the social scale. For many individuals who appear in this chapter, epitaphs are the only written sources that survive about them beyond tax rolls and church membership lists. Thus, material culture is crucial for understanding how a wide range of New Englanders thought about the afterlife.

A key text for the material turn in the humanities is the edited collection *Things That Talk* (2004). The book's talking things—glass flowers, Rorschach cards, daguerreotypes—don't really talk. They signify and suggest, indicate and insinuate, but they speak only metaphorically.[108] Talking gravestones, of course, don't actually talk either, but viewers experienced their epitaphs as something much closer to speech or communication with the deceased. When John Collins commissioned an epitaph that says, in effect, "dear wife, when I die I hope our souls unite in endless joy," he was making palpable—literally having carved into stone—his desire to communicate with the dead. When people visited Truro Cemetery in the center of the small fishing village and read the Collins stone, they heard his voice in their head addressing his dead wife, and they experienced firsthand his depth of loss and hope for reunion.

They experienced the marker, therefore, as a religious object, one that may not have had "agency" in the way literary scholars of materiality use the term but one that certainly had "power."[109] Gravestones had the power to incite iconoclastic violence during the English Reformation and Civil War, and they had the power to inspire people to consider the largest questions of their Protestant faith: what happens to our loved ones when they die, can we communicate with them, are they watching us, will we join them? The first-person voice rendered in stone made those questions only more urgent.

CHAPTER 4

Voices of the Dead in the
American Enlightenment

In 1798, Albany was a prosperous town of roughly five thousand inhabitants, a place energized by having been named New York's permanent state capital the year before. Evidence of a vibrant civil society was everywhere: in the Tontine Coffee-House; in voluntary associations such as the Albany Mechanics Society, one of the Early Republic's first trade unions; and in the four newspapers the reading public supported. Beneath a sign adorned with the head of Benjamin Franklin, the very emblem of American learning and science, knowledge-seekers stepped into the Albany Bookstore on State Street and purchased copies of the *Albany Centinel*, the most recent entry into the town's crowded newspaper market.

Published twice a week, on Tuesdays and Fridays, the four-page *Centinel* was crammed with dispatches, essays, and advertisements that testified to the desires of Albany's citizens for enlightenment. A reader who purchased the issue of January 26, 1798—or who perused a copy, gratis, at the Coffee-House—learned about the seemingly endless wars in Europe and the recent debates in the state legislature (it was hard to tell which were bloodier). The reader could enjoy a long essay about democracy, with examples from Greece and Rome demonstrating the dangers of demagogues in a republic. Scientific advances were on display in a notice for Jedidiah Morse's *American Gazetteer*, a compendium of facts promising a "much more full and accurate Account" of the nation's natural history, including "New Discoveries, on the American Continent." And if the reader were a woman, she found several items directed especially to her, including advertisements for a dancing school "for young

Ladies," for cloth "of the most fashionable colours," and for help wanted, "a woman to take care of two small Children in a respectable Family."[1]

Amid all this evidence of commerce and curiosity about the world, readers also discovered an article, nearly a full column long, titled simply, "A Ghost." Datelined New-Gaol in the Fields, New York City, from two weeks earlier, the piece offered "a true and surprising account of the apparition or ghost of a woman, that has appeared several nights past in the New-Gaol, to the great terror and affright of the prisoners."[2] The story turned out to be more complicated than it first appeared, as discussed at greater length below. But the important point here is that this "true and surprising account" was published without any editorial intervention suggesting that the story was fictional, or for entertainment only, or worthy of derision. It was not tucked into a corner of the newspaper reserved for oddities; it immediately followed a short piece on the Dutch role in the European wars. "A Ghost" was a straight, unironic apparition sighting, following conventions stretching back to the first printed ghost narratives in sixteenth-century England. But it appeared at the end of a century of enlightenment, in a newspaper, a medium historians credit with helping to usher in modernity.

How to explain the seeming contradiction? By turning to scholarship that, in the last decade or so, has reinterpreted the relationship between the Enlightenment and the supernatural. Until recently, historians equated the Enlightenment with secularization and the "disenchantment of the world," to use Max Weber's famous phrase. Focusing largely on French *philosophes* and the hostility toward religion that some of them displayed, these historians constructed an Enlightenment that birthed the "rise of modern paganism," as one influential study was subtitled.[3] In this interpretation, the Age of Reason began the inexorable decline of religion and the supernatural that supposedly became a defining feature of modernity.

If this older school of thought fit awkwardly with important religious developments in eighteenth-century Europe such as the emergence of Pietism in the German states and Methodism in Great Britain, it was even less persuasive in the American context. In the mainland British colonies, the *philosophes* had very little impact and the religious revivals later called the First Great Awakening demonstrated the unabated—indeed, growing—influence of religion and the supernatural in daily life. But historians have not responded simply by saying that the Enlightenment had no impact on religion in America. Rather, recent innovative work points to the ways that religion and the

Enlightenment were intertwined and mutually constitutive. Evangelical Protestants, for example, defended their religious practices "by appropriating an enlightened language of experience, certainty, evidence, and sensation."[4]

Central to this new interpretative angle is print culture, which is ironic because the secularization thesis also rested on print, specifically its importance in disseminating new ideas about science, religion, and skepticism. More recent understandings of print, however, demonstrate that there is no inevitable connection between the growth of a public sphere of newspapers and journals on the one hand and a decline of the supernatural on the other. In the European context, this point is made most powerfully by a definition of the Enlightenment focused on innovations in "media." This is the historian Jonathan Sheehan's term for "a new constellation of formal and technical practices and institutions" including salons, academies, lending libraries, and "new communication tools" such as journals and newspapers.[5] The Enlightenment, in this account, is no longer a set of philosophical propositions but rather a collection of tools whose uses were up for grabs. In America, the most relevant of these tools were the new outlets of print culture, especially magazines and newspapers. This print culture was multivocal; even individual publications could contain a wide range of opinions. The new media of the eighteenth century changed how ideas were disseminated, and how widely and quickly they could be spread, but the media themselves did not dictate any particular set of ideas, secularizing or not. Newspapers and magazines could just as easily circulate news about the supernatural as about the secular or scientific.

Which brings us back to the *Albany Centinel* of January 26, 1798. Twice a week the newspaper's publisher, Loring Andrews, scrambled to fill four large pages, each with four columns of densely packed type. Andrews copied articles from other newspapers and magazines—in the issue of January 26, from the *Boston Mercury* and the *Farmer's Weekly Museum*, among others—and he offered some original pieces. It is unclear what outlet Andrews cribbed "A Ghost" from, but the article appeared in almost the exact same form in some two dozen other publications. This pinching of material gave Early Republic newspapers their somewhat miscellaneous character and allowed for a wide range of opinions to sit, sometimes uneasily, side by side. The recycling of articles also helped foster a national print culture. Indeed, the two dozen reprintings of "A Ghost" appeared in newspapers from Maine to Georgia. That is why this book's geographical compass expands at this point, adding the northern colonies and states to the previous focus on New England.

Moreover, the *Centinel* was part of an explosion of print in the United States. In 1700, 68 book titles were printed throughout the British mainland colonies. By 1790, that number had increased more than tenfold, to 798.[6] The growth of newspapers was even more dramatic: the first American newspaper appeared in 1704, and as late as 1776 there were only 37 in the thirteen colonies, yet by 1798 the *Centinel* was one of 238 newspapers in the United States.[7] Many of these books and newspapers brought enlightened ideas from London and other Atlantic centers of learning to the new nation's towns and villages. Yet the growth of print culture also allowed for fresh voices to be heard: women, men without formal education, visionaries, and authors who would write anything they thought readers would pay for. With the threshold for access to the world of print significantly lowered, ideas, including ideas about communication with the dead, entered the public conversation with greater ease than in the seventeenth century.

What becomes evident, then, from an examination of eighteenth-century print culture in the northern colonies and states, is a complex range of expressions about communication with the dead. At the same time that many educated Americans adopted skeptical attitudes toward ghost belief, others used scientific methods to demonstrate that some supernatural sightings were plausible. And even though most ordinary Americans thrilled to the details of a good ghost story, they understood that wholehearted belief in apparitions could mark them as credulous rubes. Thus the characteristic stance in this period's print culture is ambivalence. Educated elites admitted that science could not unravel all the mysteries of the unseen world, just as ordinary Americans acknowledged that if they described a supernatural encounter, some people would greet their narrative with skepticism. What united people of all classes—as demonstrated by the widespread interest in stories such as "A Ghost"—was curiosity about the afterlife. Speaking with the dead, or reading about such communication in newspapers and magazines, served to both satisfy and stoke that curiosity.

Enlightenment Spirits

First, eighteenth-century ghost belief must be examined. We left the story in Salem, where minister-scientists, magistrates, and laypeople shared many ideas about the supernatural world. As the eighteenth century progressed, however, educated elites—first in Europe, then in the American colonies—began to express skepticism about interventions from the spirit world. Some thinkers of the "radical Enlightenment" questioned the very existence of spirits, but such figures remained a tiny minority.[8] More common was moderate skepticism: supernatural interventions were possible but very rare.

In early Enlightenment England, elite belief in ghosts weakened. Freethinkers associated with the court of Charles II began to express skeptical ideas in the 1670s and 1680s: these men were the "sadducists" that Joseph Glanvill and other transatlantic thanatologists worked so hard to counter with their investigations into the spirit world. Because the freethinkers' skeptical ideas were tainted by association with "Hobbism" and sadducism, few orthodox Church of England members dared voice them. As a result, skepticism remained largely an oral, elite phenomenon in the last decades of the seventeenth century, relegated to figures such as Edward Montagu, the 1st Earl of Sandwich, who was said to be "very scepticall" about the existence of spirits.[9]

Even among those who believed in an active spirit world, however, a new motivation for collecting and publishing ghost stories appeared at the turn of the century, a motivation that would only grow as the century progressed: the desire to entertain. This is first visible in the *Miscellanies* published in 1696 by John Aubrey, an English antiquarian and folklorist. Aubrey's purpose in collecting stories from the humble was similar to that of folklorists ever since: he hoped to gather evidence of traditional ways before they disappeared. His book consists of twenty-one chapters on topics including dreams, omens, and visions. Also noteworthy are chapters on apparitions and "Converse with Angels and Spirits." Some of Aubrey's stories are recycled from older sources, including Glanvill; others are fresh. The point is not that Aubrey was skeptical about the world of spirits; far from it. But Aubrey did not compile his collection to prove the existence of spirits, as did Glanvill and other anti-sadducists. Instead, in the book's dedicatory letter to the Earl of Abingdon, Aubrey revealed his motivation: that the stories "might be somewhat entertaining."[10] By the end of the eighteenth century in both England and America, this would become the dominant goal of ghost-story collectors, many of whom remained agnostic, as it were, about the reality of spirits, so long as their stories sold.

But before that could happen, learned elites on both sides of the Atlantic had to embrace a more skeptical attitude toward spirits, or else ghost stories would remain the polemical tools of the anti-sadducists. This process began in early eighteenth-century England. In the century's first decade, the controversial French Prophets—a millenarian group that claimed miraculous powers, including raising the dead—galvanized opposition to what most

English elites viewed as spurious claims of supernatural intervention. Soon thereafter, in 1712, Jane Wenham became one of the last people sentenced to death in England for witchcraft. Her sentence was commuted, but not before the case came to symbolize for elites the credulity of ordinary people and provincial magistrates. Combined with the increasing acceptance of a Newtonian universe that operated on predictable principles, the furor over the French Prophets and the Wenham case prepared the ground for learned skepticism about the spirit world. These views converged in the publication of Francis Hutchinson's *Historical Essay Concerning Witchcraft* (1718), which is frequently cited as one of the first books by a mainstream religious figure (as opposed to a Baruch Spinoza or Balthasar Bekker) to express skepticism about the existence of witchcraft, and by extension the world of spirits.[11] This was the period when moderate skepticism about the spirit world became acceptable among learned elites.[12]

Ministers and other educated residents of the British colonies learned about these skeptical ideas the same way most members of the English literati did: by reading about them. Although it was too late for Cotton Mather and his cohort to change their minds about the world of spirits, a new generation of educated men came of age after Salem, with the works of Hutchinson and others setting the intellectual tone of "supernatural rationalism" that would mark the eighteenth century.[13] Emblematic of this generational shift is Mather's nephew, Josiah Cotton, a graduate of Harvard College and son of a minister, though he himself never became a pastor.

A decade after Hutchinson's full-throated condemnation of spurious witchcraft prosecutions (including Salem) was published in London, Cotton finally got his hands on the volume. He was moved to write a letter to the author, a bishop in the Anglican Church of Ireland. Cotton began his 1729 letter with an apology: "If I had seen your Book concerning Witchcraft ten Years ago I had not been so long in paying my Respects, but having never seen nor heard of it till I borrow'd it within these few months I take this Opportunity to render my unfeigned Thanks for the Pains you have taken to undecieve Mankind." Skeptical books such as Hutchinson's were "very scarce in New-England," but "Idle stories concerning Witches are Endless." This situation frustrated an enlightened man such as Cotton. As he explained to Hutchinson, it was not only New England's rabble who believed in ghosts and witches but also some educated men. Cotton admitted that in the provincial context of the colonies, even he grew up believing in ghosts and witches: "such Notions I did (as it were) suck in with my Mothers Milk."[14]

Through education, however, Cotton was able, in his telling, to rise above the ghost stories of his youth and adopt the skeptical stance he and Hutchinson shared. This did not mean that Cotton simply ignored belief in the spirit world as a harmless diversion. Rather, he set about combating such ideas; his 1729 letter to Hutchinson prefigured a more extensive intellectual project. In 1733 Cotton penned a fifty-six-page essay, "Some Observations Concerning Witches, Spirits, & Apparitions, Collected from Divers Authors." Though the piece was clearly intended for publication, Cotton never quite finished it.[15]

In the essay, Cotton railed against the degree to which the "Common People" were liable to "to suck in the Wildest Errors & imbibe the grossest Notions" about ghosts and witches. This was a fairly common position for New England's men of learning to take by the 1730s. But the crucial point is that Cotton did not ascribe such beliefs to some timeless oral folk tradition. Rather, *print culture* was the culprit. Specifically, Cotton blamed books by Joseph Glanvill and other anti-sadducists for keeping alive—indeed spreading ever more widely—belief in ghosts. Cotton first made his case without naming Glanvill. "Too many otherwise good & worthy men," Cotton wrote, "have contributed their Parts & Laboured hard to instill & uphold those Notions. Some Divines have done it [promoted the world of spirits] in order to confute the Sadducism & Atheism of the present Age."[16]

Cotton then went after Glanvill directly: "Here I cannot but make some Remarks upon a certain Book called Sadducismus Triumphatus. It contains so many stories of Witches, Apparitions, & haunted Houses, with such subtil arguments & solutions to confirm them that it is enough to haunt & infect a whole Town or Countrey." It is no coincidence that the fourth edition of Glanvill's book had been published in London a few years earlier, in 1726. It took Cotton ten years to get his hands on Hutchinson's skeptical tract, but readers scooped up the new edition of *Saducismus* from booksellers in England and the colonies. It was a simple fact: people wanted to read stories about ghosts and witches. "Hence," Cotton continued, "Books replete therewith are greedily sought after & quickly bought up. If there come forth a Pamphlet entitled Strange News . . . it is exceedingly taking [i.e., captivating] & gains the firmest assent. And Books of this sort shall have a third & fourth Impression"— just like *Saducismus*—while pious books are neglected.[17] This is how ordinary people would "imbibe" and "suck in" their errors: by participating in the expanding market of print culture.

In this Cotton mirrored the opinions Hutchinson had expressed a decade earlier in his *Essay Concerning Witchcraft*. Hutchinson likewise blamed books, not an unchanging substratum of popular beliefs, for the widespread interest in ghosts and witches. Hutchinson listed more than two dozen books that had been published in the years since the coronation of Charles II, all of which promoted the world of spirits: titles by Glanvill, More, Baxter, and numerous others. Even though many of these volumes had been written by ministers and their intended audience was fellow ministers, they actually reached a much wider reading public. According to Hutchinson, "these Books and Narratives are in Tradesmen's Shops, and Farmer's [sic] Houses, and are read with great Eagerness, and are continually leavening the Minds of the Youth, who delight in such Subjects."[18]

In both England and New England, then, men of learning in the early eighteenth century saw books as a source not only of scientific knowledge and skeptical discourses but also of foolish stories about ghosts and evil spirits. Print culture did not inevitably lead to the disenchantment of the world; quite the opposite. When ordinary farmers and tradesmen snapped up books about the spirit world, they used the alleged tools of modernization to "imbibe" the "Wildest Errors" about the relationship between heaven and earth.

But the "Common People" that Cotton and Hutchinson accused of being so credulous actually held a nuanced range of beliefs. One of Cotton's tenants in Plymouth, Massachusetts, refused to pay rent because the house he leased from Cotton was allegedly haunted by a ghost (this conflict accounted for Cotton's bile in his essay about the supernatural). Neighbors were summoned to court to report on the house's strange lights and sounds. Some agreed with John Clark, the aggrieved tenant, that "because of such unusuall noise in the house . . . he nor no body allse could live in it because it was haunted with evill spirits." Others weren't so sure. Isaac Robinson thought the "Pale Blewish Light"—usually a sure sign that a ghost was near—was in fact caused by "the light of the moon." Similarly skeptical was Bethia West, who conducted a little empirical experiment that would have made Francis Bacon proud. West had heard the rumors about the haunted house, which she could see from her own home. Knowing that the dwelling was abandoned after Clark had moved out in terror, she was surprised one day to see a light in the empty house and wondered whether it might have a supernatural source. Thinking more about it, West "moved the Candle of[f] our Kitchen Shelfe" and "perceived plainly" that the light "was nothing else but the reflection of our Candle over to [the supposedly haunted] house."[19]

Still others started off skeptical about the rumors and then became convinced that the house did indeed hold a ghost. Mary Holmes had lived in the house "for the Space of above half a Year without the least Dread." Her sister-in-law, who also lived there, reported being frightened by a strange light. Holmes, knowing the door to the house was locked, "made light of her talke." But then the next time her sister-in-law reported a mysterious light, which happened "Speedily after the Death of my Child," Holmes declared that "I became some what affected therewith."[20] It is unclear why Holmes changed her mind after her child died. Did she think that the supernatural light was evidence that her child was trying to communicate with her from beyond the grave? The sources offer no further explanation, but the larger point is that the residents of Plymouth held a range of views about the supernatural. Some believed that spirits of the dead could return to this world, others were skeptical, and still others moved from one position to the other depending on their personal circumstances. Some Plymouth residents even followed the methodology of Baconian empiricism by investigating possible cases of supernatural intervention to look for other, natural explanations.

If we were to take Cotton and Hutchinson at their word, the ordinary women and men of the eighteenth century believed everything they read, including the ghost narratives of Glanvill and others. In reality, the period's print culture reveals a much more ambiguous story, with evidence of skepticism and ghost belief coexisting and nurturing one another. As the century progressed, however, and increasing numbers of colonists were exposed to the ideas of thinkers such as Cotton and Hutchinson, the balance tipped toward the skeptical, at least in the world of print.

Ghosts in Print

These trends are evident in an examination of magazines, newspapers, and books published in the eighteenth-century northern colonies and states. Some of this material first appeared in Britain (especially England, and to a lesser extent Scotland and Ireland), but much of it is original to America. For the most part one should not draw a bright line between fiction and nonfiction: eighteenth-century readers generally made less of a distinction between the two categories than do readers today.[21] Some of these stories were clearly intended to be read as fictional, others as factual, but most could be read on the tantalizing border between the two.

This discussion begins with skeptical sources and then moves on to stories that seem to demonstrate ghost belief, in order to invert the older narrative of a secularizing eighteenth century. Still, despite the continued popularity of seventeenth-century texts such as *Saducismus*, skepticism about ghosts and other supernatural beings dominated the print culture of the eighteenth-century colonies, given that most newspaper and magazine editors were firmly in the enlightened camp. Speaking with the dead in the form of ghosts was therefore the subject of much humor and mockery in the period's newspapers and literary magazines. This may not be a surprise, but perhaps less expected is the authors' apparent need to continue mocking ghost belief. Skeptical authors wrote against a backdrop of vibrant popular interest in communicating with the dead. Through their efforts at humor, the literati attempted to demonstrate the absurdity of ghost belief, but they never quite succeeded. Their jokes reveal the very anxieties and desires that led people to believe in the possibility of communicating with the dead.

Take, for example, one type of humorous story repeated over and over on both sides of the Atlantic: a person seems to see or hear a ghost, but it turns out to be something entirely nonthreatening. These stories invite the reader both to laugh at the first-person narrator's excessive fear of ghosts and to share in the narrator's increasing dread as all signs point toward a supernatural visitor. "The Morning Apparition," which appeared in the *New England Magazine of Knowledge and Pleasure* in 1758, is an early example of this kind of story. The narrator lies in bed and all is silent. Not even a gnat disturbed the peace; "No ticking Death-worm told a fancy'd Doom." He drifts off to sleep and then suddenly hears a noise. The door opens and the narrator sees "a tall, thin Form" at the foot of his bed, which conforms with the conventional early modern description of ghosts as gaunt, even emaciated. The narrator is certain it is a ghost with a message from the afterlife. His bones tremble, his limbs are bathed in sweat. Will he have the chance to communicate with the dead? No, it's only Master Jones, the night watchman, "Who wav'd his Hand, to banish Fears and Sorrow, / Well charg'd with Toast and Sack, and cry'd Good-Morrow."[22] Even though the narrator is ultimately portrayed as silly for fearing that the night watchman is an apparition, the dramatic buildup toward the punch line makes sense only in a culture where creaking doors in the night might signal the arrival of a ghost.

Versions of this story remained a staple of American magazines and newspapers for many decades.[23] In countless variations on this theme, the fear-inducing noise is caused by a smuggler in a white sheet, a lover accidentally locked in a closet, a runaway slave stowed away on a ship, a farmer's daughter sleepwalking, and, most commonly, a "Poor Pussey Cat."[24] In all these versions, the anxieties and uncertainties of the age regarding the supernatural are on display. Surely ghosts are laughable, the literati say, until one is lying in bed at midnight listening to the floorboards creak.

A strategy to distance the reader from the person mocked in these stories, which therefore made it easier to laugh at the joke, was to set the story in another, ideally Catholic, country. As a Catholic, the person who was the butt of the anecdote was virtually by definition superstitious. In a 1783 story, a French farmer happens upon a deflated hot-air balloon in his field, thinks it is a ghost, and sprinkles it with holy water to vanquish the spirit.[25] In another, a French ventriloquist deceives a recent widow into thinking that her dead husband's ghost is speaking. Her emotions thus heightened, she agrees to give the ventriloquist her daughter's hand in marriage, and the reader is invited to laugh at Catholic credulity.[26]

Despite the literati's laughter, many Protestant Americans remained convinced of the possibility of speaking with the dead. This in turn provoked the enlightened to try to discredit these beliefs through means more direct than humor alone. Skeptical writers in American magazines and newspapers joined a transatlantic conversation explaining away ghost sightings by saying they resulted from a variety of natural causes. Again, their urgency to prove the fallacy of ghost belief unwittingly demonstrates the depth of the beliefs against which they contended.

In the second half of the eighteenth century, the literati's theories about ghosts became increasingly psychologized and internalized. Many elites began to see ghost sightings as the product of a disordered mind: an internal rather than external phenomenon.[27] For example, Benjamin Rush, the towering figure of American medicine at the end of the eighteenth century, explained the appearance of ghosts as the result of guilt. In his essay "On the Different Species of Phobia" (1787), Rush asserted that even though most people afflicted with "Ghost Phobia" were servants and children, he knew of "a few instances" of "men of cultivated understandings" who harbored such fears. These were usually people who suffered guilt from the deliberate or inadvertent harm they had caused others: physicians who had injured their patients, rulers who had executed the innocent. Just as a phobia was, in Rush's words, "a fear of an imaginary evil," Ghost Phobia was a fear of an imaginary supernatural being that resulted from the troubled workings of a guilty mind.[28]

But the most common psychological explanation of ghost sightings blamed tales told by childhood nursemaids. Gendered stereotypes were never far beneath the surface of these explanations. In a 1739 *Boston Evening Post* article, the author asserted that while some ghost sightings were the result of a "distemper'd Imagination," most resulted from ghost stories internalized at an early age. These sightings, the author asserted, could be attributed to "a motly Mixture of the low and vulgar Education: Mothers and Grandmothers, Aunts and Nurses, begin the Cheat, and from little Horrors and hideous Stories of Bugbears, Mormoes and Fairies . . . they train us up by Degrees to the Belief of a more substantial Ghost and Apparition."[29] Significantly, although the author blamed an entirely female cast of characters for telling foolish stories, he noted that "they train *us* up"—men, that is—to believe in ghosts. Whereas telling children ghost stories may have been the special province of women, ghost *belief* did not pay attention to boundaries of sex.

Likewise, a piece written for the *Pennsylvania Mercury* in 1786 by "H" was set against a backdrop of widespread belief in ghosts. The author complained that many people were continually "frightening themselves with a thousand horrible apprehensions of things that never did, nor can exist, but in their own imaginations." "H" blamed "those who have the care of our infant state" for this situation, because "principles engrafted upon young minds never fail to take deep root." As a result, "we"—again, men included—"tread the same beaten tract" of false belief.[30]

From here the author moved on to a gendered critique of the literature that filled American minds with thoughts of ghosts. Whereas in the first half of the eighteenth century the printed works at fault were anti-sadducist writings, in the second half of the century the culprit was imaginative literature. It was not only "the nurses of our infant years" but also "several pious and grave nurses" who took care to "augment the terror of our apprehension, and have cultivated it with a truly superstitious and pedantic industry." Here "H" referred to the leading figures of the eighteenth-century Graveyard School of poetry and prose, who were famous for their funereal themes and melancholy tone: the "celebrated mothers [James] Hervey and [Edward] Y[oun]g" who "taught grown minds to fear." Again and again "H" tried to feminize the male writers of the Graveyard School, calling them "the nurses of the Herveyan system." But the author's attempt to denigrate the Graveyard poets foundered on the very popularity of their writings on both sides of the Atlantic: editions of their books were counted in the dozens.[31] As "H" admitted, the reader of Graveyard poetry "quakes and shudders at every line, and sucks it in with the same eagerness as the tender infant does its first milk and prejudice."[32]

"H" and other enlightened authors of the eighteenth century sought to marginalize and mock ghost belief, and there is no doubt that their efforts bore some fruit. Writers who tried to make the case for legitimate ghost sightings in this period had to contend with the skepticism that dominated the world of print. What these less skeptical authors had on their side was a great deal of popular interest in communicating with the dead.

Before and After Cock Lane

The widespread curiosity about the afterlife into which Graveyard School authors tapped was the reason why eighteenth-century newspapers, alongside their more regular fare of politics and shipping news, occasionally carried unironic stories of ghost sightings. Such articles did not appear with enormous frequency in American newspapers; perhaps every year or so a story was published in one newspaper and then reprinted in others. In the first decades of the 1700s these stories sound like they could have been from the sixteenth or seventeenth century, as they hewed closely to the narrative conventions of the earliest English ghost narratives.

For example, a homegrown American story that first appeared in 1729 resonated with a century and a half of printed ghost narratives. The *New England Weekly Journal* reported that a man from Ipswich, Massachusetts, had been in Nova Scotia when "there appeared to him an Apparition in Blood & Wounds." The ghost told the man that he had been "murdered by one —— who was at Rhode-Island" and asked the man to go to Rhode Island and charge the murderer with the crime. When the man made his way to his hometown, the apparition appeared again with the same message: go to Rhode Island. "He accordingly set out for that place on Thursday last." This story about supernatural justice was reported without editorializing.[33]

Indeed, straight news stories such as this sometimes indicated that the ghost sighting had convinced a skeptical person of the spirit world's reality. This was the case in a 1737 article from Worcester, England, carried in the *Boston Gazette*. Newspaper readers learned that there had been a "hideous outcry" in the Worcester debtor's prison after a man jailed there suddenly found his cell lighted at midnight as if with twenty candles. Peering into the corner, he saw "the Apparition of one Turner, who was executed the Day before, in the Habit in which he went to be executed in." The terrified prisoner cried out, which caused the ghost to "vanish in a Flame of Fire out of the Window." The debtor reportedly had never before been one to entertain the reality of apparitions, but "he now confidently affirms the abovesaid Relation to be Matter of real Fact."[34]

Many in America and England continued to believe that the ghosts of those executed or murdered frequently haunted the living, because they had suffered bad deaths and their souls returned to earth seeking justice. Such were the underlying beliefs behind a news story carried first by Philadelphia's *American Weekly Mercury* in 1737 and subsequently reprinted by at least four newspapers in New York and New England.[35] The report originated in Williamsburg, Virginia, where an indentured servant shot and beat a man to death. He might have gotten away with the crime, except that he voluntarily confessed. Why did he turn himself in? Because he had been "terrify'd (as he says) by the Apparition of the murder'd Man," and as a result "he could not rest till he discover'd [i.e., revealed] the Murder." He went to the courthouse and confessed that very day. The person reporting this story evinced a mixture of skepticism and belief that was typical of the period: "He gives a frightful Account of the Apparition of the murder'd Man's tormenting him; which seems incredible, and as if the Man was out of his Senses; but that the Circumstances of his whole Account of the Fact, the Pertinency of his Answers, and his Behaviour in the Examination, shew him to be otherwise."[36]

The writer's tone prefigures a chronological development in newspaper reports of ghost sightings. Later in the eighteenth century, such stories often included acknowledgment of the skeptical climate—at least among the educated—regarding the spirit world. This was especially true after London's 1762 Cock Lane ghost proved to be a fraud. It is hard to overstate the attention the Cock Lane ghost received in England, from members of all classes; the affair also received a good deal of notice in the colonies. It marks an important turning point in the literati's attitudes toward ghosts.[37]

In January 1762, London newspapers published startling accounts of "Scratching Fanny," the spirit that would later be called the Cock Lane ghost. Fanny Lynes, engaged to marry a wealthy stockbroker named William Kent, had died in 1760. Two years later the local parish clerk, Richard Parsons, reported that his house in Cock Lane, London, where Lynes and Kent had briefly lodged, was haunted by Lynes's agitated spirit. When the ghost returned she dropped a bombshell: she hadn't died of natural causes. Kent had poisoned her.

Suddenly London's residents could not get enough news about the Cock Lane ghost. The story was reported in at least eight newspapers and four magazines. The rabble and the renowned alike flocked to Cock Lane to hear the ghost's nocturnal knocking. As one newspaper reported, "The clergy and laity, the nobility and commonality . . . continue their nightly attendance on the invisible agent."[38] Demonstrating the widespread belief in the ability to communicate with the dead through ghostly visitations, a Methodist minister, John Moore, conducted an interview with the ghost using a system of knocks: one for yes, two for no. The evening of January 12 he began the questioning:

> "Did you die naturally?"—Two knocks.
> "By poison?"—One knock.
> "Did any person other than Mr. Kent administer it?"—Two
>   knocks.[39]

As Rev. Moore's role indicates, when the educated showed up at Cock Lane, they came not merely to mock the beliefs of ordinary people. At first, numerous respectable men and women believed in the ghost or at least thought the story was plausible. This group included Moore; Thomas Broughton, the secretary of the Society for Promoting Christian Knowledge; William Legge, Earl of Dartmouth; the Duke of York; and numerous others. Of course, many remained skeptical about the ghost, but their opinions—at least as reflected in the world of print—did not outweigh those who believed the ghost might be real.[40]

This changed after the Lord Mayor of London launched an inquiry, which determined that the whole thing was a hoax. The parish clerk had concocted the story to gain revenge on Kent, with whom the clerk was involved in a lawsuit. Suddenly, it seemed, the prevailing opinion among members of polite society was that they had always known the Cock Lane ghost was a fake and that ghost reports in general were almost always manufactured (Figure 11).

A similar trajectory can be traced in America's print culture. The first report in the colonies was published some three months after the story broke in London, a typical lag for the period. The *Boston Evening Post* carried an account that reported the details of the case with a minimum of editorial intervention. A "great knocking" had been heard in Cock Lane, to the "great terror of the family." A clergyman asked the spirit whether anyone had been murdered, and there was no response, but when he asked whether someone had been poisoned, "it knocked one and thirty times." The next night "five Clergymen of great reputation" repeated the experiment. The article's author comfortingly concluded that because of the ministers' "indefatigable care we

Figure 11. *English Credulity; or, The Invisible Ghost* (1762). An anonymous etching mocks the ministers and humble women surrounding the bed where the Cock Lane ghost appears, holding a mallet to knock in response to questions. One woman says, "I never shall have any rest again." Prints and Photographs Division, Library of Congress, PC1-3838.

doubt not of being able very soon to unravel this tremendous story."[41] Colonial newspapers followed up with articles about the hoax being discovered and the perpetrator found guilty.[42]

After the deception was uncovered, "Cock Lane" became a byword in colonial newspapers for any kind of credulity regarding the supernatural world. The *New York Gazette* reported a case from Quebec in which an imprisoned man claimed to have seen a ghost. The article's author, however, doubted that it was an apparition: "this story must be consigned to the same future incredibility, in which many others stand, which for a time were receiv'd by some understanding and good men, however disbelieved by others" such as "the

scratching and thumping ghost of Cock-Lane, for which one knave was pilloried and some that were no knaves were fined."[43] In another article, the author used Cock Lane to stand in for gullibility in an entirely unrelated
political matter. "Reconsider the tale of the Cock Lane apparition," the writer
suggested. "How greedily swallowed by the town, how generally admitted by
the superstitious, and half credited by men of sense and understanding."[44]

This is not to say that after Cock Lane belief in ghosts simply withered
away in America. Outside the world of print culture, one still finds evidence
of supernatural interventions in the natural world. Take, for example, a case
recorded by the Baptist minister Isaac Backus in 1789. In July of that year
Backus received a disturbing letter from a man in Pembroke, Massachusetts:
"Vary alaraming is the Circumstance of the famely of Mr. John Mcfarland
Junr. of this town." One of McFarland's sons had been under the influence of
an "Evel Spirit." Backus hurried to Pembroke, where he learned that the young
man had seen a ghost. A "voice" informed the man that "the ghost that appeared to him was from Halifax in Nova Scotia, where he was last winter,
and helped to release a woman from two robbers; but that she is since dead,
and now came to compel him to go there to be a witness against them; and
he accordingly set off the 27th." Based on the ghost's words, the man was going
to travel all the way back to Halifax. It was, according to Backus, "a strange
affair," but it was hardly singular in the second half of the eighteenth century.[45]

In the world of print after Cock Lane, however, when writers introduced
ghost stories they generally acknowledged the skepticism they assumed would
greet the news, even as many authors persisted in reporting such cases. These
articles appeared in newspapers, a medium notable for its multivocality. The
period's newspapers were typically devoted to politics and warfare in Europe
and the North American colonies, the classic topics of a modernizing public
sphere, but they did not shy away from the marvelous. Whether the editors
who ran these later ghost stories believed them or were using them simply to
sell newspapers is largely beside the point. Rather, in the print culture of the
late eighteenth century, plausible-seeming ghost stories flourished and found
a ready audience.

A story from Philadelphia demonstrates the late-century interplay between
skepticism and belief. In this case, the newspaper editor, Mathew Carey, was
downright contemptuous about the ghost story he reported, but many people
were convinced that the tale was true. Carey started off with a gendered rant
about people who believe in ghost stories: "All the *old women* in the city, as
well *males* as *females* (for let the philosophers argue as they will, there are cer-

tainly *male old women*; i.e. those males who delight in the marvellous—the prodigious—the supernatural . . .) are highly regaled by the following *amazing story* of a vengeful sprite." He then related the account: on a ship docked in Philadelphia, sailors found a skeleton with all the flesh rotted away, so they buried the remains in the city's potter's field. The dead man's ghost, upset by such a humble burial and "taking this neglect in high dudgeon," visited the ship's sailors with all the "apparatus befitting a ghost of consequence": white sheets, pallid countenance, and much scratching and scraping. The ghost named his murderer: the mate of a vessel soon to arrive in Philadelphia. Carey mocked the story relentlessly even as he reported it.[46]

There the matter would seem destined to end, the enlightened editor having cut to shreds an absurd story told by superstitious sailors. Except that Carey's wit and sarcasm gained little traction along the docks of Philadelphia. When George Feinour, the ship's mate accused by the ghost, arrived in Philadelphia nine days later, he found public opinion inclined to accept the ghost's account. As a result he felt compelled to write an open letter to a different newspaper, the *Pennsylvania Packet* rather than Carey's *Evening Herald*. Feinour stated, "A false, malicious, and scandalous report was circulated . . . that I had murdered a sailor who came from Cape-Nicola-Mole [Santo Domingo], in the brig Eagle." Because of "the proneness of some, and credulity of others, to believe whatever is marvelous, however Improbable, many weak persons were induced to credit this idle, absurd, and ill-founded tale, that the Ghost of the sailor appeared to captain Agar, his mate, his boatswain, and his ship's crew" and stated that Feinour had killed the man in order to steal his gold watch.

One might imagine that by the late eighteenth century a well-respected ship's mate could simply ignore a supernatural accusation, but instead Feinour included with his letter to the newspaper three affidavits sworn before a magistrate and a certificate from a physician. The affidavits swore that the deceased man seemed to have died from fever and flux, and the physician's certificate stated, "I had every reason to conclude that the death of the person was occasioned by a dysentery."[47] Even as Feinour ranted against the credulity of those who would credit such a tale, he marshaled the services of elite professionals to help him counter the power of stories passed from mouth to ear.

Another late-century story that embodies the complex interplay of skepticism and belief is the one with which this chapter begins. "A Ghost" appeared in more than twenty American newspapers from Maine to Georgia in 1798. The first reports out of New-Gaol in the Fields in New York were remarkable.

One of the debtors in the jail, whose title of "Capt." indicates his respectable status, insisted that "for several nights past, the apparition of a woman has haunted the gaol from room to room." She was "encircled by a radiant light, dressed in a white flowing robe and a turban on her head, seemingly of a pleasing but dejected countenance." Three other debtors provided corroborating evidence of the "beautiful woman, arrayed in white," whose robe "seemed to be tinged with blood." They said that "almost every night about twelve o'clock, there appears a large ball of fire at intervals, which illuminates every room in the gaol for a time."[48]

A follow-up article a few weeks later made it clear that this extraordinary report generated a great deal of discussion in the many towns where it was published. "A thousand tongues" have "vociferated" the question, "I wonder what it means," in response to the original article. The author of the second article had an answer to that question: it meant nothing. He proceeded to debunk the original report. He alleged that a young woman was desperate to raise money for the release of her husband, a debtor in the jail. Therefore, she "conjured up the ghost; and trusting the secret with a confidential Printer, the account was printed before it was lisped abroad, and immediately put into the hawkers hand for sale." The ruse was a great success: the ghost story sold enormous numbers of copies and "the multitude flocked about the jail." Once again the hawkers were there to greet the credulous, with further printed reports of the ghost's activities. The woman thereby raised enough money to get her husband out of jail, at which point "Miss Puss was let out of the bag" and the "abashed multitude" slunk off to their homes.[49]

From this distance it is impossible to tell what actually happened at the New-Gaol in New York, but the newspapers of the Early Republic were fascinated by the original ghost story, with at least twenty-one reprinting it, and the same number carrying the second, debunking piece. It is also difficult to know what the editors of these newspapers thought about the affair. Were they as "abashed" as those who gathered at the jail when they learned that it was a fraud? As the editors of the Newark *Centinel of Freedom* put it in their reprint of the exposé, the original "appears to be nothing but a cock and bull story." The editors' greatest concern was for those they believed had lesser intellectual capacity: "We most sincerely hope that the relation of this wonderful affair has not frightened any old women or children out of existance, or turned any old maids into jack-a-lanterns."[50] Nothing in the original report, however, indicated that the "multitude" that went to the jail in curiosity, nor the "thousand tongues" that repeated the story after reading it in the newspaper, were primarily old women and children. Men (certainly male newspaper editors) seem to have been equally fascinated by the story, at least until the exposé appeared. But at least one author was understanding toward those who believed the original story, putting the incident in the context of people's curiosity and lack of knowledge about the afterlife: "If we must be somewhat credulous with respect to the next world, our ignorance of what we cannot see may in some measure plead our excuse; and thus the belief of . . . a Newyork Ghost, may be forgiven."[51]

This was precisely the dynamic that kept alive a great deal of belief in the supernatural, despite the skeptical elements of Enlightenment thought. People could not know for certain what happened after death, and so, in ways not unlike what they had done for centuries, they looked to stories of unusual coincidences and messages from the other side as evidence about the afterlife. The main difference from earlier narratives was a greater attention to the enlightened, skeptical climate in which the stories circulated.

Accounts of messages from the afterlife appeared with some regularity in the magazines and newspapers of late eighteenth-century America. A classic sort of story with a long pedigree concerned a person who receives supernatural notice of the distant death of a loved one, which later proves to be correct, as in the account of Joseph Beacon's ghost that so fascinated the Mathers and others at the end of the seventeenth century. One such story appeared in the *Freeman's Journal* of Philadelphia, and when it was reprinted in 1787 in the *Worcester Magazine* it was headed, "To those who delight in the Marvellous." The author, M. W., contrasted the skeptical intellectual climate of the literati with the popular desire to learn about the supernatural: "In this age of infidelity, any Notices given us from the World of Spirits, when sufficiently proved to be genuine, are not to be overlooked." This is similar to the motivation that animated Joseph Glanvill, Richard Baxter, and others a century earlier to search for verifiable accounts of the supernatural: to counter a perceived wave of religious "infidelity." If anything, this motivation was even more intense at the end of the 1700s, after a century of skeptical writings had put on the defensive those who believed in the possibility of supernatural intrusions into daily life.

M. W. proceeded to tell his tale. Levin Milby left England on his ship to trade in the Carolinas. His brother-in-law Elias West, "a man of truth and credibility," went to bed one night and saw Milby's face at his window. The spectral form said, "Elias, I am dead—I died in Carolina, and have sent my son Natty home to his Mammy." Elias told five men about this, but they tried to convince him it was all a dream. Eight or ten days later, however, word arrived of Milby's death, just as West had foretold. Whether it was a dream or an actual ghost, the author left it to the reader to decide. "If it be called a dream," M. W. wrote, "the matter is still the same. Here was a true notification from the Invisible World." The lesson, according to the author, is that "the soul of man is not circumscribed by this present state."[52]

The same lesson was present in similar stories in *The American Oracle* by Samuel Stearns, who was not only a physician but also the official astronomer of Massachusetts and Vermont. Stearns published the *North-American Almanack* annually from 1771 to 1784 and traveled widely in Europe. His *American Oracle* of 1791 was, as its subtitle indicates, "An Account of Recent Discoveries in the Arts and Sciences." The book was a work of Enlightenment learning, yet it drew deeply on belief in the supernatural.

Stearns argued that all must admit that apparitions appear in Scripture. He acknowledged the skeptics of his age by writing, "many suppose that neither the angelical nor the diabolical spirits, nor the ghosts of persons deceased, are suffered to appear in the present age." But Stearns was not deterred by the skeptics. "It is evident by the testimonies of persons of the best credit and reputation," he asserted, "that apparitions have been seen of late." He then offered just two of the many "recent proofs" he could marshal. First, a young Englishman who was at sea, "being at cards in the cabin, stopped playing all at once, and gazed with astonishment. The company asked, what he was gazing at? and he said that his father appeared to him." When he arrived back in England, he learned "that his father died at the instant that he made his appearance." The second involved a man whose mother "appeared to him on his vessel in the West Indies." He wrote down her supernaturally delivered words, and they turned out to correspond exactly with what she said to those who attended her deathbed, which occurred while he was at sea and was thus impossible for him to have known by natural means.

Not only did shipboard supernatural events offer a way to prove that stories could not have been faked, but they also embody the collective fears of Americans and Britons whose loved ones too often were separated by months-long communication delays while they were at sea or in locales scattered around the Atlantic. Stearns and others believed stories that offered a comforting connection across those distances. Stearns himself represents a kind of learned and well-traveled American open to supernatural intervention. He allowed that some people thought they saw apparitions when they did not, but "from my own experience and observation," that is, by his own careful and scientific method, he knew of their existence, "having seen not less than five in the day-time, and when I was not thinking of any such things."[53] Thus, even in the decades after the Cock Lane ghost, when elite skepticism became ever more fashionable, some enlightened authors retained a belief in the lively interplay between residents of this world and the afterlife.

Visions of the Dead

Another genre in the print culture of late eighteenth-century America was similarly open to a range of readings, from metaphorical to literal: accounts of visions describing visits to heaven and hell. Such narratives had proliferated in the previous century during the English Civil War and Interregnum, when a breakdown in control over the press allowed a multitude of visionary pamphlets to be published.[54] In the 1740s, when young New England converts joined the Whitefieldian revivals by the thousands, visions of heaven and hell also abounded, but in general they did not make their way into print.[55] By contrast, toward the end of the century, as print culture expanded and catered more to popular tastes, accounts of visions became a staple of booksellers' offerings. These narratives were just as multivocal and ambiguous as they had been in England, and they followed the pattern set a century before: an individual takes ill, appears to die, travels to heaven and hell with an angel, sees familiar people, and revives to tell the tale. Such visionary stories peaked in popularity between 1780 and 1810.[56] They offered readers two ways of imagining communication with the dead. First, they described meetings with deceased friends and relatives in heaven and hell, and even though the visionaries did not often speak with these souls, they were able to report details about their condition. Second, the visionary was portrayed as someone returned from the dead; those who spoke with the visionary after the supernatural experience were, in some ways, speaking with the dead, or at least one who had visited the other side.

A small minority of visionaries brought back stories of their travels to hell.[57] Sarah Alley of Duchess County, New York, for example, saw the "horrid pit" of hell, surrounded by many people with "fire flaming out of their mouths and eyes." Suddenly, Alley spied someone she knew. "One man that I saw I knew well, and on my asking him what was the occasion of his being in torment, he answered, not because I have not done justly between man and man, but I have not been faithful to my God."[58] He then told Alley to warn his family to have faith in God so they could avoid his fate. This was a conventional message, to be sure, but the messenger was highly unconventional: a woman who had spoken to a dead man in hell.

Most visionaries of the 1790s, however, spoke with or saw individuals in heaven. Jane Cish saw Jesus and a "multitude of saints and angels" but did not mention any specific acquaintances by name.[59] Nine-year-old Hannah Coy of Windsor, Vermont, returned from a journey to heaven with a report that "she saw one of their neighbors in heaven, that died a little before, who was a deaf and dumb man, but he could sing now and speak, and praise God as well as any of them."[60] And Thomas Say of Philadelphia, when he visited heaven, was able to watch events transpire on earth. He saw "a negro, named Cuffee, belonging to the Widow Kearney, . . . die in the brick kitchen, and when they were laying him out, his head fell out of their hands upon the board, about six inches," a detail meant to add verisimilitude to the account. After Cuffee died, his soul entered heaven. "No sooner did the negro's soul appear to me, but it was clothed in a garment of unsullied white. I beheld him with joy."[61] Say was thus able to report that Cuffee's soul resided happily in heaven. In an age when print culture was rapidly expanding its reach, these messages from heaven, which earlier would have achieved only local fame, now spread across the country and in some cases across the Atlantic to offer believers and skeptics alike evidence of what the afterlife looked like. All of this took place a half century before Spiritualism offered Americans regular glimpses through heaven's "gates ajar," and even before Emanuel Swedenborg's eighteenth-century visions of a "modern heaven," complete with reunions and conjugal love, gained more than a miniscule audience in America.[62]

Nonetheless, one should consider the skeptical portion of the reading public that evaluated these narratives. A publication that illustrates the delicate balance between skepticism and belief is the anonymous *True Narrative of a Most Stupendous Trance and Vision* (1793). The author set his story within the context of popular interest in ghost stories and other supernatural narratives: "A great part of mankind, in every age, are pleased with the marvellous. Stories of witchcraft, fa[i]ries, hobgobblins, revelations, visions and trances always excitce [*sic*] the attention of the superstitious." This was the author's intended audience; he wrote "for the pleasure and advantage" of those who enjoyed the marvelous.[63]

The narrative began like all others in the genre. The visionary, in this case a man from Sharon, Connecticut, lost consciousness. His friends tried to revive him, but to no avail. For three days and three nights he was without a pulse, yet his body remained warm. This corporeal heat gave his friends hope, and their patience was rewarded when his soul returned to his body, and he awakened with a remarkable story of a visit to the afterlife. He explained to his friends that an angel took him to heaven, where he saw countless more angels: "A vast assembly of saints joined them in their solemn and delightful worship: some of whom he had known in this world and could call them by name." Like so many other visionaries, he saw and communicated with the souls of those he had known on earth. His angelic companion also took him to see the "sulphureous flames" and "horrid dungeon" of hell. The visionary's soul at last returned to its body, where the man found his friends weeping over his presumed corpse and delighted to learn of his supernatural travels.[64]

As the anonymous author put it, "The story of this remarkable trance and stupendous discoveries had a most rapid circulation, and produced much conversation and various opinions." These "various opinions" were the period's divergent attitudes, ranging from skepticism to belief, toward visions of heaven and hell. The visionary was prevailed upon to give a public lecture. But in this case the visionary speaker was subjected to a withering cross-examination by the local minister. The pastor asked the heavenly traveler if he saw Scotland while on his journey across the globe. "Yes, sir, I did." What did it look like? "Scotland, Sir, is a very level country—a very plain level country indeed." Aha, the minister retorted, Scotland is in fact mountainous! And so it went, with the poor visionary reporting that the Euphrates River is in Germany and making other mistakes about geography and astronomy. After this surprising twist in the story, in which the reader's expectations for a remarkable vision are confounded, the author's lesson was obvious: "let all enthusiasts and religious impostors take warning. . . . Modern accounts of witchcraft, revelations, visions, trances and apparitions, may be swallowed down easily by the ignorant and superstitious."[65]

Here is a narrative that took what became the defining stance of the late eighteenth and early nineteenth centuries: the desire to have it both ways, to be read and enjoyed by both skeptics and believers in the supernatural. Remember that the narrative begins by stating that it is "for the pleasure and advantage" of those who "are pleased with the marvellous." Perhaps the author hoped to snare credulous readers with his generic title and alluring opening paragraph, only to surprise them with the twist that the vision turns out to be false. On the other hand, some readers may have ignored the author's moralistic framework and believed the visionary's account of the afterlife, despite a few post-vision mistakes on a geography quiz.

This textual ambivalence appeared again and again in the late eighteenth century. Gothic fictions, for example, could be read either as delightfully frightening tales or as guides to what really happens when an apparition arrives and the dead speak. Newspaper accounts of hauntings, such as the female ghost in the debtor's prison, left it to the reader to decide whether to credit the supernatural tales. And many books, especially in the early nineteenth century, told gripping ghost stories to demonstrate, paradoxically enough, that ghosts don't exist.

Perhaps the best example of this last category is Richard Johnson's *False Alarms*, first published in 1802 and popular enough to warrant a second edition in 1809. Subtitled *The Mischievous Doctrine of Ghosts and Apparitions, of Spectres and Hobgoblins, Exploded*, the book ostensibly aims to demonstrate the folly of ghost belief, yet it does so through a series of chilling ghost stories. *False Alarms* begins without editorial intervention. Aside from the subtitle, no framing device tells the reader how to interpret what follows; the reader simply plunges right into the story of Mr. Howard and his children. Three "gentlemen" who are Howard's friends come to dine with the family, and the children participate in the dinnertime conversation. The discussion is so animated that the group forgets to light candles as evening approaches, so they are gradually enveloped in darkness. A scratching is heard, the noise grows louder, and suddenly "they beheld what they supposed an apparition, clothed in white, and crawling on all-fours." The children are "struck with terror," the men are "very much astonished," until they realize that it is the "barber's boy" who was looking for Howard's wig in the basement and stumbled in the darkness.[66]

Howard wonders aloud why the children were so frightened by the sounds in the darkness, especially given that "the servants in the house had been strictly forbidden ever telling them stories of ghosts and spirits." The men debate this for some time, offering various natural and psychological explanations for why people still fear ghosts. This reminds Howard of a ghost story from his childhood, which he proceeds to tell, of a maid who was frightened out of her wits by what she thought was a ghost but which turned out to be a leg of mutton. One of the guests offers a scientific explanation for the maid's fright, which reminds another guest of a ghost story about two men frightened by what they believe to be an apparition in Westminster Abbey.[67]

And so the book goes, with original and classic ghost stories interrupted only by brief interludes offering rational explanations for the seemingly supernatural events narrated therein. This method found an analogue in Gothic fiction. *False Alarms* employed something like Gothic fiction's "explained supernatural," a technique most commonly associated with the English novelist Ann Radcliffe but practiced by numerous writers on both sides of the Atlantic in the late eighteenth century. Radcliffe gained the scorn of critics, most influentially Sir Walter Scott, for explaining away the seemingly supernatural occurrences in her novels. These critics argued that Radcliffe should have had the courage of her convictions and allowed the supernatural events to stand on their own.[68]

What these critics missed is how the technique of the explained supernatural, whether used by great writers such as Radcliffe or moralizing hacks such as Richard Johnson, was a brilliant marketing ploy. These works, written at a time when readers' views on the supernatural ranged from the accepting to the skeptical and every point in between, could be read with pleasure by all, wherever they stood on that spectrum. Publishers and authors responded to this range of belief with ambivalent texts open to multiple readings. They did so in books such as *False Alarms* and in newspaper articles such as "A Ghost," which Albany's readers likely greeted with a wide variety of responses in 1798. In the multivocal print culture of the new United States, these texts reflected and shaped the pervasive curiosity about the afterlife.

CHAPTER 5

Eighteenth-Century Imaginative Literature

Grief-stricken, a young mother addresses her dead child: "Speak, Menander, let thy mother once more hear the voice that was her last comfort." It is no use; he cannot respond. "I will still keep him," the despondent mother cries, "if he will not speak to me I shall still behold him—I will still have my child." Having recently lost her husband and another child to illness, she is bereft and falls into a deep slumber. While the bereaved mother sleeps, a friend dresses the dead child for burial and places him into a coffin, which is then brought to the churchyard. The mother awakens in a panic, runs to the burial ground, and sees the tiny coffin next to an open grave. "In agony she tore the lid from the coffin—pressed him to her heart, and returned home." Back in her house, she continually kisses the corpse and will not let him go. Because he can no longer eat, she likewise refuses food. Her body cannot withstand the combination of grief and lack of sustenance. "She once more pressed him with redoubled force to her breast, again kissed his putrid cheek—and slept her final sleep."[1]

"The Dead Infant; or, The Agonizing Mother" was published as a three-paragraph fictional vignette in the *New-York Weekly Magazine* in 1796. This brief narrative and many short fictions like it are emblematic of new directions in American representations of speaking with the dead in the eighteenth century's final decades. First, "The Dead Infant" appeared when American magazines were finally flourishing, after several decades that had justified Noah Webster's exasperated 1788 declaration that "the expectation of *failure* is connected with the very name of a Magazine."[2] By 1800, editors had launched something like one hundred magazines in America, and only two had lasted as long as eight years.[3] Still, the fact that a hundred magazines had been started demonstrates the widespread interest in cultivating the new nation's literary culture. The *New-York Weekly Magazine*, founded in 1795 (and, naturally, shuttered in 1797), was a "Miscellaneous Repository" of fiction in prose and poetry. It was also, as the first issue's masthead trumpeted, "Calculated for Instruction and Rational Entertainment" and "the Promotion of Moral and Useful Knowledge."[4]

Those enlightened goals, however, ran smack into the second new development epitomized by "The Dead Infant": readers' taste for all things Gothic. The genre of Gothic fiction became popular in Britain starting in the 1760s and in America a couple of decades later. Gothic literature explored themes of death and romance and the supernatural, exciting in its readers powerful emotions and a pleasing sense of terror. It is no coincidence that this vignette's main character is a young woman, as Gothic fiction often featured female protagonists and strongly appealed to young female readers. Because of this, many educated men scathingly criticized Gothic literature as frivolous and even dangerous. In "The Dead Infant," Gothic touches include the focus on the child's corpse, the mother's "maniac rage" that leads her to pry open the coffin, and the multiple kisses she plants on his "putrid cheek." Very little is "Rational" in "The Dead Infant"; indeed, most scholars see Gothic literature as a reaction *against* Enlightenment rationalism.[5]

But if "The Dead Infant" was avant garde in appearing in an American magazine and embracing the Gothic, it also demonstrates numerous continuities with earlier Protestant representations of speaking with the dead. Eighteenth-century imaginative literature maintained the traditions of ghost narratives, puritan elegies, and talking gravestones by focusing on the deceased's voice. In "The Dead Infant," the story's very first words are the mother's cry of "Speak, Menander." She wants nothing more than to hear her child's *voice*. His lack of voice is what causes her to cling desperately to his corpse: "if he will not speak to me I shall still behold him." Such desires link the fictional mother with centuries of Protestants who so wanted to hear their deceased loved ones speak that they imagined them doing so in elegies, dreams, and ghost visitations. Furthermore, eighteenth-century poetry and short fiction continued and even intensified earlier tendencies toward portraying women as especially open to communication with the dead. Finally, the mother's plea of "Speak, Menander" directly addresses the dead, using the same device of apostrophe so frequently found in earlier elegies and talking gravestones. Although "The Dead Infant" is not the kind of "Conversation with the Departed" that Cotton Mather advocated, the story represents a similar desire for communion with the dead. By exposing ever more readers to that desire and thereby legitimizing it, eighteenth-century imaginative literature facilitated the emergence of the nineteenth-century cult of the dead.

Friendship in Death

In the first half of the eighteenth century, before the birth of Gothic literature, the most widely read text describing a network of relationships between heaven and earth was *Friendship in Death* (1728), by the English poet, essayist, and fiction writer Elizabeth Singer Rowe. The book enjoyed tremendous transatlantic popularity, appearing in at least five American editions and nearly fifty in Britain before the end of the eighteenth century.[6] First reprinted in the colonies in 1747, *Friendship in Death* consists of, as the subtitle puts it, "Twenty Letters from the Dead to the Living." The letters are clearly meant to be fictional, but in the manner of the best fiction they resonate with readers' deepest desires. The eighteenth century remained a time of very high mortality, and countless people who had lost loved ones turned to Rowe for comfort and for knowledge about what the deceased might be experiencing. The living characters in the book do not speak to the dead, but the dead communicate with the living, telling them about the afterlife and assuring them they can maintain relationships with the deceased.

Two of the most striking letters in *Friendship in Death* describe ghosts interacting with the living. In these letters Rowe does not engage in metaphysical speculation, the way transatlantic thanatologists did, about how the dead were able to appear on earth. There are no debates about astral spirits versus demonic delusions. Rowe simply imagines what the dead experience when they return to visit their loved ones. In one letter, Clerimont tells his beloved Leonora that she is not mistaken in her belief that she had seen his ghost several days before. Clerimont describes the scene. He knew she was heading out for a stroll one fine evening as the sun was setting. So he positioned himself where he was certain she would walk. In that spot "I seated my self in a human, and as I thought, a very agreeable Figure and Dress, and as much as possible, disguising the Splendor of Immortality, I imitated my mortal Form." Leonora did indeed witness the ghost. She did not approach

Clerimont's spirit, but neither did she run away in fear. Instead she headed calmly back to her house and told her brother what she had seen. But the kill-joy dismissed her account, saying "'twas all the Effect of the Spleen." Cleri-mont assures Leonora that she is right and her brother wrong. From his vantage point in heaven, Clerimont also explains that this encounter shows why people should not be afraid of ghosts: the dead return because they want to see the people they loved in life.[7]

In the book's other ghost encounter, Serena descends from heaven to warn her brother that his death is near. She appears to him as she looked when alive, so he calls out "Sister!" and tries to embrace her. This breaks the rules of ghostly interactions, so Serena evades his grasp and places herself on the opposite side of a canal. There he cannot touch her, but he can hear the "Golden Lute" she strums melodiously. The purpose of Serena's letter is to offer her brother "Proof that all was real, and neither a Dream, nor a waking Reverie, as you have per-suaded your self."[8] To the delight of readers on both sides of the Atlantic, Rowe portrays the dead as concerned about the affairs of the living, able to return to earth, and eager to communicate with their loved ones.

Readers also wanted to learn details about what awaited them in heaven, and Rowe's voices from beyond the grave helped sate that curiosity. One letter reveals that "the Language of this charming Region is perfectly musical and el-egant, and becoming the fair Inhabitants, who are fresh and rosy as the opening Morning." Another letter, from the deceased Delia to the living Emilia, brims with rapturous descriptions of the afterlife. As Delia informs her dear friend, "Here are a thousand Beauties un-reveal'd, and a thousand Delights un-nam'd among the Race of Men. We drink at the Fountain Head of Happiness, and bathe in the Rivers of immortal Pleasure." Fulfilling the fantasy of many who had lost loved ones, Delia tells Emilia about how well her dead brother is doing in heaven. He was the first spirit in heaven to welcome her, and when she first saw him, "Life and Celestial Bloom sat smiling on his Face, a Wreath of unfad-ing Flowers circled his Head, and a golden Lute was in his Hand." The "inno-cent Passion" she had felt for him while he was alive has been rekindled and "has taken eternal Possession of my Soul."[9] This is a portrayal of heaven far from the earlier emphasis on the beatific vision, with the saints' single-minded devotion to God's glory. It is a social heaven, one in which earthly relations are reestab-lished, a place where "Passion" between human souls is not out of place.

This image of a glorious and blissful heaven could lead the dead to chas-tise the living for excessive and unnecessary grief.[10] Such is the case in the letter to the Countess of ——, from her only son, who died when he was two years old. The boy is happy to have an opportunity to speak with his grieving mother, but he admonishes her for her sadness. He explains that in the afterlife his celestial self moves about with agility and enjoys the incomparable beauty of heaven. He says to his mother, "if you could conceive my Happiness, instead of the mournful Solemnity with which you interr'd me, you would have celebrated my Funeral Rites with Songs, and Festivals."[11] This was a powerful message to the middle-class mothers who mourned the loss of their children with increasing intensity in the eighteenth century: temper your sadness, remember the glories of heaven.

Indeed, it was such a powerful message that some mothers used it to foster in their own children laudable sentiments about religion and the afterlife. In 1774, Mary Cranch of Braintree, Massachusetts, sent her ten-year-old daughter a copy of Rowe's book. In her accompanying letter, Cranch urged her daughter to imitate Rowe: "try to write like her; but endeavour to be as good." She continued, "when you have read some of it, send me what you think of it—of every Letter write your thoughts, & send them to me."[12] There is evidence that as other girls read *Friendship in Death*, they adopted its language of sensibility into their own letters and diaries.[13]

With such a strong market for the volume, it is hardly a surprise that Rowe inspired at least one book-length American imitator, shortly after the first American edition appeared. Published by Benjamin Franklin in 1750 but penned by an unknown author, *Letters from the Dead to the Living* were written "in Imitation" of "Mrs. Roe's" letters. The author states, "I am well aware of how far I fall short of that excellent Lady." Unfortunately this is true, not simply conventional eighteenth-century authorial modesty. The book has a distinctly provincial flavor: not nearly as gracefully written as Rowe's letters and much more didactic. One dead man who speaks to his daughter does so "to deter her from indulging a lazy indolent Course of Life."[14] Nonetheless one can see the book's appeal, with its descriptions of heaven and its assertion that a delightful afterlife beckons.

Other writers circulated manuscript copies of their tributes to Rowe. One such group was the circle of female Philadelphia poets who coalesced around the "attic evenings" salon of Elizabeth Graeme Fergusson, including Hannah Griffitts, Susanna Wright, and Sally Norris Dickinson. Enamored with Rowe's book, the Philadelphia coterie shared imitations among themselves, including Dickinson's "To Sylvania—from her Freind Fellicia lately Deceas'd,— being a Poetical Imitation of Mrs Rowe's Letters from the Dead, To the Living." Like Rowe's letters, Dickinson's poem comforts the living: Fellicia dwells in "feilds of Light—and Pure Ambrosial air, / (Where I am Safe arrived my Mortal friend)." But in addition to these soothing words, and departing from the tone that dominates Rowe's letters, the dead Fellicia has a stern warning for Sylvania: "And o, my friend, The Path you Resent [i.e., recent] tread, / Will lead you Everlastingly-Astray." Fortunately, it is not too late for Sylvania to reform her erring ways. Her deceased friend tells her:

> But if Perhaps—(as far as leave To Tell)
> I now discribe This Ever-blooming-Place,
> And hint the Joys, which In our Bosoms dwell,
> I may urge you forward In the Glorious Race.[15]

This is didacticism with a softer touch than in some early eighteenth-century elegies in which ministers appropriate the voices of the dead. Because Dickinson wrote for friends, her imagined ghostly words of advice likely came across as less condescending than ministerial attempts at the same. Either way, Dickinson's letter in imitation of Rowe uses her friends' curiosity about the afterlife to tempt them to improve their behavior.[16] It was an appropriate homage to Rowe and *Friendship in Death*, the most popular eighteenth-century portrayal of relationships between heaven and earth.

Secrets and Phantoms

One might think that in the century of the Enlightenment, some seventeenth-century elegy conventions such as speaking with the dead and addressing the deceased's shade would diminish. Instead, those conventions remained strong, even increasing in frequency in the second half of the eighteenth century. And although most attention to early American elegy has been directed toward those authored by seventeenth-century puritans, the form did not merely survive into the eighteenth century, it gained new relevance.[17] In the latter half of the century, innovations included a strong tie between elegy and the formation of the new nation, increasing use of the newly fashionable language of sympathy and sensibility, and the strong influence of the Gothic, especially as seen in the ghosts and phantoms and graveyards these poems increasingly featured. Throughout the century, gender remained central to elegy's mourning function, as some women were portrayed as harboring a "secret wish" that their deceased loved ones would return to life.

At the start of the eighteenth century, a number of New England elegies continued the earlier tradition of employing dead women's voices. Several, however, attempted to appropriate such voices for didactic purposes, with only mixed poetic results. Given the power of the deceased's voice as rendered in elegy, and in light of the frequency with which women spoke from heaven in mourning poetry, some ministers sensed an opportunity to teach lessons about proper female behavior.

Previously, when women spoke from beyond the grave in elegies, they directed their words at family members, neighbors, or a combination of the two, without respect to the sex of the listeners. In early eighteenth-century didactic elegies, however, deceased women spoke only to other women. On February 3, 1713, seventy-one-year-old Elizabeth Hutchinson died "Suddenly."[18] Four days later she was buried in Boston's South Burying Ground and memorialized in an elegy written by the prolific puritan poet John Danforth. In the poem, soon published as a broadside, the author represents the deceased as speaking directly to women—young women in particular—with advice about how to live a holy life:

> Her Life was Speaking, and Her Death not Dumb
> She gives Instruction from the very Tomb;
> She calls aloud; "LADIES, BE READY; Mind Me;
> "I've Gone before; But Leave the WAY Behind Me.
> "LADIES! Be Lesson'd, by My Silver Hairs,
> "To Banish from your youth all Carnal Fears
> "Of Dying soon, if You are Early Pious."[19]

Hutchinson instructs the living "from the very Tomb," a phrase that reveals the ambiguities in how people thought about the location of the dead. According to mainstream Protestant theology, which Danforth well knew as a Harvard-trained minister, if the deceased is speaking it is from heaven, to which place angels whisked the soul immediately after death (at least for those not predestined to hell). But when searching for a way to describe the location of Hutchinson's postmortem lecture, Danforth, perhaps unthinkingly, settled on "from the very Tomb." Given that the poem was in all likelihood delivered at the graveside, the phrase makes sense, as the speaker could have gestured at the coffin while he ventriloquized her voice. But it also shows how graveyards were widely considered to be locations where the dead might be heard.

Hutchinson's words themselves are relatively conventional: women, learn from my experience and embrace Christ when you are young. Danforth also has Hutchinson refute something he thinks young New England women believe: that if a person was pious at an early age, she risked dying young. Harnessing the special power accorded to the words of the dead, Danforth mobilizes the deceased woman's voice against what he considered to be a problematic lay belief.

For didacticism, though, no New England minister could top Cotton Mather, who saw bereavement as a moment when mourners might be open to lessons about pious behavior. Therefore in funeral sermons and elegies he frequently urged listeners and readers to avoid sin—and to avoid activities that weren't exactly sins but that distracted them from Christian duties. Such was the case when Sarah Leveret, wife of the Massachusetts governor, died in January 1705. For her burial Mather wrote a poem that has Leveret offer advice from heaven to the "Virgins" listening to and reading her words:

"Rather to Churches than to Balls repair;
Perfume you[r] Closets too with Daily Prayer.
Foul Cards let your Fair Hands throw by with Scorn
But Write and Work as for high purpose born.
Let pearly Tears (at which lewd wretches scoff)
Of Penitence wash your Black Patches off."[20]

In just six lines Mather uses Leveret's voice to criticize a whole range of alleged female vices: dancing at balls, using perfume, playing cards, and wearing black beauty patches to cover smallpox scars. Reflecting fears about female idleness, vanity, and sexual allure, Mather's appropriation of Leveret's voice clumsily turns a gathering to mourn the dead into an occasion for a stern lecture. Perhaps in life Leveret had inveighed against the sins of youth. But even if she did, Mather's elegy represents the most extreme example of a minister ventriloquizing the dead to advance a campaign of behavior modification.

In the first third of the eighteenth century (1701–33), the didactic poems by Danforth and Mather were among the eight elegies published in New England that represent the dead either as speaking (three) or being spoken to (five).[21] Then fashions changed. Twenty-five years passed (1734–58 inclusive) without a single elegy published in New England that communicated with the dead. The form itself remained popular; fourteen elegies were published in those years. It is always difficult to explain an absence, and in this case the exercise is complicated because the convention of speaking with the dead returned forcefully to elegies in the last third of the eighteenth century. Could there have been a connection with the Great Awakening? If that explanation carries any weight, the impact was only temporary.

Starting again in 1759, published elegies returned to the technique of speaking with the dead. Influenced by the increasingly emotional, expressive styles of English poetry, New England elegists wrought verses that breathed deep sighs and were bedewed with tears. And more than ever they addressed the deceased's shade, often at the funeral itself, with the corpse's presence seemingly inviting communication with the dead. For example, Thomas Russell had been the very embodiment of the new nation's civil society when he died in Boston in 1796. President of the Society for Propagating the Gospel, leader of the Massachusetts Humane Society, Russell was mourned by many when he died. In fact, his elegy was not merely spoken by its author but also set to music and "sung after the Eulogy" by the entire congregation:

> Shade of departed worth! we come
> To pour our sorrows o'er thy hallow'd bier;
> To mourn thy unexpected doom,
> That draws from grieving virtue many a tear.[22]

In this case the elegist's "we" was not a figure of speech in which the author spoke for the audience. Instead, the assembled mourners joined voices, standing in front of Russell's earthly remains on his "hallow'd bier," and sang to the deceased's shade.

A similar scene played out at the funeral for George Whitefield, the great revivalist preacher, or at least as the funeral played out in the imagination of an anonymous elegist. As with Russell's funeral, the corpse was central to the mourners' experiences and closely tied to the desire to communicate with the dead:

> 'Tis so, blest shade! a thousand groans arise,
> And strangers pay the tribute of a tear,
> The heavy drop streams from a thousand eyes,
> And feeling mourners croud around thy bier.
> Virtues like thine must bloom around thy bust,
> And bid the generous friend of virtue mourn,
> Full many a sigh will consecrate thy dust,
> Full many a bay will shade thy hallow'd urn.[23]

These verses are awash with imagery that draws power from Whitefield's corporeal presence, as suggested by a crude skull-and-crossbones woodcut on the poem's title page.

The speaker tells Whitefield that mourners crowd around the bier, presumably to glimpse the preacher's holy remains. This presumption is strengthened by the subsequent lines, in which the speaker tells Whitefield's shade that "many a sigh will consecrate thy dust." In other words, mourners' sighs and moans will render his corpse holy. Whitefield's name, the speaker asserts, will impart a "grateful odour," a phrase redolent of the medieval and early modern Catholic "odor of sanctity" that supposedly distinguished the blessed remains of saints from the decomposing flesh of the masses.[24] And finally, the "bust" and "urn" likewise function as stand-ins for Whitefield's body, especially for future generations who will not be able to enjoy the presence of his actual body. Scholars have long known that Whitefield's corpse inspired fascination in a way reminiscent of Catholic relics, with people entering his tomb years after his death to take pieces of the preacher's clothing and bones.[25] What they have not remarked on is the way this interest was connected to a desire to represent communication with him, or at least with his shade.

Such is also the case in the most famous elegy for Whitefield, authored by Phillis Wheatley. Like the anonymous elegy, Wheatley's is decorated with a woodcut, but this one makes even clearer the importance of Whitefield's body. The berobed divine lays atop his bier, peaceful face and ample belly fully visible outside—almost floating above—his coffin. As an advertisement in the *Essex Gazette* described the woodcut, the elegy is "Embellished with a plate, representing the posture in which the Rev. Mr. Whitefield lay before and after his interment at Newbury-Port."[26] By collapsing time from both "before and after his interment" into one image, the woodcut helped readers imagine the great man's body lying in state for people to view and lying in a tomb awaiting resurrection. The presence of Whitefield's body in front of the reader invites conversation with the departed (Figure 12).

Wheatley's poem indeed conjures Whitefield's presence by speaking directly to the dead man. The speaker begins by addressing Whitefield with a powerful, if conventional, bodily image:

Hail, happy saint, on thine immortal throne,
Possest of glory, life, and bliss unknown;
We hear no more the music of thy tongue,
Thy wonted auditories cease to throng.

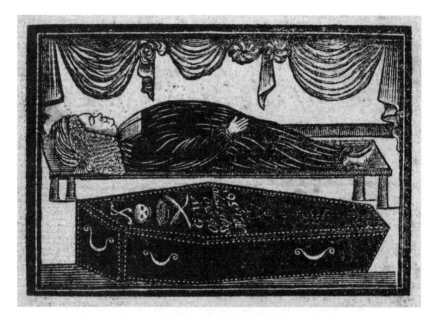

Figure 12. From the title page of [Phillis Wheatley], *A Poem, By Phillis, a
Negro Girl, in Boston. On the Death of the Reverend George Whitefield*
(Boston, 1770). Whitefield's corpse invites interaction with the viewer. The
coffin bears the inscription "G W / Ob. 30 / Sept. 1770 / Æt. 56."
Beinecke Rare Book and Manuscript Library, Yale University.

Whitefield's musical tongue has been silenced by death, but readers can imagine its silky tones in a sermon Wheatley places in his mouth. This is not the
same kind of rhetorical device where the deceased is represented as speaking
from heaven. Instead, Wheatley paraphrases words Whitefield said (or plau-
sibly could have said) while alive.

Given that this was "the poem that arguably . . . led to her eventual freedom," in the words of Wheatley's biographer, it is appropriate that Wheatley—
still enslaved at the time of the poem's writing—has the figure of Whitefield
deliver lines that explicitly put "Africans" on par with "Americans":

"Take him my dear *Americans*, he said,
"Be your complaints on his kind bosom laid:
"Take him, ye *Africans*, he longs for you,
"*Impartial Saviour* is his title due:

"Wash'd in the fountain of redeeming blood,
"You shall be sons, and kings, and priests to God."[27]

As Cotton Mather knew when he had the deceased Sarah Leveret deliver a lecture about female vanity, one of the great advantages of writing an elegy featuring the speaking dead is that the poet gets to decide what the person says. Wheatley knew this too, and her version of Whitefield has him addressing "Americans" and "Africans" as equals, urging both to take the "Impartial Saviour" for their redeemer. She employs the dead Whitefield to make the case that people of European and African descent are equally entitled to share in Christ's blessings.

With the Whitefield elegy and numerous others published in the next few years, Phillis Wheatley became the best-known elegist in late eighteenth-century New England. During her career she wrote nineteen elegies that survive, eleven of which communicate with the dead.[28] Her 1773 collection gained a broad readership in England and America and was reviewed in British periodicals such as the *Gentleman's Magazine* and the *London Magazine*.[29]

More recently, Wheatley has once again gotten a great deal of attention, but scholars have left almost entirely unremarked her penchant for communicating with the dead.[30] One literary scholar who does mention Wheatley's use of the technique neglects to see it as part of a broader poetic convention: "Astonishingly, the speaker claims to have been a witness to her heavenly admonitions."[31] But Wheatley's technique is astonishing only when removed from the context of more than a century of New England elegies that communicate with the dead.[32] Thus the arresting tally: hundreds of pages of literary analysis, but only a few paragraphs on a device Wheatley uses in eleven of her nineteen elegies. What does it mean when a poetic convention is so widespread as to become invisible?

Answers emerge when one examines Wheatley's elegies and listens to the conversations with the dead they imagine. Wheatley's poems are especially revealing of the reasons why people were so eager to read about the speaking dead. Many mourners, as Wheatley's elegies demonstrate, wished that their recently deceased loved ones would return to life. This was a dangerous view to voice in ordinary writing and conversation, given that it meant the mourner was not resigned to God's will. But in poetry, one step removed from daily speech, it was safer to make such a suggestion.

Take, for example, the elegy Wheatley wrote for the Boston merchant Thomas Hubbard, whose daughter Thankfull had recently died. Thankfull herself had lost her husband, Thomas Leonard, only one year earlier. Thus Wheatley describes the young woman as "She, who late wish'd that Leonard *might return*."[33] Given that Thankfull knew what it felt like to desire a loved one to return from the dead, she was in a good position to offer advice from heaven to those who mourned her own death. Wheatley has the dead woman speak eleven lines. Thankfull addresses her parents, expressing the conventional sentiment that they would not be sad if they knew how happy she is in heaven. Then Wheatley's Thankfull Hubbard Leonard reveals her parents' secret:

> "Amidst unutter'd pleasures whilst I play
> "In the fair sunshine of celestial day,
> "As far as grief affects an happy soul
> "So far doth grief my better mind controul,
> "To see on earth my aged parents mourn,
> "And secret wish for T——l to return."[34]

It grieves Thankfull (to the extent that those in heaven can be sad) that her parents secretly wish for her to return from the dead. The mourning parents have to keep this desire hidden, as it goes against the dictates of proper mourning; it questions God's will. Thankfull's advice, by contrast, draws on a legacy going back to Cotton Mather. As Wheatley has Thankfull tell her parents, "'Let brighter scenes your ev'ning-hours employ: / 'Converse with heav'n, and taste the promis'd joy.'" Conversation with the departed would give her parents a taste of Thankfull's heavenly bliss, without the problematic desire for their daughter to return from the dead.

A similar "secret wish" is unveiled in another Wheatley elegy, this for the twelve-month-old Charles Eliot, who died in 1773. Though only an infant, Wheatley's Eliot speaks in mature, confident language. He tells his parents that he is glad he died before his soul could be tainted with sin: "Thanks to my God, who snatch'd me to the skies, / E'er vice triumphant had possess'd my heart, / E'er yet the tempter had beguil'd my heart." Wheatley realizes that such reassurances could not simply remove the pain of a child's death. And so, as someone who herself had witnessed death at close range since her Middle Passage voyage, which suffered a mortality rate twice as high as the average shipment of slaves from Africa to America, she has the parents express the depth of their anguish by addressing the child directly. They describe their attachment to their son's ghostly memory:

"Delightful infant, nightly visions give
"Thee to our arms, and we with joy receive,
"We fain would clasp the *Phantom* to our breast,
"The *Phantom* flies, and leaves the soul unblest."[35]

Here is how much Charles Eliot's parents miss him: every night they have visions of holding him in their arms, but then the "phantom" departs and they are left with nothing but their grief. Whether dream, vision, or something else, these nightly encounters with the infant's apparition are momentarily comforting, until reality sets in.

Wheatley was not the only poet who explored the idea of a secret wish for the deceased to return. Indeed, another poem written after little Charles Eliot's death, this one by his aunt, Ruth Barrell Andrews, covers similar ground. Andrews, a white woman in the same coterie of female Boston poets as Wheatley, has her speaker insist it's a good thing the infant died with "soul unsullied" by life's inevitable sins, and therefore it does not make sense for his mother to wish that he were still alive:

Of this we'r[e] sure!—then can you want again
Your darling Charles, to pass one hour of pain?
Or wish in your imagination wild,
One dear embrace from you[r] departed child?

Andrews recognizes that some bereaved women wished to embrace the ghost or spirit of their dead children. But Andrews simultaneously says that such a desire is merely the fancy of an "imagination wild," reminiscent of the bereaved mother's "maniac rage" in "The Dead Infant."[36]

Elegies by Wheatley and others thus offer a window onto grieving practices that people did not usually report in diaries. Perhaps this was because the intensity of grief prevented some people from recording their full feelings, either because they did not want to seem like they were questioning God's will or because their anguish made writing in a diary a low priority. Wheatley's bereaved do not adopt what had long been the culturally sanctioned pose of resignation to God's will. Was this artful invention or careful reportage? Either way, the elegist does not shy away from representing intense grief.

In this, Wheatley was on the cutting edge of a gendered change in attitudes about proper mourning behavior. For over two centuries, (male) Protestant ministers had urged restrained mourning. But by the second half of the eigh-teenth century, in tandem with more vociferous expressions of grief in Grave-yard School and proto-Romantic literature, increasing numbers of middle-class men and especially women began to celebrate the public expression of mourn-ing. They participated in a public culture of sympathy, heeding works such as Adam Smith's *Theory of Moral Sentiments* (1759) that lauded sympathy as the defining feature of humanity.

Smith's *Theory of Moral Sentiments* begins with the argument that humans use their imagination to feel what others feel. Significantly, one of Smith's first examples of such fellow-feeling involves a mother and her sick or dying baby. "What are the pangs of a mother," Smith asks, "when she hears the moanings of her infant that during the agony of disease cannot express what it feels?" It is the mother's "idea of what it suffers" that causes her such anguish, even though the baby "feels only the uneasiness of the present instant, which can never be great."[37] Thus, when Smith seeks to illustrate sympathy at its most natural, he almost unthinkingly reaches for the highly gendered mother-infant relationship, the same one explored by Wheatley, Andrews, and so many other late eighteenth-century elegists.

With sympathy exalted as the finest of all human sentiments in the sec-ond half of the eighteenth century, women and men expressed their grief in ever more elaborate and public ways. Gravestone epitaphs grew longer and more emotional. After a pause during the Revolutionary War, when austere funerals were briefly in vogue, large funerals again dominated public space in towns and cities.[38] And poetic tributes to the dead proliferated, with elegists such as Wheatley in high demand among the urban literati.[39] Historians of sympathy and sentiment have connected these evolving forms of expression to the rise of the middle class, arguing that "the white women in Wheatley's circle participated in and relished public displays of grief or mournfulness to deflect attention from the political implications and responsibilities of their increasing wealth."[40] Perhaps, but given that public displays of grief quickly moved down the social ladder, the new expressive style may have had less to do with class and more to do with the broader cultural shift signaled by Adam Smith.

All this attention to sympathy meant that elegists such as Wheatley went to great lengths to represent a continuing relationship between the living and dead. Survivors had sympathy for the dead, as Smith suggested; residents of heaven likewise had sympathy for the living. One of Wheatley's strategies for representing this connection was to portray the deceased trying to make physical contact with the living. In "On the Death of a Young Lady of Five Years of Age" (1770), the poem's speaker addresses the grieving parents: "Perfect in bliss she from her heav'nly home / Looks down, and smiling beckons you to come." Here the dead girl does not speak to her parents, but she connects with them in a way almost as powerful: she smiles and beckons them to join her. One can easily imagine her little index finger slowly curling, wordlessly inviting her parents to a heavenly reunion. The deceased makes a similar connection with the living in the poem Wheatley wrote for Rev. Timothy Pitkin when his wife died in childbirth. The poem's speaker tells the grieving husband that "Thy spouse leans downward from th' empyreal sky" to speak with him.[41] This is an image that would only grow in popularity, becoming widespread in the nineteenth-century cult of the dead.

The dominant scholarly method in recent decades has been to analyze Wheatley's poetry in light of her identity as a person of African descent and a slave.[42] Could the permeable boundary between this world and the afterlife in Wheatley's elegies be the result of her African heritage? Probably not. Leaving aside the fact that she was only eight years old when torn from her homeland, the more important point is that Wheatley was schooled in her art by the same body of literature consumed by Anglo-American elegists: the Bible, first and foremost; classical authors including, as she put it, "Ovid, Horace, Virgil, &c."; the great Alexander Pope; and a century of puritan New England elegists.[43] In all these sources Wheatley encountered communication with the dead. It would be more surprising had she *not* employed such a conventional device in her many elegies. Moreover, Wheatley undoubtedly gained authority by ventriloquizing the voices of Boston's elite.[44] Wheatley's poetic achievement was to combine the convention of speaking with the dead with a willingness to represent powerful emotions that sometimes went beyond the dictates of proper mourning, such as the "secret" desire to have one's spouse or child return from the dead. Wheatley's popularity as an elegist in the 1770s was owing to this: she worked within the conventions of her time even as she pushed against the boundaries of acceptable mourning practices.

Revolutionary Elegies

Wheatley was a versatile poet who addressed a wide range of topics, including the imperial crisis that upended Boston. In poems such as "On the Death of General Wooster," "On the Capture of General Lee," and, most famously, "To His Excellency George Washington," Wheatley employed her talents to shape the public discourse about the crisis and the war that followed. In this she was hardly alone; poetry in broadside and manuscript was an important part of the polemics on all sides of the issue. Revolutionary elegies were a significant subset of this larger poetic debate.[45]

Many of these elegies communicated with the dead, especially those who were considered heroes of the patriot cause. When General Joseph Warren was killed during the Battle of Bunker Hill in June 1775, the Revolutionary War had its first great martyr. Warren had been one of the most active patriots in the years leading up to the war; it was he who sent Paul Revere and William Dawes on their immortal midnight ride. After Warren was killed in battle at age thirty-four, newspapers spread word of the tragedy throughout the thirteen colonies. In New Jersey, one person moved by the reports was Annis Boudinot Stockton, a poet and fierce patriot. Stockton's manuscript elegy, "On hearing that General Warren was killed on Bunker-Hill, on the 17th of June 1775," can be dated to late summer of that same year.

Stockton's elegy not only speaks to the dead man's ghost but also glorifies his corpse and his grave, asserting the power of his remains. The poem's speaker first addresses Thomas Gage, commander of the British forces in North America. Reflecting rumors that British soldiers desecrated Warren's corpse, Stockton writes, "But boast not Gage, tho' he unburied lies, / Thousands of heroes from his dust shall rise." Clearly Stockton means this metaphorically, but it is nonetheless striking that the speaker proclaims that Warren's corpse—despite being unburied and perhaps mutilated—will spawn a generation of revolutionary heroes. The rest of the poem continues to focus on his holy bones. Addressing the dead man's ghost, the speaker states:

> For thee, blest shade, who offer'd up thy life
> A willing victim in the glorious strife,
> Thy country's tears shed o'er thy sacred urn,
> Sweeter than dew-drops in a vernal morn,
> In rich libations to thy mem'ry pour,
> And waft their odours to the heav'nly shore:
> Nature herself, fresh flowret wreaths shall weave,
> To scatter daily on thy honor'd grave;

> While all the brave and all the good shall come,
> To heap unfading laurels on thy tomb.[46]

Stockton sets the colonies' grieving inside a metaphorical graveyard. Warren's country weeps "o'er thy sacred urn," places flowers "on thy honor'd grave," and piles laurels "on thy tomb." Proximity to the corpse and communication with the dead are central to Stockton's vision of a mournful nation. Stockton's use of apostrophe allows her a more intimate relation with Warren, his bones, and his soul than if she described him in the third person.

This focus on the corpse is appropriate for an age in which elegy on both sides of the Atlantic was increasingly influenced by the language and themes of early Gothic literature. This should come as little surprise, given that both elegy and Gothic fiction were animated by death and tried to find meaning in loss.[47] Both also drew upon the tropes and conventions of the Graveyard School of English poetry and prose, as exemplified by Edward Young's *Night Thoughts* (1742–45), Robert Blair's *The Grave* (1743), James Hervey's *Meditations Among the Tombs* (1746–47), and, most influentially, Thomas Gray's *Elegy Written in a Country Churchyard* (1751).

By having the reader contemplate death and decay, these works produce a pleasurable melancholy in the reader, provoking deep feelings that, ideally, encourage the reader to accept Christian teachings and express sympathy with the living and dead. Graveyard poetry of the mid-eighteenth century contains macabre images of the sort that will soon fill the pages of Gothic fiction. *The Grave*, for example, features a "new-made Widow" crawling "o'er the prostrate Dead," weeping as she clings to the grass on his grave, where "she thinks / She sees him."[48] And in Young's *Night Thoughts*, a graveyard throbs with the presence of ghosts and spirits: "This is Creation's melancholy Vault, / The Vale funereal, the sad Cypress gloom; / The land of Apparitions, empty shades."[49] As one scholar argues, such images combine to "forge imaginative relationships between the reader and the dead."[50]

Like Graveyard poetry and Gothic fiction, American elegies toward the end of the eighteenth century employ ghosts and corpses to heighten readers' emotions. Rather than merely addressing the shade of the deceased, some elegies invoke images of actual ghosts to convey the continuing bonds between the living and dead. John Trumbull, who would later gain fame as a member of the Connecticut Wits poetic circle, published a broadside elegy in 1771 to memorialize a fellow tutor at Yale College. Buckingham St. John had drowned off the coast of Connecticut when his "frail skiff" foundered in a storm. Trumbull's speaker settles down by the moonlit sea to meditate on his dear friend's death. But this won't be a solitary contemplation; soon the poem's speaker is joined by another figure:

> Slowly I view a whiterobed shade ascend.
> That says, "I once was St. John! from the bounds
> Of unknown realms beneath the dreary wave,
> Where ever-restless floods in nightly rounds,
> Roll their dark surges o'er my watry grave."[51]

The ghost, clad in white as convention dictated, continues to speak for many stanzas, describing the dramatic impact of the tempest, the "trembling sailors" who managed to stay aboard the boat, and St. John's soul as it parts from his body. The overall effect is to make the ghost much more of an actual presence in the poem compared with elegies that simply address the deceased's shade. For Trumbull and his readers, imagining St. John's ghost was an attempt to assuage the pain of his loss.

A final example illustrates the start of a trend toward reading elegies for enjoyment and edification rather than as a way to mourn a specific individual. In colonial New England, elegies had been almost entirely occasional poems, that is, poems written for a specific occasion. In the 1740s, Graveyard School poets demonstrated the appeal of elegies unmoored from the particularities of a single deceased person. Toward the end of the eighteenth century, similar poems began to appear in America. The anonymous author of *Effusions of Female Fancy, by a Young Lady, Native of America* (1784) collected several poems by herself and a male friend and published them, to be sold "by all the Booksellors and Printers in York, Baltimore, and Philadelphia."[52]

It is fitting that the collection's longest poem, filling twelve pages, is "An Elegy; In a Country Church Yard, in Imitation of Gray." Published in 1751, Gray's *Elegy* quickly became ubiquitous in England and before long in America too. One bibliographer has found one hundred imitations of Gray's *Elegy* published in the Anglo-Atlantic world by 1831.[53] Nor was the poem's popularity limited to elites; in 1781 Samuel Johnson remarked that "the common reader" held the poem in high esteem.[54] These were the same people the author of *Effusions* addressed: middle-class women and men who consumed poetry in books, magazines, and newspapers. But Gray's American imitator went far beyond the original in her portrayal of communication with the dead.

Gray's *Elegy* reflects on the life and death of a single individual, addressed once as "thee" and once with "thy." The poem thus includes some interaction with the dead, but it is a minor feature of the 128-line original.

By contrast, the version in *Effusions* is centrally concerned with the relationship between the living and dead that plays out in a churchyard. The poem is divided into six "Nights." In "Night the First," the speaker walks through a churchyard while "The moon lends aid to scan the speaking tomb." The poet thus indicates that talking gravestones are going to be vital to the elegy. Gothic touches abound, with a "moss grown tomb" here, and there a girl for whom death "caus'd the cherry to desert her cheeks." The speaker then hears her name "with faintness cried" and, surprised, turns to see an old grave marker:

> This stone declares "Here rests retired from toil,
> "A sailor who of't plow'd the wat'ry deep,
> "Who of't experience'd fortune's frown and smile,
> "And left the troubled seas in earth to sleep."

Ironically, this stone does not fit my definition of a talking gravestone; it describes the sailor in the third person. But in the poem, the stone speaks to the narrator and "declares" its message, suggesting that some people experienced their visits to graveyards as opportunities to interact with the dead.[55]

This sense is confirmed during "Night the Second," when the speaker returns to the graveyard once again to "converse with the silent dead." This time her communication with the deceased is more direct. She sees a fisherman's marker and says, "But yet poor fisherman fear not your doom, / Heav'n will receive you, Heav'n no man scorns." Chancing upon the stone of a beloved family man, the speaker says aloud that the tears of his wife and children cannot "e'er restore you to their arms again." On the fourth night the speaker encounters her loving brother's stone, which inspires her to address the dead:

> Adieu dear brother lov'd departed shade,
> May you to heav'ns exalted throne ascend,
> Where dire misfortune never dare invade,
> But blessings infinite on all attend.

The sentiment is conventional, but if the scene is based at all on the way people actually behaved in graveyards—and there is no reason to think otherwise—then the author confirms that visiting a burial ground was an important way that people maintained connections with the dead.[56] This had been articulated in New England elegies going back to the middle of the seventeenth century. But as the nineteenth century neared, this practice became even more prominent in the literature that growing numbers of middle-class readers consumed in the expanding marketplace of print.

Lovers Tragedie

The many American literary magazines that popped up like mushrooms (and frequently disappeared just as quickly) in the 1780s and 1790s were truly miscellaneous in character. Indeed, many proclaimed the fact in their title or subtitle, such as the *Monthly Miscellany* (Bennington, Vermont, April to September 1794); the *Literary Miscellany* (Philadelphia, October to November 1795); and the *New Star: A Republican, Miscellaneous, Literary Paper* (Concord, New Hampshire, April to October 1797). Like newspapers but even more so, magazines featured a plethora of distinct voices in their pages: some skeptical, others embracing the supernatural. Literary magazines were known to plunder stories and poems from English sources, but to a great extent they relied on the "Favors" or contributions of "the Fair Daughters and the Sons of Literature," as the *New Star*'s editors phrased it in their solicitation of original material.[57] Because these "Fair Daughters" and "Sons" were local residents, their poems and stories form a portrait of literary taste among middle-class readers.[58]

Gothic poems and short fictions stand out as being among the most popular sort of imaginative literature for these late-century readers. With its interest in the supernatural, Gothic fiction frequently explored the relationship between the living and dead. The Cock Lane ghost was a crucial factor in Gothic fiction's emergence. Although "Scratching Fanny" proved to be a hoax, the 1762 affair demonstrated the reading public's fascination with the supernatural, as English consumers snapped up newspapers, magazines, books, and broadside ballads that featured the ghost. Following the smashing commercial success of the first Gothic novel, Horace Walpole's *Castle of Otranto* (1764), writers and printers hurried to fulfill the public's seemingly insatiable desire for supernatural fiction. But although Gothic fiction was born in a ghost hoax, and despite its deep imbrication in market relations, its rise did not signal the secularization of literary tastes. Ghost stories sold because many people still believed in ghosts—or believed enough to make such stories entertaining.[59]

Figure 13. James Gillray, *Tales of Wonder!* (1802). Four well-to-do women, portrayed as ugly and ridiculous, share a reading of M. G. Lewis's Gothic classic, *The Monk* (1796). Image © Victoria and Albert Museum, London.

Because of its supernatural subject matter, Gothic fiction was sharply criticized by enlightened elites on both sides of the Atlantic. Male taste-makers wished that readers—especially women, the dominant consumers of the Gothic—would choose more "profitable" subjects. Although plenty of men read and enjoyed Gothic fiction, the genre's perceived feminization led to much mockery, such as the English caricaturist James Gillray's satirical drawing, *Tales of Wonder!* (1802) (Figure 13). Four well-to-do women huddle around a table as one reads aloud from M. G. Lewis's Gothic classic, *The Monk* (1796), a book (in)famous for its "openly avowed supernaturalism."[60] Gillray portrays as ugly and ridiculous these women who tremble at the story of a bleeding nun's ghost. He seems to suggest that these women would be better off reading works of Christian piety.[61]

Likewise, writing at the height of England's Gothic craze, the educator John Burton warned women away from fiction that might lead them to believe in supernatural beings. In his popular 1793 conduct manual, *Letters on Female Education and Manners*, which saw editions published in England, Ireland, and America, Burton told young women that "Spectres and Apparitions" were generally products of overheated imaginations. Therefore, "if, as we have reason to think, they are only creatures of the fancy, how unwise is our conduct, to wander in the regions of fiction, for new and unusual objects of alarm!" Burton's advice to women about Gothic fiction was unequivocal: "It will be a proof of good sense, and consequently, of a proper degree of female fortitude, to reject such fabulous tales."[62]

Many young, middle-class women brushed aside such stodgy admonitions as they pursued the latest fashionable fictions, including much that was Gothic. Their access to such literature was facilitated by the decreasing price of print and especially by the explosion of lending libraries, which circulated a wide range of imaginative literature. Benjamin Franklin established America's first library in 1731, and between then and 1790 another 110 were opened. But then in the 1790s the United States witnessed the opening of a remarkable 266 new circulating libraries.[63] These institutions catered to female as well as male tastes. Consider the motto of Robert Bell's Circulating Library in Philadelphia: "Where Sentimentalists, whether Ladies or Gentlemen, may become Readers."[64] In light of this broader access, some scholars see Gothic fiction as an example of the democratization of reading, with market demand—driven by female interests—winning out over top-down dictates about what people *should* read.[65]

Though Gothic fiction emerged in England in the 1760s, it took a little longer to gain traction in America, as readers were initially preoccupied with the imperial crisis and Revolutionary War. But starting with the new literary magazines of the 1780s and continuing with the many newspapers that carried imaginative literature, countless poems and short stories explored the desire to communicate with the dead. A subset features a person's recently deceased lover who returns with a message from heaven. This section focuses on twelve of these short Gothic fictions (eleven in verse and one in prose) published in America in the last quarter of the eighteenth century.[66] Seven of these works originated in Britain (including two traditional ballads), the other five in America. The ghost is female in only three of the pieces; in the other nine the dead man returns. Perhaps this reflects supernatural fiction's predominantly female audience. Female readers may have been especially moved by the tale of a woman who had experienced her lover's death.

Elite contempt did not stop American women and men from enjoying Gothic tales about the ghosts of returned lovers. One such story is "The Ghost of Edwin," which appeared in the *Massachusetts Magazine* in 1792. Laura's lover Edwin has gone to the Indies. She understandably worries about his safety and wonders, "O when shall wedlock make us one?" Each night she watches the sun set and repeats her plaintive question. But one night she is greeted by an unwelcome figure. "At last the ghost of Edwin came, / Pale as the snow on winter's cheek." He tells Laura that he has been consigned to a "watery grave." Tears flow down Laura's cheeks as she tries to touch the specter: "To grasp his much lov'd form she strove," but of course she cannot reach him. She groans, "Then dy'd amid the leafy grove, / So death has made these lovers one."[67] The poem reflects the desire for reconnection after death. Reunion in the afterlife makes "these lovers one."

In "Jamie's Dream; or, Mary's Ghost" it is a female ghost that returns, but again the poem expresses the wish for reunion after death. Mary is dead and Jamie is lying in his bed when he hears a voice: "Dear Jamie, weep for me no more." Jamie is much more agitated about the ghost's appearance than was Laura in "The Ghost of Edwin." Jamie "started up with wild surprize" and "sweat did drop from every pore." He is appalled to see his beloved in this ghostly state. With good reason, it turns out: Mary has returned to tell him that he is about to die: "That thou must soon unite with me; / Prepare, for soon will toll the knell / It's mournful requiem for thee." But Jamie's opinion changes when Mary tells him that heaven will be amazing. Part of heaven's glory will be that "We soon shall meet when thou are dead, / To live united evermore."[68] The reader is left to imagine the joyous reunion of these two lovers in heaven.

Whereas the reader is invited to believe that the ghosts appearing to Laura and Jamie are real, some poems in this period offer a more ambiguous position on the reality of apparitions. As we have seen, many late eighteenth-century elites explained away ghosts as figments of a disordered imagination or guilty conscience: internal rather than external phenomena. This is the meaning ascribed to the ghosts that appear in several works in this sample. In "Harriet's Ghost," an original American story that first appeared in 1775, Moloch has killed Harriet in a horrible manner, garroting her with a "fatal Cord." Harriet is portrayed as blameless, with a loving husband and infant daughter. Harriet returns to haunt Moloch—or does she? "'Twas Dead of Night, when Sleep had clos'd / The perjur'd Moloch's Eyes, / He dreamt he saw, such Pow'r has Guilt, / Poor Harriet's Ghost arise."[69] The speaker asserts that guilt has the power to conjure specters. The rest of the poem, however, continues *as if* the ghost were real, allowing the reader to ignore the first stanza and concentrate on the subsequent nine in which Harriet's "ghost" condemns Moloch for his evil deeds.

A similar dynamic is at work in "Edwin's Ghost," which originally appeared in the London *New Lady's Magazine* in 1789 and was reprinted in New

York's *Weekly Museum* in 1799. Mary has been "false" to Edwin, having committed an unspecified act of duplicity. Something about the events, and Edwin's subsequent death, has left Mary in a state of unease. "Deep silence hush'd the midnight scene; / Sweet sleep had seal'd each wearied eye; / And sooth'd to rest the wretch's woes— / But Conscience, Mary, wak'd with thee!" Mary awakens only to find a "pale spectre" beside her bed. He cries out to her: it is "thy Edwin true!" He tells her that she will no longer be able to sleep, owing to her pangs of conscience: "Guilt-haunted she the scene broods o'er, / A Ghost in ev'ry shade she sees." Mary is not literally haunted but "guilt-haunted." Again, though, if the reader wishes to focus on the "ghastly" aspects of Edwin's visage and his macabre statements to Mary, she is free—even encouraged—to do so.[70]

Readers may have downplayed the degree to which guilt accounted for the apparitions in light of their own desire to speak with their deceased loved ones. The poem "Henry and Selima" plays on this desire. Horatio's fiancée Selima has, to his great grief, just died. He contemplates suicide, but instead of killing himself, he embraces her lifeless body: "He clasp'd her cold and breathless corpse, / He clasp'd it o'er and o'er." He also speaks to her: "Oh! Solitude, with thee I'll dwell! / My Selima, Adieu!" But unlike most readers who may have spoken to their departed lovers, Horatio gets a reply. Selima's ghost appears with a comforting message, of sorts: "No longer weep, no longer sigh, / No longer now complain; / But seek my grave, for there thou'lt find / Relief from all thy pain." Horatio lies down on her grave, cries out "My love I come," and dies.[71] Again it is left to the reader to imagine the young lovers reunited in heaven.

Beyond the twelve works in the sample, another subset of Gothic fiction involved the reader in the emotions of communicating with the dead: poems and short stories that portray speaking with the dead in a burial ground, such as *Effusions of Female Fancy*. These American works from the 1790s were deeply indebted to the Graveyard School, and they also resonated with the practice of visiting burial grounds to remember one's departed friends. Even though these pieces predated the rural cemetery movement of the 1830s, many Americans in the late eighteenth century enjoyed contemplative walks through churchyards. These visits, as represented in fiction, often culminate in conversations with the dead.

The narrator of an original story in Boston's *Gentlemen and Ladies' Town and Country Magazine* visits a graveyard to consider human mortality rather than remember a particular individual. At each grave he passes, the narrator expresses sympathy for the dead and reflects on the meaning that can be wrung from the cryptic words on the marker, not unlike the speaker in Gray's *Elegy*. He reads the epitaph of an eleven-month-old child and addresses the deceased infant: "Happy babe! immortality is thine after a short trial, and a few pangs." Next he sees the stones of several ministers. Again he is inspired to speak to the dead men: "Sleep on, blest shades; though you are now chained in your narrow prisons, darkness your habitation; yet, this is not your abiding place— your everlasting home." He imagines the souls of these holy men flying up to heaven, and he addresses them: "Leave me not in your rapid flight, ye holy spirits! May I never lose sight of your transporting bliss—of your flaming love!"[72] Even though Protestants had long ago abandoned purgatory, the belief in graveyards as a site of souls and ghosts persisted, making those spaces especially fruitful for communication between heaven and earth.

Another common device in these works is to have the individual or collective dead in the graveyard address the person strolling through the grounds. The entire poem "The Church Yard" is in the first-person-plural voice of the buried dead speaking to a visitor: "O Thou! by Fortune or Reflection led, / To view this gloomy mansion of the dead." The dead urge the visitor to look out for them. "Let not the voice of impious Mirth presume / To break the hallow'd silence of the tomb."[73]

By contrast, in "Lines Occasioned by . . . the Grave-yard of the Church of Wicacoe," the eighteen-year-old poet Anna Young imagines one specific deceased person, who seems to be a woman, addressing the narrator and her female companions. As the speaker is walking among the graves with her friends in an old Swedish burial ground near Philadelphia, she suddenly hears a voice: "But hark!—a note from heaven's own choir I hear!" The dead woman says to the visitors, "My sisters, tho' unseen, / I long have watched you on this pensive green!" The spirit tells them that she lived sixty years before dying. Her body now lies in the earth but her soul has been released to heaven. The spirit goes on for sixty-four lines, offering the speaker and her companions conventional advice for living a meaningful life: be kind, compassionate, virtuous. This will allow them to have good deaths and ascend to heaven like her: "Kind angels shall your dying hour attend, / And sister spirits o'er your shades shall bend. / Their choral songs your trembling souls shall cheer, / Disperse death's horrors, and the prospect clear."[74] From the afterlife the speaker thus receives a comforting message: directions on how to live so as to ensure a place in heaven. Given their supernatural source, these were indeed words to heed.

But the most frequent device in these works is to have the bereaved speak with the dead. In "The Rural Mourner: A Sentimental Fragment," an original piece written for the *Massachusetts Magazine* in 1791, Eliza's cheeks are bedewed with tears for her beloved Edward; she is the very portrait of enlightened sympathy. She sits by his grave and remembers all his virtues: compassion, modesty, even his skill at singing and dancing. The memories leave her feeling empty, wishing for his presence. She sees a wilted flower, which inspires her to address her dead lover directly: "Yes, Edward, such was thy fate! Thou didst fade as the flower. Thine head was bowed to the high command of the angel of death." He cannot, of course, respond; the piece, without the spooky details of Gothic fiction, sets up no expectation that his ghost is going to appear. So Eliza conjures him herself. She imagines him saying, "Eliza, I knew thy love, cherish my memory, and be happy."[75] Even without apparitions, visitors to churchyards could have conversations with the dead.

Similarly, in another original "fragment," this one published in New York's *Weekly Museum*, a literary magazine aimed at female readers, a graveyard's peaceful setting contrasts with the protagonist's agitation. In the trees "little songsters of the grove" sing merrily; in the vales lambs bleat contentedly. But Amelia feels anguish because "my *Philander* sleeps in the silent dust." With a nod to Gothic sensibilities, the narrator thinks about the deceased's corpse: "cold are the clods which cover his once faithful breast." In this state Amelia addresses a long speech to her dead lover. Gazing at his tombstone, she asks him, "is this white stone an emblem of thy innocence, the only *momento* [sic] of thy lovely youth;—no, tho[u] livest in the soul of Amelia." Because he continues to live in her soul, she promises to plant willows and strew the grave with flowers. "Nightly will I visit thy grave," she vows.[76]

Amelia then voices a belief that the spirits of the dead remain around their loved ones, an idea that would become ever more deeply entrenched in the first half of the nineteenth century. "If the spirits of the just watch round their surviving friends," Amelia says, "surely thou art my guardian angel." She addresses his ghost directly: "Dear shade thou knowest the anguish of my soul."[77] These statements are worth lingering over. At first, Amelia indicates that she is not sure whether to believe in the presence of the dead: her declarations are preceded by the conditional "if." *If* the "spirits of the just"—souls in heaven— "watch round" the living, then "surely" he is hovering near her. But her subsequent direct address of the dead undermines the "if"; she speaks to the dead because she wants to believe that Philander's spirit is there. That is why she will visit the grave every night.

Protestant ministers were uncomfortable with belief in the presence of departed spirits, but the idea would nonetheless become a cornerstone of the cult of the dead. Female writers and readers thus drove important changes in Protestantism at the end of the eighteenth century. Although the *Weekly Museum* "fragment" is a fictional vignette, it derived its power from being a plausible representation of lay Protestant beliefs about the presence of the dead. Burial grounds, full of talking gravestones, might just be sites of immanence: places where the spirits of the dead hovered, awaiting communion with the living.

*   *   *

One must be careful about reading too literally the words of Eliza, Amelia, and the dozens of other fictional speakers examined in this chapter. In the last two sentimental fragments, for example, it is impossible to know what the anonymous authors believed about the possibility of actually communicating with the dead in graveyards. Nor do we know what the magazines' publishers, Isaiah Thomas and John Harrison, thought about these ideas. A combination of literary ambition, financial incentive, and sincere belief motivated the writing and publishing of short fiction in the new nation's magazines. Still harder to discern is what readers took away from these stories. What kind of "Knowledge and Rational Entertainment," as the *Massachusetts Magazine* promised to deliver, did literary-minded women and men derive from fictions about communication with the dead? Did readers shed a tear, smile with condescension, skip to the next story?

Despite these uncertainties, several things are clear. Writers and readers used imaginative literature to explore the boundary between the living and the dead. In belles lettres people could express or read about ideas too dangerous to broach in ordinary conversation or diaries, such as the secret desire that the dead would return to earth, or the wish to hear a child's voice one more time, or the hope that spirits of the dead hover around the living. These ideas seem to have been especially appealing to women, in light of the plethora of female protagonists in Gothic short fiction, the numerous female speakers in elegies, and the many stories about interactions with the dead that appeared in magazines catering to women.

As with newspapers, magazines were a new form of knowledge production and dissemination in the eighteenth century, but they did not necessarily lead to secularization or the disenchantment of the world. They were too multivocal for that. Of course, countless magazine articles and fictions in the 1780s and 1790s embodied the rational spirit of an enlightened century. But next to essays about politics sat Gothic fictions about shades of the dead flitting about graveyards. As Chapters 7 and 8 will show, ideas expressed in imaginative literature that were too far outside mainstream Protestantism to be revealed in diaries and letters began, in the nineteenth century, to appear in private writings. This is when earlier ideas finally coalesced into the cult of the dead. Before then, communication with the dead represented a relatively minor part of Protestants' overall religious experiences. But in the late eighteenth and early nineteenth centuries, several new sects put speaking with the dead and revelations about heaven at the very center of their beliefs and practices: Swedenborgians, Shakers, Mormons, and others. These religious movements were started by visionaries such as Mother Ann Lee, about whom it was said that "when she speaks in unknown tongues, the living people cannot understand her; yet the dead understand her, for she talks to them."[78]

CHAPTER 6

Revelations and New Denominations

In a year of remarkable events, one of the most unusual was Jemima Wilkinson's death and subsequent rebirth as the Public Universal Friend, a vessel of the Holy Spirit. In October 1776, the twenty-three-year-old resident of Cumberland, Rhode Island, contracted a severe fever and took to her bed, seemingly for the last time. Soon she experienced the "Shock of Death," and then, perhaps even more shockingly, two angels appeared. They told Wilkinson that "the Spirit of Life from God, has descended to the earth" to "assume the Body which God had prepared, for the Spirit to dwell in." The Holy Spirit would inhabit Wilkinson's reanimated body in order to "warn a lost and guilty perishing dying world, to flee from the wrath which is to come."[1] With that mandate, the Public Universal Friend rose from bed, never again to use the name Jemima or any female pronouns for self-reference. The Friend immediately began preaching about the revelation the angels had brought, eventually convincing hundreds of followers to move to New York's Finger Lakes region to create a society where they could follow their prophet's teachings.

One of the most distinctive aspects of the American religious landscape from the Revolution to the Civil War was the proliferation of new denominations such as the Public Universal Friends. This was the defining component of the "antebellum spiritual hothouse," a phrase that evokes the fertile environment in which new religions multiplied rhizomatically and flowered abundantly.[2] But the proliferation of denominations actually began before the antebellum period, in the middle of the eighteenth century. New Light Separate Congregationalists formed new churches during the Great Awakening; challengers arose to Calvinist orthodoxy, including Freewill Baptists and Universalists; and numerous groups emerged based on prophetic visions and revelations. In the second half of the eighteenth century this last group included Swedenborgians, Shakers, and Public Universal Friends. During the antebellum period revelations spawned the Millerites, Mormons, Hicksite Quakers, and many others.

For some Americans, especially those in older mainline denominations who felt themselves under siege from the upstarts, this new reality seemed like a "realm of confusion and religious anarchy," as the Congregationalist Julian Sturtevant wrote in 1829.[3] For many others, however, the plethora of new groups was exhilarating, as it afforded them a range of options for spiritual satisfaction. In a post-Revolutionary society that celebrated the ability of ordinary people to make choices based on their own interests, religious seekers were freer than ever to explore new spiritual possibilities. This is what one historian calls the antebellum period's "populist principle of theology," the insistence that "the unlearned, even more than the learned, could discern theological truth."[4] Some unlearned individuals—Jemima Wilkinson, Ann Lee, Joseph Smith—had revelations that turned them into prophets. Many thousands more chose to follow these visionaries and their bracing new teachings.

Building on the widespread Protestant desire to maintain connections with the dead, theological populists took that interest in unforeseen directions. Ann Lee and the Shakers insisted that the living could lead the dead into the Shaker fold, while departed spirits could bring messages about the afterlife. Joseph Smith and the Mormons did not communicate with the dead in the same way, but they did create links between people and their deceased kin, based on the ritual of baptizing the living in the name of the dead. And Emanuel Swedenborg, though hardly unlearned (he was a member of Europe's intellectual elite), experienced decades of communication with angels and the dead, which some of his adherents interpreted to mean that they too could converse with the departed.[5]

These three prophets and their new denominations reinterpreted relationships between heaven and earth to such an extent that they did not gain huge numbers of adherents in the antebellum period. Even the Mormons, the most numerically successful of the three, numbered only about 28,000 by 1850, compared with 1.6 million Methodists and 1.4 million Baptists. Shakers and Swedenborgians were yet more marginal; they had perhaps 5,000 members between them.[6] But for believers, prophetic revelations gave them exactly what they wanted: a more powerful relationship with the dead.

Enlightenment Visionary

For the first fifty-plus years of his life, Emanuel Swedenborg was an unlikely candidate to be a visionary. He was born into a prosperous Stockholm family in 1688; his father was a Lutheran minister; he himself was a man of science. As a young man, Swedenborg studied mathematics, and in the 1730s he became an accomplished metallurgist, publishing six papers on the topic. Turning his scientific curiosity toward anatomy, Swedenborg trained with leading medical authorities in France and Germany, and he authored highly respected books of natural philosophy.[7]

There were signs, however, that Swedenborg's interests went beyond his physical surroundings. Like the late seventeenth-century thanatologists, Swedenborg explored natural philosophy in part to learn about the invisible world. When he went abroad to study anatomy, one of his goals was to discover the human soul's physical properties. This quest was interrupted in 1744 by a spiritual crisis that manifested itself in dramatic fashion: suddenly Swedenborg could converse with angels.

Throughout Christian history, theologians had considered angels to be God-created beings that served as messengers from God to humans. For Catholics, angels were generally *not* the souls of the deceased that had ascended to heaven.[8] Protestant theologians were even clearer on this issue, insisting that the souls of the dead inhabited celestial realms alongside angels but that the two orders of beings remained separate. Protestants found evidence for this in the New Testament book of Hebrews, which describes "the spirits of just men made perfect," that is, the souls of the righteous deceased, as being distinct from "angels" (Heb. 12:22–23).

When Swedenborg began to talk with angels in 1744, however, he learned that angels were the spirits of deceased humans who had gone through a process of instruction before they were admitted to heaven. Swedenborg described this system in the book that became his most widely read: *Heaven and Hell* (1758; English translation 1778). In the first stage of the process, the deceased person's spirit closely resembled his or her earthly self and thus was recognized by friends and relatives. After a happy reunion the spirits of the dead would talk with one another and resume the friendships they had enjoyed on earth. Then the spirits began to receive the knowledge of truth that allowed them to become angels and enter heaven. Thus for Swedenborg, and in contrast to eighteen centuries of Christian teachings, "there is not a single angel who was created [as] such from the beginning" by God; rather, "all . . . are from the human race."[9]

Swedenborg said he had the ability to communicate with both kinds of supernatural beings: the spirits of the deceased and the angels into which the righteous were transformed. Early in his career as a visionary, Swedenborg frequently spoke with the spirits of people he had known in life, whereas his later conversations (which continued until his death in 1772) were typically with angels who did not correspond with individuals he recognized from earth. In his *Memorabilia*, which described his spiritual experiences from 1747 to 1748, Swedenborg wrote that "it has been granted me to speak and converse with many persons whom I have known during their life in the body; and this not merely for a day or week, but for months, and sometimes for nearly a year,—speaking and conversing with them just as if they were on earth."[10] These were not the imagined conversations that authors sometimes represented in Anglo-American elegies, or the mental communication of Cotton Mather's "Conversation with the Departed," but rather literal speech with the spirits of the dead.

Thus Swedenborg was innovative in two important respects: his ideas about angels being the souls of the deceased saw no precedent in Protestant theology (though there were antecedents in popular belief), and he connected visionary experiences with Enlightenment science more effectively than any other figure.

Nonetheless, scholars have given Swedenborg too much credit for inventing the "modern heaven." This is the phrase helpfully coined by heaven's leading historians to describe the "thoroughly anthropocentric" heaven of the nineteenth century and later, which replaced the theocentric medieval and early modern heaven. Whereas the earlier heaven emphasized the beatific vision—the unendingly blissful viewing of God's glory—modern heaven is marked by four characteristics: it is only thinly divided from earth; it is a continuation of material existence on earth; saints engage in activities; and it is a social heaven, with human love replacing the beatific vision. All four of these criteria are found in Swedenborg's heaven. Scholars argue that Swedenborg was the "first" to provide "a vigorous alternative to an ascetic, theocentric heaven."[11]

But as previous chapters have shown, the idea of a social heaven long predated Swedenborg, appearing in everything from puritan elegies to Elizabeth Singer Rowe's *Friendship in Death*.[12] In fact, it is more accurate to say that Swedenborg didn't so much invent the modern heaven as vividly describe a heaven that was already well on its way to becoming modern in the second half of the eighteenth century. This, then, was the source of Swedenborg's appeal: he offered detailed descriptions of heaven that resonated with broader ideas about the afterlife.

Those who encountered the Swedish seer's ideas almost always did so via the printed word. During Swedenborg's nearly three decades as a visionary, he feverishly wrote volume after volume of what he learned from spirits and angels. His magnum opus was *Arcana Coelestia* (*Heavenly Mysteries*), published in Latin between 1749 and 1756; when translated into English the book filled twelve large volumes. Next came *Heaven and Hell*, and then about fifteen more books before he died. Most of these works were published in England because of the looser controls on the press than in Sweden. But even in England Swedenborg's writings barely registered on the cultural seismograph during his lifetime. The first volume of the *Arcana*, for example, created nary a tremor: it sold only four copies in its first two months.[13] This is hardly surprising given that Swedenborg did nothing to establish a church or even a following. When he died in 1772 his believers could be counted on one hand.

But then, very slowly, Swedenborg's writings began to attract adherents. Given the widespread curiosity about the afterlife in England and America, Swedenborg's claims of communication with spirits and angels gained the attention of a small number of religious seekers. A few of these proved to be outstanding organizers. In 1773 John Clowes, an Anglican clergyman in Manchester, declared himself a disciple of Swedenborg (though he never left the Church of England). Manchester was a hotbed of dissenting religious practice, with a century-long tradition of Quaker influence that resulted in the formation of the Shaking Quakers or Shakers, and a more recent overlay of Methodist energy.[14] Within five years of his conversion, Clowes established the world's first Swedenborg society just outside Manchester. But unlike the city's Methodists, with their vigorous preaching, and the Shaking Quakers, with their dramatic bodily manifestations of the Holy Spirit, Swedenborg's followers adopted a religious practice seemingly better suited to the Age of Reason. They established reading circles.[15]

Such was the strategy of the group's first missionary to the American colonies, James Glen, a wealthy Scot. In 1784 Glen sailed for Philadelphia and used his ample funds to purchase a large advertisement in the *Pennsylvania Gazette*. Readers learned that they could head to Bell's Book Store and hear Glen deliver a lecture explaining how "the earliest of the Human Race held

Converse and Communication" with angels, knowledge of which had been lost until Swedenborg recovered it.[16] No record survives of how many attended America's inaugural Swedenborg meeting at Bell's Book Store, but it was enough to start a reading circle. The Philadelphia circle probably resembled the London gathering described by a woman in a 1785 letter: "They meet once a week in order to converse upon the subject of [Swedenborg's] writings; they are of different Denominations, but united in promoting the translating and sale of his Books."[17] Translating texts, selling books, and discussing ideas: Swedenborg societies promoted quintessentially Enlightenment forms of intellectual sociability, except geared toward parsing the words of a visionary who spoke with angels.

From Philadelphia interest spread to Baltimore, where in 1800 adherents dedicated the first American temple of the New Church (as the denomination called itself, in opposition to the "Old" Catholic and Protestant churches). From Baltimore the denomination expanded to New York, Boston, and beyond. By 1830 Swedenborg societies could even be found in some small towns in the Midwest and Upper South such as Dayton, Ohio, and Abingdon, Virginia. Still, the number of New Church members remained vanishingly small in the Early Republic. In 1820 the twelve U.S. societies claimed just 230 members; by 1840 that figure had increased only to 850.[18]

These figures, however, understate Swedenborg's influence in America. They count only those individuals who formally joined Swedenborg societies, but that was not how most people expressed their interest in Swedenborg. Rather, religious seekers read Swedenborg's numerous books and the journals dedicated to explaining his ideas. Starting with *The Temple of Truth*, founded in 1801, and continuing with several others, Swedenborgian magazines taught interested Americans about the mystic's ideas in short, informative articles. Moreover, the best-selling *Heaven and Hell* reached far beyond the circle of committed members.[19]

Popularizers such as the editors of Swedenborgian magazines correctly guessed that an audience could be found among mainstream Protestant parents mourning the deaths of their children. For some bereaved readers, Swedenborg offered a glimpse into heaven. In 1813, for example, New York's *Halcyon Luminary* offered an excerpt from *Heaven and Hell* that the editors titled "An Account of Infants, or Little Children, in Heaven." The editors introduced the selection with a brief explanation. "Many pious persons," they wrote, "having expressed their anxiety to know the real estate and condition of infants, or little children, after their departure from this life; it is with particular satisfaction we lay before our readers the following pleasing account given by Emanuel Swedenborg."[20]

Likewise, Boston's *New Jerusalem Magazine* published an original article in 1827 that contrasted Swedenborg's revelations with older and increasingly unpopular Calvinist ideas about predestination. This was a major part of Swedenborg's appeal: his contention that heaven was not reserved for a small number of the elect. Swedenborg's views thus fit with the populist tenor of nineteenth-century American Protestantism and the widespread challenges to Calvinism.[21] According to the article's author, Calvinists believe that the souls of only a small percentage of infants enter heaven; the rest are subject to the "vindictive justice" of hell. The writer argued that such beliefs were, thankfully, disappearing, not least because they were so difficult for grieving parents to accept. Swedenborg offered an attractive alternative.[22]

Did bereaved parents who embraced these ideas try to communicate with their deceased children, in imitation of Swedenborg's conversations with spirits and angels? One might think so, at least in light of the scholarship that sees Swedenborg as a precursor to séance Spiritualism.[23] In reality the matter was more complicated.

From the beginning, Swedenborg and New Church officials expressed misgivings about people attempting to replicate the master's visionary experiences. As Swedenborg asserted in *Heaven and Hell*, "at the present day to talk with spirits is rarely granted because it is dangerous." Evil spirits lurked everywhere, and they were eager to deceive people into thinking they could receive heavenly messages. Swedenborg warned that some individuals think they hear spirits, "but such persons are visionaries and enthusiasts; and whatever spirit they hear they believe to be the Holy Spirit, when, in fact, such spirits are enthusiastic spirits. Such spirits see falsities as truths."[24]

And once the New Church was organized in the 1780s, the denomination's leaders came out against continuing spirit communications. Simply put, most Church officials did not want additional revelations to challenge Swedenborg's authority.[25] Robert Hindmarsh, the energetic Manchester disciple who did more than anyone to spread Swedenborg's teachings, wrote *Rise and Progress of the New Jerusalem Church* between 1824 and 1834. In more than five hundred densely packed pages, Hindmarsh included virtually nothing on new spirit manifestations. To the contrary, he did his best to debunk visionary claims. A group in Avignon, France, led by the mystical Count Grabianka of Poland, claimed "immediate communication with heaven." Hindmarsh dismissed them as being under the influence of a "Jesuitical scheme and

contrivance." Likewise with visionaries such as the "impostor" Richard
Brothers, the "false prophetess" Joanna Southcott, and the "notorious impostor" Ann Moore.[26] All earned Hindmarsh's scorn.

In the United States, the official line was much the same. For example,
in 1827 Boston's *New Jerusalem Magazine* described how New Church
members had to counter outsiders' perception that they sat around all day
talking with the dead: "Whenever we meet with a person who has heard any
thing about Swedenborg and the New Church . . . we are obliged to answer a
great many questions upon this point. He inquires whether we do not set
chairs and dishes for our friends who have left the natural body." No, the
patient New Churchman would respond, we don't set the table for our dead
friends; in fact, "no class of people would be more unlikely to do such things
than the believers in those doctrines" of Swedenborg. Only those like Swedenborg whose spiritual senses have been "opened" can speak with spirits and
angels.[27]

But even denominational leaders could not assert that ordinary people
could *never* communicate with the dead. As the author of the *New Jerusalem
Magazine* article continued, "We believe that a few of [Swedenborg's adher-
ents] have been favoured with visions of short duration, but for their own particular benefit, and therefore unsuitable for public examination."[28] So the
door remained open; followers could have visions. Again, this could be traced
back to Swedenborg's writings. Although he insisted that most visions were
"dangerous" because of the ubiquity of evil spirits, Swedenborg conceded that
he was not uniquely qualified to speak with the dead. Such power was "rarely
granted," Swedenborg insisted, but that little phrase opened a Pandora's box
of adherents who believed that they too could communicate with the dead.[29]

Manchester was the center of such spiritualistic activity. As early as 1784
an English New Churchman reported that "several persons in Manchester are
having open communication with the spiritual world and receive ocular and
auricular proofs of the statements of Swedenborg."[30] Also in Manchester, Rev.
John Clowes reassured a visionary correspondent that "you have no need to
be afraid of supernatural communications, which a merciful Providence may
vouchsafe."[31] Clowes was less supportive of a woman who in 1820 sought to
form a new denomination based on her visions. According to Clowes, this
woman asserted "that she had immediate open communication with heaven,
that she frequently saw and conversed with the Lord Himself." Most troubling,
"she was expressly commanded by Him to establish a New Church, which

was to be called the *New Church New*, to distinguish it from what was commonly called the New Church." Here was the antinomian threat of continuing visions written in boldface. It would be impossible to prevent dozens of new prophets from arising if Church officials countenanced each message from heaven. So Clowes and others shut her down.[32]

The most prolific Manchester visionary, however, was James Johnston. Like Swedenborg, this textile worker spoke with spirits and angels for more than two decades. And also like Swedenborg, Johnston filled hundreds of pages with transcriptions of his heavenly conversations. Starting in 1817 and continuing until his death in 1840, Johnston recorded a lengthy series of vibrantly detailed visions. Some of the beings he conversed with were angels, with names like "the King" and "the Prince," but others were the spirits of people recently deceased, Johnston's friends and acquaintances. In April 1817, Johnston spoke with the spirit of Rev. William Cowherd, an Anglican curate and devoted Swedenborgian who had died in Manchester just eleven months earlier. The spirit warmly welcomed Johnston: "Mr. Cowherd shook me friendly by the hand; and after a few words passed between us, he stood upon the stool and asked the news." Johnston also conversed with the spirit of his employer's wife, Mrs. Horrocks, who brought information about her heavenly condition.[33] Thus at least some English followers of Swedenborg were attracted to the visionary's writings precisely because they believed—contrary to the position of most New Church officials—that the master provided a model for their own conversations with the dead.

Evidence that American Swedenborgians engaged in spirit communication is weaker, though not entirely absent. Scholars have suggested that in the United States, Swedenborg's followers generally did not communicate with heaven before the emergence of séance Spiritualism.[34] But in New Church magazines one finds occasional examples of openness to continuing revelations. In May 1813, the *Halcyon Luminary* revealed that the New York society was riven into two factions: those who believed in continuing "supernatural communications" with the dead, and those who disparaged those visions using the "reproachful" term "New Lights." The author supported these "New Light" visions, though he disliked the term, because it was meant to be derogatory. Addressing the rival faction directly, the author asked, "wherefore all this cry against New Light in *spiritual* things, for are we not exhorted to grow in the knowledge, as well as in the grace, of our Lord and Saviour Jesus Christ?" We should therefore be open to "fresh discoveries of truth" via visions, the author insisted.[35] How many members of the New York society actually communicated with the dead remains unclear, but it was enough to generate controversy.

A similar tone marks an article in the *New Jerusalem Church Repository*, the Philadelphia society's official organ from 1817 to 1818. This piece used a vision that occurred in Philadelphia nearly a century earlier to defend communicating with the dead. The article recounted Thomas Say's 1725 vision, which had been the subject of two books in the 1790s.[36] The vision was well-known in the city; the magazine editors claimed that "almost all the old inhabitants of Philadelphia are familiar" with it. In Say's vision, he traveled to heaven and communicated with three recently deceased men he knew from life. The New Church magazine decided it was worth repeating this story because it showed that relationships between heaven and earth were possible. Drawing on this broader culture of visionary narratives, the Philadelphia editors asked, "If a man has a soul, capable of perceiving, *after death*, the objects of the spiritual world, where is the difficulty of believing, that, for wise purposes, God, in his goodness, has permitted that even *during their lives*, some individuals should have been so prepared for the transition, as to have had their spiritual eyes opened?"[37] This example does not provide evidence of Philadelphia New Church members communicating with the dead, but at the very least it demonstrates that some were open to the possibility. Such is also the case in articles from Cincinnati's *Herald of Truth* and New York's *New Jerusalem Missionary and Intellectual Repository*.[38]

The most dramatic and controversial instance of Swedenborgian communication with the dead occurred in 1844, within a family that included several leading New Church members.[39] Samuel Worcester (1793–1844) founded Boston's Swedenborg society in 1818, and before long Samuel and his brother Thomas became New Church ministers. The brothers remained leaders among Boston's Swedenborgians until June 1844, when Samuel heard about spiritualistic activity in New York City. There, in the words of his daughter Sarah P. Worcester (1821–1884), "my father's spiritual sight was opened, and he saw and conversed with Swedenborg and some other spirits."[40]

This deceptively bland statement appears in a remarkable document, a defense of Samuel that Sarah wrote and had printed as a three-page circular, with "To" and a blank space at the top, where Sarah could fill in the names of various recipients. Such an elaborate and expensive defense of her father was necessary because, as she put it, many Swedenborgians "regarded him as insane" for his belief in communication with the dead. Even those who didn't think he was crazy assumed that Samuel "was deceived by evil spirits." Sarah tried to set the record straight by narrating in just-the-facts prose what her father experienced in New York. When he arrived in New York in June 1844, "the Lord was pleased in His Divine Mercy, to open his spiritual sight, and enable him to see, with more clearness than he had ever beheld any earthly friends, the kind and good spirits by whom he was surrounded." This continued until Samuel died on Christmas Day 1844. During the six months of Samuel's supernatural communication, several others also had their "spiritual sight" opened, including his wife back in Boston, their daughter Sarah and son Samuel H. Worcester (1823–1891), and three or four individuals outside the family.[41]

Two things are significant in this story. First is an offhand remark Sarah made in the printed defense of her father. She mentioned that "from early childhood he had been in the habit of frequently seeing his mother, who was removed from this world when he was very young; and her influence assisted him in resisting the temptations to which children and young men are exposed."[42] Samuel's mother died in 1797, so he was "frequently seeing" her in the first decade of the nineteenth century, before he learned anything about Swedenborg, and long before historians imagine Americans having that kind of relationship with the dead. With her presence protecting him from "temptations," Samuel's mother effectively served as a guardian angel, a theologically suspect being for Protestant writers. Second, even among Swedenborgians, the Worcester family's spirit communications were controversial. Many considered Samuel insane or deluded.[43]

Aside from the detailed Worcester documents, only scattered evidence remains about American New Church visionary practice, but enough exists to suggest that Manchester was not the only place where Swedenborg's followers were interested in communicating with the dead. The New Church's official position—that members should heed Swedenborg's warnings about spirit communication—has hidden some of the broader interest in continuing visions that occasionally bubbled up from members. The official view is what led to the Worcesters being ostracized. But even if many New Church leaders and some members were skeptical of those who claimed that they, like Swedenborg, conversed with spirits and angels, this was a denomination that recognized its founding figure as a visionary of rare talent. And it was a denomination that appealed to some who themselves wished to speak with the dead. Both statements also apply to another group with deep roots in Manchester's fertile religious culture.

Shaker Visions of the Dead

Like the Swedenborgian New Church, the United Society of Believers, as Shakers called themselves starting in 1826, originated with revelations from heaven. Also like the New Church, these revelations started with one revered founder: "Mother" Ann Lee. But unlike New Church officials, Shaker leaders were much more open to continuing revelations. This allowed the group to tap into a deep well of curiosity about the dead and the afterlife among members and potential converts.

Shakers are often viewed as having inhabited a world apart from mainstream Protestantism, owing to the practices that emerged from Ann Lee's revelations: celibacy, religious dancing, communal living—and especially communicating with the dead. This assessment contains more than a grain of truth, but it is also true that Shaker spirit messages evolved in tandem with broader antebellum attitudes toward heaven and the dead. Shakers drew their members from the society in which they lived; after all, they couldn't reproduce themselves by bearing Shaker babies. As a result, Believers held fast to many of the ideas about death found in the dominant Protestant culture. Like other antebellum Americans, Shakers believed that the dead would be reunited in heaven with departed friends and family members. They also manifested "a refusal to allow the dead to disappear from the living community," as one historian describes mainstream antebellum Protestant beliefs.[44] For non-Shakers this sentiment took concrete form in locks of the deceased's hair and posthumous mourning portraits and photographs. For Shakers it expressed itself in spirit messages from the dead.

But even Shaker spirit communications were not that far outside mainstream American culture. In fact, such interactions drew upon earlier Anglo-American traditions of speaking with the dead. Believers shared with other Americans an intense desire to know about the state of deceased friends and family members. This shared culture of curiosity about the afterlife is apparent when non-Shakers flocked to witness communication with the dead during the revival of Shaker spiritualistic activity that began in 1837. Because such contact with departed spirits was at the center of Shaker religious practice, and because it drew thousands of spectators and generated numerous published descriptions, the Shakers and their departed friends demonstrate the widespread interest in speaking with the dead.

The Shakers arose from the same religious ferment in northern England that nurtured Swedenborg's first followers. Mid-eighteenth-century Manchester, already home to numerous Quakers, was buffeted by the winds of the transatlantic Pietist revival and became a center of the emerging Wesleyan Methodist movement. Led by Jane and James Wardley, a group of Manchester's religious enthusiasts came to be called Shaking Quakers in reference to the way their bodies trembled when filled with the Holy Spirit. Ann Lee and her husband, Abraham, joined the Wardleys' society, probably in the late 1760s. By the early 1770s, Ann Lee was at the center of the group's activities as a result of her "visions and revelations of God." In 1774, Ann Lee, her husband, and several other Shakers emigrated to America, both to escape persecution and to spread their faith. Lee and her small band soon purchased a tract of land at Watervliet, a few miles northwest of Albany, New York.[45]

The early Shakers' key beliefs focused on the confession of sins to an elder, the practice of celibacy, and the presence of the Holy Spirit in their worship.[46] The Holy Spirit's presence resulted in the Believers' eye-catching bodily manifestations of piety, including ecstatic dancing and whirling, as well as miraculous healing, speaking in tongues, and communicating with the dead. The very first accounts of the Shakers in America asserted that speaking with departed souls was one of the Believers' most distinctive practices.

According to the former Shaker Valentine Rathbun, Believers told potential converts dramatic stories of their powers to bridge the boundary between this world and the next. When someone showed interest in their teachings, "they tell him, that they see angels, and converse with them, and hear them sing, and sing with them; and the spirits of just men made perfect, they also freely converse with." Thus they claimed to speak with both angels and departed souls. The Shaker with the greatest talent for speaking with the dead was Ann Lee. Believers asserted that "she speaks seventy two tongues, and that when she speaks in unknown tongues, the living people cannot understand her; yet the dead understand her, for she talks to them."[47] The ex-Shaker Amos Taylor, who lived in five different communities for a total of ten months, offered readers in 1782 an important detail that Rathbun did not mention: the purpose of communicating with the dead was "for the redemption of departed spirits."[48] Believers could bring the dead posthumously into the Shaker fold. Given the success the Shakers had in gaining converts in New England's hill country in the early 1780s, these powers evidently appealed to many.

Taylor's observation was corroborated by outside observers in the 1780s. According to William Plumer, who visited several Shaker villages in 1782 and 1783, if the dead confessed their sins to the Shakers they would "become new born souls & live forever in full & open vision with God."[49] And in the words of an anonymous observer in 1787, the Shakers "carry on very frequent dialogues with both angels, devils and departed souls—a party of them being employed now in preaching to the Indians and negroes who have died since the beginning of time."[50] The informant reveals that "a party" of Believers— not just Ann Lee herself—spoke with the dead. Indeed, by this point Lee herself was a three-year resident of the spirit world, having died in September 1784.

A generation later, when elderly Shakers looked back on the early years of Ann Lee's ministry in America, among the things they remembered most clearly were Lee's powers to speak with the dead. Mary Tiffany described the first time Lee visited Enfield, Connecticut, when the prophetess said to her, "I see your deceased kindred all around you." Tiffany asked if it was her mother or her child. Lee replied, "It is all your kindred, both upon your father's and mother's side; they are nearer to you than I am." Moreover, when Shakers remembered those early years they recalled that Lee was not the only one with the gift of communicating with the dead. One Shaker remembered that a Believer named John Hocknell went into a trance and spoke in tongues. When he came out of the trance, he said, "I saw the souls of three men, whom I knew while I was in England. They came to hear the word of God; but they had not finished their sufferings, and therefore were sent back to hell again."[51] That people remembered these stories thirty years later suggests that the Shakers' ability to communicate with the dead strongly influenced new converts' decisions to join.

Speaking with the dead remained an important aspect of Shaker worship into the antebellum period, but it became significantly more frequent and widespread in the late 1830s and early 1840s, during the revival that Believers called "Mother Ann's Work" and that historians refer to as the "Era of Manifestations." This upsurge of spirit communication started in Watervliet in 1837 and quickly spread to the eighteen other Shaker communities from Maine to Kentucky. Bodily expressions of visionary communication with the dead continued and intensified. Among the most arresting examples of this came when Shakers channeled the spirits of dead Indians: some fictional, some historical such as Tecumseh. Visionists spoke in unknown Indian languages— "O ka na vah si ne tu tri le ni"—and danced Indian dances.[52] The visions and spirit communications at Watervliet and elsewhere reverberated in the supercharged religious atmosphere of the Second Great Awakening.

In this context, non-Shakers learned of the spirit communications and wanted to see the proceedings for themselves. Shakers had always allowed visitors from "the world"—so-called "worldlings"—to observe their public meetings, as a way to lure potential members.[53] Even before the Era of Manifestations, non-Shakers were interested in watching Believers dance, sing, and speak with the dead. At the remote Sodus Bay settlement, forty miles east of Rochester, New York, Esther Bennett noted matter-of-factly one Sabbath in 1835 that "We have quite a goodly number of spectators." Twice in 1837 Anne Buckingham at Watervliet reported, "Great many of the world here to meeting."[54]

Soon after Mother Ann's Work began in mid-August 1837, a member of the Shakers' central ministry observed a spike in public interest. Already by September 3, Rufus Bishop reported "a great concourse of spectators at the public meeting today." Within a few months the meeting house was so crowded with spectators—up to hundreds at a time—that the Shakers could barely dance as they usually did. They also had trouble hearing what the visionists said, "as there was such rustling among the world [i.e., the spectators] for the purpose of getting a better chance to hear what was said, and to see such as were in trances on the floor."[55] These entranced Shakers were the ones communicating with the dead.

Surely some visitors came to scoff at the Shakers and their unusual practices. But most observers' reports during the Era of Manifestations are respectful, such as the dispassionate 1841 account by "C. B.," a mill girl who watched the Believers communicate with the dead.[56] The Shakers themselves described the spectators as mainly attentive. "The world gave as good attention as we could expect," Rufus Bishop wrote after one public meeting, "and many seemed to be struck with awe."[57] Non-Believers' interest in Shaker spiritualistic activity demonstrates that although these practices were outside the Protestant mainstream, they resonated with the beliefs and curiosities of numerous "worldlings."

Conventional antebellum Protestant attitudes toward death and the afterlife made Shaker beliefs seem less odd than they appear to many readers today. Indeed, Shaker beliefs, though distinct, emerged from and built upon mainstream concerns. First, antebellum Americans were enthralled with heaven. Since the seventeenth century, lay Anglo-Americans had embraced an image of heaven that focused on the reunions between departed friends and family members. This is the long tradition that Swedenborg's followers drew on and helped expand in the nineteenth century. When residents near

Shaker communities—and tourists just passing through—learned about the Believers' spiritualistic revival, they wanted to see for themselves. They strained to hear the visionists' words so they could learn about the next world.

Second, Euro-Americans in the first half of the nineteenth century lavished emotional and religious attention on their loved ones' corpses. In this they shared the attitudes of peoples in almost all times and places; rare indeed is the society that treats corpses with disregard.[58] But it is fair to say that antebellum Americans invested corpses with greater significance than those who came before them. In particular, they were more reluctant to say farewell to the dead than were their seventeenth- and eighteenth-century counterparts, keeping tokens of the deceased's body and commissioning paintings and photographs of the corpse. These artifacts demonstrate how powerfully people wanted to maintain connections with the deceased, and thus reveal why Shaker claims to speak with the dead generated interest among non-Believers.

Drawing on these broader attitudes, Shakers themselves sometimes exhibited "relic behavior": activities that implicitly recognize the power of human remains but do not go as far as Catholic beliefs regarding the efficacy of prayers assisted by saints' relics.[59] Like other nineteenth-century Americans, Shakers occasionally described corpses in terms that resonate with accounts of medieval saints. When the Shaker David Darrow died at Union Village, Ohio, in 1825 at the age of seventy-five, friends remarked that his corpse appeared "beautifull beyond discription." The "brightness of heaven" seemed to illuminate his remains. Indeed, his corpse "surpassed any thing they ever saw of the kind" because it "emitted no odors." Darrow's loved ones connected the sanctification of his corpse with their continued access to him in the spiritual world. At the funeral, one man insisted that Darrow was "not gone" but rather would remain "the spiritual lead & protector of this people."[60]

An even more dramatic example of relic behavior occurred in 1835, when the Shaker central ministry decided to move the corpses of Mother Ann Lee and her brother, Father William Lee, from Watervliet's North Farm to its main burial ground. The primary reason for doing so was probably to put their bodies in closer proximity to recent Shaker leaders such as Lucy Wright, who had died in 1821. But a secondary motivation may well have been to allow Shakers contact with the holy bones of Mother and Father.[61]

The disinterments began on May 9, 1835, when Shaker leaders dug up Lucy Wright's grave, found her coffin, and opened it to examine the remains. Fourteen years after Wright's death, "the body had retained its shape pretty much," according to Rufus Bishop. Two days later, Bishop and numerous other elders "took up the bones" of Ann Lee, William Lee, and another early Shaker, William Bigsby. The elders carefully examined these powerful links with the Founding Era of American Shakerism. "We found them in a better state of preperation than was expected," Bishop wrote, "notwithstanding they had lain in the sand more than half a century. Even the bones of the fingers & toes were in pretty good shape."[62]

While carpenters prepared three small coffins for the remains, other Shakers "had free access to view the bones of these venerable messengers of peace & salvation" who "waded through sore afflictions, privations & cruel persecutions, both in England & America for the good of lost souls."[63] The language of martyrdom connected these holy bones to both medieval saints and the Protestant martyrs of the English Reformation. Even though Mother Ann and Father William had not been killed for their faith like the Marian martyrs, they had been persecuted by mobs of angry opponents in England and America. These attacks gave the Shakers a martyr complex they carefully cultivated in subsequent decades, when they liked to see themselves as standing apart from mainstream American culture.[64]

During the reinterment process, Shakers beheld the "marks of their suffering" inscribed on the very bones of Mother Ann. "On the left side of Mother's scull," Bishop wrote, "could be seen a fracture, said to be made when she was dr[a]gged down stairs feet foremost by her persecutors, when at Petersham [Massachusetts]." The next day, after examining these tokens of persecution and perseverance, the Shakers reinterred the remains in Watervliet's main burial ground.[65]

To be clear, the Shakers' relic behavior does not mean they invested these bones with the same powers that Catholics did. Instead it shows how closely linked they were to mainstream Protestant American beliefs in the corpse's sanctity: before, during, and after interment. As discussed earlier, some visitors engaged in relic behavior when they entered George Whitefield's tomb. For decades after Whitefield died in 1770, devoted pilgrims occasionally cut off bits of clothing that covered the corpse; one especially zealous visitor absconded with Whitefield's arm bone.[66] Emerging from a similar impulse but practiced much more widely, many antebellum Protestants treasured locks of hair from their deceased loved ones. Such tokens helped maintain connections between the living and dead. By speaking with the dead, Shakers merely took to its logical end the widespread Protestant desire to blur the line between this world and the next.

Because a funeral was the most highly charged moment when a corpse was visible, Shakers believed that such rituals were especially open to communication between heaven and earth. Nonetheless, Shaker funerals proceeded much like those of non-Believers, at least to start. According to the 1845 Millennial Laws compiled by the New Lebanon ministry, "when the spirit is departing and a person is breathing the last, all present should kneel in prayer." Shakers were then supposed to wait an hour before laying out the corpse, perhaps to make sure that the person was dead. The deceased was dressed in "a shirt and winding sheet, a handkerchief, and a muffler if necessary,—and for a female add thereto a cap and collar."[67] This sort of home preparation was standard among antebellum rural Americans, for whom the professionalization of undertakers was still decades away.[68]

A Shaker funeral quickly became distinctive, however, when participants started speaking with the dead. This was not uncommon, especially during the Era of Manifestations. Take, for example, the funeral of Sarah Fairchild, who died a difficult death when she was only thirty-two years old. Her friends and family members gathered around her the morning of April 12, 1838, expecting her to die soon. Instead, "to the astonishment of all she had to struggle between life & death about 25 hours!! In this space of time she had between 80 & 90 spasms or convulsion fits!" This must have been exceedingly unpleasant for Fairchild's loved ones to witness; perhaps the violence of her death inspired the outpouring of spiritualistic activity at her funeral, which occurred the next day. During the service Elleyett Gibbs, one of Watervliet's most active visionists, received a "Farewell Song" from "Sarah herself," which she then sang to the assembled mourners. Gibbs then "went into Vision & saw Sarah again singing & dancing with life & activity."[69] After Fairchild's terrible death, this must have been a comfort to all.

Dorothy Kibbee's 1839 funeral similarly brought news that the deceased was in a better physical state in heaven. Shortly after the elderly Kibbee died, Rufus Bishop was "viewing her corpse, in company with a number of Sisters." Like virtually all nineteenth-century Americans, Shakers wanted to view the body of a deceased friend to admire the corpse's beauty. While they were thus engaged, Kibbee's friends called for Saphrona Smith, known for her ability to communicate with the dead. The mourners were not disappointed. Smith "came into the room under powerful operations, went around the corpse which lay on a beadsted [sic] almost as swiftly as tho' she was carried by a whirlwind." After this dramatic entrance she reported that Kibbee's spirit was there in the room, along with that of five other recently deceased women. The "inspired instrument," as Shakers called those who communicated with the dead, had good news. Although Kibbee "had been unable to walk without crutches for upwards of eight years," Smith reported that "she is very active now."[70]

At other funerals, visionists not only saw how the deceased was getting on in heaven but also channeled the person's voice, as in this book's opening when a Shaker woman proclaimed through a medium, "I am not dead."[71] In another instance, during the service for forty-one-year-old Lucy Clark at New Lebanon in December 1839, "the Spirit of the deceased spoke through Zillah P. at the funeral, & thanked the Elders, and all the family for kindness she had received from first to last, & especially during her last sufferings which had been lengthy." Later, at the graveside, "she thanked them [the mourners], through H. Godwin, for their kindness in burying her lifeless body."[72] That same year, an old woman named Mary Robinson died at Watervliet and spoke to the mourners through a young female visionist named Sarah Simons. "Although my spirit has left the body," said Simons as Robinson, "I am not alone. I have found Mother and obtained the privilege of making some communications to the brethren and sisters. I desire the family would all receive my thanks, love, and blessing, for I feel as if I could not leave this house until I had returned my thanks to you all."[73]

Although the spirits of deceased men sometimes spoke at funerals, the vast majority of examples in the sources are women, often elderly, speaking through visionists who were teenaged girls. This fits the broader pattern of Shaker spirit communication in the period. One historian has found that more than two-thirds of all visionists during the Era of Manifestations were female, a fact connected to the nineteenth-century stereotype that women and girls were especially receptive to spirit messages because they were said to be more "passive" than men. Supposedly "active" men resisted the influx of spirits, whereas "passive" women possessed bodies and minds that were more easily taken over by spirits.[74]

Even though Shaker women had more prominent religious roles than their counterparts in mainstream Protestant denominations, they were shut out of certain public functions such as dealing with political leaders and writing theology.[75] And to the extent that Shaker women did have power, it did not go unchallenged by rank-and-file male Believers. Several controversies in the first decades of the nineteenth century saw men rebel against being "entirely ruled by women," as a Shaker man named Angell Matthewson put it.[76] Women and girls may have found serving as inspired instruments so satisfying because of the storytelling involved in their spirit messages. Storytelling was a way of "doing theology" for Shaker women, given that formal theological writing was off limits for them.[77]

The storytelling potential of Shaker spirit narratives was especially evident when visionists brought longer messages from loved ones. Inspired instruments often received these outside the context of funerals, perhaps because they had the time to receive more complex messages. Numerous such communications received by visionists in Enfield, Connecticut—representative of a very large body of sources from all Shaker villages—demonstrate Shakers' powerful desires to learn details about their loved ones' eternal states and the physical reality of heaven. In 1843 Esther Markham received a message from her mother, Sarah Markham, via an unnamed inspired instrument. The deceased woman described some of her activities in heaven. "I help [Mother Ann] lay away her choice things and sometimes I carry some to her dear children [on earth] to comfort them." This task had a personal connection to her living daughter. "Yea, I have brought unto you when you did not know it beautiful things from your Mother [Ann] to sooth[e] your spirit and strengthen your body."[78] Thus did the visionist comfort Esther with news that her dead mother retained a powerful connection to her, serving as a guardian angel.

Through the inspired instrument Sarah also told Esther that she was, unsurprisingly, happy in the heaven: "Much hath been my joy since I departed this life, I have not seen a moment that I wanted to return back to earth again." Perhaps worried that this might make her daughter eager to have her own time on earth come to an end, the deceased woman warned, "I would not have you feel anxious to leave on earth because that I have told you about so many pretty things."[79] This raises an intriguing issue. Were Shakers ever tempted to end their own lives in light of the frequent descriptions of heaven's glories that they received? It is hard to know. Suicide does not seem to have been especially frequent among Shakers.[80] Nonetheless, when Elizabeth Hanford committed suicide by hanging herself from a tree in March 1838, during the height of Mother Ann's Work, the central ministry responded harshly. Hanford was buried "without any funeral honors," and elders and eldresses "labored to convince the Brethren & Sisters that the late Suicide was a work of the devil & a very heinous sin in the sight of God & all good people."[81] In this the Shakers mirrored mainstream antebellum Protestant views about suicide: societal leaders stridently condemned suicide as the ultimate sin, while ordinary men and women may have been more sympathetic to their friends and loved ones who killed themselves.[82]

Most Shaker spirits, however, did not feel the need to warn the recipients of their messages against suicide. They took it for granted that their loved ones on earth could learn about heaven and not be tempted to kill themselves. Such was the case when Rozina Allen contacted her brother Abner through a visionist in 1843. Rozina had been dead for over three decades, yet her sixty-seven-year-old brother was still eager to learn about her situation in the afterlife.[83] One of Rozina's tasks in heaven was to keep watch over her living loved ones. She assured her brother, "I have many times seen you and have poured on love comfort and the balm of consolation on your spirit to make you cheerful and happy." In contrast to Sarah Markham, who worried that her daughter might be tempted to kill herself, Rozina Allen practically begged her brother to join her in the spirit world: "I have called you home to dwell with me that you may prepare yourself and make ready to help me in the trying scenes that is coming in heaven and on earth. I have sounded and sounded aloud for thee to come for I stood in great need of thee."[84] Rozina's spirit would have to be content with speaking to Abner through a medium; her brother would not die for another twelve years.

Given that Shakers lived in nonprocreating, nonbiological "family" units, many of their closest relationships were with individuals unrelated by blood. The messages the Enfield Shakers received from their closest friends were as deeply personal as those sent by blood relations. Anna Granger, for example, received a message from a close companion who had died the previous year. A visionist brought Granger words "written on a little stone" by Lovicy Wood, who was only twelve years old when she died in 1842.[85] "I do rejoice and give thanks to you," Wood told Granger, "for your tender care of me in sickness and in health." Wood also revealed some details about heaven and her relationship with "Mother Sarah," probably Sarah Harrison (1740–1796), a leading early member at the Hancock, Massachusetts, settlement. According to Wood, Mother Sarah "gives me precious Fruit to eat and healing wine to drink to nourish and cherish my spirit."[86]

Aside from the comfort of hearing from loved ones, this was probably the most important aspect of Shaker spirit narratives: they showed the living what they could hope to experience in heaven. For antebellum Americans, this was an exciting prospect. Driven by consumer interest, print culture abounded with images of heaven. A viewer of such engravings and lithographs could surmise that heaven was filled with clouds, winged angels in filmy gowns, and famous figures such as George Washington. Plus, heaven was surprisingly close, usually situated just beyond the clouds.[87]

Taking that proximity as their cue, Shaker visionists related details about life in the spirit world. The Enfield narratives include descriptions of the afterlife's soundscape: "the heavens doth ring with the sound of mighty Trumpets," Elder Nathaniel wrote. Accounts of heavenly garb: Rozina Allen wore "a white pure Robe" and a "Crown on my head." And, especially, descriptions of daily activities: "I do shout sing and dance" with Shakers on earth, Lovicy Wood related; "rejoicing daily in the God of my salvation" is how Sarah Markham filled her time.[88] This is not the domestic heaven of Victorian parlors that scholars associate with séance Spiritualism after 1848.[89] Rather, it is a more traditional early modern Protestant heaven of trumpets, singing, and the beatific vision, combined with distinctive Shaker details such as dancing and talking with Mother Ann.

Most Protestants, of course, did not learn about heaven by communicating with the dead. But numerous published vision narratives, for example, demonstrate that interest in heaven was not confined to Shakers alone. And, more broadly, mainstream Protestants consumed depictions of heaven in poetry, short fiction, and visual media. As with other elements of their communication with the dead, Shaker visions of heaven drew on antebellum America's broader culture of death. There is no question that for Shakers, the boundary between this world and the next was more permeable than it was for most Americans. But Shaker beliefs about death and the afterlife bore more than a family resemblance to the attitudes of mainstream Protestants.

Baptizing the Dead

Like Ann Lee, Joseph Smith built on widely shared ideas and anxieties about the dead to create a new religion at once familiar and idiosyncratic.[90] Whereas the Shakers emerged from industrializing England's cauldron of religious ferment, the Mormons were forged in the fires of upstate New York's Burned-Over District. In this region Smith was exposed to opponents of Calvinism such as Universalists and Freewill Baptists, the hermeticism and folk magic of Pennsylvania German migrants, and products of the antebellum spiritual hothouse such as Shakers and Swedenborgians. On a more mundane level, Smith also had firsthand experience with the death of loved ones like all of his contemporaries. These ingredients, and many more, came together in Mormonism in the 1820s.

Like the Shakers and the New Church, this was a denomination founded on revelations. Smith experienced what would later be called his "First Vision" of God in 1820, when he was only fourteen years old; three years later the angel Moroni told Smith the location of the golden plates on which the Book of Mormon was engraved. Over the next twenty years, until his death in 1844, Smith experienced more than one hundred revelations.

What Smith learned via revelation spawned a religion that was deeply concerned with exploring the relations between the living and dead. In one historian's formulation, Mormonism's central goal was the "attempted conquest of death."[91] As an American religion founded in the 1820s, Mormonism drew on emerging ideas about companionate marriage, sentimental family relations, and the nearness of the deceased in heaven to create the novel doctrine of the "eternal family." The family was at the center of God's plan for salvation, and the living were linked by family ties through deceased kin back to Adam.[92] This doctrine found its fullest expression in a ritual that proved extremely popular with ordinary Latter-day Saints: baptism for the dead. This rite did not involve speaking with the dead, so it differed from Shaker and New Church practices, but it did forge powerful bonds between the living and deceased, which accounted for its popularity.

Joseph Smith did not learn about baptism for the dead all at once in a single revelation but rather in several visions. In 1836, "the heavens were opened" to Smith and he saw, among others in the "celestial kingdom," his brother Alvin, who had died in 1823.[93] But how could that be? Alvin had died before he could be baptized into the Mormon Church—before there was a Mormon Church into which to be baptized—and Smith's teachings as of 1836 were that only those who had received baptism for the remission of sins could enter the celestial kingdom. A partial solution to this conundrum emerged by 1838, when Smith learned via revelation that Jesus himself preached to the dead. Perhaps that allowed them to become Mormons in the afterlife.[94]

Before Smith could fully work out the implications of the dead receiving the gospel, a woman had a startling vision of heaven. And thus the story once again returns to Manchester. Brigham Young and seven other young apostles sailed to England in April 1840, charged with spreading word of Smith's revelations. Manchester's religious culture was as volatile as it had been a century earlier, when it had birthed the Shakers. Ann Booth, a newly converted Mormon, told Young about a vision she had on March 12, 1840. Young devoted nearly a thousand words to the vision in a letter to his wife back in the new Mormon central settlement of Nauvoo, Illinois.

What is most striking about Booth's vision is its demonstration of the lively relationship that Manchester's religious seekers maintained with the dead. Booth saw a Mormon in heaven baptize John Wesley, the Methodist founder dead for nearly a half century, and then Wesley began to baptize others "for the remision of sins and the gift of the Holy Gost," that is, into the Mormon Church. Wesley baptized Booth's uncle, her grandfather, her sister, and her mother: "all these had lived and died Methodest," and now it appeared they were becoming Mormons in the afterlife. Booth also spoke with the dead: "My grandfather then came to me and Blest me saying 'the Lord bless [you] forever and ever, art thou come to see us deliverd?' My mother then came to me and clasped me in hir arms and kissed me three times and said 'the Lord Almighty Bless the[e] for ever and evere.'"[95]

Joseph Smith almost certainly learned about Booth's vision in June 1840 via Young's letter. There is no evidence that the vision decisively shaped Smith's ideas about the relationship between the living and the dead, but it must have confirmed his sense that the dead could receive the gospel and even baptism. Two months later, at the funeral of Seymour Brunson, Smith delivered his first discourse on baptism for the dead. No contemporary account of the sermon survives, but there were reports of supernatural activity at the funeral: the "R[o]om was full of Angels that came after [Brunson] to waft him home" to heaven.[96] In this electric atmosphere Joseph Smith first explained that the living could be baptized on behalf of their deceased ancestors, a practice also known as vicarious or proxy baptism. Smith thus outlined a "heavenly family tree" that connected the living with their dead ancestors all the way back to God.[97] One Mormon recorded his wife's reaction to Smith's words: "a more joyfull Season She Ses She never Saw be fore on the account of the glory that Joseph Set forth."[98]

What Smith set forth that day had its origins in both his own revelations and an ambiguous passage in Paul's first epistle to the Corinthians. In that letter, Paul insisted on the key Christian doctrine of the resurrection of the dead, about which some in Corinth remained skeptical. Frustrated, Paul asked his readers, "Else what shall they do which are baptized for the dead, if the dead rise not at all? why are they then baptized for the dead?" (1 Cor. 15:29). This passage has generated a cottage industry of exegetes; by one count, theologians have offered more than forty different interpretations.[99] Some have argued that Paul used the term "baptism" metaphorically, to mean martyrdom

or grief for the deceased, whereas others have insisted that Paul was criticizing the residents of Corinth who baptized the living in the name of the dead.
What virtually no one argued, though, was that Paul was *advocating* baptism
for the dead.[100]

That is until members of the Ephrata Cloister in eighteenth-century Pennsylvania made such a claim. The German Pietist Conrad Beissel established
Ephrata in 1732 as a communal, celibate setting to await Christ's Second Coming. Six years after Ephrata's founding, one of Beissel's followers used 1 Corinthians 15:29 to argue that early Christians had practiced vicarious baptism.
Convinced by the logic, Beissel led his followers down to Cocalico Creek for
baptism by immersion. Emanuel Eckerling was baptized on behalf of his deceased mother, Alexander Mack was immersed for his dead father, and a movement was born. As a nineteenth-century historian put it, vicarious baptism
"struck the popular fancy" and gained a "firm foothold" in the region, not
just among Ephratans but also among other German Pietists. Indeed, the practice survived longer than the community, lasting into the 1830s.[101]

It is possible that Ephratan proxy baptism directly influenced the Mormons. The German Pietist Peter Whitmer Sr. lived in Cocalico Township, on
the very river where Beissel's followers immersed the living for the dead, before moving close to Smith's base of Palmyra. Four of Whitmer's sons were
among the "Eight Witnesses" who attested that they had seen and handled
the golden plates upon which the Book of Mormon was engraved; maybe they
told Smith what they had observed on Cocalico Creek.[102] It is more likely,
however, that Beissel and Smith developed their interpretations of 1 Corinthians 15:29 independently. Either way, the point is that among their adherents the practice "struck the popular fancy." In fact, that phrase is too weak
to describe what took place after Smith announced the doctrine at Seymour
Brunson's funeral. The Mormons at Nauvoo experienced a full-fledged frenzy
of proxy baptisms.

Located on swampy ground adjacent to the Mississippi River, Nauvoo was
a sickly environment, rife with malaria and other diseases. As thousands of
Mormons arrived in their new homeland in the early 1840s, hundreds died
each year, especially in the peak malaria months of August and September.
In 1843, for example, 435 people died out of an estimated population of 13,200,
for an extremely high death rate of 33 per 1,000.[103] By comparison, even an
unhealthy urban setting such as Boston featured a crude death rate below 20
that year.[104] Surrounded by death, and sharing in the widespread antebellum
beliefs about the nearness of heaven and the dead, ordinary Mormons in

Nauvoo embraced the opportunity to renew the connections with their deceased family members that proxy baptism offered.[105]

Numbers tell part of the story: in 1841, the first full year of baptisms for the dead, Mormons performed the ritual 6,818 times. This in a town with roughly 2,500 adults.[106] The deceased were close relatives of the living, not distant ancestors. The largest category was uncles and aunts (24 percent of all proxy baptisms), followed by grandparents (23 percent), parents (15 percent), and siblings (14 percent). Cross-sex baptisms were allowed (Brigham Young would ban them after Smith's death). In 1841, 43 percent of all vicarious baptisms involved men baptized for dead women and girls or women baptized for deceased men and boys. And there were some true champions of proxy baptism. An otherwise unremarkable Saint named Nehemiah Brush was immersed in the Mississippi River 111 times in 1841. Sarah Cleveland was the woman most dipped; she brought forty of her deceased relatives into the Mormon fold.[107]

But even those extraordinary numbers do not fully convey ordinary Saints' enthusiasm for proxy baptism. Letters, diaries, and poems complement the figures. Take, for example, Joseph Fielding's letter to one Brother Robinson, written at the end of 1841. Fielding wrote that "when I have listened to the teachings of the servants of God under the new covenant and the principle of Baptism for the Dead the feelings of my soul were such as I cannot describe." He contrasted the glorious possibility of eternal life for the deceased with the terrors of Calvinist predestination. Simply put, under Joseph Smith's new dispensation, "the sting of death is gone."[108] In the same year, J. H. Johnson published a poem titled "Baptism for the Dead" in the Nauvoo newspaper. Among its eight breathless verses was this:

> And we for them can be baptized,
> Yes for our friends most dear!
> That they can with the just be rais'd,
> When Gabrials' trump they hear.[109]

Johnson's exclamation point captures the exhilaration of this moment in Mormon history, just a year after Smith had announced the doctrine of proxy baptism.

Ordinary Saints reached out to their living relatives across the country, begging for information about their deceased kin. Jonah Ball wrote to his family, "I want you to send me a list of fathers relations his parents & Uncles

& their names, also Mothers. I am determined to do all I can to redeem those I am permitted to." Likewise, Sally Carlisle Randall pleaded with her kin, "write me the given names of all our connections that are dead as far back as grandfathers and grandmothers at any rate. I expect you will think this [baptism for the dead] is strange doctrine but you will find its true." "Strange" but "true": ordinary Mormons did not merely recognize that proxy baptisms were a radical departure from mainstream Protestantism, they positively reveled in the fact that they had access to this new ritual for connecting the living and the dead. Not incidentally, baptism for the dead was open to women as well as men, and not restricted to an elite priesthood as with many other Mormon rituals.[110]

In their desire to connect with deceased loved ones, lay Mormons' concerns were not all that different from those of their Prophet, Joseph Smith. It was not merely that Smith's first inkling about preaching to the dead came in a vision about his dear, deceased eldest brother, Alvin. Rather, many of Joseph's ideas about the dead were tightly bound to his own emotional connections to his family members. Frequently at funerals Smith showed empathy for his adherents' grief by opening up about his own sadness. At the burial of twenty-four-year-old Ephraim Marks, Smith delivered an address. As recorded in Wilford Woodruff's diary, the Prophet said, "it is a vary solumn & awful time. I never felt more solumn. It calles to mind the death of my oldest Brother who died in New York & my Youngest Brother [Don] Carloss Smith who died in Nauvoo."[111]

Even when Joseph did not mention his brother by name, it was not hard to discern Alvin's spirit lurking behind the Prophet's words. In October 1841, after an exciting year of baptizing the dead, Joseph was still clarifying the doctrine's implications. In an address on the topic, "which was listened to with intense interest by the large assembly," Smith used a family-based metaphor to demonstrate Mormonism's superiority to "sectarianism," his term for mainstream and especially Calvinist Protestantism. Imagine, Smith urged his sizable audience, "the case of too [sic] men, brothers, equally intelligent, learned, virtuous and lovely, walking in uprightness and in all good conscience." Then imagine, Smith continued, that "one dies, and is buried, having never heard the gospel of reconciliation, to the other the message of salvation is sent, he hears and embraces it and is made the heir of eternal life. Shall the one become a partaker of glory, and the other be consigned to hopeless perdition? Is there no chance for his escape? Sectarianism answers, 'none! none!! none!!!' Such an idea is worse than atheism."[112] In this story, is Joseph the "heir of eternal life" and Alvin "consigned to hopeless perdition"? His listeners, who knew Joseph's family history, likely made the connection.

Likewise, the Prophet's funeral sermons often mentioned his deceased father, the "Presiding Patriarch" Joseph Sr., who died only two days after the first proxy baptisms in September 1840. When talking about the death of a missionary who had recently died in England and was therefore interred far from Nauvoo, Joseph Jr. painted an indelible portrait of the value of being buried close to loved ones, which the next chapter will call "burial *ad familiares*." According to one diarist, the Prophet stated that "should he die he Considered it would be a great Blessing to be buried with the saints & esspecially to be buried with his father." Smith explained the reason behind this desire: "He wanted to lie by the side of his father that when the trump of God should sound & the voice of God should say ye Saints arise that when the tomb should birst he could arise from the grave & first salute his father & say O my father! & his father say O my son!! as they took each other by the hand."[113] It is a telling moment: Joseph imagines that the first thing he will do on the Day of Resurrection is not gaze upon Christ but rather lovingly grasp the hand of his reanimated father. Once again Smith's family focus made an impact on ordinary Saints. One Mormon woman recorded that her husband described this as "the sweetest sermon from Joseph he ever heard in his life."[114]

Rank-and-file Mormons were just as concerned as Joseph with reuniting with their departed loved ones. As the editors of the Nauvoo newspaper put it in 1842, "we are frequently asked the question, what has become of our Fathers?"[115] Or consider the question that one woman called out during Smith's famous "King Follett Discourse," his 1844 sermon in front of thousands in which he fully elaborated on the relationship between the living and the dead. This unnamed woman cried, "Will Mothers have their Children in Eternity?"[116] These were the same questions that many antebellum Protestants asked themselves, and their ministers, and their God in prayers. Those who were drawn to Mormonism were attracted in no small part because Smith seemed to have the answers. As he confidently declared in the King Follett Discourse, "I will open your eyes in rel[ation] to your dead."[117] In antebellum America, Smith could not have framed his unorthodox teachings in a more appealing fashion.

* * *

Wilford Woodruff and his wife, Phebe, were exceptionally dedicated Mormons. Wilford traveled more than fifty thousand miles spreading the Mormon gospel between 1834 and 1844; Phebe did not tabulate her mileage the way her husband did, but she too traveled from Ohio to England to Maine. When the Woodruffs moved to Nauvoo in the early 1840s, they, like most of their coreligionists, enthusiastically embraced the new doctrine of proxy baptism. On a Monday in August 1844, Phebe and Wilford walked together to the Mississippi River, where each was baptized for five "dead friends," as Wilford called them. These were among the thirty-six dead friends in whose name Wilford was immersed through 1844.[118]

One reason why the Woodruffs and other Mormons flocked to the waters for proxy baptism was the sense of connection they felt with their deceased loved ones. In this their ideas resonated with the beliefs of countless other antebellum Americans, even if their means of acting on that connection drew ridicule and condemnation from evangelical and mainline Protestants.[119] Baptism for the dead did not spread beyond the Mormons. But Wilford and Phebe also expressed their ideas about the dead in ways that were more typical of mainstream Protestants. In June 1844, Wilford was traveling in Boston when he received the awful news of Joseph and Hiram Smith's assassination. Like many antebellum Americans confronted with a confounding loss, as Chapter 8 will show, Wilford penned a diary entry in the form of a prayer spoken to the deceased: "Peace be to thy ashes, the most glorious resurrection to thy bodies and the American gentile nation to answer for thy blood before the bar of God."[120]

An expression of Phebe's grief that resonated with broader Protestant norms is one that took a characteristically female form: a poem written after the death of a young child. Phebe and Wilford's two-year-old daughter, Sarah Emma, died in Nauvoo in July 1840, while Wilford was away proselytizing in England. Without her companion, Phebe descended into blackest grief, even composing (but not sending) a letter in which she said that Sarah Emma would be alive if Wilford hadn't been away from home. Three months after her child's death, Phebe salved her sorrow by writing a poem that imagines her "lovely child" looking down from heaven, and then making closer contact:

Or if permitted, to the earth descends,
And gladly mingles with her earthly friends;
Although unseen her happy spirit near,
May hear the sigh, and see the falling tear,
May with concern behold maternal grief,
And fondly wish to sooth and give relief.[121]

These lines contain nothing that is distinctly Mormon. As the next two chapters demonstrate, hundreds of similar poems—asserting that deceased loved ones could return as guardian angels—appeared in magazines, newspapers, and diaries in the first half of the nineteenth century. Like Shakers and Swedenborgians, Latter-day Saints held beliefs about the afterlife, based on prophetic revelations, that put them outside the mainstream of Protestantism, even as they drew on the antebellum cult of the dead for ideas about relationships between heaven and earth.

CHAPTER 7

Religious Objects, Sacred Space, and the Cult of the Dead

Isaac Jocelyn's four teenaged sisters adored him. They comforted their five-year-old brother when he fell, taught him how to read, and cherished his "beaming" eyes and "exquisite" lips. Because the children in the comfortably middle-class Jocelyn household did not have to be apprenticed out or take in piecework to contribute to the family economy, they spent much time together. Indeed, the Jocelyn girls' key domestic task was taking care of their three younger siblings. So when little "Iky," as the girls called him, grew danger-ously ill in February 1839, his sisters were at his bedside, nursing him and fear-ing the worst. The family called a doctor, but he had no cure. On February 12 Isaac died, lying on his side as though he were sleeping.[1]

The Jocelyn family immediately mobilized and, as if they had long awaited this moment, began to fashion objects that would help them maintain a rela-tionship with the dead boy. For this task the family was better prepared than most. The father, Nathaniel, was a skilled portrait painter who would later gain fame for his likeness of Cinqué, leader of the Amistad rebellion. But in this regard the Jocelyns differed from other middle-class families more in de-gree than kind, more in artistic skill and training than in the impulse to generate material responses to death.

The family's New Haven, Connecticut, home quickly became an atelier. With the corpse as his muse, Nathaniel began to paint Isaac's likeness the morning after the boy died and worked on the image for four days (Figure 14). On day three, according to fourteen-year-old Elizabeth, Nathaniel "took a pro-file by a reflecting instrument," trying to get the likeness just right. Neigh-bors came to pay their respects and view what one called "a scene he had never

Figure 14. Nathaniel Jocelyn, *Isaac Plant Jocelyn* (detail), 1839. Though
Iky was painted while dead, his eyes shine with life, encouraging
communication with the bereaved. Oil on canvas with pine wood
support panel and gilt frame. Gift of Foster Wild Rice, 1960.51.1,
Connecticut Historical Society.

seen before, a father painting his dead child."[2] This was indeed unusual, but
only because the father was doing the painting. In the 1830s posthumous
mourning portraiture, in which an artist sketched a corpse to produce a painting of a living child, became so popular among middle-class families that
artists advertised their services in newspapers.[3] And portraiture was not the
only way the Jocelyns preserved Iky's image. The sculptor Hezekiah Augur
took casts of Isaac's head and hands to produce lifelike, three-dimensional
representations.

All of this was done to maintain a connection with Isaac in heaven. Before the boy's burial, each surviving family member "cut off a lock of hair, and arranged them in his hands," hoping Isaac would bring physical tokens of their love to heaven. After the boy was buried in New Haven's fashionable Grove Street Cemetery, his family continued to commune with him. They regularly walked to the cemetery, stood near his remains, and imagined him as something other than inert matter: "it seemed almost cruel, to leave him there, and go home without him." At home they gathered around Augur's plaster cast of Isaac's head and face, and when Nathaniel put Isaac's "cloth cap he used to wear" onto the cast "it looked very much like him," wrote eighteen-year-old Margaret. In Elizabeth's account, this was an act of religious adoration: "After we had looked at it, till the idea of himself, was fully impressed, on our minds, we had prayers, and then retired."[4]

For years the Jocelyns marked Isaac's birth and death dates like religious holidays. On the day that would have been Isaac's sixth birthday, Elizabeth composed what was essentially a prayer to the dead boy in heaven: "Happy little Isaac! thou art far from all temptation and sorrow and pain,—and could'st thou speak to us, thy words would be [']Weep not for me, ye loved ones—oh! weep not for me.[']" In 1840, thirteen-year-old Frances noted, "Elizabeth was invited to Julia Pecks to-day but she did not go for one year ago to-day our little brother Isaac died." A decade later Frances reported that Nathaniel's portrait of Isaac still had the power to evoke a connection with the boy: "While taking dinner my eye rested upon the portrait of my dear little brother whose merry voice had in former Thanksgiving days mingled with ours but its music is now hushed and his little form laid in the grave."[5]

With the exception of Isaac's head and hands rendered in plaster, which were uncommon but not unique tokens of the dead, the Jocelyn family's use of material and spatial markers to maintain a connection with the deceased was standard for the time.[6] The painting, locks of hair, graveyard visits, handwritten prayers to the dead: all were common components of middle-class Protestant deathways in the antebellum North.

These practices and more constituted what I argue was a cult of the dead, a religious complex that in the early nineteenth century emerged from Protestantism but contained lay- and especially female-driven elements distinct from mainstream Protestantism.[7] These beliefs included five ideas: corpses deserved adoration, departed souls turned into angels, souls returned to earth as guardian angels, graveyards harbored spirits of the dead, and praying to the dead was a legitimate form of religious communion.

Where did these beliefs come from? The best explanation combines ante-cedents from previous centuries with vast intertwined changes in economy, society, culture, and theology. We have already seen some of the beliefs that came to constitute the cult of the dead: the idea that spirits inhabited grave-yards and the belief that representing communication with the dead in po-etry and epitaphs was acceptable, even desirable.

Developments in the late eighteenth and early nineteenth centuries en-abled earlier, inchoate beliefs to coalesce into a true cult of the dead. Families began to reduce their fertility toward the end of the eighteenth century, with the urban middle class leading the way and others following. As increasing numbers of men found employment outside the home, women played a larger role in domestic affairs, especially in inculcating piety in children. With some-what smaller families, middle-class parents and especially mothers devoted more emotional energy to child-rearing, and family bonds developed more in-tensely in the context of new ideals about companionate marriage and affec-tionate parent-child relations. Mortality rates remained high, and thus the increased devotion to family members generated great anxiety about their sur-vival. The growing middle class also had more time and money to spend on reading; this both stimulated and was shaped by the explosive growth of print-ing. More than ever before, print culture addressed the interests of increas-ingly educated women, with an abundance of women's magazines, sentimental fiction, and religious memoirs. Building on earlier trends, sentimental litera-ture taught readers that powerful expressions of emotion were evidence of re-fined sensibility. Finally, as Calvinism became less dominant in Protestant belief, mourners grew ever more confident that the souls of the dead were in heaven. Taken together, these transformations set the stage for the antebel-lum cult of the dead.[8]

In using the phrase "cult of the dead," and in calling its participants "cult-ists," I reject all modern connotations of a "cult" as a religion that is "strange or sinister," in the words of the *Oxford English Dictionary*. Instead I employ the *OED*'s neutral, religious studies definition: a "form or system of religious worship or veneration, esp. as expressed in ceremony or ritual directed toward a specified figure or object."[9] For many nineteenth-century Protestants, even before the advent of séance Spiritualism, the figures toward which they di-rected those ceremonies were deceased loved ones, *in addition to* the worship of God.

My identification of an antebellum cult of the dead builds on Robert Orsi's definition of religion as "a network of relationships between heaven and earth."[10] Historians have been more comfortable applying this concept to Catholicism and the so-called traditional religions of Africans and American Indians than to Protestantism.[11] By contrast, scholars have tended to portray Protestantism as a system of beliefs (internal, intellectual) rather than an assemblage of relationships, practices, and material expressions (external, bodily).[12] That has been changing in recent decades, and as part of the more recent trend this chapter offers an interpretation of Protestantism that focuses on the material and spatial components of communication with the dead.

My argument about the cult of the dead is a significant departure from the many historians who see a broad trend toward secularization in antebellum deathways. On gravestones, the nineteenth-century willow-and-urn motif allegedly represented a turn away from the vigorous piety expressed in colonial death's heads and winged cherubs.[13] Nondenominational rural cemeteries, in this interpretation, focused less on religious concerns than on a secularized sentimentality and a penchant for promenading.[14] Likewise, the corpse itself was "transformed from a sacred object exclusively within the interpretive jurisdiction of religion into a symbolic commodity on the marketplace of ideas."[15] By making use of mourning costume and other material tokens of grief, "a middle-class man or woman was believed to establish very clearly the legitimacy of his or her claims to genteel social status" rather than express powerful religious beliefs.[16] The Jocelyn family would have found all this incomprehensible, as they sat around Isaac's plaster head topped with his old cloth cap, praying to God and communing with Iky in heaven.

Mourning Embroidery

Like a plaster head or a gravestone, a mourning embroidery was a "religious object": it focused the mind in prayerful contemplation, both for the person crafting it and for viewers; it recalled the presence of the deceased, sometimes through communication with the departed; and it reminded viewers of important theological precepts. Popular from the end of the eighteenth century through the first decades of the nineteenth, mourning needlework is a rarely examined source, one that demonstrates interest in communicating with the dead. Drawing on the visual and literary conventions of gravestones, epitaphs, and elegies, mourning needlework was an entirely female response to death. These objects are material reminders of women's and girls' desires to maintain connections with the departed and thus evidence for the cult of the dead.

First, some terminology. "Needlework" and "embroidery" are general terms for adding ornamentation to cloth using colored thread. "Samplers" are the pieces worked by girls in the colonial period and Early Republic to practice their stitching. Usually featuring an alphabet, numerals, a few simple images, and a didactic verse or two, plain-stitch samplers were crafted by girls as young as five years old from "all classes" of society.[17] On the other hand, "fancywork" embroidery, elaborate pictorial compositions made from expensive threads of silk and other materials, were strictly the domain of elite girls and young women and were usually undertaken in private girls' schools and female academies. A subset of both plain and fancy needlework were mourning pieces, wrought to memorialize deceased family members.

The primary motivation for creating a mourning piece was to give lasting material expression to feelings of grief, loneliness, and resignation to God's will: in other words, to create a religious object for the domestic sphere. One imagines that the many hours spent in deep concentration on a mourning piece helped a woman literally work through her grief, while the many years viewing it displayed in a place of honor in the house brought a sense of artistic accomplishment along with a continued connection with the deceased. But there were other, more practical returns on the investment of time and money. A finely wrought mourning piece was a material expression of middle-class gentility and sensibility, visible to all visitors.[18]

Despite the potential for these sources to offer a window onto the experiences of a wide range of women, historians have spent little time analyzing needlework.[19] Building on the few who examine mourning embroidery, this section focuses on the cultural and theological meanings of the texts and images.[20] Both samplers and fancywork mourning pieces sometimes included intimate conversations with the departed. But unlike gravestones, which were relegated to burial grounds, where such conversations could occur only occasionally, these religious objects remained within the domestic sphere, ready to renew the connection with the dead at a moment's notice.

This section analyzes 189 examples of mourning embroidery created in the northern United States before 1850.[21] Mourning needlework existed in England and North America in the eighteenth century, but its popularity exploded in the United States after 1800 (Figure 15), partly because George Washington's 1799 death inspired a large number of memorial prints that served as templates for mourning pieces.[22] Also a factor was the rise of girls' schools and female academies, which into the 1830s almost always taught ornamental needlework. Between 1790 and 1830, 182 female academies

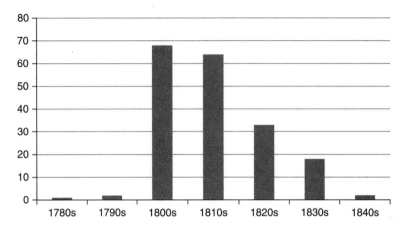

Figure 15. Mourning embroidery by decade. When a source gives a
date range rather than a particular year, the midpoint is entered into
the database. For example, 1810–20 becomes 1815. The thirteen
embroideries listed as "early 1800s" are assigned the date of 1812,
the median of all other dates.

opened in the United States.[23] By the 1830s, however, reformers sought to
move female education away from a focus on embroidery and other genteel
"accomplishments," resulting in a steep decline in mourning embroidery by
the 1840s.[24]

Mourning needlework embraced many of the conventions of gravestone
iconography and epitaphs with some important differences. Whereas talking
gravestones comprise some 30 to 40 percent of all Cape Cod stones in the first
two decades of the nineteenth century, talking *embroideries* are much less common. Only 14 of the 189 mourning embroideries (7.4 percent) represent the
deceased as speaking or being spoken to (Figure 16). Even after omitting those
works that do not have an epitaph, only 12 percent (14/116) of the embroideries with epitaphs speak with the dead.[25]

Why were gravestones so much more likely than needlework to communicate with the dead? It may be that stone markers' location in the cemetery
was an important reason why mourners commissioned talking gravestones.
Euro-Americans had long believed that graveyards held the spirits of at least
some of the dead (the returned dead, or the recently buried), and many
nineteenth-century Americans maintained a sense of graveyards as spiritually
charged spaces. In light of such sentiments, with the corpse as a locus of piety

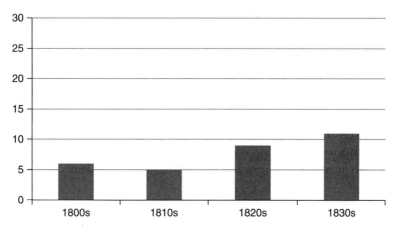

Figure 16. Talking embroidery as a percentage of all mourning embroidery.
Embroideries from the 1780s, 1790s, and 1840s are too few for
meaningful results.

and grief, gravestones that represented the dead as speaking or being spoken
to made sense. The proximity of the corpse was crucial to the fiction of talking gravestones.

Without that proximity, mourning embroideries more frequently opted
for third-person epitaphs such as this, by an unknown maker at Miss Field's
School in Boston, c. 1815, memorializing the death of fifty-year-old Hannah
Smith:

> Weep not ye dear surviving friends
> for all her pain and sorrows end
> she soars ware joy[s] celestial are
> to reap an endless harvest there.[26]

The text's speaker addresses the reader, urging her or him to picture the dead
woman's soul soaring in heaven, so an imaginative connection exists between
the living and dead, but no communication passes between them. Even outside the graveyard, though, people maintained a relationship with the dead.
Nineteenth-century American Protestants imagined that heaven was nearby,
just above a neighborhood's houses in some depictions.[27] Thus mourning needlework that spoke with the dead reflected the imagined nearness of departed
spirits.

In the 1810s, Susan Winn stitched a more effusive memorial at the Moravian boarding school in Lititz, Pennsylvania, as did Sarah Gould of Huntington, Long Island. Winn was fifteen when she attended school in Lititz and crafted a memorial to her sister who had died a decade earlier as an infant. Hand-written in blue ink on the monument are the lines, "Sacred to the Memory of / my dear Sister / CAROLINE WINN. / Sweet be Thy sepulchral rest / Sister dear! supremely blest! / May the ties which us unite / Be renew'd in realms of light! / Erected by Susan Winn."[28]

Sarah Gould likewise maintained a connection with her siblings through her mourning embroidery. Attending Huntington Academy in 1815, Gould created a mourning sampler much simpler than Winn's fancywork. It is a true sampler, with capital and lowercase letters of the alphabet, numerals, and an image of a dog in front of a church (Figure 17). Ten-year-old Gould crafted the sampler for her brother Egbert, who had died two years earlier at age twelve, and her sister Janet, who died at nineteen in the year Gould stitched the sampler. The words embroidered onto the linen backing speak to the dead and include a suggestion of the dead themselves speaking. This is what Gould originally stitched:

My Brother and my Sister dear.
For you we drop the mourning tear.
And from your tombs I hear you say
Prepare for death. make no delay.
The old must die the younger may.

But then her brother James died in 1820 and her sister Levinia died in 1825. For Gould, her sampler was a living memorial, a true religious object, so she revised the first line, squeezing in two small esses to make "My Brothers and my Sisters dear." Gould had indeed learned from her siblings that "the younger may" die.

Given that much antebellum poetry communicated with the dead, it makes sense that some embroiderers dipped into the deep pool of published mortuary verses. Lydia Platt, for example, combined her own lines with several borrowed from Samuel Taylor Coleridge. Platt's original lines speak to the dead while Coleridge's do not. Platt also changed Coleridge's words, because his lines did not capture the full measure of her tragic experience of losing six children in six years. The embroidery begins with a rhythmic roll call of the dead:

Figure 17. Sarah Gould mourning sampler (1815). Ten years after Gould
stitched this sampler she updated it when her sister Levinia died. Courtesy
of the Huntington Historical Society, Long Island, New York.

TO THE MEMORY OF
John Platt who departed this life october 25 1842
Eliza Platt who departed this life september 30 1843
Mary Platt who departed this life may 10 1844
Ann Platt who departed this life may 11 1845

Alice Platt who departed this life october 13 1846
William Platt who departed this life July 26 1847.[29]

Each child does not need elaborate praise for the lines to generate their power; like a war memorial, the embroidery makes its point merely by listing the names and death dates of the deceased.

Platt's final verse quotes Coleridge's "Epitaph on an Infant" (1796) in its entirety.[30] The English poet's words, though beautiful, did not fully express Platt's desire to communicate with her children. She thus turned to the epitaphic tradition and created something original:

Farewell my daughters and my sons
your earthley race you soon have run
youve left a world of sin behind
a crown of glory for to find.

Platt's "earthley race" is a phrase that does not appear in the Bible. Rather, it is a fairly common paraphrase of several passages by Paul that appeared in popular hymns such as "Christ, Of All My Hopes the Ground."[31] In 1 Corinthians 9:24, for example, Paul compares life to a foot race to convey the dedication and hard work it takes to receive the relatively rare "prize" of admission to heaven. In the nineteenth century, by contrast, most American Protestants believed that young children were certain to go to heaven because they died before they had sinned.[32] Paul's assertion is therefore a much more exclusive vision of admission to heaven than Platt likely believed.

Given that most talking samplers were meant to be decorative, they usually included images—like Platt's weeping willows—that conveyed their meaning at a glance. Because mourning embroideries typically devoted a lot of space to images, most left little room for words, at most a stanza or two of epitaphic poetry. An exception is the devastatingly simple mourning sampler that Mary Ann Dewhurst stitched for her daughter Caroline, who died before her third birthday after a long and painful illness (Figure 18). Using nothing but basic cross-stitching and monochrome silk thread on linen, Dewhurst crafted a religious object, a material expression of her grief, with an eight-verse mourning poem. Whereas most mourning embroidery draws from the visual tradition of gravestones, Dewhurst's sampler looks more like an open book or broadside elegy. It is more a "stitched text" than a sampler proper.[33] Dewhurst's sentiments could not be squeezed into the corner of a mourning piece; she needed the entire surface to express her grief.[34]

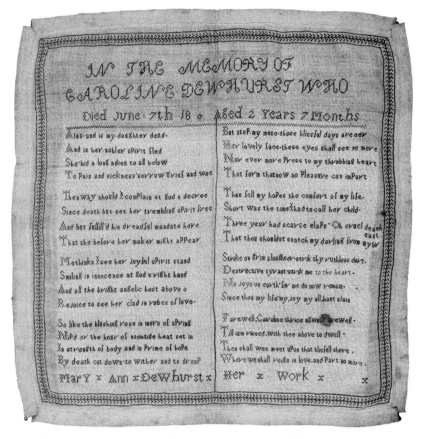

Figure 18. Mary Ann Dewhurst mourning sampler (likely 1818). Dewhurst
speaks to her deceased three-year-old, promising that mother and daughter
will reunite in heaven. Courtesy of Historic New England, Boston.
Gift of Mrs. Evelyn L. Dunn, 1948.96.

Like Anne Bradstreet's elegy for her granddaughter Elizabeth a century
and a half earlier, Dewhurst's poem tries to reconcile grief with acceptance of
God's will. Whereas Bradstreet asks her deceased granddaughter "why should
I once bewail thy fate," Dewhurst directs a similar question to herself: "why
should I complain at gods decree." Dewhurst knows that she should not question why God has chosen to take her daughter, because "death but set her
trembling spirit free." Still, the phrasing of her question indicates that she does
"complain at gods decree" and is trying to will herself to feel otherwise. One

strategy Dewhurst uses is to imagine her daughter in heaven: "Methinks I see her joyful spirit stand / Smiling in innocence at gods right hand."

But Dewhurst's attempt to assuage her sorrow is not fully successful. Unlike many other elegies, which typically proceed from grief to resignation, Dewhurst cannot keep herself from returning to sad memories of her daughter, focused on her bodily absence. After imagining Caroline in heaven, Dewhurst compares her daughter to a rose "By death cut down to wither and to droop." She will no longer be able to hold her faded rose in her arms. "Her lovely face these eyes shall see no more / Nor ever more Press to my throbbing heart / that form that now no pleasure can impart." Dewhurst thus invokes a powerful physical bond between mother and child, and she seems far from resignation when she laments, "No joys on earth for me do now remain."

At this moment of deepest anguish, Dewhurst turns in the climactic final stanza to address her dead daughter:

Farewell Caroline thrice again Farewell
Till i am raised, with thee above to dwell
Then shall wee meet upon that blisfull shore
Where we shall reign in love, and part no more.

She bids her daughter multiple farewells, but clings to the certainty that they will be reunited in heaven, where mother and daughter will "reign in love." Again, the poet takes this phrase from hymns rather than the Bible. Perhaps the most popular hymn to use the phrase is Charles Wesley's "Come, And Let Us Sweetly Join" (1740).[35] In the hymn, Christ sits at God's right hand, just where Dewhurst asserts Caroline is "smiling in innocence," and where Dewhurst will join her. Together they all will "reign in love," a vision of heaven that privileges familial affection.

Like Lydia Platt and Mary Ann Dewhurst, the women and girls who stitched mourning pieces were surrounded by religious language, in the Bible (especially the Book of Psalms); in hymns by Watts, the Wesleys, and others; in popular mourning poetry; in sermons both read and heard; and on gravestones. From these sources, girls and women who had lost loved ones crafted material expressions of their grief. These were religious objects that contained powerful messages even as they provided an attractive accessory to a parlor and, in the case of fancywork embroidery, attested to the maker's gentility and sensibility. Especially for embroiderers who chose to speak with the deceased, their mourning pieces were a tangible connection to a dead person imagined

as not that far away: in a nearby heaven or even, perhaps, in the very room
where the mourning embroidery hung.

"I Kissed the Clay"

Whereas mourning embroidery's popularity peaked early in the nineteenth
century, the corpse's power as a religious object only grew in the antebellum period. Even more effectively than mourning embroidery, the corpse
demonstrates the period's intensifying cult of the dead. In contrast to the
many scholars who argue that the corpse lost much of its religious significance in the nineteenth century, this section contends that activities surrounding human remains demonstrate the religious yearnings of antebellum
Protestants, especially women, who desired to maintain connections between heaven and earth.[36] The corpse represented the final opportunity on
earth to have a physical interaction with a loved one, contact that could prefig-
ure continuing communication with the dead in prayers, poems, and graveyard visitations.[37]

In the colonial period, people also had powerful interactions with corpses,
as female family members were usually in charge of preparing the dead for
burial. Once the body was washed and shrouded, however, it was ordinarily
placed into a coffin that was then screwed or nailed shut. The coffin was not
left open and people did not view the corpse, even though the body was typically kept in the family's best room for two or three days before burial, both
to allow mourners to pay their respects and to ensure that the person was actually dead. It seems that the closed coffin became standard early in the seventeenth century, in deference to puritan worries that survivors might otherwise
be tempted to pray for the dead like the hated Catholics.[38]

At some point toward the end of the eighteenth or beginning of the nineteenth century—the evidence is unclear—it became increasingly common to
leave the coffin open between death and burial. Families still usually waited
two or three days before burying the dead; at four days, the Jocelyn family's
period of viewing Isaac was longer than most, but then again Nathaniel was
trying to get his painting just right. When excessive heat or an unusually noi-
some corpse made hasty burial necessary, loved ones found this troubling
because during the time between death and burial they hoped to use the corpse
as a way to commune with the dead. They did so either by leaving the coffin

open or by relying on new coffin features such as a hinged or removable panel that allowed mourners to view the deceased's face and upper torso.[39]

For cultists, looking at the corpse blurred the line between life and death, helping to create relationships between heaven and earth. For example, in 1832, Sarah Connell Ayer of Eastport, Maine, mourned her husband's unexpected death. The day after he died she wrote, "I went down into the parlour to look at all that was now left of my dear husband. There was a smile on his countenance, he look'd pleasant and natural." Several decades before the Civil War made chemical embalming widely available, mourners hoped that their loved ones would look "natural," which helped sustain the illusion that the person was not quite dead. Ayer continued, "I felt as if he was conscious I was near him, that he would open his eyes once more upon me, and speak to me. I could not realize that he was dead, that he would never again look upon me, that I should never hear his voice again."[40] Confronted with the deceased's familiar face and hoping to commune with the dead, some mourners sensed that the corpse might come back to life.

Seventeen-year-old Mary Ware Allen of Northborough, Massachusetts, had a similar response when her close friend Lucy Gassett died of consumption in 1836. Allen wanted to view the corpse, so she headed to her friend's house. "I went and saw the lifeless remains of one who was once dear to me, & who still is, for I do not think she is dead, but sleeping, and she looked as if she was in a sweet sleep, so calm and so free from distress." She knew the truth but couldn't keep herself from writing, "I do not think she is dead," so intense was her continued connection with Gassett. Like Ayer, Allen also commented on her friend's appearance, observing that "her countenance was very natural."[41] This was the same word that Margaret Jocelyn used to describe Isaac's corpse: "he never looked more natural than when he died."[42] For some mourners, a corpse was even more "natural" than a living body.

Antebellum Protestants most frequently described natural-looking corpses as "beautiful," especially when the deceased was an infant, child, or young woman. Beautiful corpses abounded in sentimental fiction, but they were more than a literary trope.[43] Rather, they were part of the lived religion of many middle-class mourners. When Mary Allen saw the corpse of a neighbor's infant son in 1838, she declared that he was a "beautiful picture of death." Gazing at him was nothing but a pleasure: "I could have looked at that sweet picture all the afternoon."[44] Emotions were more complex when the deceased was one's own child, but nonetheless most parents likewise considered their children's corpses beautiful. When Fanny Appleton Longfellow's eighteen-month-old daughter died, the mother declared the corpse "a most holy and beautiful thing": a religious object.[45]

Sometimes the bereaved described even the elderly in similar terms. Elizabeth Pierce was twenty-two in 1826 when her maternal grandmother, Sarah Tappan, died in her eightieth year. "I never saw so beautiful a corpse as was Grandma's on Sunday morning," Pierce recorded in her diary. "She died just about the time that her Lord & Saviour rose from the dead, on Easter Sunday." Like the crucified Christ, Tappan's corpse inspired religious adoration in those who viewed it. Pierce held a lamp while five people eased the body into a coffin. At that moment it was almost as if Tappan were alive: "A sweet smile was upon her countenance, & I never saw any thing so heavenly as her appearance when she was placed in the coffin. She seemed to smile & say 'Now I am going to sleep sweetly in the grave, as I told you before.'" This imagined conversation with the departed was but one facet of an intense, three-day communion between Pierce and her grandmother's corpse. As the body awaited burial, Tappan's open coffin "remained in the north room" where Pierce "spent the greater part of my time contemplating it, with unmingled pleasure." Even when she was not viewing the corpse, its presence in the house increased Pierce's spiritual fervor. At night she could barely sleep, as "a most delightful series of texts & verses of hymns, like a golden chain between me & heaven, came into my mind."[46] Tappan's corpse forged links between Pierce and heaven; it was an object as palpable as a golden chain and just as effective in connecting Pierce with her departed grandmother.

Indeed, a corpse's palpable quality gave it extra power as a means of inspiring religious thoughts. Elizabeth Pierce did not record whether she stroked or kissed the corpse, but many others did. Louisa Jane Trumbull of Greenfield, Massachusetts, was only ten when her four-year-old brother Johnny died, but she was already an avid journal keeper who wrote often about death. In this she was not unusual; in one study of forty-four antebellum children diarists, "no single theme appeared as frequently as death."[47] Even though Johnny did not look as "natural" as Louisa hoped, she still wanted to kiss his corpse: "He was dreadfully pale, and his lips were very white. I kissed his sweet forehead, it was cold, and felt like marble, and a sweet smile was on his pale lips."[48] Susan Huntington's recollection was more uniformly positive after her husband died in 1819. She had been led out of the room during his final hours to shield her from witnessing anything too upsetting. "When the intelligence was brought me that the conflict was over," she wrote, "it was good news; I kissed the clay, as pleasantly as I ever did when it was animated by the now departed spirit." This physical contact with his "clay"—his mortal remains—led Huntington into a reverie about how his spirit now resided in heaven.[49]

But perhaps the clearest example of the corpse's hold on the cultist imagination appears in the diary of Louisa Park of Newburyport, Massachusetts. In 1799 she married John Park, a physician; the very next year he left on an extended tour of duty aboard a U.S. Navy sloop-of-war. Dr. Park left behind his young wife and ailing infant son, Warren. For five months the child battled illness after illness until finally he succumbed, just a week past his first birthday. Immediately, Louisa missed her son's physical presence. "At bedtime, instead of my charming boy, my lovely babe, to clasp me around the neck and kiss off the silent tear that would fall for the absence of his father," all that remained was his corpse. She was determined to touch him, but there was no response: "Though I wept & pressed him, he could not look at me."[50]

Over the next several months, as if to compensate for the lack of physical interaction with her son, Park began to focus ever more attention on his corpse and what she imagined was happening in its tiny coffin. One day she walked past the crypt that held the body. "It wrung my heart, and I would have given anything to have unlocked the door, and once more beheld my little Warren." Park imagined her son's entombed body as if it were an object of veneration inside a chapel: "What a satisfaction it would be to me, how much pleasure I should take if I could, every day, enter his gloomy mansion and there indulge in meditation and give vent to the feelings of my heart."[51] Park's emotions were not the same as a Catholic's in the presence of holy relics; she hoped for "meditation," not intercession. Nonetheless, thinking about her son's lifeless body stimulated Park's religious fervor.

A month later, the feelings persisted. Park focused simultaneously on her son's corpse and his soul. Thinking about the tomb in which her son lay, she composed a prayer spoken directly to his spirit: "Oh, how I long to visit that sacred repository, and shed the bitter tears of disappointed affection on thy cold cheeks!" Louisa Adams Park was a mainstream Protestant: daughter of a Congregational minister, she adhered to her father's teachings and once wrote of Universalism that "I can have charity for all professions, excepting this."[52] Moses Adams must have taught his daughter that once the soul departed the body, the corpse was nothing but inert matter, food for worms. Nonetheless, Park and many other middle-class women (and some men) found in corpses inspiration for meditation, adoration, prayer, and communication with the departed: in short, for relationships between heaven and earth.

To be sure, some writers (usually men) criticized what they saw as excessive attention to corpses. Their arguments varied. For William Bentley, the Unitarian minister of Salem, it was an ominous sign of religious enthusiasm when people showed up to view the exhumed remains of a charismatic preacher in nearby Rowley. Four months after the preacher died in January 1801, the town disinterred his corpse to make way for a monument. "A new kind of zeal was displayed. The Bell was tolled & the assembly were invited of all ages to come & see the corps which was exposed to public view, in a high state of putrefaction. This is a new kind of curiosity, & a new way of exciting it."[53] Another man, a Boston sexton writing in the late 1840s, worried that women who looked at decomposing corpses—the way Louisa Park wished to do— would be emotionally scarred by the sight. "There is a morbid desire," the sexton wrote, "especially in women . . . to descend into the damp and dreary tomb—to lift the coffin lid—and look upon the changing, softening, corrupting features of a parent or child—to gaze upon the mouldering bones; and thus to gather materials, for fearful thoughts, and painful conversations, and frightful dreams!"[54] However, such complaints did not stop cultists from adoring corpses or opening coffins to commune with the remains.

Thou Art Gone to the Grave

Even those most dedicated to viewing corpses, such as Louisa Park and Elizabeth Pierce, understood that their loved ones' remains needed to be buried. Antebellum Protestant funerals retained most of their essential characteristics from the previous century. Mourning costume and coffin hardware became more elaborate among the growing middle classes, and a greater number of processions used horse-drawn hearses rather than carrying the coffin by hand, but these were relatively superficial changes.[55] Ministers continued to deliver funeral sermons: puritan antipathy to such discourses had long given way to the ministerial belief that funerals were excellent occasions for driving home key religious tenets. And, as in the eighteenth century, some ministers ventriloquized the voice of the dead as they addressed the bereaved.

Numerous funeral sermons survive in which the minister, for didactic and rhetorical purposes, spoke the imagined words of the departed to the assembled mourners. In 1808, the Boston minister Joseph Buckminster presided over the funeral for Massachusetts governor James Sullivan. Buckminster addressed the governor's offspring: "you, dear children; your father's voice cries to you from his tomb, [']live not for yourselves!['']"[56] Three years later in Epping, New Hampshire, Rev. Peter Holt imagined a similar—but longer—message from the deceased Rev. Timothy Upham. "Could your dear pastor now speak to you from the realms of glory," Holt asked, "would he not address you in language like this? [']My dear people! for whom I have spent my strength to promote your best interest; I have delivered to you the message of my master, in whose presence I now am. Be not forgetful of the doctrines you have heard; they are your life; and of your improvement, you must render an account.['']"[57] Many more examples could be cited.[58] In all of them, the words from the dead are clearly meant to be fictional rather than reportage about direct communication with the deceased. Nonetheless, as in the eighteenth century, ministers used this rhetorical strategy for a reason: it stirred the congregation's emotions, tugging on the bands that connected the living with the dead, especially in the presence of the corpse.

By occasionally ventriloquizing the dead, ministers said what laypeople wanted to hear: that funerals maintained rather than severed connections between the living and dead. Funeral hymns had the same effect. Hymn-singing was as old as the Protestant Reformation; Martin Luther himself was a prolific composer of hymns. Increasingly widespread musical literacy in the eighteenth century, however, made hymn-singing a much more satisfactory emotional and auditory experience than it had been previously. Isaac Watts and Charles Wesley wrote dozens of beloved hymns in the eighteenth century, but they were only the most famous of many composers. The nineteenth century witnessed an explosion of hymnals, with each Protestant denomination publishing its own version of popular sacred songs.[59]

Nineteenth-century funerals almost always featured hymns, sung in the church during the funeral service, at the graveside during the burial, or both. The ability of sacred song to help maintain a relationship with the deceased is best seen in the diary of Janis Van Wagoner, a twenty-year-old woman from New Berlin in central New York. In the summer of 1838, two of Van Wagoner's close female companions died, the first unnamed friend from consumption, the second, Susan, from an excruciating illness that left her delusional at the end. On July 31 of that year, the first friend died. Van Wagoner went to view her corpse, which caused her to think about the young woman's "pure spirit" taking its "flight to that heavenly clime to which she has been so long desirous of hastening." Two days later, Van Wagoner attended the funeral. "We have committed our friend to the silent tomb. We sang at her grave, Scotland 'Thou art gone to the grave' &c &c."[60]

"Scotland" (or more properly SCOTLAND) was the tune; in this period, worshippers sang a great number of hymns but used only a small number of tunes, so the music could more easily be memorized. The hymn was "Thou Art Gone to the Grave, But We Will Not Deplore Thee" (1818), by the Anglican bishop Reginald Heber; "deplore" simply meant to bewail or lament. This was one of the most popular funeral hymns of the first half of the nineteenth century: it appeared in seventy hymnals published in England and the United States before 1848, including about 40 percent of those in the 1840s.[61] At least one young woman so loved the hymn that she copied the whole thing into her commonplace book.[62] She and Janis Van Wagoner and many thousands of others responded powerfully to Heber's hymn at least in part because all four verses speak directly to the dead. The first is sung as follows:

> Thou art gone to the grave, but we will not deplore thee;
> Though sorrows and darkness encompass the tomb;
> The Savior has passed through its portals before thee,
> And the lamp of his love is thy guide through the gloom.[63]

When they joined their voices together, Van Wagoner and her fellow mourners addressed the deceased woman lying right in front of them and told her that they would not lament her death because Christ was leading her to a better place. It was the perfect hymn for the cult of the dead.

Two months later, Van Wagoner's dear friend Susan died a hard death, unable to give her friends "the satisfaction of ever knowing that they were recognized." Funeral hymns were again central to the mortuary ritual. "We sung at her grave Mount Vernon, so often spoken of by her, and very appropriate for the occasion, but it was with aching hearts that we sung. She who had been so passionately fond of singing, and always with us was now laid in the grave, her voice was now silent in death."[64] The hymn was almost certainly "Sister Thou Wast Mild and Lovely" (1833), using the tune MOUNT VERNON. Written by Samuel Francis Smith, a young Baptist minister from Boston, this hymn was newer than "Thou Art Gone to the Grave." Still, by the 1840s it appeared in about 20 percent of all hymnals. And like "Thou Art Gone," all four verses of "Sister Thou Wast Mild and Lovely" address the dead:

Dearest sister, thou hast left us!
Here thy loss we deeply feel;
But 'tis God that hath bereft us,
He can all our sorrows heal.[65]

Sung in the sacred space of the graveyard, the hymn betokened a connection between the living and dead that persisted long after the words disappeared on the breeze. Indeed, four months after the funeral, Susan visited Van Wagoner's dreams: "I dreamed last night of being with Susan, and enjoying her good society once more but soon found that it was no reality." This inspired Van Wagoner to address Susan's spirit: "Dear girl! I fondly desire that we meet in a better world than this."[66]

The sacred songs that Van Wagoner enjoyed in 1838 were only two of the many Protestant funeral hymns that apostrophized the dead. This was not solely a nineteenth-century phenomenon; at least four of Charles Wesley's eighteenth-century funeral hymns have one or more verses that address the dead. His "Ah, Sister in Jesus, Adieu!" (1746), "Thanks Be to God Alone" (1746), "Happy Soul! Thy Days Are Ended" (1749), and "Ye Virgin Souls, Arise!" (1749) all increase their emotive power by representing communication with the departed.[67]

In the nineteenth century, in addition to the two hymns that Van Wagoner sang, many other composers wrote funeral hymns that address the dead: Thomas Dale's "Dear as Thou Wast, and Justly Dear" (1819) and James Montgomery's "Go to the Grave, in All Thy Glorious Prime" (1823) and "Rest from Thy Labour, Rest" (1832) are just a few examples. In a century when the corpse increasingly became the main attraction in mortuary rituals, it is fitting that funeral hymns likewise directed attention to the deceased's physical remains and the soul that was escaping its confines.

Material Memory

Other material traces of the deceased—some the actual remains of corpses, others simply representations thereof—became treasured keepsakes in the nineteenth century. Unlike embroidery, which usually included text to help guide the viewer's interpretation, other material connections with the deceased relied on the corpse's numinous power—that is, its association with the holy— to effect a continuing connection with the deceased.

Hair was the material most commonly used to remember the dead. Euro-American colonists brought from their home countries traditions of using hair for memorial purposes. By contrast, almost all African and American Indian groups had religious prohibitions against using hair in such a way.[68] Among Euro-Americans, hairwork's popularity increased with the rise of sentimental culture in the late eighteenth century and grew even further as the nineteenth-century cult of the dead took root. The Jocelyn family practiced an uncommon form of hair memorialization when they cut hair from seven living family members and placed the locks in Isaac's hands. Mourners more typically cut locks from the dead or dying and then used a variety of means to invest the bodily remains with symbolic power.

Whereas family members occasionally snipped locks from a dying person, they more frequently took hair from the corpse. Sometimes the hair was simply kept in a safe place; because hair could be obtained for free, this was a good option for the less affluent. But middle-class women preferred the security and beauty of incorporating it into jewelry, and they liked how such pieces kept their loved ones' remains close to their bodies. Rings, breast-pins, and brooches all could be purchased with small enclosures for holding the hair of the dead. Sometimes the hair was woven into a bracelet, if there was enough of it. This painstaking, time-consuming project was ordinarily undertaken by professional hairworkers who advertised in newspapers and magazines, but occasionally mourners did the work themselves or sent it out to a skilled neighbor. Hair bracelets became so popular that by 1844 a women's magazine could note that "sentimental bracelets, composed of hair . . . are now considered indispensable."[69] In fact, one of hair's attractions was its versatility as a medium of expression. While Mary Wallace Peck was attending Litchfield Female Academy in the 1820s, two of her friends died. Peck glued their hair into intricate patterns surrounding the mourning poetry she wrote for them in her friendship album.[70]

Historians generally emphasize the claims on gentility that middle-class women made when they displayed finely wrought mourning jewelry.[71] There is undoubtedly truth to the assertion, but such tokens of the dead also held considerable religious power.[72] The language that some mourners used to describe physical remains made hair seem like a sacred relic. When Fanny Appleton Longfellow's infant daughter died, the bereaved mother described how she "cut a few locks from her holy head."[73] It bears repeating that Protestant theologians insisted that human remains were not "holy." As Rev. William Bentley put it, "I have a most settled enmity to all ceremonies for the Dead.

Let their memories live but let their ashes be forgotten."[74] Even mourners who did not describe corpses as "holy" behaved in ways indicating that that was how they thought of human remains. After the death of Louisa Jane Trumbull's grandmother in 1832, she received a report from two female cousins: "We have had 2 or 3 letters from them they said they had cut off all her hair as almost every one would wish for a lock."[75] It is a striking image: the old woman's corpse left almost entirely bald after eager grandchildren sought tokens for each member of a large family.

Such behavior makes sense in light of hair's ability to evoke a sense of religious connection with the dead. On the twelfth anniversary of her mother's death, Eliza M. Spencer of Sandisfield, Massachusetts, remembered the powerful moment when the dying woman "requested me to cut off her hair." As Spencer wrote, "O I shall never forget the calm and mournful manner in which she said, 'My children, remember me when I am gone—each one reserve a lock of my hair and as often as you see it, think how you all stood around my bed this evening.'" Spencer took that charge to heart, and when she looked at that lock of hair twelve years later she was inspired to compose a poetic prayer to her mother:

> Yes Mother, dear Mother, I'll remember thee long;
> Thy joys and thy sorrows, thy smiles and thy frowns,
> I'll remember thy prayers and thy rapt moving lays [i.e., songs]
> That oft broke the silence of happier days.[76]

Spencer continued to communicate with her mother even though the elder woman's prayers and songs lived only in memory.

What explains hair's power to maintain relations with the dead? Partly its tactility: for years after a person died, the mourner could touch the springy, silky locks. Receiving such a token, therefore, was a long-term commitment. In the words of a mother describing the hair bracelet she sent to her deceased daughter's friend, "I am sure you will value it, and *always* wear it for her sake."[77] Hair was more than simply an aide-mémoire. For that purpose it was a fairly impoverished source, as all it provided in a literal sense was evidence of the deceased's hair color and texture. More than that, though, hair offered a physical connection—wrapped around one's wrist, pressed against one's chest—to the corpse's "holy head" from which it had been taken.

More so than hair, a painted likeness was the gold standard for recalling the deceased's features, at least until the invention of photography. But even portraits had attractions that went beyond the utilitarian, and cultists responded to them with fervor akin to that inspired by hair memorials. Posthumous mourning portraiture became popular in the United States in the 1830s, though there were antecedents in North America and Europe.[78] After 1830 watercolors and oil paintings of the dead, especially of children, grew dramatically in popularity among the upper-middle class. Such families typically hired an artist to sketch the subject either as the child was dying or soon after death. But in almost all cases the child was represented as living. Indeed, as with Isaac Jocelyn, artists portrayed deceased children in blooming health, with ruddy cheeks and twinkling eyes.

One partial exception to that rule appears in several surviving paintings that depict children in heaven. The miniature watercolor that Clarissa Peters Russell crafted c. 1845 features five children from an unknown family (Figure 19).[79] Three living children form a tight group in the painting's lower tier; two deceased children float just above their siblings. A clearer representation could not be found of cultists' insistence that souls hovered near their living family members. On the painted ivory surface, perhaps a millimeter separates the older deceased child's torso from the oldest living child's head. Even accounting for perspective, the dead are extremely nearby. Their ontological status remains unclear, however. Without wings, they do not seem to be angels; perhaps the way they blend into the surrounding clouds suggests they are souls. In any case, they look very much alive, aware, and ready to communicate.

Even more dramatic portrayals of the imagined connection between living and dead appeared on upper-middle-class women's mourning jewelry. Fashionable women on both sides of the Atlantic commissioned pieces that represented graveyard visitors experiencing the presence of the dead, though these pieces were too small to depict the deceased's face with any specificity. At just over an inch in length, a mourning pin in memory of a nineteen-year-old woman captivates the viewer with a bold sense of movement and narrative (Figure 20). The dead woman bursts from her grave marker to greet her grieving mother; the artist even affixed a tiny piece of ivory broken off from the obelisk to show how eagerly the deceased wants to maintain contact with the living. Crafted in c. 1789, the pin includes chopped hair—presumably from the dead woman—in the paint. When the grieving mother wore the object, she kept close to her heart both the physical remains and painted image of her daughter. Similar designs appeared on rings, brooches, and lockets.[80] One such ring depicts the soul of fifteen-year-old Eliza Clark emerging from her tomb and ascending to heaven as her enraptured mother looks on (Figure 21).

Figure 19. Mrs. Moses B. Russell (Clarissa Peters Russell), *Five Children*
(c. 1845). Two deceased children hover just above their living siblings.
Watercolor on ivory, 4⅝" × 3⅜"; 6¹⁄₁₆" × 4¾" (framed).
Collection of Amelia J. Zoler.

Figure 20. Artist unknown, *Memorial for S. C. Washington* (c. 1789). A nineteen-year-old woman bursts from her grave to reunite with her grieving mother. Watercolor, chopped hair, gold wire, and pearls on ivory; 1⅛16" × 1¹¹⁄16". Yale University Art Gallery, ILE1999.3.18.

Figure 21. Gold mourning ring, Great Britain (c. 1792). Eliza Clark's soul emerges from her tomb while her mother watches, enraptured. Museum number 918-1888. Image © Victoria and Albert Museum, London.

One need not rely only on the objects to get a sense of how some middle-class mourners used paintings to evoke a religious connection with the dead. In addition to the Jocelyn family, others described the power of such images. In his autobiography, which he addressed to his children, the Presbyterian minister Lyman Beecher outlined the mourning process after the death of his month-old daughter, Harriet, in 1809. Lyman's wife, Roxana, took care of Harriet while the infant suffered from whooping cough, but after a week the baby died. According to Lyman, "after the child was laid out, she looked so very beautiful that your mother took her pencil and sketched her likeness as she lay. That likeness, a faint and faded little thing, drawn on ivory, is still preserved as a precious relic."[81] By using the phrase "precious relic," Beecher did not mean that the ivory miniature had the potency of Catholic saints' bones. Nonetheless, he implied that some numinous power resided in the object. Similarly, in an example from somewhat later than the others, the artist Shepard Alonzo Mount of Long Island described the reaction to his portrait of his deceased infant niece, Camille. In a letter to his son, Mount wrote, "all the family seem'd surprised, and delighted with it . . . Joshua and Edna [the parents] would sit before it for an hour together and Mr. and Mrs. Searing [the grandparents] are in raptures with it. I have framed it and hung it up for all to see and love—for next to the dear babe herself—it is now the idol of the family."[82] Beecher's miniature was a "relic"; Mount's oil portrait an "idol." In both cases, representations of the dead were objects of religious adoration.

Images could also prompt communication with the dead. Following the death of fifteen-year-old Louisa Sedgwick in Stockbridge, Massachusetts, her mother recorded in her diary that "the following lines were written by Mrs Dr Adams on seeing Louisa's picture." Adams wrote a twenty-line poem speaking to the dead girl:

Thou hast left us gentle sister
When thy sky was bright and fair;
Ere thine eye had lost its lustre
Or thy soul been chilled by care.[83]

The image evidently does not survive, but in 1841 it inspired Adams to communicate with the dead. Joanna Bethune, a Presbyterian in New York City, felt a similar impulse seven years after the death of her husband when she penned "Lines suggested by looking at the Portrait of my beloved Husband."

The poem includes thirty-eight lines addressed to the dead man, including these:

> Six lovely babes to us were given;
> Three passed before thee into heaven.
> Those dear loved ones thou now hast join'd;
> Three, with thy widow, left behind.[84]

When Bethune looked at her husband's face rendered in paint, she not only thought of her family being reconstituted in the afterlife but also desired to communicate with her husband's spirit in heaven.

The clearest example of this dynamic comes from the pen of Sarah Brown Ruggles of North Providence, Rhode Island, a Baptist churchgoer. Alongside her mainstream Protestant beliefs, she too behaved as if a portrait allowed for communication with the deceased. Her husband, George, died in December 1833, not yet thirty years old. Two months later she continued to use her diary as an outlet for grief and to record prayers to her dead husband: "My George, my love. As I gaze upon thy portrait & cannot refrain from calling upon thee, how thankful amidst all my sorrow, do I feel that thou art at rest, where no sorrow can assail thee & where thou art I humbly hope, at rest."[85] As grief-stricken Sarah gazed at the painting, she could not "refrain from calling upon" her husband and addressing his soul in prayer.

Further evidence of portraiture's numinous power comes, ironically, from the medium that would all but replace it: photography. Louis Daguerre unveiled his eponymous photographic technique in 1839 and almost immediately western Europeans and North Americans recognized the medium's potential for representing the dead—not least because corpses sat still for the many minutes it took to render a clear image in the earliest daguerreotypes. More importantly, mourners now had a new way of capturing an image of their deceased loved ones, something many families wanted. And photography quickly became less expensive than portraiture, so families further down the social scale could afford postmortem likenesses of the dead.[86]

A subset of daguerreotypes in the 1840s are images of the living holding images of the dead. Like phony spirit photographs after the Civil War—but without the trickery—such meta-images document the continuing relationships between the living and the dead, *and* between the living and objects that represented the dead. In 1845, for example, the artist William Matthew Prior painted a mourning portrait of an unknown child with a penetrating

Figure 22. Unidentified photographer, *Mother and* Baby in Blue *by William Matthew Prior* (c. 1850). A mother documents her relationship with both her deceased child and a posthumous mourning portrait. Sixth-plate daguerreotype. Collection of David A. Schorsch.

gaze and a delicate bow mouth. Curators have dubbed the painting *Baby in Blue* for the arresting color of the baby's dress. Several years after Prior completed the likeness, the grieving mother, evidently hoping to memorialize her relationship with both her deceased child and the portrait, commissioned a daguerreotype in which she holds the painting (Figure 22).[87] Other daguerreotypes show mourners holding photographs, rather than paintings, of the deceased.[88]

Much more common, however, were daguerreotypes that displayed the actual corpse, either on its own or being held by the bereaved. These were most frequently commissioned when a child died; parents were especially eager to preserve a likeness of a loved one who had not yet sat for a photograph. But cultists in the 1840s sometimes wished to capture a photograph of a deceased adult, and occasionally the adult corpse was even posed in the arms of a family member.[89] Other daguerreotypes incorporated human remains. Unsatisfied with merely an image of the corpse, some mourners incorporated a lock of the deceased's hair into the daguerreotype case.[90]

Mourning embroidery, corpses, hair jewelry, posthumous mourning portraits, and postmortem daguerreotypes were thus religious objects in addition to being emblems of gentility and sensibility. This is reinforced by the concept of the "sacred gaze," which is "the manner in which a way of seeing invests an image, a viewer, or an act of viewing with spiritual significance."[91] When Elizabeth Pierce spent days communing with her grandmother's corpse, when Lyman Beecher and Shepard Alonzo Mount described images of the dead as "precious relics" and "idols," when Sarah Ruggles prayed to her husband's portrait, these objects and acts of viewing clearly had "spiritual significance." In middle-class homes filled with other visual tokens of piety—including illustrated primers, pamphlets from the American Tract Society, and framed lithographs of biblical scenes—emblems of grief helped maintain a continuing relationship with the dead. Not every antebellum Protestant experienced intense acts of communion with the material culture of mourning; some women undoubtedly wore hair jewelry simply because it looked good. But for many pious Protestants, such objects were the material expressions—indeed, the material foundations—of the cult of the dead.

Sacred Space of Memory

Graveyards were another repository of religious objects, filled with corpses and—for those who could afford them—the stone markers that allowed mourners to locate their loved ones' remains and use them as a focal point for piety. Scholarly discussions of antebellum burial grounds have been dominated by rural cemeteries: the large, exquisitely landscaped, nondenominational cemeteries such as Cambridge's Mount Auburn (1831) and its many imitators. But even before the rural cemetery movement, mourners in village churchyards throughout the northern United States expanded earlier English and American ideas of graveyards as places of communion with the dead. One scholar sees rural cemeteries creating "new rituals of memorial visiting."[92] In fact, such rituals emerged toward the end of the eighteenth century, fifty years before the rural cemetery movement.

Historians generally portray rural cemeteries as secularized departures from earlier churchyards, based on several factors. Gravestones with willow-and-urn and neoclassical motifs replaced earlier death's heads and cherubs. Rural cemeteries were nondenominational, which supposedly indicated a diminished attachment to religion. And urban residents, before the advent of municipal park systems, turned to rural cemeteries as "pleasure grounds" where they could promenade, picnic, enjoy nature, and engage in courting rituals.[93]

Without denying that pleasure-seekers used graveyards for secular purposes, this section builds upon the smaller number of historians who insist on rural cemeteries' predominantly religious character.[94] These scholars show that symbols such as crosses and Bibles abounded in rural cemeteries. And they demonstrate that the nondenominational character of rural cemeteries reflected Protestant unity more than lack of religious attachment. Going beyond that, I maintain that antebellum graveyards were, in effect, the cult of the dead's open-air cathedrals. As the English poet Felicia Hemans represents a parent speaking to a dead child, "Thy grave shall be a blessed shrine."[95] Cultists considered cemeteries to be sites of immanence: spaces that offered access to the divine. Cultists thought of the divine as God or Christ, *and* the deceased's soul or spirit. Graveyards were thus places that sustained relationships between heaven and earth.

Two topics from previous chapters bear repeating here. First, Cape Cod's talking gravestones were all in burial grounds founded before Mount Auburn. Rural cemeteries also held talking gravestones, but in doing so they were following rather than shaping epitaphic conventions. The talking gravestones in churchyards assumed that people visited the burial grounds in which they stood: not merely by having epitaphs, which implied readers, but in the very words carved into the stones, which frequently urged people to visit. "My bosom friend come here and see / Where lays the last remains of me," Azubah Handy's 1819 stone implores her husband.[96] Talking gravestones also address the dead's soul or shade. Given the connection with the deceased that their words and images represented, such stones were religious objects, with the power to conjure the dead in the imagination.

Second, Gothic fiction often took place in burial grounds. When lovers returned from the dead, they usually did so in a cemetery. Poems frequently situated speaking with the deceased's soul or ghost in cemeteries. Imaginative literature offered some of the first descriptions of souls returning as guardian angels to hover over the grave or near loved ones. Burial grounds hummed with activity—of the living and dead—in late eighteenth- and early nineteenth-century imaginative literature. Again, this predated and helped pave the way for the rural cemetery movement.

Another antecedent to Mount Auburn was the "reformed cemetery." Like rural cemeteries, reformed cemeteries were nondenominational, larger than typical churchyards, and situated outside the center of town. The first was New Haven's New Burying Ground (1796), later called the Grove Street Cemetery—the very graveyard where Isaac Jocelyn's family had him interred and visited his remains. Indeed, family ties were at the heart of the New Burying Ground's most important innovation. James Hillhouse gridded his six-acre tract into lots that families could purchase and hold *in perpetuity*. Before New Haven, families had no expectations that their loved ones' corpses would forever remain untouched. Even burials marked with stones might be disturbed during future interments. By the turn of the nineteenth century many began to find this intolerable. With the emerging cult of the dead's interest in corpses, mourners viewed grave violation—whether by anatomists seeking cadavers or sextons trying to find room for new burials—with increasing disgust. Hillhouse's solution was a cemetery organized as a corporation with numerous owners to guarantee the organization's enduring existence. It was to be, in Hillhouse's words, a "sacred and inviolable" site.[97]

With the rise of the middle-class companionate family toward the end of the eighteenth century, it seemed only natural for Hillhouse to organize his cemetery by family lots.[98] Whereas medieval and early modern Catholics craved burial *ad sanctos*—"near the saints" and thus inside the church and close to relics—nineteenth-century Protestants wanted nothing more than burial *ad familiares*, "near the family."[99] I have coined this phrase to suggest the religious fervor with which families sought union in death. The use of family lots became enormously popular, imitated in other reformed cemeteries such as Buffalo's Franklin Square Cemetery (1804), Syracuse's First Ward Cemetery (1819), and Philadelphia Cemetery (1827). The designer of Philadelphia Cemetery made clear that his graveyard was meant to sustain continuing relations between the living and dead: the site allowed mourners "to cherish those tender feelings that connect the living with their deceased friends." Burial *ad familiares* subsequently became a central feature of Mount Auburn and the other rural cemeteries founded in the 1830s and 1840s.[100]

The Jocelyns were not alone in their desire to visit the family lot as a way to commune with the dead. Catherine Henshaw of Leicester, Massachusetts, was in her early twenties when her sister's husband died. One Sabbath evening in April 1805 she and several others made a pilgrimage to the dead man's grave: "Towards night all took a walk down to the grave yard to see, perhaps for the last time, the small spot of ground that now contains the relics of our late friend and brother, who, one short year ago was cheerfull and gay, whose countenance wore a pleasing aspect, but now lies numbered with the dead."[101] Here Henshaw used the term "relics" to mean "remains," but the solemnity of the account suggests the reverence with which the group contemplated the young man's "pleasing" face, now visible in imagination only.

What Henshaw implied Hannah Syng Bunting of Philadelphia made explicit. In April 1827 the young Methodist woman wrote, "The scenes of eternity were brought very near this afternoon on visiting the sad, solitary spot where the sacred relics of my cousin, D[aniel] Ellis, lie." The proximity of her beloved cousin's "sacred" corpse was powerful: "Various emotions swelled my bosom." The location's beauty was also important. "I could scarce imagine," she wrote, "a more lovely picture: the sun just declining; a river murmuring slowly by the mansions of the silent dead." Several years later Bunting described visiting the remains of a female friend: "I went with Hannah to gaze on the hallowed spot where our dear D. sleeps in sweet repose."[102] The language is sentimental and also religious: the corpse's location is "hallowed." Thus, before the rural cemetery movement, mourners—especially women—generated demand for beautiful, holy sites where they could contemplate the remains of the dead.

Sarah Connell Ayer likewise communed with the dead long before rural cemeteries existed. In 1808, she and her cousin John had something resembling a supernatural encounter during an evening visit to the cemetery where several family members were buried. "The Moon cast a pale light on the surrounding tombs, and I expected almost to see the spectre of some departed fellow Mortal." She did not quite anticipate seeing a ghost; she "almost" expected it, indulging some Gothic thoughts. But she and her cousin also had a more pointed purpose: "We sought and found the grave of his departed Mother, and watered her graves with tears of love." For cultists such as Ayer, graveyard visits were central to their piety. As she later wrote when she had to move to Eastport, Maine, "I shall leave Portland with regret. Here I have spent the first ten years of my married life, 'tis the birth-place of my children, four of which lie in the grave-yard, a spot to which I love to resort."[103] The children were buried *ad familiares*; the move to Eastport threatened the family's post-mortem continuity.

As Ayer's sentimental language of watering graves with tears suggests, mourners' ideas about graveyards were influenced by the poetry, short fiction, and essays that filled antebellum magazines. These pieces traced their roots back to the Graveyard School and to turn-of-the-century English and American Romanticism. The desires of antebellum mourners, in turn, shaped that literature: ordinary middle-class readers, not some distant literary elite, contributed most of the sentimental pieces to American magazines. One example of this large body of writing is an anonymous 1820 essay written for the *Club-Room*, a Boston literary journal. "The Village Grave-Yard" starts realistically, describing a visit to a churchyard one fine October evening on a trip to an unfamiliar town. The narrator seeks out the burial ground, attracted to the graveyard's blurring of the boundary between life and death: "something human is there." As the sun sets, the protagonist dozes. Suddenly, the ground shakes and "subterraneous cries and groans issued from every part of the grave-yard." Still in a dream-like state, the narrator sees figures "clad in the garments of death" rise from the ground and stand next to their graves. An angel appears, urges the narrator to behold the power of heaven, and banishes the dead back to their graves.[104]

We know that this story resonated with women and men, not only because it was reprinted or excerpted a half-dozen times in other publications, and not only because teachers read it to their female students, but also because at least one middle-class reader of the *Club-Room* copied a long passage into her commonplace book.[105] Anna Eliza Heath was in her early twenties and living in Brookline, Massachusetts, when she read "The Village Grave-Yard" and was moved by its sentimental descriptions of the burial ground. Calling her excerpt "The Grave," Heath found especially memorable a passage that begins, "I never shun a grave-yard—the thoughtful melancholy which it inspires, is grateful rather than disagreeable to me," and includes the assertion that "something human is there." Indeed, Heath acted on this belief that something human resided in burial grounds. In March 1825, just three months after her beloved sister Mary died, Heath traveled to the city. "As I went to Boston, I passed the tombs." Heath's proximity to the graveyard inspired her to pray to her dead sister: "Mary, we shall never see you again." Heath noted that winter's gloom was giving way to spring's beauty, but it was happening, she told her dead sister, "while thou art silently returning to dust."[106] Thus did literature like "The Village Grave-Yard" cater to women and men who, before rural cemeteries, communed with the dead in sacred spaces of memory.

The common practice of visiting the dead was one factor that helped generate the rural cemetery movement, as mourners desired sites whose solemn beauty would reinforce the spiritual sensations experienced there. Another important consideration was health concerns. In the early nineteenth century, most American men of science believed in the miasma theory of disease transmission, which held that rotting flesh and other organic matter released disease-bearing particles into the atmosphere. In other words: if something smelled bad, it was probably spreading disease. Officials in New York, Boston, and elsewhere therefore suspected that the foul odors emanating from crowded urban graveyards were to blame for epidemics of yellow fever and cholera in the 1820s. Rural cemeteries, with their spacious grounds located at a city's periphery, helped alleviate concerns of graveyards as vectors of disease.[107]

Equally important, though, was the desire to create a place away from the urban maelstrom that would allow the living to commune with the dead. Proponents of rural cemeteries frequently cited this in their arguments. In an 1826 *Boston News-Letter* article, Abel Bowen advocated for a cemetery outside the city. There, city residents could pass their "most pleasant and improving hours in 'converse with the departed,'" visiting often to learn "the lesson of our own mortality; and, that, from those we love, even death itself cannot separate us."[108] At the 1831 "consecration" of Mount Auburn, Judge Joseph Story made a similar argument for the intense relationship between living and dead that physical proximity to human remains facilitated: "As we sit down by their graves, we seem to hear the tones of their affection whispering in our ears. We listen to the voice of their wisdom, speaking in the depths of our souls. . . . We feel ourselves purer, and better, and wiser, for this communion with the dead."[109]

After Mount Auburn's founding, the already robust genre of graveyard poetry and prose describing such "communion with the dead" positively exploded in American magazines. With titles such as "Our Parents Sleep There," "My Mother," and "My Mother's Grave," poems and essays explored how burial grounds could help the living maintain relationships with the departed. As one man wrote in *Godey's Magazine and Lady's Book*, America's highest-circulation magazine in the 1840s:

Amid a sculptured sylvan scene,
Where silence reigned profound and dread,
I stood, and 'neath the willow green
Held sweet communion with the dead.[110]

The dead were not distant and unreachable but immediately present around their graves, insisted cultist poets. For example, an anonymous writer in the *New-York Mirror* describes a man standing beside his mother's grave. The speaker asks the dead woman, "Wilt thou not hover round my path, and bless thy suppliant child, / And guide me while I yet may roam the world's unfriendly wild?" He answers his own question definitively: "I know thou wilt!"[111]

Considering only the poems and essays inspired by Philadelphia's rural cemetery, Laurel Hill, one finds dozens of examples in the late 1830s and 1840s, most asserting the site's religious power. These pieces appeared in outlets ranging from *Mechanics' Magazine* to *Godey's*, from the working-class *Subterranean* to the *Episcopal Recorder*. Some of these poems and essays merely described a sense of religious solemnity and contemplation in Laurel Hill, but many others insisted that communion with the dead took place there. Authors of the latter were certain that visitors to rural cemeteries could experience the presence of the dead. In one poem the speaker says that a person can interact with the spirits of the dead there: "Here may you sit, secluded from the world, / And commune with the shades."[112] Another writer, taken by Laurel Hill's natural beauty, asks the reader why burial grounds are so gloomy: "Ought we not, rather, to inquire, how may the living be most pleasingly invited to hold communion with the dead?" The answer: go to a place of "delightful seclusion" like Laurel Hill.[113] No wonder that when an upper-middle-class tourist such as Sarah Brown Ruggles arrived in Philadelphia, she, like many others, "hired a carriage" and visited Laurel Hill.[114]

In diaries such as Ruggles's, written by middle-class girls and women in the 1830s and 1840s, one finds evidence of intense graveyard encounters with spirits of the dead. Several months after Ruggles's husband died, his remains—like a magnet—drew her again and again to the cemetery. This earned her a rebuke from her physician, who feared her grief endangered her health. As Ruggles wrote, "unable to go to Church, but ride to the Burying Ground, with cousin Susan & my boy. There is a loadstone [*sic*] to draw me there, that I know not how to resist, tho the Dr. warns me to avoid it. Oh! my George, my husband! thy grave, thy grave!"[115] How could she resist, when a cemetery visit promised an experience of George's presence?

When a graveyard visitor encountered the deceased's spirit, it could lead the mourner to worry that her experience was heterodox. Such was the case with ten-year-old Louisa Jane Trumbull, who thought she might have felt her deceased brother's presence at his funeral but then reconsidered: "It snowed all day until Johnny's coffin, was let down into the ground, when the sun broke through the clouds, and everything looked beautifully. ~~Perhaps it was Johnny's happy little spirit so bright.~~"[116] Trumbull evidently felt she should not believe that her brother's spirit was there in the graveyard to brighten the proceedings.

Others expressed no such ambivalence. In 1831, Eliza M. Spencer taught school in Sandisfield, in western Massachusetts. She was twenty-eight years old and engaged to Chauncey Hawley from Norfolk, Connecticut. Against all of Spencer's expectations, her fiancé sickened and died. Spencer never married, throwing herself into teaching, religion, and a lifelong interaction with Hawley's spirit and memory. She could not, however, visit his grave as often as she wished; Norfolk was a fifteen-mile horse ride from Sandisfield and required an overnight stay to make the trip worthwhile. Therefore, when she did visit Hawley's remains her experiences were especially powerful. A year after his death, she recorded one such visit in her diary: "Last Friday rode to N[orfolk] and Saturday went to visit the grave of C[hauncey]." She had little desire to join her friends in their ramble around diminutive Pond Town Cemetery. "While my companions wander from stone to stone, I felt irresistibly chained to one little spot. O how strong the tie that binds the mourner to the clods of the burial sod." Lying on the ground above her lover's corpse, she thought of Jesus and Hawley: "While reclining upon the grave of my friend musing upon life's broken dreams, many, many a mournful sweet remembrance rushed upon my mind and I felt that I had at least one example which I was not afraid to follow, by indulging the swelling grief. 'Jesus wept.'" Either while she lay atop his grave or when she returned home, she composed a poem addressed to his spirit:

> Forgive the secret wish that now would wake
> Thy peaceful relics from their tranquil rest,
> Forgive the prayer that would have kept thee here
> O spirit blest.[117]

As in a prayer to Jesus, Spencer addresses Hawley as "O spirit blest." And like the speakers in Phillis Wheatley's elegies, she has a "secret wish" for him to return, all inspired by his corpse.

The following year, Spencer made another Friday ride to Norfolk for a Saturday visit to the graveyard. This time she ditched her lighthearted companions. Again she lay on top of the grave, separated from Hawley's corpse by only a few feet of soil, and now she wrote explicitly about the impact of his presence: "The conscious proximity of that dear friend who slept beneath the turf on which I was reclining made everything seem familiar, and completely banished from my bosom that undefinable and unpleasant trepidation which almost invariably pervades it, when treading the soil 'where human skulls are lodged below.'"[118] Here Spencer made a literary allusion worthy of a Massachusetts schoolmistress. The quotation is from a classic of the Graveyard School, James Hervey's "Contemplations on Night," in a passage where Hervey gently chides those who fear ghosts but who don't fear God. If a schoolboy has to "cross the spot where human skulls are lodged below," he "scarce touches the ground" as he speeds through the allegedly haunted acre.[119] The feeling that a graveyard might be haunted is what explains Spencer's "undefinable and unpleasant trepidation" when she enters a burial ground, even if she agrees with Hervey that one should pay more attention to God than ghosts. Ironically, it is the "conscious proximity" of her lover's corpse that brings her to that realization.

A cultist with similar experiences was Adelia Lamb of Berlin in central Connecticut. Born in 1802, Lamb remained childless through her long marriage. She never lacked for family connections, though, maintaining close relations with siblings and parents, living and dead. For Lamb, a graveyard was a holy space for cultivating those relationships, the "blessed shrine" that the poet Felicia Hemans described. Lamb agreed with Eliza Spencer about the character of the typical burial ground: "if it is gloomy it is also sacred," because it was a place to commune with the dead.[120]

It was also sacred because it was a site of burial *ad familiares*. The Beckley (or Beckley Quarter) Cemetery in Berlin is a small burial ground that by the 1830s held just shy of one hundred Beckley burials.[121] Adelia (Beckley) Lamb thus was surrounded by family when she visited the graveyard. As she noted one Sabbath evening in 1836 after a visit to the holy site, "We have just returned from the graveyard, the spot where all my fore-fathers are inter'd, the spot made dear and sacred, to me, by the remains of my dear Father, and two lovely brothers." After her mother died two years later, she felt an even stronger connection to the location. In March 1840, Lamb composed some reflections on the coming change of season: "Oh I long, for the sweet month of May that I may visit the sacred spot where repose the ashes of my Parents, and brothers." The spot was "sacred" because her mother's departed spirit seemed to remain there, just above the grave. As she wrote after another Sabbath evening visit, "The grave of a Mother, oh! what a spot for a child to visit and reflect. Oh how many, many, thoughts of the past come home to my heart. I could linger all night by her side, it seemed as if her pure spirit was hovering around me while I sat weeping on the green turff."[122]

Like other cultists, Adelia Lamb was a pious Protestant. She may have been more open to religious experimentation than some of her contemporaries; her diary records attendance at Presbyterian, Baptist, and Unitarian services. But there is no evidence that she got her ideas about graveyard interactions with departed spirits from Emanuel Swedenborg, the source scholars usually cite for belief in a permeable boundary between heaven and earth.[123] Lamb never mentioned Swedenborg in her diary. Rather, three centuries of Protestant popular belief in burial grounds as sites of haunting, two centuries of talking gravestones, a century of Graveyard School poetry, and many decades of sentimental and Gothic literature had prepared the way for Adelia Lamb to think of Beckley Cemetery as a place where her mother's "pure spirit" seemed to hover around her.

*　*　*

Traditionally, scholars have written about Protestantism as a religion of belief rather than practice, of interiority rather than materiality, of the "absence" rather than "presence" of supernatural beings. Even though the portrayal of Protestantism as a religion of "absence" was always a caricature, the term nonetheless aptly describes a long genealogy of writing about Protestantism.[124] Scholars of material religion have been working hard over the past two decades to change that. Emphasizing the material, visual, and tactile aspects of Protestantism, they have insisted that religion is much more than a list of tenets or creeds to which a believer adheres. They have shown that communion silver, images of Christ, and church buildings are constitutive—the very stuff—of Protestant religious experience.[125] However, scholars of material religion have spent less time examining the religious objects that connected the living with the dead.

Historians have overlooked the significance of such objects, and other expressions of the cult of the dead, in part because of the cult's largely female constituency. Had ministers, theologians, and leading male literary figures been more active participants, those antebellum figures might have identified the cult's distinctive beliefs, and perhaps even codified or named them, and historians would have paid more attention. But with the cult's key texts being women's spiritual journals, which historians generally perceive as formulaic,

and sentimental consolation literature, which literary scholars have until recently denigrated, the cult's key beliefs have gone largely unnoticed and our
understanding of Protestantism has thus been incomplete.

The four Jocelyn sisters were devout Protestants, members of New Haven's
North Congregational Church.[126] There they were exposed to a version of
Nathaniel Taylor's "New Haven Theology": Jonathan Edwards updated for
the nineteenth century.[127] Historians of religion have written shelves of books
about Calvinism in America. They have, by contrast, spent little time study-
ing the religious objects and sacred spaces that helped connect the Jocelyn
sisters and thousands more like them to their deceased loved ones. In so doing,
scholars have overlooked changes to Protestant belief and practice driven
largely by women. Embroidery, paintings, photographs, locks of hair, and
graveyards all have their historians, but scholars have not seen how those objects, taken together, point to the emergence of a cult of the dead decades
before the advent of séance Spiritualism. When the Jocelyns gathered around
Iky's plaster head, they filled its blank eyes and alabaster-white lips with their
memories of the living boy; they created a religious object; they communed
with the dead.

CHAPTER 8

Ghosts, Guardian Angels, and Departed Spirits

Mary Heath's death in 1824 left few marks on the public record. John Pierce, the minister of the liberal Congregational church her family attended in Brookline, Massachusetts, recorded only that the twenty-year-old woman died of "diabetes," which meant that she passed excessive amounts of urine in her final illness.[1] If Mary Heath's death caused only minor ripples in public, it generated powerful waves of emotion for her older sister. Anna Eliza Heath made a brief appearance in the previous chapter, when a glimpse of Mary's burial plot caused Anna to compose a prayer to her dead sister. That was but one moment in the postmortem relationship that Anna maintained with Mary.

Perhaps Anna was especially emotional about her sister's death owing to a sense of guilt. "I was not near to witness her quiet exit," she lamented in her diary. Eight years Mary's senior, Anna regretted that she had been unable to offer comfort and counsel as her sister lay dying. More problematically, from the perspective of the dominant Protestant model of proper mourning, she also could not fully accept God's will: "How much I wished, I still wish, for christian resignation."[2]

Her faith tested, Anna directed her devotional fervor toward a figure less inscrutable than God: her sister Mary. Anna Heath did not cease to worship God; she continued to do so, with vigor. But in addition to God, a new supernatural being existed, not for Anna to worship but to speak to, pray to, and beg for comfort. This connection between the living and dead even manifested itself in church. In April 1825, four months after Mary died, Anna rode to Boston with her aunt and uncle to hear a fast-day sermon. Their destination was New South Church, also known as Sixth Congregational. This was the first time Anna had been to worship in Boston since Mary died, and she struggled to reconcile her grief with the cultural script of moderate mourning. "I gave all my attention to the services as long as I had any command of myself, that I might not <u>cherish</u> sorrow by thinking of her, but at length my feelings got the upper hand, and knowing Mr. Howe [her sixty-year-old uncle] would disapprove such weakness, I strove so violently to repress emotion, that the conflict almost overpowered me." In this agitated state, surrounded by judgmental male authority figures including her uncle, her minister, and her God, Anna turned to a more sympathetic being: "Almost, & I believe the <u>very</u> last time I was there, Mary accompanied me to Church; & she seemed to be present with me now."[3]

Two weeks later, Anna again gained comfort from Mary, this time at home. On a day when she was "weighed down by depression," Anna apologized to her dead sister for missing her final hours: "Oh Mary, Mary! how could I leave you so unthinkingly!" To console herself, Anna told Mary about the relationship they maintained. "You are ever present to my thoughts. . . . In solitude I commune with you, in the social circle you are near." And then she articulated the cult of the dead's principal article of faith: "It is a delightful idea, that departed spirits are commissioned by God to execute purposes of mercy on earth; & that you are present with us tho' invisible, active in accomplishing errands of love."[4]

The dead are "present with us tho' invisible." Anna Heath and other participants in the cult of the dead did not perceive this conviction to be in conflict with their strong Protestant beliefs. But this was a concept that people almost never heard from the pulpit in Sunday sermons or read about in devotional classics. As Samuel Whelpley, a Presbyterian clergyman in Morristown, New Jersey, phrased the standard ministerial line in 1807, "at death, we drop all converse with those we leave behind us."[5] Or in the 1817 words of Henry Holcombe, pastor of the First Baptist Church in Philadelphia, a dead person "neither can, nor if permitted, would, return to us."[6] According to these ministers, postmortem interaction between the living and dead was impossible. By contrast, lay women and men generated the idea that the dead are present though invisible, combining mainstream Protestant tenets about heaven and God's omnipotence with popular belief in a permeable boundary between this world and the next.

In other words, Anna Heath and her ilk offer historians an opportunity to test Robert Orsi's contention that the definition of religion should include "all the special suprahuman beings with whom humans have been in relationship in different times and places."[7] Anna Heath undoubtedly believed that Mary was a "suprahuman being": her spirit could return to earth to perform "errands of love"; Anna could communicate with Mary's soul. Heath's religion therefore offered the "presence" most scholars have not seen as part of Protestantism.

The previous chapter examined the material and spatial expressions of connections between the living and dead. This chapter focuses on the immaterial: ideas about spirits of the departed, emotions about the dead, and beliefs about ghosts. For ghost belief, newspapers provide ample (though not unambiguous) evidence. For the presence of departed spirits, two types of sources document such beliefs: diaries and popular sentimental literature. Both have strengths and limitations. Diaries provide unparalleled insight into the lived religion of antebellum Protestants, as many women—and a few men—described their efforts to maintain relationships with the dead. These documents were generated by people with sufficient time and education to keep detailed diaries: members of the comfortable middle class.

Imaginative literature, especially poems and short fiction in magazines aimed at a largely female audience, complements the diaries. The popularity of sentimental literature, with some cherished pieces reprinted dozens of time, demonstrates the widespread interest in these beliefs. In fact, a reciprocal relationship existed between lived religion and imaginative literature, with each influencing the other. People's private expressions of belief were shaped by what they read in magazines and books; authors wrote about what they believed and experienced, including the sense that their loved ones' spirits hovered nearby. Overlooked by historians, the pervasive belief that the beloved dead were present though invisible long predated séance Spiritualism and was a key factor in that movement's rapid growth after 1848.

A Well-Authenticated Ghost

In sixteenth- and seventeenth-century England and its American colonies, ghosts were the most common way people interacted with the dead, either in encounters they believed to be real or in ghost stories, which could be greeted with skepticism or wholehearted acceptance. By the nineteenth century, ghosts were no longer the primary means of interacting with the dead. Skepticism among most members of the literati, combined with the Cock Lane ghost and other high-profile hoaxes, put those who still believed in ghosts on the defensive. At the same time, the antebellum cult of the dead, with its insistence that the dead were present though invisible, meant that ghosts were no longer as necessary to maintain connections with the departed. In the nineteenth century, the dead were less frequently imagined to return as ghosts and more commonly thought of as souls or angels hovering around mourners such as Anna Heath, "accomplishing errands of love."[8]

Nonetheless, ghost narratives abounded in antebellum print culture. In some ways this was merely a continuation of the dynamic from the late eighteenth century, when publishers of newspapers, magazines, and books worried less about the moral or ideological implications of the ghost stories they printed than whether they would find a paying audience. Printed ghost narratives retained the ambivalent stance that many of them displayed toward the end of the previous century: authors presented accounts in ways that could appeal to skeptics and believers and everyone in between.

There were some important changes in the nineteenth century, however. First, evidence for ghost belief became increasingly rare outside print culture. Whereas eighteenth-century diaries and letters occasionally described ghost belief, such expressions became almost nonexistent in the nineteenth century. This does not mean that such belief disappeared among all classes. Rather, it suggests that among the educated the topic was confined to the realm of imaginative literature. Second, the rise of the penny press in the 1830s and 1840s offered a new outlet for printed ghost narratives that appealed to working men and women. Editors of cheap newspapers almost never believed such stories, but they knew that ghost tales found an eager audience among urban readers who could afford only a penny for their news.

Scholars have paid almost no attention to sincere ghost belief among nineteenth-century Euro-American Protestants. Virtually all of the work has either analyzed fictional representations of ghosts or offered philosophical explorations of haunting's metaphysics.[9] But nineteenth-century ghost narratives help demonstrate how some people imagined relations between the living and dead. The accounts that appeared in nineteenth-century newspapers, magazines, and books display numerous continuities with those from the late eighteenth century. The educated men who dominated the publishing industry remained quick to offer natural explanations of supposedly supernatural occurrences. They pointed to diseases that caused people to lose their rational functions and see specters.[10] They cited guilt as a factor that induced ghost sightings; a murderer was often described as believing that he was haunted by the person he had killed.[11] If someone reported seeing a ghost, editors usually explained away the sighting as being the result of more humdrum circumstances: talking about ghosts before bedtime or receiving a blow to the head.[12]

Many nineteenth-century writers continued the earlier practice of associating ghost belief with women, in particular old or lower-class women. One man scoffed at the "absurd stories" about ghosts that "old women tell to children," while another described the "maiden aunt of a great family, who is one of those antiquated sibyls, who . . . is always seeing apparitions."[13] Others mocked the "fables of old women" and the "persons of weak intellects" who believed in ghosts.[14] Continuing the long tradition of criticizing nurses for the effects of their stories on impressionable children, some male writers pointed to "tales of the nursery" as the root of ghost belief.[15] It is difficult to ascertain whether these writers were at all justified in believing that nurses inculcated middle-class children with belief in the supernatural.

At the same time, gendered critiques of credulous old women were sometimes used to smuggle thrilling ghost stories into print. This was a continuation of the late eighteenth-century posture of ambivalence, in which publishers cared more about sales than ideological consistency. An 1829 newspaper article, originally printed in the *Boston Patriot*, made fun of the "trembling old women and timid maidens" who believed a ghost story in circulation. But that mockery came only *after* the story built suspense with realistic details, including this deadpan opening: "For several evenings last week the town of Waltham had a supernatural visiter [*sic*], who appeared in the edge of the wood, near the plain."[16]

Nonetheless, most members of the literati mocked ghost belief, which makes the continued appearance of straight news reports about ghosts all the more surprising. But perhaps that surprise should be tempered, given the publishing industry's intense attention to audience in the first half of the nineteenth century. If a segment of the population wanted to read about ghost sightings, then at least some newspaper editors would meet that demand. As always it is almost impossible to discern how readers responded to newspaper stories about ghosts, but some of the accounts include descriptions of how local people reacted to the ghosts themselves, suggesting continued curiosity about phenomena that blurred the line between this world and the next.

Early in the century, for example, a story appeared that was reprinted in dozens of newspapers around the country. Breathlessly headlined "Apparition!!!" the item originated in South Carolina but attracted readers throughout the North. The story's widespread dissemination is noteworthy because the narrative is written as if the Enlightenment had never occurred; this was a first-person account that Joseph Glanvill would have loved. In fact, it included exactly the kind of corroboration by trustworthy witnesses that Glanvill considered the gold standard for establishing authenticity.

The story quoted an affidavit, "sworn to and signed, this 18th day of July, 1803, by Wm Gragg, before me, John Nixon." This is what William Gragg testified: "On or about the 20th of June last, as I lay meditating before day, I saw plainly the appearance of a young woman, by name of Tabitha Ashley, standing by my bed-side." Ashley had been dead four months, and like so many other returned souls, Ashley's ghost brought a message from the afterlife. "The apparition said to me, 'Will you go to my father's house, and read and pray with them, pray mightily with them, and warn them to prepare to meet their God in heaven?'" Gragg said he would, but then he lost courage. Ten days later the ghost appeared again, urging him to do as she desired. This time Gragg really did deliver the message, and the ghost's final message was simply, "Now I am satisfied."[17] In New York's *Mercantile Advertiser*, as in so many other newspapers, the piece appeared without editorial comment, one item on a page full of shipping news and auction notices directed toward the city's men of commerce.

Several years later, another ghost story from the South appeared in northern publications: fourteen newspapers and one magazine. According to a witness in a civil trial in Maryland, Thomas Harris's ghost appeared and took sides in a complicated property dispute. One historian sees political motivations for the widespread interest in the case, with Federalists using it to embarrass Republicans, because the judge and three of the four attorneys in this strange case featuring ghostly testimony were Jeffersonian Republicans.[18]

But the political stakes would have been opaque to most readers. The front-page, three-column account that appeared in the *Northern Whig* of Hudson, New York, like most other versions, did not mention the party affiliations of anyone involved in the case. Instead, the story devoted nearly two full columns to the ghost's multiple appearances and especially its words. William Briggs testified that he asked Harris's ghost, "why not go to your brother instead of me," given that the message concerned Harris's brother. The ghost responded, "ask me no questions," and then proceeded to lay out his opinions about the property dispute. Some readers of the *Northern Whig* undoubtedly chuckled at this story, but there was nothing in the article's presentation that pointed them toward a skeptical interpretation. Rather, the editor offered it as an "authentic account of a remarkable trial" and allowed readers to make up their own minds.[19]

Similar ambivalence appeared in headlines about an 1831 incident in Albany: "Ghost or No Ghost" in the New York *American*, "Extraordinary—If True" in Cooperstown's *Watch-Tower*.[20] A sixteen-year-old girl had been suffering seizures for about eighteen months when she began to hear a mysterious knocking in her bedroom. The *Albany Argus* first reported this as a ghostly visitation, but the *Albany Evening Journal*'s editor declared that it was merely a case of "severe spasmodic affection." The editor further put the story within a skeptical framework by invoking the most famous ghost hoax of all: "Every one remembers the story of the London Cocklane ghost. . . . The same scene is now enacting in Albany."[21]

But newspaper accounts also reveal a great deal of popular interest in the case, even beyond the fact that numerous papers carried the story. As with the Cock Lane ghost, respectable citizens tried to figure out whether the knocking was supernatural. According to one account, "a gentleman" and "two or three neighbors" sat next to the girl's bed during the night and, to their astonishment, heard a "sudden and powerful" knocking.[22] In another newspaper, even a skeptical editorial noted that "the case has excited the fears of some, and the curiosity of many."[23] A few weeks later, when the knocking resumed after a brief respite, the New York *Evening Post* reported that "public interest and curiosity have once more been awakened."[24] One Philadelphia reader wrote a letter to the editor saying the story demonstrated the "superstitious fears of the ignorant and vulgar."[25] The reader was haughty and judgmental, but he had a point: outside the circle of those who wrote newspaper articles and letters to the editor, some people still believed the dead could return.

This was likewise evident in the 1842 case of a "Well Authenticated Ghost" that appeared in newspapers from Georgia to New Hampshire. Two men were at Samuel Mann's deathbed in North Benton, New Hampshire. As the deathbed watchers described in a deposition, they heard a groan that could not have come from the dying man. Suddenly the room was bathed in an "unearthly crimson colored light," which allowed the watchers to see a "strange looking man." They had no idea who the ghost was, but Samuel Mann did. Even though the ghost did not speak, its presence was enough to drive the dying Mann to a dramatic confession: forty-four years ago, he cried, he had murdered a person whose ghost now stood before him.[26]

Again, most interesting about the case are the varying reactions it generated. Some opted for outright scorn: "what somewhat impairs the credibility of that story is the well known fact, that they [the watchers] were both under the influence of 'blue ruin' at the time. In such a state it is no wonder they were troubled with *spirits*."[27] Whereas the Philadelphia editors who wrote that piece blamed the ghost on cheap gin, those closer to the source attributed it to the credulity of local residents. In the *New-Hampshire Patriot*, a letter writer found the story ridiculous, "as is the light in which it is regarded by sensible people of all parties and all sects throughout the community."[28] Despite this writer's contempt, "sensible" citizens of North Benton from across the ideological and religious spectrum believed the watchers.

Articles about an 1845 ghost sighting in Dixboro, Michigan, demonstrate the new role of the penny press in responding to and stoking public interest in the supernatural. As the dramatic growth in American newspapers continued unabated through the 1820s, papers typically cost six cents per copy, a price too high for many working-class readers. In 1833, Benjamin Day began publishing the *New York Sun* and charged only a penny per issue. To the surprise of all observers, Day's low-margin, high-volume business model proved a smashing success. Catering to popular tastes, the *Sun* featured true crime, sensational trials, and the marvelous. By 1835 it was the most widely circulated newspaper in the world and imitators soon appeared in cities from Boston to New Orleans to Cincinnati.[29]

In 1846, two of those imitators carried accounts of the Dixboro ghost. Isaac Van Woert moved with his wife and sons from central New York to Dixboro, not far from Ann Arbor, in the summer of 1845. As reported under the headline "A Genuine Ghost Story," the account included the kind of specific details and expert corroboration that Glanvill looked for nearly two centuries earlier. In a statement "duly sworn to before William Perry, Esq., at Ann Arbor," Van Woert declared that "on Saturday night, Sept. 27th, between 7 and 8 o'clock, I was standing in front of the window . . . when I saw a light." It was a woman holding a candle. He then saw this woman "dressed in white" nine times over the next six weeks. She was a talkative spirit; "in all her conversation she used the Irish accent," like so: "they have kilt me, Oh they kilt me."[30]

The ghost's words terrified Van Woert. The spirit claimed that she had once lived in the house that Van Woert's family now occupied and that she had been murdered for her money. Combining elements of the supernatural with true crime, the story was a perfect fit for the penny press. As one newspaper's editors wrote, "The earnest manner of the deponent induced an examination of the corpse of the person indicated as having formerly dwelt in the house; and the coroner's jury, after a careful scrutiny, returned a verdict of death by poisoning."[31] That was it: no mockery, nothing but straight reportage as if the story were about disorderly conduct in a local tavern. The editors ran the piece because it appealed to those across the spectrum of belief, from skeptics who shook their heads in derision to believers who wondered at the supernatural, and all in between.

In antebellum America, ghosts represented one way that some people thought about communicating with the dead, even as many readers consigned them to the realm of imaginative literature. Ghosts, simply put, were not a central part of the cult of the dead. In previous centuries, ghosts had sometimes brought welcome messages from the dead and offered comfort to grieving family members. But they were also dangerously unpredictable. They could haunt a house, terrify its residents, wreak havoc. In the nineteenth century, therefore, people interested in conversation with the departed turned to kindlier versions of the dead. For cultists, loved ones more frequently returned as guardian angels, present though invisible among the living.

The Angell Guardian

Guardian angels are older than Christianity itself. In fact, early Christians inherited the idea of personal, protective angels from Judaism and other religions of the ancient eastern Mediterranean. As angels became increasingly central to both learned and popular Catholicism during the Middle Ages, guardian angels received ever more attention. Theologians such as Aquinas and Bonaventure debated key issues such as whether God assigned each person an evil, fallen angel (demon) in addition to a good angel.[32] But interest in guardian angels was hardly limited to theologians. By the thirteenth century, the Catholic liturgy included a prayer to one's guardian angel, and in the fifteenth century some books of hours used by the laity were devoted entirely to these protective beings.[33] One such book contained this intimate prayer for people to offer:

> Praise to you, with joy,
> My guardian, and love;
> I cannot say sufficiently
> How good you are to me.[34]

In short, guardian angels played an active role in medieval Catholic piety and theology.

One might think that the Protestant Reformation would have banished these figures of Catholic veneration. But Protestants could not overlook the biblical foundation of such beliefs. As one English reformer pointed out, the Bible mentions angels more than 260 times.[35] And Protestants conventionally understood several of these texts to describe the existence of guardian angels. In his epistle to the Hebrews, for example, Paul asks rhetorically about angels, "Are they not all ministering spirits, sent forth to minister for them who shall be heirs of salvation?" (Heb. 1:14). Christians, in other words, have angels who care for them on earth.

What remained an open question for Protestants was whether God assigned a *particular* guardian angel to each person, or whether a person received the aid of a changing cast of angelic characters over the course of one's life. The danger of the particular guardian angel, reformers feared, was that it could lead to the type of veneration that should be reserved only for God. After all, Catholic prayers to specific guardian angels were not unlike prayers to saints and the Virgin Mary. Starting with Calvin, most reformers took a position of studied agnosticism on the question of particular guardian angels, in light of Scripture's opacity on the topic. As Calvin put it in his *Institutes* (1536), "whether or not each believer has a single angel assigned to him for his defence, I dare not positively affirm."[36] Underlying Calvin's attitude was a fear that too much focus on guardian angels would lead people to worship them.

In seventeenth- and eighteenth-century England and its American colonies, ministers generally followed Calvin's lead. In sermons such as John Bayly's *The Angell Guardian* (1630) and in theological treatises such as Richard Baxter's *The Protestant Religion* (1692), English ministers agreed that good angels protected believers from evil, but they hedged on the issue of particular guardian angels.[37] And even though one scholar flatly states that "angels were scarce in Calvinist New England," the reality was otherwise.[38] Ministers such as Increase Mather, Cotton Mather, and Samuel Willard published tracts and delivered sermons about protective angels, and around their deathbeds dying laypeople sometimes witnessed guardian angels readying to escort their souls to heaven.[39]

Ministers and laypeople, however, seem to have diverged on one crucial issue: the origin of guardian angels. As discussed earlier, Protestant theologians through the eighteenth century were unanimous in their opinion that angels and the souls of the deceased were distinct entities.[40] Human souls did not become angels. God created angels before time; the souls of the dead became the "spirits of just men made perfect" in heaven (Heb. 12:23). Ministers such as Jonathan Edwards always maintained the distinction between "angels" and "saints." In the *Works of Jonathan Edwards Online*, the Northampton minister uses the phrase "angels and saints" 28 times, "saints and angels" 113 times.[41] They were separate supernatural beings.

By contrast, some lay Protestants began in the eighteenth century to assert that the souls of the dead could return to earth as guardian angels. This necessarily implied that human souls became angels in heaven, contrary to mainstream Protestant theology. Evidence for this belief is fragmentary and scattered in the eighteenth century, so much so that historians have entirely missed this development. Virtually the only scholars who have noticed the conflation of angels and souls see it as a part of "modern popular culture" and consider it an "indirect consequence" of Swedenborg's writings.[42] There are two problems with this statement. First, the conflation of angels and souls started long before the twentieth century. Second, Swedenborg was not the ultimate source for this belief. Several examples predate Swedenborg's publications, and others date to the second half of the eighteenth century when Swedenborg remained largely unknown. Instead, it might be more accurate to say that Swedenborg tapped into an inchoate lay Protestant interest in maintaining connections with the dead, an interest that occasionally expressed itself as the belief that souls became angels, which allowed the dead to return as guardian angels.

The oldest example I have found dates to 1697. It comes from the pen of the English poet and essayist Elizabeth Singer Rowe, author of *Friendship in Death* (1728). Rowe asked her brother-in-law to posthumously publish her letters and previously unpublished poems. The collection includes a series of letters from Elizabeth Rowe to her close friend and patron, Grace Thynne. In a 1697 letter, Rowe informed Thynne that she was desperately ill. Thinking about the relationship between this world and the next, Rowe asserted the permeability of that boundary: "I can hold up my head no longer, but yet, Madam, I'll stay to tell you (for perhaps I may never write to you more) that the cold embraces of death shall never freeze up the kindness I have for you: No, the sacred flame shall glow in my breast to eternity. I'll be your guardian angel, and leave paradise to converse with you."[43]

Thirty years before she published *Friendship in Death*, Rowe believed a dead person's soul could return to earth as a guardian angel and "converse" with the living. Rowe's avowal of this belief is not at all "literary" or imaginary, and certainly not ironic. It is an earnest statement of fact. Readers sensed Rowe's sincerity in *Friendship in Death*, which helped account for the book's transatlantic popularity. Though the letters in the 1728 collection were imagined, they reflected beliefs that united author and audience. And one of those beliefs included the dead returning as guardian angels. As a young man writes to his sister from heaven, "I have often, since I left the World, had the Priviledge to supply the Place of your Guardian Angel. I have been an invisible Witness of your Tears for my Death; and to allay the Excess of your Grief for me, I have been at last permitted to let you know that I am happy."[44] Rowe almost certainly did not invent the idea that deceased loved ones returned as guardian angels. More likely, she put to paper an emerging belief; pre-1697 examples probably remain to be found. But at the very least, in nearly fifty English and five American editions before 1800, *Friendship in Death* exposed readers to an idea that was gaining traction within an ever-widening circle of women and men.

Belief in guardian angels found occasional expression in fiction and elegiac verse through the rest of the eighteenth century. As the Philadelphia Quaker poet Hannah Griffitts wrote in 1759 as part of an unpublished elegy addressed to her mother on the ninth anniversary of her death, "Oh, still attend, my Guardian-Angel Thou, / Watch o'er my steps, direct me where to tread."[45] Or consider a scene in the anonymously authored English novel *The History of Clorana* (1737) that portrays the deathbed of Bellmont. The dying man comforts his beloved with these words: "if I have one Thought upon Earth, 'tis center'd in Amelia, and I could with Pleasure receive the Almighty's Commands to be Amelia's Guardian Angel, to hover perpetually round her, to prevent the Evils of the Day, and the Dangers of the Night."[46] Like many other expressions of this desire, this one includes the suggestion that it is only at God's command that a person's soul could return to earth as a guardian angel.

In the nineteenth century, the expression of these beliefs in print became only more widespread. *Monima; or, The Beggar Girl* (1802), the "widely read" novel by Martha Meredith Read of Philadelphia, features a title character who does not merely hope for a guardian angel to protect her. Twice she actually calls down her mother's spirit from heaven. In the first instance, Monima is shaken after her father has nearly died from exposure to cold. "Dread and melancholy, were the predominant sensations of her harrassed soul. She invoked the spirit of her mother, to hover over, and bestow a nerve on her nerveless mind." In the second, the villain De Noix is trying to force Monima to yield to his sordid propositions. Monima cries out to heaven, "Oh! gentle spirit of my mother, hover over and guard your ill fated child!"[47] These were not empty, ritualized expressions. Rather, Monima's words gained force by drawing on the increasing practice of maintaining relationships between heaven and earth.

Deceased parents weren't the only ones who could protect the living. Numerous poems and essays asserted that dead children would return to serve as their parents' guardian angels. One poem, "Addressed to a Mother, on the Death of Two Infants" (1807), proved very popular among pious readers: it was reprinted in American magazines at least a dozen times before 1850. The poem presents itself as an authentic expression of consolation for a real mother, whose children died on September 19, 1803, and December 19, 1806. The speaker comforts the bereaved woman by assuring her that her children's souls "oft" return as guardian angels:

> Oft in the stillness of the night
> They smooth the pillow for thy bed;
> Oft, till the morn's returning light,
> Still watchful hover o'er thy head.[48]

The anonymous author's explicit reason for penning these lines is to help the mother reach a state of Christian resignation: do not cry; your children remain near. Implicitly, the author demonstrates just how thin was the veil between this world and the next.

Again and again, poems in antebellum magazines make similar claims.[49] But whereas the previous examples demonstrate certainty that the dead could return as guardian angels, others express this belief with some diffidence, phrased either as a question or as a statement preceded by the poetic "methinks." In a short fiction by Ann S. Stephens, editor of the *Ladies' Companion* literary magazine, the protagonist learns via a letter that her sister is dead, and yet she senses her sister's presence in the room. This leads her to ask, "Who shall affirm that this was all a phantasy, or that the dead may not sometimes linger about the living, to guard and to bless them? May they not, come and hover about us in seasons of sorrow and trial, to breathe the music and purity of another world within the soul?"[50] Or as the speaker of a poem in the abolitionist *Liberator* says to a dead brother, "Thou art not here, and yet / Methinks thy presence is around us still!"[51] These lay authors were attracted to the idea of guardian angels but, perhaps influenced by ministerial discomfort with those figures, had reservations about embracing their presence.

Still, most representations of guardian angels in sentimental literature unflinchingly asserted the existence of such suprahuman beings.[52] But the strongest evidence for guardian angels' importance to lay Protestants comes from the diaries and letters of women (and a few men). A dialectical relationship existed between imaginative literature and lived religion: people yearned for continuing relations with the dead; some came to believe their loved ones would return as guardian angels; a few of those wrote about those ideas in fiction and poetry; others read those ideas; the circle widened. For a demonstration of this mutually reinforcing relationship one need look no further than Anna Heath, who believed that her sister Mary was "present with us tho' invisible." Immediately after penning that phrase, Heath copied from a Unitarian magazine these lines in which a man tells his dying beloved he expects her to return as a guardian angel: "The force of virtue lasts beyond the grave, / Still shalt thou watch, console me, guide & save!"[53] Thus beliefs expressed in imaginative literature about guardian angels had real consequences for lived religion, and vice versa.

In the decades before séance Spiritualism, numerous mourners wrote in their diaries and letters that they felt or hoped to feel their loved ones' spirits near them. Some, like Mary White, believed themselves to be on the verge of sensing the deceased's presence. Ten days after her daughter Fannie died in 1844, the sounds of other children singing hymns caused White to write, "I . . . seem to feel that she will soon again be here & mingle her voice with those who are sad without her."[54] In her grief, White was uncertain about what she was experiencing; she "seemed" to feel that her daughter's spirit would soon return. Other mourners, perhaps hoping to emulate models from popular sentimental literature, tried to will themselves into a belief that their loved ones would return as guardian angels. A Congregationalist from West Baldwin, Maine, Mary Richardson Walker was working as a missionary to the Indians in Oregon Territory when she learned of her mother's death. "May I believe her spirit does indeed hover over her sorrowing child," Walker wrote.[55] With this petition the bereaved woman demonstrated how strongly she wanted to believe in the presence of the dead.

Still others felt that their loved ones had returned as suprahuman beings, but they were concerned about whether their impressions could be fully trusted. Adelia Lamb wondered about the authenticity of her sense that her mother was her guardian angel: "I have the impression that her sainted spirit is always near me; guiding me in whispers in the path of duty, be it so, if it is only a vision of my fancy it is a happy vision."[56] And a year after Louisa Trumbull's brother Johnny died, she too found herself hoping his spirit remained near: "Some persons think that the spirits of departed friends hover around us. I know not why we should not indulge the thought as it is pleasant and I do not think it will do any harm to indulge the thought . . . . . ."[57] The eleven-year-old girl's six dots at the end of the sentence suggest her ambivalence. She had learned from books and conversations that some people believed the deceased could return as guardian angels. She had also, evidently, received the message—perhaps from her parents or minister—that such a belief was problematic. Thus her defensive stance that it wouldn't do any harm to "indulge the thought."

Others harbored no such concerns. In 1837, after the death of her fourteen-month-old daughter, Mary Wilder Foote wrote a cathartic letter to a friend. Foote described the actions that she and her husband were taking to ensure that the infant girl would remain their guardian angel: "We both realize her nearness to us, and, in our strong efforts to keep our lives pure enough for her ever to encamp about us, we may realize a better blessing than her presence with us on earth could have been."[58] This was a path to Christian resignation that was, to put it mildly, a long way from what Protestant ministers had long encouraged. Similarly, when Mary Ware Allen of Northborough, Massachusetts, was nineteen years old, her aunt died. No distant relation, her aunt was like a "second mother" to Mary. Thus it is not surprising that Mary maintained a relationship with her after death: "I love to think that her pure spirit is near me, to guide and to cheer, and to whisper of hope and of perfect love. . . . I think of her with purer and deeper pleasure than even while she was here." Appropriately enough, the family had her buried "in the shades of Mt. Auburn," a fine place to contemplate the woman's presence as a guardian angel: "her pure spirit was indeed there."[59]

Although women made up the large majority of the cult of the dead, men were not without their representatives. By the 1810s even a few ministers expressed the idea that the spirits of the dead hovered around them.[60] But there are more examples from lay men such as Dr. John Park. The previous chapter discussed Louisa Adams Park, who had powerful desires to commune with her infant son's corpse. Louisa's extant diary is actually not in her hand; her husband transcribed it in 1848, thirty-five years after she had died, because it was falling apart from being read so much. For John, transcribing the journal was an act of communion with his dead wife, whose spirit kept watch over him so many years after her death. At the end of the diary Dr. Park addressed his dead wife directly: "Spirit of my departed Louisa! Hast thou not been near me, in my silent and retired room, while I have been transcribing the record of thy pure and devoted attachment? . . . It seemed to me thou wert present."[61]

This was a high standard of postmortem contact to match. When cultists described their continuing relationships with the deceased in print and letters and conversations, they created the expectation among some that they too would be able to experience such communion. This was the hope of Sarah Brown Ruggles of Providence, whose daughter Alice died soon after her seventh birthday. The day that Alice died, Ruggles signaled her interest in maintaining a connection with her child. "My sweet Alice!" she exclaimed in her diary. "How can I ever accustom myself to your absence!" Almost daily Ruggles wrote about her grief, but her experiences did not meet the standard she had internalized: "one month ago my darling resigned her holy spirit to Him who gave it. Oh that I could more sensibly feel her guardian spirit among us!"[62] Whereas Anna Heath felt that her dead sister was nearby, "accomplishing errands of love," and Mary Allen could confidently assert that her aunt's "pure spirit is near me," Sarah Ruggles yearned for a stronger sense that Alice had become her guardian angel. But for those who did experience that sensation, guardian angels were an important—though hardly the only—means by which antebellum Protestants conceptualized a continuing relationship with the dead.

Praying to the Dead

Sally Hersey frequently prayed to the dead. She was neither a Catholic nor a Spiritualist but rather an unexceptional Congregationalist woman living in central Massachusetts in the first third of the nineteenth century. Like virtually all women and men of her time, she suffered the deaths of children, siblings, and friends; eventually she also lost her dear husband, Calvin. Because parting with these loved ones was so painful, she continued to communicate with them after they died, in dreams, prayers, and her two-hundred-page spiritual journal. It is only this last fact that made Hersey unusual: that she so fully documented her efforts to maintain a connection with loved ones after they died.

Born Sarah Read (or Reed) in Worcester in 1768, Sally, as she called herself, married Calvin Hersey when she was twenty-three and moved with him a few miles west to the small town of Leicester. Soon she joined the Congregational church there, as evidenced by a "covenant and Articles of faith" she copied into her journal before her first child was baptized in 1793.[63] Sally Hersey was a generation older than many of the young women and girls who participated in the cult of the dead, and her handwriting and spelling strongly suggest that she did not attend a female academy the way so many upper-middle-class girls did in the nineteenth century. Perhaps for this reason her language was less sentimental than some other female diarists, and her participation in the cult of the dead had some distinctive elements. For one, Hersey never described the spirits of her loved ones as guardian angels. Instead, Hersey focused her energies on praying to the dead.

When Hersey prayed to God, she used the direct address that convention dictated. "God grant that we may all be prepared to dwell with the[e] in endless felisaty," she begged in 1826.[64] Prayer was thus an intimate act, one that brought believers into close contact with the divine. Caricatures of stern puritans and their distant Old Testament God notwithstanding, Protestants had always prayed in such a fashion. To take an earlier model prayer almost at random, consider one composed by the English puritan Lewis Bayly for his enormously influential *Practice of Pietie* (1612). Bayly designed this prayer to be offered when a person first awakens: "O God . . . be mercifull unto mee, and blesse me, and cause thy face to shine upon me: fill me with thy mercy this Morning, so shall I rejoyce and be glad all my daies."[65]

Like Bayly's, Hersey's pronouns are noteworthy. Again following convention, she addressed God using the "thee" and "thy" pronouns that had long disappeared from standard English but remained in the language of prayer. Taking their cue from the King James Bible, nineteenth-century Protestant prayer guides universally used such pronouns.[66] But the curious fact is that in Elizabethan English, "thee" and "thy" were the *informal* pronouns; "you" and "your" were formal. Why did the King James Bible's translators opt for the familiar form when passages addressed God the Father? Because, as one historian observes, "all supernatural beings were so addressed" in written English.[67] As a result, this was the wording that was standard in epitaphs and elegies addressed to the dead, such as Phillis Wheatley's "On the Death of Dr. Samuel Marshall" (1771): "Thy Lucy sees thee mingle with the dead, / And rends the graceful tresses from her head."[68] Hersey and other cultists, however, moved the formulation from the realm of imaginative literature to the prose form of prayers. By praying in the self-consciously archaic words of the King James Bible, nineteenth-century Protestants signaled that they were speaking the language of communication with supernatural beings, language outside ordinary time and experience.

Sally Hersey adopted this intimate yet archaic language in her prayers to God—and in her prayers to the dead. Granted, Hersey and other participants in the cult of the dead probably would not have used the word "prayer" to refer to their exchanges with deceased loved ones. Plus, she and others (with a few exceptions discussed in the next section) did not ask the dead to do anything for them, even though most prayers to God are petitions. But three considerations justify the term's use. First, such writings fit most definitions of "prayer," such as this appropriately inclusive formulation: prayer is "human communication with divine and spiritual entities."[69] Cultists considered deceased loved ones to be "spiritual entities"; directly addressing them in writing undoubtedly qualifies as "communication." Second, the term describes the earnest interaction with supernatural beings common to both traditional Protestant prayer and conversations with the departed. In fact, Protestants had long conceived of prayer as conversation with God, as the Church of England minister John Preston did in his popular *Saints Daily Exercise* (1629): "Now, you know how acquaintance growes amongst men; it is by conversing together, by speaking one to another. . . . So it is in this: when wee come to the Lord; and are frequent, and fervent in this duty of calling upon him, we grow acquainted with him."[70] Third, petitioning was not the only kind of prayer. In the eighteenth century, Isaac Watts categorized eight kinds of prayers, including prayers of adoration, confession, thanksgiving, and blessing.[71] To be clear, Hersey and other cultists who used such forms did not think of their deceased loved ones as equivalent to God. Nonetheless, they engaged in communication with the dead aptly described as prayer.

The first death Hersey recorded in her journal was her mother's. In 1819 Hersey and her mother made the sixty-mile journey to Beverly to be with Hersey's sister when she gave birth. Her sister's delivery of a "lovely blooming son" strengthened the intense bonds of shared female experience. Hersey stayed ten days, "visited the graves of my dear departed sisters Eleanor and Charlotte," and bid her mother and sister adieu. Shortly after her return to Leicester, Hersey was shocked to learn that the blooming son was dead and her mother was dying of "the disentarys." She hurried back to Beverly but it was too late: when she arrived the funeral hearse stood awaiting her mother's coffin. "My heart died within me," Hersey wrote.[72]

It is possible that Hersey communicated with her mother in the years immediately following that funeral, but no evidence thereof survives. The first extant record of Hersey's conversations with her departed mother dates from 1826, on the seventh anniversary of her death. "Oh my mother," she cried in the language of the King James Bible, "was thou here coulds[t] thou know the pangs that have rent my heart within these seven years past, thy tender heart would bust but thou art beyond the re[a]tch of earthly troubles, happy in the injoyment of thy redeemer." Imagining her mother's sympathy was comforting because Hersey had indeed had a rough few years. As she recalled, "I have been call'd to mourn the loss of two verry dear sisters, and a dear and much loved child sence her death."[73]

If this was Hersey's first postmortem communication with her mother, it may have been triggered by the death of that "much loved child," her son Austin. Born in 1797, Austin sought brighter economic prospects in North Carolina some time before 1818, when he was in his late teens or early twenties. In 1825, after not having heard from her son for seven years, Hersey received the letter every mother with far-flung children dreads. Austin had traveled to meet friends in Philadelphia, where he took ill and died. Hersey was grateful to learn that Austin died a good death, but for years it haunted Hersey that she had not been there. "Oh that I could have seen him but for one short hour, could I have heard from his own lips that his peace was made with God," she lamented. Twelve years later she still thought about how "far from all his dear relations his moldren [moldering] body lyes."[74] Distance rendered burial *ad familiares* impossible.

Austin's death ushered in fifteen years of regular communication with the departed. About a year after Hersey received that terrible letter, on the fourth of July in 1826, her family went to Worcester to celebrate fifty years of American independence. Hersey stayed home, alone, and prayed to her son. "Dear departed shade I shall behold the[e] no more in the land of the living but I shall soon follow the[e] to the land of silence." If Hersey could not see Austin in life, she could conjure him in death. "How oft do I call to mind thy blooming countenance, thy smiles, thy tender affectionate behaviour to thy parents and friends, the joy that aluminated thy countenance when we met, and the gloom that overspread thy face when we parted. All is present to my view." If on the fourth of July Hersey most missed *seeing* Austin, later that month, on the first anniversary of his death, Hersey imagined *hearing* his dying words. "I almost felt, that I could here him say my dear parents, my much loved brothers, and sisters, where are you in this trying hour, no one of you present to wipe the cold sweat from my dying face."[75]

For the rest of her life, Hersey treated Austin's death day as one of religious commemoration. She thought about her son at other times—"he is ever in my mind, not a day passes over my heart but I think of his dear departed shade"—but on the thirtieth of each July she took the time to write a prayer in her journal.[76] Marking death days was a common practice among participants in the cult of the dead. People observed the death days of their spouses, children, siblings—and especially their mothers. The Philadelphia Quaker Hannah Griffitts offered the most elaborate commemorations: each year from 1751 to 1803 she composed a death day elegy, many of which apostrophized her mother's soul.[77] Jemima Brewer of Wilbraham, Massachusetts, wrote the death day observance furthest removed from the person's death that I have found: "55 years today; my Mother ceased to live. O Eternity what a thought. She died the year she was 43. I hope and desire to meet her in Heaven."[78] Cultists sometimes marked such occasions with prayers to the dead, as Eliza Spencer did in 1835: "The [thirteenth] anniversary of the day when death first entered our dwelling and summoned my mother away—O Mother! Where? What? Shall we yet meet? Shall we know each other there? Shall we sing together? Shall we yet mingle our voices in the praise of God?"[79] These sources testify not only to the length of time that the living maintained relations with the dead but also to the especially strong bond between women and their deceased mothers. Because mothers were usually in charge of inculcating their children with Christian piety, adult children associated their mothers with intense spiritual connections.[80]

Sally Hersey's prayers to Austin were the reverse: the mother survived, lamenting the adult child she had reared in the faith. Most of Hersey's death day prayers to Austin focused on her inability to see him in this world. Almost certainly without a portrait of her son, and thus unable to gaze at his likeness, Hersey had a visual sense of Austin's presence in her dreams. As she told him on the second anniversary of his death, "oftimes I see the[e] in my dreams blooming in health, with that cheerfull smile on thy countenance, that has so often made my heart glow with pleasure, but when I a woke I fear'd it all a delusive dream."[81] In dreaming of the departed, Hersey joined countless other cultists. After Elizabeth Prentiss of New Bedford, Massachusetts, lost her daughter, she wrote to a friend that "I dream about her almost every night."[82] Likewise, Susan Allibone of Philadelphia explained how "in my dreams I am with my mother,—I hear her speak, and look upon her, but in the morning I awake, and do not, as once I did, feel her kind arm around me."[83] Dreams of the dead—and specifically those featuring conversation with the departed—were common enough that an early nineteenth-century dream interpretation book considered them as their own category. "To dream of talking with dead folks," the guidebook informed readers, "is a good auspicious dream, and signifies a boldness of courage, and a very clear conscience."[84]

Figure 23. Hersey family gravestones, Rawson Brook Burial Ground, Leicester, Massachusetts. Sally Hersey's simple marker (center), squeezed between those of her husband (left) and daughter (right), demonstrates her powerful desire for burial *ad familiares*. Photograph by the author.

Hersey did not record dreams featuring the other family members to whom she prayed, but, as with her son, she marked their death days with annual entries in her journal. By the mid-1830s she regularly observed at least four such occasions: in addition to Austin's July 30, she solemnized March 22 for her husband, Calvin; June 27 for her daughter, Elvira; and December 6 for her mother. When she addressed Calvin, she focused on the comfort she used to receive from his voice, now silenced. With Elvira, who died at age thirty-one, Hersey recalled their bodily contact as the young woman lay dying: "I seem to feel the pressure of her feverish hand, while she besought me not to mourn for her."[85]

It may have been Elvira's death in 1833 that prompted Hersey to move to Hawkesbury, Upper Canada (now Ontario), to seek refuge with her sons Charles and Zephaniah. The 1830 U.S. Census had Sally and Calvin still living in Leicester, with two young adults who may have been Elvira and her husband.[86] But then Calvin died in 1831, and Elvira two years later, so at age sixty-five Sally journeyed some four hundred miles to be with her sons, who had moved to the frontier lumber town of Hawkesbury to seek their fortunes. As she told her husband in 1840, on the ninth anniversary of his death, "thy Sarah is wandering in the wilderness," unlike Calvin, who had "reached the Celistal Citty."[87] Borrowing from Bunyan and the Bible, she connected her geographical isolation to her spiritual yearning to reunite with her loved ones in heaven.

On February 21, 1850, Sally Hersey's wait was over; she died of unknown causes. She had long been upset by how far she lived from her family members' bones. Soon after moving to Hawkesbury, on what would have been her forty-third wedding anniversary, she thought of Calvin and lamented that "God has taken him home to him self, and left me a lonely widdow wandering in a far country four hundred miles from my dear native home, and from the graves of my dear husband and beloved daughter."[88] Yet somehow Sally received her wish for burial *ad familiares*. In Leicester's Rawson Brook Burial Ground, near stones for Calvin and Elvira, stands a simple marker (Figure 23): "Mrs. SARAH HERSEY, wife of Calvin Hersey, died Feb. 21, 1850, aged 81 years."[89] Ironically, for a woman who spoke so frequently with the dead, the marker does not talk.

"My Dearest Parent interceed for me"

Sally Hersey left the longest paper trail documenting the practice of praying to the dead, but other women and men generated abundant evidence for this and other forms of conversation with the departed. Although the cult of the dead reached a critical mass only in the nineteenth century, scattered sources by eighteenth-century Protestant women reveal its antecedents. Isabella Marshall Graham, for example, was born in central Lowlands Scotland in 1742. When she was twenty-five, her husband, an army surgeon, was stationed in North America. Graham followed her husband to Montreal, Fort Niagara, and finally Antigua, where he died in 1773. In a long letter to her sister, Graham described the intense communion she had, first with her husband's corpse, then with his soul in heaven. According to Graham, after a nurse prepared the corpse "I returned to our bed-chamber to take a last farewell of the dear remains. The countenance was so very pleasant, I thought there was even something heavenly, and could not help saying, 'You smile upon me, my love; surely the delightful prospect, opening on the parting soul, left that benign smile on its companion, the body.'" She continued a powerful interaction with the corpse until it was buried the next day. Still, Graham desired communication: "I wanted something supernatural, and wished ardently for a dream or vision."[90]

Graham did not get the vision she was hoping for, so she took matters into her own hands, praying to both God and her husband. As she told her sister, "I often walked out in the twilight, among the sugar-canes, and the most solitary places I could find; sometimes continuing my walk till it was quite late; during which time I conversed with God and my husband by turns; but the latter had by far the greatest share." When she prayed to her husband, "I asked him a thousand questions, told him all my doubts and fears, and often expressed an ardent desire to see him: nay, I was not without hopes of being indulged."[91]

Most eighteenth-century prayers to the dead—at least as they survive in the written record—were less elaborate than Graham's. When Lowry Wister of Philadelphia lost her three-year-old son to smallpox in 1781, she wrote a long account of his dying days. In that document she offered a brief prayer addressing her son and God: "Oh! my son my son my dearly beloved child, thy pure spirit took its flight to the mansion of eternal glory to the habitations of never ending felicity, may God in his infinite mercy grant us an admittance into the same happy regions may we be united is the fervent prayer of my afflicted soul."[92] Wister's petition to God is for a heavenly reunion; her direct address of her son aims to maintain a connection with him.

In the nineteenth century, more people offered prayers to the dead along the lines of Sally Hersey's than had been the case in the eighteenth. With her father's corpse still lying in her house, twenty-year-old Rebecca Clark of Brookline, Massachusetts, authored a prayer to her father's soul in the language of the King James Bible: "Oh My father art thou gone? Tender affectionate parent, have I lost thee? Yes for a little while we must be separate, but when ever my heavenly father pleases I shall go to you, though you can never return to me."[93] Here Clark played with the distinction between "My father" and "my heavenly father." She did not confuse the two but rather saw them both as denizens of the supernatural world. Likewise, Abigail Adams, wife of the former president, remembered not "the ladies" in general but her mother specifically. Interrupting a letter to a friend consoling her for her mother's death, Adams inserted a prayer to her own mother: "Dear departed spirit, wilt thou still be my friend in those regions of immortal bliss, to which I trust thou art translated and whither I hope ere long to follow thee."[94]

Similarly, when Sylvia Drake of Weybridge, Vermont, was thirty-seven years old, a female friend from her younger days died an untimely death. Even though the two women had drifted apart, the death stirred powerful emotions in Drake, who was inspired to compose a long prayer to her friend. It read, in part, "I mourn thy early exit tho' thou hast long ceased to be my intimate. Early a wife & mother, thy residence at a distance I seldom saw thee: but never forgot thou existed."[95] Unable to maintain a face-to-face relationship with her friend while she was alive, Drake turned to prayer to maintain a connection with the woman after she died.

Most antebellum Protestants did not ask the dead to do anything in the prayers they wrote. Sylvia Drake, for example, sought only to maintain a relationship between heaven and earth. Others, however, had more specific goals in mind. Eliza Spencer petitioned her sister for divine knowledge. In 1836 Spencer was living in Sandisfield, Massachusetts, when she learned that her sister Melissa had died in Ohio, where the young woman had moved with her new husband. Like Hersey and many others, Spencer was especially upset that she had not been at Melissa's side at the end. Distraught, Spencer began to communicate with Melissa's soul. Her interactions culminated in a prayer asking her sister to reveal heaven's secrets: "O my sister, what is it to die? What is it to part with the earthly tenement and soar away a disembodied spirit? O what is the import of the words eternity—judgment—salvation—heaven?"[96]

Such petitions blurred the distinction between souls of the departed and the supernatural beings conventionally addressed in prayer: God and Christ. Cultists did not believe the dead were on the same plane as God, but rapid switching between the figures to whom they prayed created some ambiguity. Young Louisa Trumbull, whom we have met several times, remained deeply bereaved two years after her brother's death. One spring night, thinking about how at that time of year Johnny used to plant seeds in the garden with his little trowel, Trumbull turned to her journal to compose a formal prayer to God. "Oh God," she wrote, "when I die may I be received at thy right hand and meet my dear family there. Hear me, and grant me this my most earnest prayer. I shed tears while I write. Johnny peace to thy ashes and as thy life on earth was without blemish may you be even as one of the angels of God singing praises evermore. L. J. Trumbull."[97] Signing the prayer as if it were a formal covenant, Trumbull could not help switching from God to Johnny as the objects of her supernatural communication.

Sarah Ruggles did much the same in a prayer she composed four months after her husband died. The passage ricochets from God to the late George Ruggles: "Oh Merciful God & Righteous Father! Change this wicked heart. Without thee, I do indeed feel I am powerless, & thou has manifested thy power, in taking from me, all those ties, which were so very strong, that I feel my Maker was forgotten, in comparison with my love for the creature! Oh my loved, my blessed husband! If it be, thou canst watch over the welfare of her thou loved so well, how fully assured thou must now feel, that she was thine own indeed!"[98] With barely a breath to separate the sentiments, Ruggles went from asking God to keep her from sinning to asking her husband to serve as her guardian angel.

This was exactly the outcome that Protestant reformers such as John Calvin had feared if people maintained too close a relationship with the dead: that the living would be tempted to petition the dead for supernatural aid and comfort. And although evidence of such behavior is relatively rare, the few surviving examples suggest that some cultists believed the dead could offer intercession with God, in a manner not unlike Catholic saints. In one of her annual death day elegies to her mother, the Quaker Hannah Griffitts surprisingly indicates that she believes her mother capable of supernatural action from heaven:

Amidst the chearless paths of Life I tread
Wish for the grave, and bless the hap[p]y dead;
My Dearest Parent interceed for me;
That soon my date of Life, may finish'd be.[99]

It is less arresting that Griffitts wishes to die so she can reunite with her mother—this was a commonplace among cultists—than that she prays as if her mother could convince God to shorten her span on earth. No Protestant minister or theologian would have been comfortable with such a suggestion.

To be fair, neither would have most lay Protestants. But some cultists, so bereft after suffering a loss, so convinced they could communicate with the dead, behaved as if they believed in the dead's intercessory powers. Once again Sarah Ruggles offers a vivid example. Two months after her seven-year-old daughter Alice died, Ruggles struggled to contain her grief. Returning home after a month away, Ruggles saw Alice's face in all her familiar haunts. "Memory constantly recalling to my mind my lost treasure! My Alice, my blessed one. Plead for thy poor mother!"[100] It is this last imperative that was so unorthodox. Ruggles's prayer, asking her daughter in heaven to intercede on her behalf, isn't all that far from "Holy Mary, Mother of God, pray for us sinners": the Ave Maria. Ruggles, who frequently attended Baptist services, was unusual in framing her prayer as a plea for intercession. But that was merely the logical end point of the cultist belief that the living could communicate with the dead. Why not ask them for heavenly assistance?

Spirit Land

In the 1830s and 1840s, women and men began to use a new phrase for heaven: "spirit land." One might think this demonstrates Emanuel Swedenborg's increasing influence, based on, for example, the title of one historian's chapter on the Swedish visionary, "Voices from Spirit-Land."[101] But Swedenborg never used the phrase, according to a digital search of his eighty-five volumes published in eighteenth-century England.[102] He used "world of spirits" dozens of times in his most popular book, *Heaven and Hell* (1758). "Spirit land," however, seems to have emerged independently of Swedenborg in the late 1820s and grew tremendously in use during the 1840s (Figure 24). For participants in the cult of the dead, "spirit land" suggested a heaven that was nearby and not sharply demarcated from earth; its spirits remained open to communication and could descend to earth as guardian angels. No wonder Spiritualists would make "spirit land" a fixture of their vocabulary in the 1850s.

One of the phrase's very first appearances in an American magazine was in Hartford's *Episcopal Watchman* in 1827. This use of the phrase is characteristic in that it appears in a sentimental poem that portrays a continuing relation between the living and dead. In "The Two Graves," the speaker is the older, perhaps adult brother of two siblings whose graves he visits. Throughout the poem he apostrophizes the dead children; here he addresses his dead sister: "Now thou art in the Spirit-land, / With the holy and the blest." Like other cultists, he believes in a thin line between heaven and earth:

> Still it has been to me a dear
> Though desperate delight
> To meet thee in my dreams, and hear
> Thee bless my sleeping sight.[103]

Although the phrase could function simply as a poetic substitute for "heaven," it more often signaled a specific set of beliefs about the relation be-

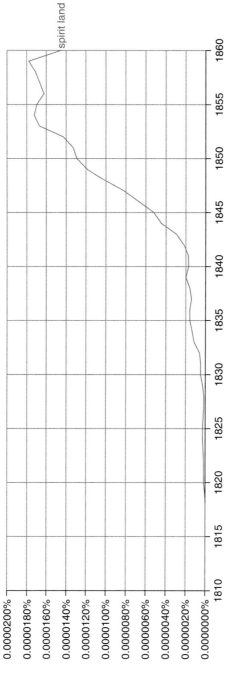

Figure 24. Increasing use of "spirit land" in books. The phrase appeared 6.5 times more frequently in 1850 than in 1840. Data courtesy of Google Books Ngram Viewer, https://books.google.com/ngrams.

tween this world and the next. In an 1832 poem called "The Spirit Land," written for the *Liberator's* literary column, the speaker is a dying young woman. She says that her dead father and sister are urging her to join them in heaven:

> My father's form among the blest
> Is saying, "Daughter, there is rest
> In the far-off Spirit Land"—
> And my sister whispers amid the throng—
> "Soul, there is peace for thee ere long,
> Hasten away."[104]

Such usages, which started as a trickle in the 1830s, gushed forth from the pens of sentimental poets in the 1840s.[105]

Diarists, too, described a spirit land that could barely contain its heavenly residents. Adelia Lamb, who in the previous chapter so loved to visit cemeteries, began in the 1840s to use the phrase in connection with both ordinary and supernatural occurrences. On the ordinary side, Lamb wrote that a woman "follow'd her little grandson to the spirit-land." In more supernatural fashion, she invoked the phrase before praying to a recently deceased member of her church: "A shadow has been cast over the pensive beauty of Autumn by the departure of a dear friend, and brother, to the land of spirits." This inspired Lamb to pray to his soul: "No brother dear tho' we miss thee from our small but love'd and cherish'd circle, . . . Yet we will not wish thee back to this changing world."[106] And Mary Ware Allen used the phrase when summarizing a popular sentimental fiction titled "Consumption." Three sisters were all dying of the dread disease. To increase the pathos, so was their mother. In Allen's words, "their dying mother, whose earthly all they were, had around her bedside three devoted attendants, ministering angels who she knew would soon follow her to the 'spirit land.'"[107] And so they did: all three sisters died and joined their mother in heaven.

Allen's quotation marks around "spirit land"—a phrase that did not appear in the original story—show the formulation's relative novelty. Quotation marks also sometimes appeared around the words in obituaries, an increasingly common feature of local newspapers. In 1844, the *Cleveland Herald* noted the death of Harriet Chapman from consumption. The obituary's author wrote that "it was the happy lot of the writer to visit the deceased during her sickness, and just before her departure to the 'Spirit-land.'"[108] Similarly, an obituary memorialized a young woman from East Corinth, Vermont, by describing how quickly her illness overtook her: "Within the short space of five days she was called from a state of comparatively good health to the 'spirit land.'"[109] Once again, the author made it clear that this was a phrase of recent vintage.

There is no evidence that any people described as heading to the spirit land were followers of Swedenborg, and indeed evidence sometimes exists to the contrary. When Fanny Lathrop of Essex, Vermont, died of consumption in 1846, her obituary described her final hours conventionally, with the exception of the new phrase for heaven: "As she came in near proximity to the spirit land, the windows of heaven seemed to be opened, and the light broke in upon her soul." The author observed not only that the "Congregational society" had lost a dear member but also that Lathrop was a Calvinist of the old school: "While many were driven about by every wind of doctrine, and in 'wandering mazes lost,' she adhered firmly to the doctrines of grace—of election—of justification by faith."[110]

A publishing phenomenon even newer than the obituary was the parlor song. Simple songs of several verses, with each verse sung to the same melody, parlor songs became tremendously popular among a wide range of Americans. Although members of the urban middle class had been purchasing sheet music since the 1790s, the industry did not really take off until the 1840s, when increasing numbers of Americans began to purchase pianos. But even people without pianos could buy and share sheet music; Lowell mill girls, rural farmers, and the urban working class all enjoyed parlor songs.[111] Such songs were meant to be sung with family members and friends, and their lyrics explored numerous sacred and secular topics. Given the growing number of cultists, it is not surprising that some of the most popular parlor songs focused on deathbed scenes, grieving lovers, the return of departed souls, and spirit land.[112]

As with hymns, countless parlor songs represent communication with the dead. In a few, singers voice the words of the dead, as in *Alone* (1848), about a man whose wife has died. The song's climax features the dead woman comforting her grieving husband:

> "Forget—forgiven all neglect—
> Thy love recalled alone;
> The babes I leave; oh, love, protect!
> I still am all thine own."[113]

Many more apostrophize the dead: *Leila Grey* (1845), *When Stars Are in the Quiet Skies* (1845), *The Burial of Mrs. Judson* (1846), and *To Mary in Heaven*

(1846), to name just a few.[114] In these songs the boundary between heaven and earth is not just permeable but downright porous. The ambiguously gendered speaker in *When Stars Are in the Quiet Skies*, for example, successfully petitions his or her beloved to return as a guardian angel:

> There is an hour when Angels keep
> Familiar watch o'er men,
> When coarser souls are wrapp'd in sleep—
> Sweet spirit, meet me then.

Many singers—especially those who had recently lost a loved one—would have experienced powerful emotions as they gave voice to key beliefs of the cult of the dead.

Because parlor songs surged in popularity during the 1840s, they adopted the "spirit land" terminology for heaven. Several songs even included the phrase in their titles, such as *The Willow Song; or, Voices from the Spirit Land* (1847) and *Voices from the Spirit Land* (1848), two entirely different songs.[115] Others featured the phrase prominently, as in the first line of *The Sister's Call* (1839):

> A voice from the spirit land,
> A voice from the silent tomb,
> Entreats with a sweet command
> Brother come home.[116]

The song's lyricist was Samuel Robbins Brown, a minister with the Reformed Church of America, a Calvinist descendant of the Dutch Reformed Church. While Brown was across the Pacific in Macau, trying to convert the locals to Protestantism, he learned of his sister's death. His song imagines her calling him home, both to his earthly residence in New York and to her abode in spirit land. It was a popular message and the song was printed in at least two editions.

Even if Swedenborg was not the main source for greater interest in spirit land during the 1840s, his work gained in popularity alongside the cult of the dead's burgeoning appetite for all things related to the afterlife. As a crude proxy for Swedenborg's growing cultural impact, the Google Books Ngram Viewer shows a marked increase during the 1840s in the percentage of books that included the word "Swedenborg," though the increase (3x) was not as great as that for "spirit land" (6.5x).[117] This is a "crude" proxy because some portion of the references to Swedenborg were critical. Nonetheless, it is undeniable that during the 1840s more Americans than ever were exposed to Swedenborg's ideas.

One reason for this was the sudden flurry of interest in Mesmerism that started in 1836 with the French medical healer Charles Poyen's lecture tour of New England. In the 1770s the Austrian physician Franz Anton Mesmer had claimed to discover "animal magnetism": a force or fluid of attraction that surrounded all living bodies. Sickness resulted if this fluid could not flow freely. Mesmer restored health or bodily "harmony" by getting the magnetic fluid moving again, massaging the body's magnetic "poles" to induce either convulsions or a deep trance. In the state of somnambulic trance, some patients could communicate with the dead because the magnetic fluid connected them with animate objects (including souls) throughout the universe. Although Mesmerism caused a sensation in Revolutionary France, it received little notice in the United States until Poyen's 1836 arrival in Boston.[118]

Adept at putting audience volunteers into the somnambulic state, Poyen convinced many observers of Mesmerism's scientific foundations. The first American magazine on the topic, *Annals of Magnetism*, began publication in Cleveland in 1838. Similar journals followed in New York (1842), Boston (1842), and St. Louis (1845). All these publications demonstrated a deep interest in Swedenborg. The *St. Louis Magnet*, for example, published excerpts from Swedenborg's *Animal Kingdom* over the course of nine issues in 1846.[119] The affinity between the systems of Mesmer and Swedenborg lay in their descriptions of a universe teeming with occult forces that connected this world with worlds beyond, forces that could be harnessed to produce bodily and societal "harmony." Although their systems differed in many details, popularizers in the United States glossed over such distinctions and focused on the commonalities, including that both offered seemingly scientific explanations for communication with the dead.[120]

The editor of Boston's *Mesmeric Magazine* likely exaggerated in 1842 when he claimed that "we have delivered seventy-five public lectures within one year in the city of Boston, and the consequence is that mesmerisers are found by scores, mesmerisees by hundreds, and converts by tens of thousands." But he accurately diagnosed a key aspect of Mesmerism's appeal when he noted that "our mesmerisees have repeatedly conversed with departed spirits."[121] This communication with the dead was not of the same sort that would be practiced by séance Spiritualists. A historian writes that one clairvoyant in the 1840s "received messages from the generalized spirits of the Second Sphere" but "he did not receive messages from individual, identifiable spirits."[122]

That clairvoyant was Andrew Jackson Davis, the most important bridge from Swedenborg and Mesmer to the spirit land of séance Spiritualism. Davis, the "Poughkeepsie Seer," was introduced to Mesmerism in 1843. Soon thereafter Davis gained local renown as a medical clairvoyant, but he would not earn a national reputation—for some as a crank, for others as a visionary—until the 1847 publication of his *Principles of Nature*. Drawing on Swedenborg and Mesmer, *Principles of Nature* outlined the various "spheres" of the universe and how communication among them was possible based on a substance called "Spirit." For Davis it was the "free, unshackled spirit" that allowed him to "communicate with spiritual substances." Some of the knowledge he received came from denizens of "spirit-land," and Davis was able to obtain that information because "I can converse with the spirits distinctly."[123]

Davis thus joined Mesmer and Swedenborg in providing scientific explanations for communication with spirit land. These explanations strongly appealed to the relatively small number of radical men one scholar calls "harmonialists," using a term Davis later applied to the quest for harmony between spiritual and earthly realms. In the 1840s harmonialists were highly educated, middle- and upper-middle-class men interested in new forms of scientific and spiritual enlightenment, even as they stood outside the mainstream of scientific and religious thought. The leading harmonialists were "virtually all men."[124] Davis and other male harmonialists would become, in the 1850s, the principal theorists of séance Spiritualism. They would explain at great length how the movement's mediums were able to speak with the dead.

For the predominantly female participants in the cult of the dead before 1848, by contrast, such intellectual scaffolding was beside the point. Sally Hersey, Adelia Lamb, Louisa Jane Trumbull, Anna Heath, and many other cultists already knew that it was possible to communicate with the dead. Theirs was not the two-way communication of Spiritualist mediums; cultists, so far as the sources reveal, did not receive answers to the questions they posed to the dead. Nonetheless they prayed to departed friends and family members, visited their graves and spoke to them, composed poems to them, sang to them. They created, as Ann S. Stephens wrote, "a beautiful charm of love to link us with the spirit land."[125]

*　　*　　*

Edward Everett started his career as a Unitarian minister and then moved into politics. In an awful coincidence, on the very first day of his term as governor of Massachusetts, his daughter Grace died. She had just turned eight. Two and a half years later, Everett still maintained a relationship with his dead daughter. In an 1838 letter to Rev. Charles Wentworth Upham of Salem, Everett consoled his friend on the loss of his son by presenting his own experience as a guide. First, Everett offered the conventional sentiment that time heals all wounds. But then Everett made a statement that would be startling if one were not familiar with the cult of the dead: "I can truly say that my views of the great mystery of our being have been greatly enlightened by the efforts I have made to maintain unbroken a connection & relationship with my little angel."[126]

What "efforts" did Everett refer to? The letter is frustratingly silent on the point. Alas, so is his detailed diary: in the 565 pages over several volumes between Grace's death and the day he wrote Upham, Everett mentioned his daughter exactly twice. On New Year's Day 1837, after a full day in church, Everett confessed his spiritual confusion. "Eternity bewilders me," he wrote. "The Question of questions is, If a Man die shall he live again? Shall his consciousness continue? Shall he know his friends? Shall I meet again my little daughter?" Tellingly, he phrased the first three questions in the third person but turned to the first person when he thought of Grace. Six days later Everett did not mark the one-year anniversary of his daughter's death, nor did he observe her birthday in his diary. Two years after Grace died, he did note that the day was "the Anniversary of our dear little daughter's departure."[127] But he never spoke to her in his diary, or wrote prayers to her, or described visiting her grave to commune with her. Nonetheless, he told Upham that he had maintained an "unbroken" connection with Grace.

This reveals an important fact about the cult of the dead: the sources undoubtedly understate its extent. For every Adelia Lamb and Sarah Brown Ruggles who had the time, resources, and inclination to record their relationships with the dead in their diaries, there must have been hundreds or thousands—based on the evidence from popular sentimental literature—who likewise maintained connections with the dead but did not write about them. Everett's exhaustive diary suggests that this bias may have been especially strong for men, who were less likely than women to record for posterity their struggles with grief.[128] Were it not for a brief mention in a letter, we would not know that Everett used a variety of "efforts" to continue a relationship with his dead daughter. Whatever acts of devotion he performed—perhaps communing with a portrait, praying to her soul, or caressing a lock of her hair—they successfully connected him with Grace in heaven.

This was the antebellum cult of the dead's ultimate goal: to continue relationships with the deceased. This desire went far beyond merely remember-
ing the dead. It demanded a much more active process, for it took a great deal
of work to "maintain unbroken a connection & relationship" with the dead.
But even if the sources do not fully reflect male participation in the cult of
the dead, Everett as a man was surely in the minority.[129] Why was that so?
First, women were in charge of the physical labor of caring for the dying, washing corpses, and shrouding them. In addition, with the rise of sentimental
culture toward the end of the eighteenth century, women also increasingly performed the emotional labor of grieving and memorialization. Finally, women
continued to dominate the private and public aspects of Christian devotion.
In the nineteenth century they were more likely than men to keep spiritual
journals, inculcate children with piety, and join churches. To cite just one telling statistic, in five revival years between 1814 and 1838 in Oneida County,
New York, women made up 63 percent of new members (918/1,458) in four
churches. And this was down from the pre-revival figure of 70 percent.[130]

Bulwarks of Christian piety and intimately involved with the dying and
dead, women saw the maintenance of relationships with those in heaven as
an outgrowth of their social roles on earth. Women therefore helped drive
important changes in Protestantism. With much broader influence than Swedenborg, Mesmer, and other male occultists, and in advance of most Protestant ministers and theologians, they pried open the door between heaven and
earth. Their desires to maintain continuing relationships with the dead created the world in which séance Spiritualism was possible.

Continuing Relationships

At age seven, Frances Ann Crowell was a young initiate into the cult of the dead. The year was 1838, and Crowell lived with her pious Baptist mother and spiritually indifferent father in a modest home in Portsmouth, New Hampshire. One evening the young girl lay in bed, wracked by fever. Her mother, Hannah, watched by the bedside in case her dear "Fannie" took a turn for the worse. Emerging from a feverish fog, Fannie heard her mother talking to someone and assumed it was a neighbor. But seeing no one else in the room, the girl leaned over and asked, "Who are you talking with, mother?"

Surprised that Fannie was awake, Hannah hesitated a moment. "Well, my dear, I was talking to the angels."

"The angels, mother! I thought they lived in heaven."

"Yes, but they sometimes come to talk with us in this world."

The girl asked her mother who angels are. "The angels," Hannah replied, "are those who once lived on this earth, but who are now called dead. Your little sister is an angel."

"So you were talking to them?"

"Yes."

"What did they say?"

"Your little sister tells me that you are to recover."[1]

Fannie did indeed get well. And four years later, after her mother died, she too began to speak with the dead. She communicated with her mother and "other departed ones," receiving advice from them and learning about the afterlife.[2] Within a few years she made the transition, like many of her generation, from a participant in the cult of the dead to an adherent of séance Spiritualism. In the 1850s, now known as Mrs. J. H. Conant, Fannie parlayed her ability to speak with the dead into a position as one of the nation's best-known mediums. Her spirit messages appeared weekly in Boston's *Banner of Light* from 1857 until her death in 1875.[3]

Unlike all the other evidence I have presented about the cult of the dead, Fannie's account of her childhood was written retrospectively. It is certainly possible that in her 1873 memoir, Mrs. J. H. Conant concocted a tale of spiritual precocity to add luster to her reputation as a medium. But it is unclear why she would feel such a need when she was already considered "the world's medium" after fifteen years of high-profile columns. And more to the point, her account fits with what we know about the cult of the dead. Conant's memoir includes many details corroborated by diaries and sentimental literature written before 1848: the mother has lost a young child, believes that her dead daughter is an angel, and asserts that communication with angels is possible; the living child maintains a relationship with her dead mother. The account's only atypical aspect is that the dead child speaks to the mother, telling her that Fannie will recover. Whereas cultists sometimes spoke to the dead, they generally did not think the deceased answered back. Such two-way conversations were typically the province of imaginative literature: ghost narratives, parlor songs, and sentimental poems.

At the same time, it makes little sense to draw a bright line between lived religion and imaginative literature. Religion, ultimately, is all about imagination. Even if one believes that God or gods exist, one (usually) can't see him, or her, or them. The faithful act as if those beings exist: praying to them, avoiding behaviors they frown upon, participating in rituals to show devotion. In the case of Catholicism, it is easy to see how figures in addition to God— saints, souls in purgatory, the Virgin Mary—are central to people's beliefs. These figures make Catholicism a religion of presence. With Protestantism it has been more common to think of God and Christ as the only supernatural beings with whom people have relationships. But for many Euro-American Protestants before 1848, relationships with the dead complemented connections to God and Christ.

From the start of the English Reformation through the seventeenth century, ghosts remained a central way that ministers and laypeople imagined interactions with the dead. No longer souls returned from purgatory, Protestant ghosts could be either angels or, more frequently, demons (ministers' favored interpretations), or souls that God allowed to return from heaven (laypeople's frequent understanding). Minister-scientists on both sides of the Atlantic investigated ghost narratives to determine which were credible and not the result of a witness drinking too much beer or being overly timorous.

Laypeople read the accounts these investigators published, snapping up books such as *Saducismus Triumphatus* and inspiring printers to publish multiple editions of favorite titles.

At the same time, both ministers and laypeople understood that many representations of speaking with the dead were imagined. Elegists in England and its colonies imagined what the dead would say if only listeners could hear them. Starting in the middle of the eighteenth century, New England gravestones featured epitaphs that represented the dead as speaking or being spoken to. Some of these stones quoted Graveyard School poets, whose works fostered the sense that in burial grounds the spirits of the dead just might make their presence felt. Gothic fiction built on Graveyard School themes but went even further in focusing on corpses and the deceased's voice. Material forms of expression such as mourning embroidery and portraits invited viewers into conversations with the departed. All of this imagined communication with the dead was important in Protestant lived religion, as it gave readers and listeners and graveyard visitors the opportunity to explore some of humanity's most vexing questions: What happens to us after we die? Will we meet our loved ones in the afterlife? Do departed souls know what we are doing, and can they offer us protection from harm?

Over the course of the eighteenth century, ghost belief diminished, especially among the educated. Ghosts never entirely faded away, as many elites had predicted. But as ghosts retained a weaker hold on people's imaginations, other ideas about the dead gained traction. Graveyards came to be seen less as the sites of hauntings by anonymous spirits than locations where loved ones' souls might make their presence felt. Protestants began to think of heaven as a place of reunion with friends and family, rather than primarily a place to adore God's majesty. Many lay women and men started to believe, contrary to more than two centuries of Protestant teachings, that the souls of the dead became angels in heaven. These supernatural beings could even return to earth and serve as guardian angels for the living. As the eighteenth century gave way to the nineteenth, such beliefs combined with several emergent ones to create a cult of the dead. Participants in this religious complex also believed that a corpse could serve as a locus of communion with the deceased and that composing prayers to the dead was a good way to maintain relationships between heaven and earth. Some of these cultists were attracted to new denominations such as Shakers and Mormons whose prophetic leaders promised closer relations with the dead. Most, by contrast, retained their affiliations with mainstream Protestant denominations.

By the time the Fox Sisters heard a dead man's rappings in their house, a large segment of the population was ready to believe that communication with the deceased was possible. This preexisting pool of potential adherents is one reason why séance Spiritualism spread in the 1850s "like a prairie fire," in one participant's words.[4] Cultists were the tinder that helped that fire burn brightly and move quickly across the landscape. But it is important to note the differences between the cult of the dead and séance Spiritualism. Both halves of the latter phrase show what was distinctive about the new practices. The word "séance," French for "a sitting," never appeared in the United States before 1850.[5] It came to describe the distinctive Spiritualist ritual in which women and men alternated seats around a table, the better to balance female and male energy as they tried to speak with the dead (Figure 25). The ritualized practice of two-way communication with spirits had no antecedent in the cult of the dead.

Likewise, capital-S "Spiritualism" distinguishes the post-1850 religious movement from other spiritualist (or, better, "spiritist") practices throughout

Figure 25. Séance table, Leipzig, Germany (1853). The alternation of men and women, with their "positive" and "negative" valences, helped facilitate the electrical currents spirits used to communicate. From *L'illustration, Journal Universel* (Paris), World History Archive/Alamy Stock Photo.

history in which the living communicate with the dead.[6] The word's upper-case "S" and "-ism" suffix also suggest the extent to which the practices amounted to an organized movement. Although Spiritualists were famously decentralized (the attempt to form a national organization floundered for decades), there were dozens of Spiritualist magazines and newspapers, and eventually hundreds of Spiritualist churches.[7] Again the contrast with the cult of the dead is telling. Cultists formed no churches and published no magazines, unless one considers the cult's official outlets to have been women's magazines filled with sentimental literature representing communication with the dead. Indeed, the phrase "cult of the dead" is my own. Participants considered themselves Baptists, or Unitarians, or Congregationalists, not cultists. But they did share consistent, definable beliefs and practices that justify using the phrase.

If significant differences existed between the cult of the dead and Spiritualism, numerous similarities remained, beyond the obvious fact that participants in both were eager to maintain relationships with the dead. Most important was the central role that women played in both movements. In the cult of the dead, women were much more likely than men to write and read imaginative literature that represented the dead as speaking or being spoken to. They were also much more likely to pray to the dead in their diaries, describe graveyard encounters with the spirits of the departed, and express the wish that their loved ones return as guardian angels. This all meant that women played an active role in shaping antebellum Protestantism. But it also meant that the cult of the dead's cultural authority was less than it otherwise might have been—at the time and in subsequent histories. Had more men been active participants in the cult of the dead some might have attempted to codify its challenges to mainstream Protestantism. Historians almost certainly would have paid more attention had male theologians and politicians and literary figures declared their adherence to the cult's tenets.

With Spiritualism as their vehicle, many women followed a trajectory similar to the one that transformed Fannie Crowell, cultist, into Mrs. J. H. Conant, medium. Such female mediums acquired an ambivalent sort of power in the second half of the nineteenth century. Many gained local renown for their spirit communications, some attracted paying audiences, and a few fashioned independent careers as traveling trance speakers. At the same time, even the most successful mediums were valued for stereotypically female qualities such as their "passivity," which supposedly allowed them to channel messages from spirits without undue influence from their own agency. For other mediums, their alleged ignorance worked in their favor, as it seemed to prove that they could not be faking their spirit messages. As one observer declared about Cora L. V. Hatch, a young medium famed nearly as much for her cascade of blond ringlets as for her ability to communicate with the dead, "her use of language is almost perfect, while it is obvious to everyone that she has not above ordinary intellect, and her years preclude the possibility of her being conversant with all the topics that come before her."[8]

Spiritualism attracted the greatest number of adherents in the two decades after the Civil War. Following a conflict in which perhaps 750,000 men died in the prime of life, parents, wives, and siblings of fallen soldiers sought out mediums to help them maintain relationships with the deceased.[9] The "Message Department" of the *Banner of Light* included letters from dead soldiers for more than a decade after Appomattox. And following the template established by the cult of the dead, imaginative literature played a crucial role in helping the bereaved explore connections between heaven and earth. The second-best-selling book of the nineteenth century—behind only *Uncle Tom's Cabin*—was Elizabeth Stuart Phelps's *The Gates Ajar* (1868).[10] In this novel, the protagonist is a young woman who has lost her beloved brother Roy in the war. Mary Cabot of Homer, Massachusetts, is disconsolate, and mainstream Protestantism—the "Evangelical church" of which she has been a member for six years—offers her little solace. Its promise of souls "standing up among the grand, white angels" is too formal and distant to provide comfort. Deacon Quirk from her church visits to offer platitudes about accepting God's will: "Afflictions come from God, and however afflictin' or however crushin' they may be, it is our duty to submit to them."[11] The whole thing leaves Mary cold.

Until her Aunt Winifred arrives from Kansas. Winifred is a bit of a freethinker, and she promises Mary she will reveal truths about Roy's state that will finally bring her comfort. Winifred begins her tutelage in a graveyard, as one might expect in a text intellectually descended from the cult of the dead. Roy's body has been brought back from the battlefield for burial in the local cemetery. Mary and her aunt visit the grave, where Mary voices her worry that her efforts to beautify the plot make no difference to Roy in heaven. Winifred gently contradicts her. "I do not feel sure that anything he has left makes no 'difference' to him."

"But I don't understand," Mary replies. "He is in heaven. He would be too happy to care for anything that is going on in this woful world."

Winifred explains that the living do, in fact, continue their relationships with their deceased loved ones. Mary has an epiphany. "But that must mean— why, that must mean—"

"That he is near you. I do not doubt it. I cannot doubt that our absent dead are very present with us."[12]

Just as Anna Eliza Heath believed forty years earlier that her sister Mary hovered around her, accomplishing errands of love, so does the fictional Mary Cabot learn that her brother is present, watching over her. Even though scholars usually describe *The Gates Ajar* as a Spiritualist novel,[13] it might better be called a cult of the dead novel. There are no séances in *The Gates Ajar*; Roy does not speak through a medium. Indeed, for the hundreds of thousands of readers who generated demand for fifty-five reprintings in twenty years, the novel showed how continuing relationships with the dead could fit with the beliefs of an "Evangelical" Protestant. As Aunt Winifred says about the afterlife, "the Bible does *not* say a great deal on this point, but it does not contradict me."[14] *The Gates Ajar* could thus appeal to both Spiritualists and mainstream Protestants.

Spiritualism reached its zenith in the latter part of the nineteenth century. The twentieth century, by contrast, was not kind to the practice of maintaining relationships between heaven and earth. Sigmund Freud, who did so much to shape both professional psychiatry and popular culture in the twentieth century, argued that the whole point of healthy grieving was to end the mourner's relationship with the deceased. As Freud wrote in 1913, "Mourning has a very distinct psychic task to perform, namely, to detach the memories and expectations of the survivors from the dead."[15] Building on this insight, Freud's highly influential essay, "Mourning and Melancholia" (1917), distinguished between "normal mourning" on the one hand and, on the other, melancholia, the "pathological mourning" that occurs when the living cannot detach from the deceased. The concept of melancholia pathologized what would have been seen in the nineteenth century as deep but fairly standard grief: "a profoundly painful dejection, cessation of interest in the outside world, loss of capacity to love, inhibition of all activity." Freud, characteristically, believed that sex was at the root of the problem: melancholia was caused by the bereaved's opposition to withdrawing her or his libido from the deceased "loved object."[16] But most popularizers did not get bogged down in those details. Instead, the message the broader culture took from Freud was that the key to healthy mourning was to end the relationship with the deceased. In other words, get over it.

Reacting against Freud and the twentieth century's "denial of death," many grief professionals in the 1990s began to argue that for some mourners, maintaining "continuing bonds" with the dead is a valuable strategy for dealing with loss.[17] According to these researchers and therapists, the living can experience continuing relationships with the deceased through objects, dreams, and a "sense of presence." Professionals describe "linking objects" as items connected with the deceased's life that "link the bereaved to the dead; in so doing, they evoke the presence of the dead."[18] Similar to how participants in the cult of the dead used locks of hair and postmortem portraits to maintain a connection with the deceased, mourners today are encouraged to keep objects that remind them of the dead. The Compassionate Friends, a grief therapy collective specializing in parents whose children have died, encourages the bereaved to communicate with the dead. One member of the group wrote a birthday letter to his son six years after the boy's death: "I haven't been able to part with the bicycle cart that I bought for you and your sister a few weeks before you died. . . . I feel close to you when I'm close to your favorite things."[19] Echoing Sally Hersey's prayers to her son Austin, this father found writing to his son an effective way to maintain a continuing relationship with the boy.

Communication with the dead occurs even more frequently online. Facebook and other social media platforms allow mourners to express their grief within a community of "friends" and "followers" whom the bereaved may or may not know personally. A high percentage of such posts directly address the dead, in a manner not unlike seventeenth-century elegies, except with emojis and random punctuation. In one study a sociologist examines twelve public Facebook memorials from 2010 and 2011, when Facebook had yet to be supplanted by Instagram and Snapchat as the social media platform of choice for teens and young adults. The twelve memorialized individuals represent a cross-section of young Americans, evenly distributed by sex, diverse in race and apparent class status, who died from a range of causes including disease, suicide, and gun violence.[20]

Of the 1,270 postings to the twelve memorial pages, 340 (27 percent) spoke with the dead. As one young man wrote to his deceased sixteen-year-old girlfriend, "you are on my mind again tonight. listening to a song that reminds me of you. just wishing I could see your face one more time. Its not easy to let go..but i know im never alone. see you soon babe." Another 267 (21 percent) requested guidance from the deceased or asked to be watched over, in effect hoping that the person would serve as a guardian angel, even when they did not use that term. A young woman addressed her deceased eighteen-year-old friend, "I know you are looking after me up in heaven. Hopefully, I can make sense of all this craziness one day. i know yr looking out for me and keeping me on track." Heavenly reunions were also a popular topic, with 49 postings (4 percent) explicitly making reference to meeting in the afterlife. And 26 messages (2 percent) described visitations from the deceased. These were not the unsettling hauntings of medieval European ghosts but rather comforting visits more like the presence cultists felt from the hovering spirits of departed friends. A woman posted to a deceased male friend, "I know that you sent that butterfly to attack my dress. It was totally you!! It worked. It totally made me laugh." Or, as another young woman instructed her dead friend, "Leave me hints to know when you are with me. i know you were with us the other night in pauls car. i could feel it. ☺"[21]

As grief professionals promote continuing relationships with the dead, and social media platforms facilitate postmortem communication, it is hardly a surprise that supernatural encounters with the dead are on the rise. According to a 2009 Pew Research Center survey of more than 2,000 U.S. adults, 18 percent say they have "seen or been in the presence of a ghost," double the figure from 1996. Likewise, 29 percent say they have felt "in touch with someone who has already died," up from 18 percent in 1996. In both categories, as one might expect in light of the cult of the dead's precedent, women are 25 percent more likely than men to report supernatural encounters.[22]

Women also make up a disproportionate share of the audience for *Long Island Medium*, the long-running show that updates Spiritualism for the twenty-first century. *Long Island Medium* was the highest-rated program on cable TV in 2012, and it's still going strong in its twelfth season.[23] Theresa Caputo, the eponymous medium, is easy to make fun of, with her white stiletto fingernails and peroxide blond bouffant. But it is clear that her spirit messages comfort the bereaved.

In one episode, two parents are in desperate pain after their daughter hanged herself in her closet. The father, in a blue blazer and button-down shirt, says, "I'll be the first to admit I'm skeptical of mediums." The mother is more open to Caputo's abilities: "I really am hoping to connect with my fifteen-year-old daughter Jenna." The medium reveals no great secret that she couldn't have known, but her spirit message profoundly moves the parents. Caputo channels Jenna: "She says, I need you to know that I take responsibility. She says, I don't want you to think or feel that you should have asked more questions or found out more. She says, I need you to stop doing that. It is not helping you to heal." The father nods vigorously, tears welling, mouth tight. "Am

I still skeptical? Not as much as I was when I walked in here today. She was able to tell us things that will put us at ease and certainly make us feel more peaceful."[24] The "she" in his last sentence is ambiguous. Who told him things that put him at ease? Jenna? Caputo? For the father, it is a distinction without a difference.

My point in drawing connections from the early modern period to today is not to flatten the many important differences between the two eras. Apostrophizing the dead in a puritan elegy is not the same as doing so in a Facebook post; Sally Hersey could not just slip into a meeting of the Compassionate Friends and feel right at home. But even though it's obvious, it bears repeating that the living almost always miss the dead, and some mourners will pursue continuing relationships with the deceased. For Euro-Americans before 1848, the dominant way of thinking about the afterlife combined Protestantism with popular beliefs that emerged from Protestantism. Today, a wider range of sources influence our reactions to death, but those sources are still filtered through similar impulses and questions.

I don't believe in ghosts. I don't believe in mediums. I don't even believe in God. So after my grandfather died, I was especially grateful for that voice mail he left. I didn't think I was going to meet "The Ghost" in heaven, so I was glad to experience the power of speaking with the dead.

NOTES

ABBREVIATIONS

AAS	American Antiquarian Society, Worcester, Massachusetts
BL	Department of Manuscripts, British Library, London
CHS	Connecticut Historical Society, Hartford
HL	Houghton Library, Harvard University, Cambridge, Massachusetts
HSP	Historical Society of Pennsylvania, Philadelphia
LC	Manuscript Division, Library of Congress, Washington, D.C.
MHS	Massachusetts Historical Society, Boston
NEHGS	New England Historic Genealogical Society, Boston
NYPL	Manuscripts and Archives Division, New York Public Library, New York
NYSL	Manuscripts and Special Collections, New York State Library, Albany
PEM	Peabody Essex Museum, Salem, Massachusetts
RIHS	Rhode Island Historical Society, Providence
RSA	Royal Society Archives, London
SL	Schlesinger Library, Radcliffe Institute, Cambridge, Massachusetts
SwL	Swedenborg Library, Bryn Athyn College, Bryn Athyn, Pennsylvania
UR	Rare Books and Special Collections, University of Rochester, Rochester, New York
WRHS	Western Reserve Historical Society, Cleveland

INTRODUCTION

1. Audio file in author's possession.

2. *A Revelation of the Extraordinary Visitation of Departed Spirits of Distinguished Men and Women of All Nations* (Philadelphia, 1869), 19. Emphasis in original.

3. *Upon the Death of the Virtuous and Religious Mrs. Lydia Minot* (Cambridge, Mass., 1668). The elegy does not state it was read in the graveyard, but that was the usual practice.

4. Jacques Le Goff, *The Birth of Purgatory*, trans. Arthur Goldhammer (Chicago, 1984); Peter Brown, *The Cult of the Saints: Its Rise and Function in Latin Christianity* (Chicago, 1981), ch. 4 ("very special dead").

5. Carlos M. N. Eire, *Reformations: The Early Modern World, 1450–1650* (New Haven, Conn., 2016), 754. On Protestantism's reevaluation of the dead, see Craig M. Koslofsky, *The Reformation of the Dead: Death and Ritual in Early Modern Germany, 1450–1700* (New York, 2000).

6. On early modern English ghosts, see Peter Marshall, *Mother Leakey and the Bishop: A Ghost Story* (Oxford, 2007); and Sasha Handley, *Visions of an Unseen World: Ghost Beliefs and Ghost Stories in Eighteenth-Century England* (London, 2007).

7. Allan Nevins and Milton Halsey Thomas, eds., *The Diary of George Templeton Strong*, 4 vols. (New York, 1952), 2:244–45 (entry of November 26, 1855).

8. Robert S. Cox, *Body and Soul: A Sympathetic History of American Spiritualism* (Charlottesville, Va., 2003), 2.

9. Ibid., 5–16; Jon Butler, "The Dark Ages of American Occultism, 1760–1848," in *The Occult in America: New Historical Perspectives*, ed. Howard Kerr and Charles L. Crow (Urbana, Ill., 1983), 58–78, esp. 71–72; Catherine L. Albanese, *A Republic of Mind and Spirit: A Cultural History of American Metaphysical Religion* (New Haven, Conn., 2007), ch. 4; John Lardas Modern, *Secularism in Antebellum America* (Chicago, 2011), 40n105; Molly McGarry, *Ghosts of Futures Past: Spiritualism and the Cultural Politics of Nineteenth-Century America* (Berkeley, 2008), 10, 45; Emily Ogden, *Credulity: A Cultural History of U.S. Mesmerism* (Chicago, 2018), 217–18. An exception is Ann Braude, who sees Spiritualism emerging from a combination of Davis's harmonial philosophy, liberal Protestantism's rejection of Calvinism, and sentimental fiction's portrayal of a nearby heaven. Braude, *Radical Spirits: Spiritualism and Women's Rights in Nineteenth-Century America*, 2nd ed. (1989; Bloomington, Ind., 2001), ch. 2.

10. I pay only fleeting attention to denominational differences. Such distinctions were undoubtedly important, but I have found interest in communicating with the dead across the denominational spectrum, from puritans to Unitarians, from Shakers to Methodists.

11. Erik R. Seeman, *Death in the New World: Cross-Cultural Encounters, 1492–1800* (Philadelphia, 2010); Seeman, *The Huron-Wendat Feast of the Dead: Indian-European Encounters in Early North America* (Baltimore, 2011). I will indicate in the notes opportunities for future research on comparisons among Euro-Americans, Amerindians, and African Americans.

12. On the nonlinearity of this narrative, see Alexandra Walsham, "The Reformation and 'The Disenchantment of the World' Reassessed," *Historical Journal* 51,2 (2008): 497–528.

13. Isaac Watts, *Death and Heaven; or, The Last Enemy Conquer'd, and Separate Spirits Made Perfect*, 2nd ed. (1722; London, 1724), 240. For laypeople's "Curiosity about the many Questions relating to the Invisible World," see Isaac Watts, *The World to Come; or, Discourses on the Joys or Sorrows of Departed Souls at Death, and the Glory or Terror of the Resurrection* (London, 1739), v.

14. *Oxford English Dictionary*, "cult," def. 2.a. Brown, *The Cult of the Saints*; Bridget Heal, *The Cult of the Virgin Mary in Early Modern Germany: Protestant and Catholic Piety, 1500–1648* (New York, 2007).

15. Susan E. Klepp, *Revolutionary Conceptions: Women, Fertility, and Family Limitation in America, 1760–1820* (Chapel Hill, 2009); Mary P. Ryan, *Cradle of the Middle Class: The Family in Oneida County, New York, 1790–1865* (New York, 1981); Steven Mintz and Susan Kellogg, *Domestic Revolutions: A Social History of American Family Life* (New York, 1988); Mary Louise Kete, *Sentimental Collaborations: Mourning and Middle-Class Identity in Nineteenth-Century America* (Durham, N.C., 2000).

16. Ann Douglas, *The Feminization of American Culture* (New York, 1977), 7 ("rigor"), 205 ("self-indulgence"); David S. Reynolds, *Faith in Fiction: The Emergence of Religious Literature in America* (Cambridge, Mass., 1981), 94 ("nonintellectual"). See also Barbara Welter, "The Feminization of American Religion, 1800–1860," in *Religion in American History: A Reader*, ed. Jon Butler and Harry S. Stout (New York, 1998), 160 (orig. pub. 1973).

17. Kete, *Sentimental Collaborations*; Karen Sánchez-Eppler, *Dependent States: The Child's Part in Nineteenth-Century American Culture* (Chicago, 2005), ch. 3; Lisa J. Shaver, *Beyond the Pulpit: Women's Rhetorical Roles in the Antebellum Religious Press* (Pittsburgh, 2012); Claudia Stokes, *The Altar at Home: Sentimental Literature and Nineteenth-Century American Religion* (Philadelphia, 2014).

18. Robert A. Orsi, *Between Heaven and Earth: The Religious Worlds People Make and the Scholars Who Study Them* (Princeton, N.J., 2005), 2.

19. Robert A. Orsi, *History and Presence* (Cambridge, Mass., 2016), 25, 4.

20. Alexandra Walsham, *Providence in Early Modern England* (New York, 1999); Jane Shaw, *Miracles in Enlightenment England* (New Haven, Conn., 2006); Marshall, *Mother Leakey and the Bishop*; Phyllis Mack, *Visionary Women: Ecstatic Prophecy in Seventeenth-Century England* (Berkeley, 1992).

21. David D. Hall, *Worlds of Wonder, Days of Judgment: Popular Religious Belief in Early New England* (New York, 1989); Douglas L. Winiarski, *Darkness Falls on the Land of Light: Experiencing Religious Awakenings in Eighteenth-Century New England* (Chapel Hill, 2017).

22. Ralph Houlbrooke, *Death, Religion, and the Family in England, 1480–1750* (Oxford, 1998); David E. Stannard, *The Puritan Way of Death: A Study in Religion, Culture, and Social Change* (New York, 1977); Gary Laderman, *The Sacred Remains: American Attitudes Toward Death, 1799–1883* (New Haven, Conn., 1996).

23. The exception being the small number who study ghosts. Peter Marshall, *Beliefs and the Dead in Reformation England* (Oxford, 2002), ch. 6; Owen Davies, *The Haunted: A Social History of Ghosts* (Basingstoke, Eng., 2007); Handley, *Visions of an Unseen World*.

24. On material religion, see David Morgan, ed., *Religion and Material Culture: The Matter of Belief* (London, 2010); David Morgan and Sally M. Promey, eds., *The Visual Culture of American Religions* (Berkeley, 2001).

25. Diarmaid MacCulloch, *The Reformation: A History* (New York, 2003), 237.

26. Colleen McDannell and Bernhard Lang, *Heaven: A History* (New Haven, Conn., 1988), ch. 7.

CHAPTER I

1. Increase Mather, *Cases of Conscience Concerning Evil Spirits Personating Men* (Boston, 1693), 19–20. This ghost sighting was also reported in the *Athenian Mercury* (London) 4,10 (October 31, 1691), 1. Mather's account was repeated verbatim in William Turner, *A Compleat History of the Most Remarkable Providences, Both of Judgment and Mercy, Which Have Hapned in This Present Age* (London, 1697), 38.

2. Jacques Le Goff, *The Birth of Purgatory*, trans. Arthur Goldhammer (Chicago, 1984).

3. Natalie Zemon Davis, "Ghosts, Kin, and Progeny: Some Features of Family Life in Early Modern France," *Daedalus* 106,2 (Spring 1977): 87–114; Jean-Claude Schmitt, *Ghosts in the Middle Ages: The Living and the Dead in Medieval Society*, trans. Teresa Lavender Fagan (Chicago, 1998).

4. Diarmaid MacCulloch, *The Reformation: A History* (New York, 2003), 12–13, 120–23, 576 (quotation).

5. Craig M. Koslofsky, *The Reformation of the Dead: Death and Ritual in Early Modern Germany, 1450–1700* (New York, 2000), 40–77, quotation at 42.

6. "The Book of Common Prayer, 1549," http://justus.anglican.org/resources/bcp/1549/Burial_1549.htm (accessed September 29, 2016).

7. "The Book of Common Prayer, 1552," http://justus.anglican.org/resources/bcp/1552/Burial_1552.htm (accessed September 29, 2016).

8. Quoted in Peter Marshall, *Beliefs and the Dead in Reformation England* (Oxford, 2002), 245.

9. Quoted in Keith Thomas, *Religion and the Decline of Magic* (New York, 1971), 591.

10. Bruce Gordon, "Malevolent Ghosts and Ministering Angels: Apparitions and Pastoral Care in the Swiss Reformation," in *The Place of the Dead: Death and Remembrance in Late Medieval and Early Modern Europe*, ed. Gordon and Peter Marshall (New York, 2000), esp. 102–4.

11. Quoted in Ronald Hutton, "The English Reformation and the Evidence of Folklore," *Past and Present* 148,1 (August 1995): 104.

12. Euan Cameron, *Enchanted Europe: Superstition, Reason, and Religion, 1250–1750* (New York, 2010), 188.

13. Ludwig Lavater, *Of Ghostes and Spirites, Walking by Night*, trans. Robert Harrison (1572; London, 1596), B2r, 163.

14. Ibid., 9, 14.

15. Others who saw women as particularly susceptible to imagining apparitions include Anthony Anderson, *The Sheild of Our Safetie* (London, 1581), H2r; and Reginald Scot, *The Discoverie of Witchcraft* (London, 1584), 461–62.

16. For example, William Perkins, *A Golden Chaine; or, The Description of Theologie Containing the Order of the Causes of Salvation and Damnation* (1591; Cambridge, Eng., 1600), 515; Andrew Willet, *Syopsis Papismi; that is, A Generall Viewe of Papistry* (London, 1592), 305–6; and John Deacon, *Dialogicall Discourses of Spirits and Divils* (London, 1601), 121–26.

17. John Aubrey, *Miscellanies*, 2nd ed. (1696; London, 1721), 86–87.

18. Frederick S. Boas, ed., *The Diary of Thomas Crosfield* (Oxford, 1935), 17.

19. John, Earl of Orrery, *The Letters of Pliny the Younger with Observations on Each Letter*, 2 vols. (London, 1751).

20. Quotations in Marshall, *Beliefs and the Dead*, 251–52.

21. Peter Marshall, *Mother Leakey and the Bishop: A Ghost Story* (Oxford, 2007), 52.

22. David Person, *Varieties; or, A Surveigh of Rare and Excellent Matters, Necessary and Delectable for All Sorts of Persons* (London, 1635), 165. See also the 1627 account of the return of the Duke of Buckingham's father in BL, Lansdowne MS 207 B/2 folio 253; and a 1650 case in Ann Fanshawe, *Memoirs of Lady Fanshawe* (London, 1829), 84–85.

23. This and the following paragraph are indebted to Steven Shapin, *The Scientific Revolution* (Chicago, 1996), ch. 2.

24. Francis Bacon, *Of the Proficience and Advancement of Learning*, ed. B. Montagu (London, 1840), 45. On the use of the discourse of "old wives' tales" to discredit ideas attributed to women and the unlearned, see Adam Fox, *Oral and Literate Culture in England, 1500–1700* (Oxford, 2000), ch. 3.

25. Thomas Hobbes, *Leviathan*, ed. C. B. Macpherson (London, 1968), 658.

26. Michael Hunter, "The Decline of Magic: Challenge and Response in Early Enlightenment England," *Historical Journal* 55,2 (June 2012): 399–425.

27. Stuart Clark, *Thinking with Demons: The Idea of Witchcraft in Early Modern Europe* (Oxford, 1997), ch. 19; Sarah Rivett, *The Science of the Soul in Colonial New England* (Chapel Hill, 2011).

28. Quoted in Michael P. Winship, *Seers of God: Puritan Providentialism in the Restoration and Early Enlightenment* (Baltimore, 1996), 61.

29. Alexandra Walsham, *Providence in Early Modern England* (New York, 1999); David D. Hall, *Worlds of Wonder, Days of Judgment: Popular Religious Belief in Early New England* (New York, 1989), ch. 2.

30. Quoted in Winship, *Seers of God*, 61.

31. Sasha Handley, *Visions of an Unseen World: Ghost Beliefs and Ghost Stories in Eighteenth-Century England* (London, 2007), 26–27; Cameron, *Enchanted Europe*, 270–84; Clark, *Thinking with Demons*, 296–300. David Hall mistakenly asserts that "in the cool mood of Restoration England, Anglicans and scientists renounced visions, dreams, and other unseen wonders, like the drummer boy of Tidworth [*sic*], as tricks of the imagination." Hall, *Worlds of Wonder*, 106. But this section shows that many Anglican clergymen remained interested in "unseen wonders." Scientists likewise did so; see, for example, Robert Boyle, *The Divell of Mascon; or, A True Relation of the Chief Things Which an Unclean Spirit Did, and Said at Mascon in Burgundy*, 4th ed. (Oxford, 1669).

32. Bodin said it was a "friend" who interacted with the spirit, but historians assume the spirit communicated with Bodin himself. Robin Briggs, "Dubious Messengers: Bodin's Daemon, the Spirit World, and the Sadducees," in *Angels in the Early Modern World*, ed. Peter Marshall and Alexandra Walsham (New York, 2006), 168.

33. Henry More, *An Antidote Against Atheism; or, An Appeal to the Naturall Faculties of the Minde of Man, Whether There Be Not a God* (London, 1655), 252.

34. Henry More, *The Immortality of the Soul, So Farre Forth as It Is Demonstrable from the Knowledge of Nature and the Light of Reason* (London, 1659), B2r.

35. Ibid., 109, 20, 19, 12–13.

36. Ibid., 286, 290.

37. On the popularity of the postmortem pact in medieval Europe, see Nancy Mandeville Caciola, *Afterlives: The Return of the Dead in the Middle Ages* (Ithaca, N.Y., 2016), 2.

38. More, *Immortality of the Soul*, 293–94.

39. Marjorie Hope Nicholson, ed., *Conway Letters: The Correspondence of Anne, Viscountess Conway, Henry More, and Their Friends, 1642–1684* (London, 1930), 214.

40. On colonists' familiarity with the Drummer of Tedworth, see Hall, *Worlds of Wonder*, 72.

41. Joseph Glanvill, *A Blow at Modern Sadducism: In Some Philosophical Considerations About Witchcraft* (London, 1668), B3v.

42. Joseph Glanvill, *Saducismus Triumphatus; or, Full and Plain Evidence Concerning Witches and Apparitions* (1681; London, 1689), 399–429, 453–63. I use the 1689 edition because it was the first to be paginated continuously.

43. Ibid., 419, 399, 410.

44. Ibid., 408.

45. For example, *A New Ballad of the Midwives Ghost* (London, 1680); *An Answer to the Unfortunate Lady Who Hang'd Herself in Dispair* (London, 1680s?); and *The Disturbed Ghost; or, The Wonderful Appearance of the Ghost, or Spirit of Edward Avon* (London, 1670s?).

46. Glanvill, *Saducismus Triumphatus*, 412.

47. The others are in ibid., 406–7, 413–14.

48. Michael Hunter, "New Light on the 'Drummer of Tedworth': Conflicting Narratives of Witchcraft in Restoration England," *Historical Research* 78, 201 (August 2005): 311–53, esp.

312–13; Jonathan I. Israel, *Radical Enlightenment: Philosophy and the Making of Modernity, 1650–1750* (New York, 2001), 399.

49. John Webster, *The Displaying of Supposed Witchcraft: Wherein Is Affirmed That There Are Many Sorts of Deceivers and Impostors* (London, 1677), 81. See also Rivett, *Science of the Soul*, 240–42; and Thomas Harmon Jobe, "The Devil in Restoration Science: The Glanvill-Webster Witchcraft Debate," *Isis* 72,3 (September 1981): 342–56.

50. Webster, *Displaying of Supposed Witchcraft*, 294, 311.

51. Increase Mather, *An Essay for the Recording of Illustrious Providences* (Boston, 1684), unpaginated preface. For letters from seven of Mather's correspondents, see "The Mather Papers," *Collections of the Massachusetts Historical Society*, 4th ser., 8 (1868): 58–61, 285–87, 306–7, 361–62, 466–69, 475–76, 480–81.

52. Mather, *Illustrious Providences*, 202. Perhaps Mather did not know of the 1673 ghost of a woman from Portsmouth, Rhode Island, whose words, as reported by her brother, were entered into legal testimony. Elaine Forman Crane, *Killed Strangely: The Death of Rebecca Cornell* (Ithaca, N.Y., 2002).

53. "Mather Papers," *Collections*, 58.

54. Mather, *Illustrious Providences*, 203, 220, 241, 243.

55. Cotton Mather, *The Wonders of the Invisible World: Observations As Well Historical As Theological, Upon the Nature, the Number, and the Operations of the Devils* (Boston, 1693), 79; Cotton Mather to Richard Waller, November 26, 1712, RSA, EL/M2/30, p. 1.

56. Mather, *Wonders of the Invisible World*, 79–80.

57. Ibid., 80.

58. Ibid., 81.

59. *Athenian Mercury* (London) 9,29 (March 21, 1693).

60. Mather to Waller, November 26, 1712, p. 3.

61. Evidence for this belief goes back to twelfth-century London. On dying declarations as an exception to the hearsay rule in common law, see John Henry Wigmore, *A Treatise on the Anglo-American System of Evidence in Trials at Common Law*, 2nd ed., 5 vols. (Boston, 1923), 3:160–87, quotation at 160.

62. Mather to Waller, November 26, 1712, p. 3.

63. Mather, *Wonders of the Invisible World*, 79–81; Cotton Mather, *Magnalia Christi Americana; or, The Ecclesiastical History of New-England, from Its First Planting in the Year 1620, Unto the Year of Our Lord, 1698* (London, 1702), bk. 6, pp. 77–78; Increase Mather, *A Disquisition Concerning the State of the Souls of Men, (Especially of Good Men) When Separated from Their Bodies* (Boston, 1707), 25; Reiner Smolinski, ed., *The Threefold Paradise of Cotton Mather: An Edition of "Triparadisus"* (Athens, Ga., 1995), 115.

64. In England, the Beacon story appeared in, for example, Turner, *Compleat History*, 34–35; and *Philosophical Transactions of the Royal Society* 29 (1714–16): 66–67.

65. Historians who have examined the "Curiosa Americana" have not discussed the seven-page letter on ghosts. See Susan Scott Parrish, *American Curiosity: Cultures of Natural History in the Colonial British Atlantic World* (Chapel Hill, 2006), 39–40; David Levin, "Giants in the Earth: Science and the Occult in Cotton Mather's Letters to the Royal Society," *William and Mary Quarterly* 45,4 (October 1988): 751–70; and Otho T. Beall Jr., "Cotton Mather's Early 'Curiosa Americana' and the Boston Philosophical Society of 1683," *William and Mary Quarterly* 18,3 (July 1961): 360–72.

66. Mather to Waller, November 26, 1712, pp. 2–4.

67. *Diary of Cotton Mather, 1681–1708* (Boston, 1911), 129.

68. *Oxford English Dictionary*, "ephialtes," def. 1, and "incubus," defs. 1 and 2.

69. *Diary of Cotton Mather*, 129–30.

70. Mather, *Disquisition Concerning the State of the Souls*, 26. Cotton Mather also discussed the case in his 1712 letter to the Royal Society, and in Smolinski, ed., *Threefold Paradise*, 116–17.

71. Schmitt, *Ghosts in the Middle Ages*, 156–58.

72. Mather, *Disquisition Concerning the State of Souls*, 27–28.

73. Mather to Waller, November 26, 1712, p. 7.

74. Mather, *Disquisition Concerning the State of Souls*, 27–29.

75. Ballads are also a deep repository of English ghost beliefs. See "Broadside Ballads Online from the Bodleian Libraries," http://ballads.bodleian.ox.ac.uk/ and the "University of California, Santa Barbara, English Broadside Ballad Archive," https://ebba.english.ucsb.edu/.

76. To compare with ghost belief among Africans and African Americans, see Newbell Niles Puckett, *Folk Beliefs of the Southern Negro* (1926; Montclair, N.J., 1968), 79–166; Albert J. Raboteau, *Slave Religion: The "Invisible Institution" in the Antebellum South* (New York, 1978), 13, 31, 83; Sylvia R. Frey and Betty Wood, *Come Shouting to Zion: African American Protestantism in the American South and British Caribbean to 1830* (Chapel Hill, 1998), 23; Jason R. Young, *Rituals of Resistance: African Atlantic Religion in Kongo and the Lowcountry South in the Era of Slavery* (Baton Rouge, 2007), 149; James H. Sweet, *Recreating Africa: Culture, Kinship, and Religion in the African-Portuguese World, 1441–1770* (Chapel Hill, 2003), 178; and Vincent Brown, *The Reaper's Garden: Death and Power in the World of Atlantic Slavery* (Cambridge, Mass., 2008); among Amerindians, see Experience Mayhew, *Indian Converts; or, Some Account of the Lives and Dying Speeches of a Considerable Number of the Christianized Indians of Martha's Vineyard* (London, 1727), 241; Constance Crosby, "From Myth to History, or Why King Philip's Ghost Walks Abroad," in *The Recovery of Meaning: Historical Archaeology in the Eastern United States*, ed. Mark P. Leone and Parker B. Potter Jr. (Washington, D.C., 1988), 183–209; and Patricia E. Rubertone, *Grave Undertakings: An Archaeology of Roger Williams and the Narragansett Indians* (Washington, D.C., 2001), 165–66.

77. John Hale, *A Modest Enquiry into the Nature of Witchcraft* (Boston, 1702), 46.

78. Mather, *Magnalia Christi Americana*, bk. 6, p. 77 ("often seen," "abroad at Sea," "much Notice"); Smolinski, *Threefold Paradise*, 117 ("Soul of the Deceased").

79. Mather, *Magnalia Christi Americana*, bk. 6, p. 66.

80. Bernard Rosenthal, ed., *Records of the Salem Witch-Hunt* (New York, 2009), 245, 616. Mary Beth Norton is uniquely keen in her analysis of the decisive role the returned dead played in Salem. My account builds on hers, with greater attention to the context of popular and learned ghost beliefs. Norton, *In the Devil's Snare: The Salem Witchcraft Crisis of 1692* (New York, 2002).

81. Cotton Mather, *Memorable Providences, Relating to Witchcraft and Possessions* (Boston, 1689), unpaginated Letter to the Reader. This book was reprinted in London in 1691.

82. Richard Baxter, *The Certainty of the Worlds of Spirits* (London, 1691), 80.

83. Ibid., 61–62.

84. Handley, *Visions of an Unseen World*, 41–47.

85. *Athenian Mercury* (London) 4,10 (October 31, 1691).

86. *Athenian Mercury* (London) 7,28 (July 2, 1692).

87. Norton, *In the Devil's Snare*, 120.

88. Rosenthal, *Records of the Salem Witch-Hunt*, 505.

89. Pendle and Leicester: Malcolm Gaskill, "Witchcraft Trials in England," in *The Oxford Handbook of Witchcraft in Early Modern Europe and Colonial America*, ed. Brian P. Levack (New York, 2013), 294. Chelmsford: *A True Relation of the Araignment of Thirty Witches at Chensford [sic] in Essex* (London, 1645). Hartford: John Demos, *Entertaining Satan: Witchcraft and the Culture of Early New England* (New York, 1982), 405; Walter W. Woodward, *Prospero's America: John Winthrop Jr., Alchemy, and the Creation of New England Culture, 1606–1676* (Chapel Hill, 2010), 226–35.

90. Norton, *In the Devil's Snare*, 121.

91. Rosenthal, *Records of the Salem Witch-Hunt*, 245–46.

92. See, for example, the woodcut that adorns *A New Ballad of the Midwives Ghost*.

93. Webster, *Displaying of Supposed Witchcraft*, 311. See also Handley, *Visions of an Unseen World*, 56–63; and Todd Butler, "The Haunting of Isabell Binnington: Ghosts of Murder, Texts, and Law in Restoration England," *Journal of British Studies* 50,2 (April 2011): 248–76.

94. Rosenthal, *Records of the Salem Witch-Hunt*, 245–46.

95. See, for example, ibid., 248.

96. Ibid., 293 ("As Red As"); Deodat Lawson, *Christ's Fidelity the Only Shield Against Satan's Malignity*, 2nd ed. (London, 1704), 99 ("Blood would fly").

97. Rosenthal, *Records of the Salem Witch-Hunt*, 293, 297.

98. Ibid., 360, 393, 616. See also Lawson, *Christ's Fidelity*, 98–100.

99. Mather, *Wonders of the Invisible World*, 97.

100. Norton, *In the Devil's Snare*, 303.

101. Joseph Ennemoser, *The History of Magic*, trans. William Howitt, 2 vols. (London, 1854), 2:455.

102. Rosenthal, *Records of the Salem Witch-Hunt*, 597. For additional evidence of divination, see ibid., 679; and Hale, *Modest Enquiry*, 133.

103. Mather, *Cases of Conscience*, 66. See also [Samuel Willard], *Some Miscellany Observations on Our Present Debates Respecting Witchcrafts* (Philadelphia, 1692), esp. 12.

104. Robert Calef, *More Wonders of the Invisible World* (1700; Salem, Mass., 1796), 227.

105. Rosenthal, *Records of the Salem Witch-Hunt*, 703.

106. On the scholarly tradition in which Salem marks the "threshold of . . . American modernity," see Sarah Rivett, "Our Salem, Our Selves," *William and Mary Quarterly* 65,3 (July 2008): 498. This is often expressed most baldly in textbooks. For example: "the events in Salem . . . accelerated a commitment among prominent colonists to finding scientific explanations for natural events like comets and illnesses, rather than attributing them to magic." Eric Foner, *Give Me Liberty: An American History*, 2 vols., Seagull 3rd ed. (New York, 2012), 1:110.

CHAPTER 2

1. William Witherel, *Upon the Immature Death of that Virtuous and Truly Religious Young Woman Elizabeth Stetson* (Boston, 1682).

2. Colleen McDannell and Bernhard Lang, *Heaven: A History* (New Haven, Conn., 1988), ch. 7.

3. Nathaniel Morton, *New-Englands Memoriall; or, A Brief Relation of the Most Memorable and Remarkable Passages of the Providence of God* (Cambridge, Mass., 1669), 155, 153.

4. Scholars have translated this as "impersonation" or "personification," but each of those terms has other meanings, so I will use the Greek "prosopopoeia."

5. Quintilian, *The Orator's Education*, trans. Donald A. Russell, 4 vols. (Cambridge, Mass., 2001), 4:51 (bk. 9, ch. 2, sections 29–30).

6. Ibid., 4:51–53 (9.2.30–33).

7. Ibid., 4:55 (9.2.38–39).

8. Quoted in Anna Linton, "Blithe Spirits: Voices from the Other Side in Early Modern German Lutheran Funeral Poetry," in *Early Modern Ghosts*, ed. John Newton and Jo Bath (Durham, Eng., 2002), 19.

9. Quoted in Gregory S. Johnston, "Rhetorical Personification of the Dead in 17th-Century German Funeral Music," *Journal of Musicology* 9,2 (Spring 1991): 187–88. See also Anna Carrdus, "Consolatory Dialogue in Devotional Writings by Men and Women of Early Modern Protestant Germany," *Modern Language Review* 93,2 (April 1998): 415.

10. Quoted in Carrdus, "Consolatory Dialogue," 418–19, 417. All translations from this article are by Jake Newsome, to whom I am grateful.

11. Peter Sherlock, *Monuments and Memory in Early Modern England* (Aldershot, Eng., 2008), 83, 88. More may be found in John Stow, *A Survay of London Contayning the Originall, Antiquity, Increase, Moderne Estate and Description of That Citie* (London, 1598).

12. David Cressy, *Birth, Marriage, and Death: Ritual, Religion, and the Life-Cycle in Tudor and Stuart England* (New York, 1997), 393. See also Raymond A. Anselment, "'The Teares of Nature': Seventeenth-Century Parental Bereavement," *Modern Philology* 91,1 (August 1993): 26–53.

13. David Kennedy, *Elegy* (New York, 2007), 4. See also Dennis Kay, *Melodious Tears: The English Funeral Elegy from Spenser to Milton* (Oxford, 1990), 1–6; and Lorna Clymer, "The Funeral Elegy in Early Modern Britain: A Brief History," in *The Oxford Handbook of the Elegy*, ed. Karen Weisman (New York, 2010), 174.

14. Clymer, "Funeral Elegy," 174.

15. Peter Marshall, *Beliefs and the Dead in Reformation England* (Oxford, 2002), 273.

16. John Phillips, *The Life and Death of Sir Phillip Sidney* (London, 1587), A3r, B4v. Kay discusses this poem but does not analyze the fact that Sidney speaks "from my grave." Kay, *Melodious Tears*, 69–70.

17. Robert Dallington, *A Booke of Epitaphes Made Upon the Death of the Right Worshipfull Sir William Buttes* (London, 1583); Phillips, *Life and Death of Sir Phillip Sidney*; Robert Fletcher, *A Briefe and Familiar Epistle Shewing His Majesties Most Lawfull, Honourable and Just Title to All His Kingdomes* (London, 1603); Joshua Sylvester, *Lachrymae Lachrymarum; or, The Spirit of Teares, Distilled for the Untymely Death of the Incomparable Prince Panaretus* (London, 1612); William Drummond, *To the Exequies of the Honourable Sir Antoyne Alexander, Knight: A Pastorall Elegie* (Edinburgh, 1638); *Justa Edouardo King Naufrago, ab Amicis Moerentibus, Amoris* (Cambridge, Eng., 1638).

18. Quoted in Andrea Brady, *English Funerary Elegy in the Seventeenth Century: Laws in Mourning* (Basingstoke, Eng., 2006), 48. See also Henry King's elegies to his wife, who died in 1624. G. W. Pigman III, *Grief and English Renaissance Elegy* (New York, 1985), 96–102.

19. Dallington, *Booke of Epitaphes*, B8v.

20. William Alexander, Earl of Stirling, *An Elegie on the Death of Prince Henrie* (London, 1613), A3v; Patrike Mackgueir, *Teares for the Death of the Most Gracious Prince Lodouicke, Duke of Richmond and Lenox* (London, 1624).

21. Leonard D. Tourney, "Joseph Hall and the *Anniversaries*," *Papers on Language and Literature* 13,1 (Winter 1977): 26. See also Tourney, *Joseph Hall* (Boston, 1979), 72–76.

22. Barbara Kiefer Lewalski, *Donne's* Anniversaries *and the Poetry of Praise: The Creation of a Symbolic Mode* (Princeton, N.J., 1973), 224.

23. Ramie Targoff, "Traducing the Soul: Donne's *Second Anniversarie*," *PMLA* 121,5 (October 2006): 1493–1508.

24. John Donne, *The Second Anniversarie of the Progres of the Soule* (1612; London, 1621), E2v.

25. Igor Kopytoff, "The Cultural Biography of Things: Commoditization as Process," in *The Social Life of Things: Commodities in Cultural Perspective*, ed. Arjun Appadurai (Cambridge, Eng., 1986), 66–67.

26. The only extended treatment of speaking with the dead in New England elegy is Adrian Chastain Weimer, "Heaven and Heavenly Piety in Colonial American Elegies," in *The Church, the Afterlife, and the Fate of the Soul*, ed. Peter Clarke and Tony Claydon (Woodbridge, Eng., 2009), 258–67. See also Jeffrey A. Hammond, *The American Puritan Elegy: A Literary and Cultural Study* (New York, 2000), 189–90, 195–96; and Matthew P. Brown, *The Pilgrim and the Bee: Reading Rituals and Book Culture in Early New England* (Philadelphia, 2007), 146, 149, 167–69.

27. Kay, *Melodious Tears*, 9–14.

28. John Canup, *Out of the Wilderness: The Emergence of an American Identity in Colonial New England* (Middletown, Conn., 1990).

29. See, for example, Kenneth B. Murdock, ed., *Handkerchiefs from Paul: Being Pious and Consolatory Verses of Puritan Massachusetts* (Cambridge, Mass., 1927), lxii–lxiii.

30. Hammond, *American Puritan Elegy*, 209.

31. Joanne van der Woude, "Puritan Scrabble," *Common-Place* 11,4 (July 2011).

32. William J. Scheick, "Tombless Virtue and Hidden Text: New England Puritan Funeral Elegies," in *Puritan Poets and Poetics: Seventeenth-Century American Poetry in Theory and Practice*, ed. Peter White (University Park, Pa., 1985), 286–302, quotation at 296.

33. *On the Death of Beulah Worfield, Who Departed This Life September 26, 1776* (n.p., 1776).

34. Brown, *Pilgrim and the Bee*, 139.

35. Gordon E. Geddes, *Welcome Joy: Death in Puritan New England* (Ann Arbor, 1981), chs. 5 and 6; David E. Stannard, *The Puritan Way of Death: A Study in Religion, Culture, and Social Change* (New York, 1977), 109–22.

36. Harrison T. Meserole, ed., *Seventeenth-Century American Poetry* (Garden City, N.Y., 1968), 488.

37. John Warren, *A Monody on the Death of the Hon. Thomas Russell, Esq.* (Boston, 1796).

38. Geddes, *Welcome Joy*, 131.

39. *A Directory for the Publike Worship of God Throughout the Three Kingdoms of Scotland, England, and Ireland* (Edinburgh, 1645), 58. Emphasis added.

40. Brown, *Pilgrim and the Bee*, 149.

41. Morton, *New-Englands Memoriall*, 154.

42. Hammond, *American Puritan Elegy*, 190.

43. "Diary of Samuel Sewall, 1674–1729," *Collections of the Massachusetts Historical Society*, 5th ser., 5 (1878): xxvii.

44. The two original poems and the third combined one are in Peter White, *Benjamin Tompson, Colonial Bard: A Critical Edition* (University Park, Pa., 1980), 168–75. The third was printed as Benjamin Tompson, *A Neighbour's Tears Sprinkled on the Dust of the Amiable Virgin, Mrs. Rebekah Sewall* (Boston, 1710).

45. Geddes, *Welcome Joy*, 131; Stannard, *Puritan Way of Death*, 113. The practice had roots in England. Marshall, *Beliefs and the Dead*, 273; Ralph Houlbrooke, *Death, Religion, and the Family in England, 1480–1750* (Oxford, 1998), 328; Kay, *Melodious Tears*, 61, 238.

46. *Oxford English Dictionary*, "hearse," def. 3.

47. Cotton Mather, *A Poem Dedicated to the Memory of the Reverend and Excellent Mr. Urian Oakes* (Boston, 1682), A2r.

48. Meserole, *Seventeenth-Century American Poetry*, 489. Cotton Mather also mentions that the Muses "saw these Lines upon his Hearse," referring to an elegy he wrote about John Wilson. Cotton Mather, *Magnalia Christi Americana; or, The Ecclesiastical History of New-England, from Its First Planting in the Year 1620, Unto the Year of Our Lord, 1698*, 7 vols. (London, 1702), 3:50.

49. Cotton Mather, *An Elegy on the Much-To-Be-Deplored Death of That Never-To-Be-Forgotten Person, the Reverend Mr. Nathanael Collins* (Boston, 1685), 2.

50. M. Halsey Thomas, ed., *The Diary of Samuel Sewall, 1674–1729*, 2 vols. (New York, 1973), 1:66.

51. Houlbrooke, *Death, Religion, and the Family*, 260.

52. Max Cavitch, *American Elegy: The Poetry of Mourning from the Puritans to Whitman* (Minneapolis, 2007).

53. Benjamin Franklin, "Silence Dogood, No. 7," in *The Papers of Benjamin Franklin*, ed. Leonard W. Labaree (New Haven, Conn., 1959), 1:26. Emphasis in original.

54. *New-England Courant*, November 5–12, 1722, quoted in Cavitch, *American Elegy*, 34.

55. Quoted in ibid., 2.

56. Scheick, "Tombless Virtue," 298; Brown, *Pilgrim and the Bee*, 139, 146, 148, 159–60; Cavitch, *American Elegy*, 34.

57. Brown, *Pilgrim and the Bee*, 159–60, 148.

58. *Oxford English Dictionary*, "to wait on or upon," def. 14.

59. Clare Gittings writes that "items buried with the dead" caused "considerable consternation among the [Protestant] clergy." Gittings, *Death, Burial, and the Individual in Early Modern England* (London, 1984), 111. See the numerous English Reformation writers who mocked burial in a monk's robe as a way for Catholics to gain forgiveness for sins. For example, Thomas Russell, ed., *The Works of the English and Scottish Reformers* (London, 1829), 312.

60. Hammond, *American Puritan Elegy*, 47 ("hundreds").

61. Geddes, *Welcome Joy*, 146.

62. From *Upon the Death of the Virtuous and Religious Mrs. Lydia Minot* (Cambridge, Mass., 1668) to Samuel Buell, *The Following Lines Were Occasioned by the Death of Richard Brown* (New London, Conn., 1770). This is image number 18 in Elizabeth Carroll Reilly, *A Dictionary of Colonial American Printers' Ornaments and Illustrations* (Worcester, Mass., 1975), 7.

63. *Upon the Death of the Virtuous and Religious Mrs. Lydia Minot*.

64. Murdock, ed., *Handkerchiefs from Paul*, xvi, 20, 7.

65. Samuel Sewall likewise kept a journal in which he copied elegies and epitaphs. Brown, *Pilgrim and the Bee*, 170–78.

66. Thomas, *The Diary of Samuel Sewall*, 1:429, 1:34.

67. Quincy's location is strongly suggested by items Sewall asked him to purchase: a "Turkish Alcoran, 2d hand" and a "Map of London" (Thomas, *The Diary of Samuel Sewall*, 1:34).

68. [Joshua Moodey], *Lamentations Upon the Never Enough Bewailed Death of the Reverend Mr. John Reiner* (Boston, 1677).

69. Thomas, *The Diary of Samuel Sewall*, 1:553–54.

70. Abram Van Engen, *Sympathetic Puritans: Calvinist Fellow Feeling in Early New England* (New York, 2015), 2. The author does briefly examine one of Anne Bradstreet's elegies (19).

71. Most historians are no longer persuaded by Lawrence Stone's argument that early modern parents did not develop intense bonds with their children because high childhood mortality made it "folly to invest too much emotional capital in such ephemeral beings." Stone, *The Family, Sex, and Marriage in England, 1500–1800*, abridged ed. (New York, 1979), 82. For the contrary view, see Erik R. Seeman, *Pious Persuasions: Laity and Clergy in Eighteenth-Century New England* (Baltimore, 1999), 58–60.

72. Robert Daly, *God's Altar: The World and the Flesh in Puritan Poetry* (Berkeley, 1978), 111, 112.

73. Randall R. Mawer, by contrast, claims that Bradstreet's elegies are practically "heretical" for their "implicit rebellion" against God's will. Mawer, "'Farewell Dear Babe': Bradstreet's Elegy for Elizabeth," *Early American Literature* 15,1 (Spring 1980): 29–41, quotations at 36. More recent scholarship rejects such an interpretation. For example, Jennifer Lynn Holley, "The Child Elegy" (PhD diss., University of Connecticut, 2012), 65–69.

74. Meserole, *Seventeenth-Century American Poetry*, 31.

75. *Oxford English Dictionary*, "content," def. 1.b., "heart's content."

76. Janice Miller Potter, "Anne Bradstreet in Winter," *PoemShape*, https://poemshape .wordpress.com/tag/in-memory-of-my-dear-grandchild-anne-bradstreet/ (accessed May 20, 2016).

77. Meserole, *Seventeenth-Century American Poetry*, 34.

78. Ibid., 382. See also Hammond, *American Puritan Elegy*, 152.

79. Ichabod Wiswell, *Upon the Death of that Reverend and Aged Man of God, Mr. Samuel Arnold, Pastor of the Church at Marshfield* (Boston, 1693).

80. Morton, *New-Englands Memoriall*, 129.

81. Weimer, "Heaven and Heavenly Piety in Colonial American Elegies," 259.

82. *Oxford English Dictionary*, "shade," def. 6.a. This sense of the word first appeared in 1616.

83. Thomas Beedome, *Poems, Divine and Humane* (London, 1641), unpaginated (document image 52).

84. Dallington, *Booke of Epitaphes*, B8v; Alexander, *An Elegie on the Death of Prince Henrie*, A3v; Mackgueir, *Teares for the Death of the Most Gracious Prince Lodouicke*.

85. Mather, *A Poem Dedicated to the Memory*, 1.

86. Perseus Digital Library, definition "praefica" from Lewis and Short, *A Latin Dictionary*, http://www.perseus.tufts.edu/hopper/morph?la=la&l=praefica (accessed May 23, 2016).

87. Mather, *A Poem Dedicated to the Memory*, 2.

88. Mather, *An Elegy on the Much-To-Be Deplored Death*, 15–16, 18.

89. Cotton Mather, *Corderius Americanus: An Essay upon the Good Education of Children* (Boston, 1708), 32.

90. The quotation is from Cotton Mather, *Cælestinus: A Conversation in Heaven, Quickened and Assisted, with Discoveries of Things in the Heavenly World* (Boston, 1723), 49.

91. Mather, *Corderius Americanus*, 32.

92. Biographical data from the elegy and Find a Grave, "Lydia Butler Minot," https:// www.findagrave.com/memorial/123835251 (accessed December 2, 2017).

93. *Upon the Death of the Virtuous and Religious Mrs. Lydia Minot*.

94. Seeman, *Pious Persuasions*, 74–77.

95. Amy M. E. Morris, *Popular Measures: Poetry and Church Order in Seventeenth-Century Massachusetts* (Newark, Del., 2005), 72.

96. McDannell and Lang, *Heaven*, 145–56. See also Philip C. Almond, *Afterlife: A History of Life After Death* (Ithaca, N.Y., 2016); Mark S. Schantz, *Awaiting the Heavenly Country: The Civil War and America's Culture of Death* (Ithaca, N.Y., 2008); and Gary Scott Smith, *Heaven in the American Imagination* (New York, 2011).

97. Witherel, *Upon the Immature Death.*

98. On ministerial efforts to rein in their parishioners' grief, see Seeman, *Pious Persuasions*, 47–50.

99. Morton, *New-Englands Memoriall*, 148.

100. Walter Hughes, "'Meat Out of the Eater': Panic and Desire in American Puritan Poetry," in *Engendering Men: The Question of Male Feminist Criticism*, ed. Joseph A. Boone and Michael Cadden (New York, 1990), 102–21.

101. White, *Benjamin Tompson*, 168.

CHAPTER 3

1. Birgit Meyer et al., "The Origin and Mission of *Material Religion*," *Religion* 40,3 (July 2010): 209. Emphasis in original. See also Sally M. Promey, ed., *Sensational Religion: Sensory Cultures in Material Practice* (New Haven, Conn., 2014); and Dick Houtman and Birgit Meyer, eds., *Things: Religion and the Question of Materiality* (New York, 2012).

2. An important exception: Mark A. Peterson, "Puritanism and Refinement in Early New England: Reflections on Communion Silver," *William and Mary Quarterly* 58,2 (April 2001): 307–46.

3. Such Catholic objects, according to Caroline Walker Bynum, don't just gesture toward the divine, they "lift matter toward God and reveal God through matter." This is beyond what Protestant gravestones did. Bynum, *Christian Materiality: An Essay on Religion in Late Medieval Europe* (New York, 2011), 35.

4. This gloss of David Morgan's work is from Birgit Meyer and Dick Houtman, "Introduction: Material Religion—How Things Matter," in *Things*, ed. Houtman and Meyer, 12. See Morgan, *Visual Piety: A History and Theory of Popular Religious Images* (Berkeley, 1998); and Morgan, *The Sacred Gaze: Religious Visual Culture in Theory and Practice* (Berkeley, 2005).

5. Cotton Mather, *Cœlestinus: A Conversation in Heaven, Quickened and Assisted, with Discoveries of Things in the Heavenly World* (Boston, 1723), 49.

6. Morgan, *Visual Piety*, 3.

7. Quoted in Peter Marshall, *Beliefs and the Dead in Reformation England* (Oxford, 2002), 298.

8. George Strode, *The Anatomie of Mortalitie*, 2nd ed. (1618; London, 1632). See also George Abbot, *A Sermon Preached at Westminster, May 26, 1608* (London, 1608), 3; Nicholas Byfield, *The Cure of the Feare of Death: Shewing the Course Christians May Take To Bee Delivered from These Feares About Death* (London, 1618), 27; and Francis Rodes, *Life After Death: Containing Many Religious Instructions and Godly Exhortations* (London, 1622), 74.

9. John Weever, *Ancient Funerall Monuments within the United Monarchie of Great Britaine, Ireland, and the Ilands Adjacent* (London, 1631), 8, 42. See also John Cotton, *A Modest and Cleare Answer to Mr. Balls Discourse of Set Formes of Prayer* (London, 1642), 20.

10. Edward Pearse, *The Great Concern; or, A Serious Warning to a Timely and Thorough Preparation for Death* (1671; London, 1678), 86–87. See also Philip Pain, *Daily Meditations; or, Quotidian Preparations for, and Considerations of Death and Eternity* (Cambridge, Eng., 1668), 6.

11. *Oxford English Dictionary*, "conversation," def. 2; "converse," def. 4.

12. M. Halsey Thomas, ed., *The Diary of Samuel Sewall, 1674–1729*, 2 vols. (New York, 1973), 1:364. Emphasis added.

13. Ibid., 1:364. The two relevant senses of "awful" are "worthy of, or commanding, profound respect or reverential fear" and "solemnly impressive; sublimely majestic." *Oxford English Dictionary*, "awful," def. I.2, I.3.

14. Kenneth A. Lockridge, *The Diary and Life of William Byrd II of Virginia, 1674–1744* (Chapel Hill, 1987), 44.

15. David H. Watters, *"With Bodilie Eyes": Eschatological Themes in Puritan Literature and Gravestone Art* (Ann Arbor, 1981), 71–74.

16. Mather, *Cælestinus*, 49. Increase Mather likewise urged his readers "to be daily Conversing with Heaven while on Earth." Mather, *Meditations on Death, Delivered in Several Sermons* (Boston, 1707), 147.

17. For example, Mather, *Cælestinus*, 39.

18. Cotton Mather, *A Father Departing: A Sermon on the Departure of the Venerable and Memorable Dr. Increase Mather* (Boston, 1723), 29.

19. Mather, *Cælestinus*, 41, 50. The "weep not" clause paraphrases Luke 23:28.

20. John Shower, *The Mourners Companion; or, Funeral Discourses on Several Texts* (London, 1692), 66; Isaac Watts, *Death and Heaven; or, The Last Enemy Conquer'd, and Separate Spirits Made Perfect*, 2nd ed. (1722; London, 1724), 62.

21. Mather, *Cælestinus*, 39.

22. Reiner Smolinski, ed., *The Threefold Paradise of Cotton Mather: An Edition of "Triparadisus"* (Athens, Ga., 1995), 147.

23. Mather, *Cælestinus*, 92.

24. Smolinski, *Threefold Paradise*, 147.

25. Erik R. Seeman, *Pious Persuasions: Laity and Clergy in Eighteenth-Century New England* (Baltimore, 1999), 47–48.

26. William Cooper, *A Sermon Concerning the Laying the Deaths of Others to Heart* (Boston, 1720), 13.

27. Watts, *Death and Heaven*, 240, 239.

28. Early American Imprints database.

29. Seeman, *Pious Persuasions*, 174–77; Thomas S. Kidd, *The Great Awakening: The Roots of Evangelical Christianity in Colonial America* (New Haven, Conn., 2007), 268–70.

30. Samuel Buell, *The Happiness of the Blessed in Heaven; or, The Saint with Christ in Glory* (New York, 1760), vii, 15–16.

31. Ibid., 18.

32. Colleen McDannell and Bernhard Lang, *Heaven: A History* (New Haven, Conn., 1988), 153–56.

33. *The Confession of Faith and Catechisms, Agreed Upon by the Assembly of Divines at Westminster* (London, 1649), 65–66.

34. Richard Sibbes, *A Glance of Heaven; or, A Pretious Taste of a Glorious Feast* (London, 1638).

35. Richard Baxter, *The Saints Everlasting Rest; or, A Treatise of the Blessed State of the Saints in Their Enjoyment of God in Glory*, 2nd ed. (1650; London, 1651), 97–102; William Gearing, *A Prospect of Heaven; or, A Treatise of the Happiness of the Saints in Glory* (London, 1673), ch. 22.

36. Mather, *Meditations on Death, Delivered in Several Sermons*, 48. See also Increase Mather, *Meditations on the Glory of the Heavenly World* (Boston, 1711), 84; James Hillhouse, *A Sermon Concerning the Life, Death, and Future State of Saints* (Boston, 1721), 75; and Benjamin Colman, *Reliquiae Turellae, et Lachrymae Paternae: The Father's Tears over his Daughter's Remains* (Boston, 1735), 47–48. For a similar development in England, see Philip C. Almond, *Heaven and Hell in Enlightenment England* (Cambridge, Eng., 1994), 100–105.

37. John Gill, *The Glorious State of the Saints in Heaven*, 3rd ed. (Boston, 1756), 28.

38. Peter Powers, *Heaven Ready for the Saints* (Boston, 1773), 15. See also Oliver Noble, *The Knowledge, or Well-Grounded Hope, That, We Shall Go to Heaven When We Die, Is the Best Support in Every Calamity and Trial of Life* (Newburyport, Mass., 1781), 12; Ezra Stiles, *A Funeral Sermon, Delivered Thursday, July 26, 1787, at the Interment of the Reverend Mr. Chauncey Whittelsey* (New Haven, Conn., 1787), 20; and George Whitefield, "Christ's Transfiguration," in *The Works of the Reverend George Whitefield*, 7 vols. (London, 1771–72), 5:453.

39. McDannell and Lang, *Heaven*, ch. 8.

40. "Deacon John Paine's Journal," *Mayflower Descendant* 9 (1907): 138.

41. Ebenezer Parkman, "Memoirs of Mrs Sarah Pierpont; late amiable Consort of James Pierpont A.M. of New Haven," AAS, June 15, 1735.

42. Jonathan Willis Diary, MHS, November 18, 1744.

43. Daniel King Diary, PEM, August 13, 1767. See also Lydia Prout Diary, NEHGS, October 20, 1716.

44. Douglas L. Winiarski, *Darkness Falls on the Land of Light: Experiencing Religious Awakenings in Eighteenth-Century New England* (Chapel Hill, 2017), 253.

45. Joseph Fish, *The Church of Christ a Firm and Durable House: Shown in a Number of Sermons on Matth. XVI. 18* (New London, Conn., 1767), 139.

46. Quoted in Ann Marie Plane, *Dreams and the Invisible World in Colonial New England: Indians, Colonists, and the Seventeenth Century* (Philadelphia, 2014), 93.

47. To compare dreams of the dead among African Americans, see Albert J. Raboteau, *Slave Religion: The "Invisible Institution" in the Antebellum South* (New York, 1978), 12; Henry Louis Gates Jr., ed., *The Classic Slave Narratives* (New York, 1987), 466; Mechal Sobel, *Teach Me Dreams: The Search for Self in Revolutionary America* (Princeton, N.J., 2000), 42–48; and Jonathan W. White, *Midnight in America: Darkness, Sleep, and Dreams During the Civil War* (Chapel Hill, 2017), 95; among Amerindians, see Michel Perrin, *The Way of the Dead Indians: Guajiro Myths and Symbols*, trans. Michael Fineberg (Austin, Tex., 1987), 105; and Plane, *Dreams and the Invisible World*, 164–65, 172.

48. Quoted in Plane, *Dreams and the Invisible World*, 150.

49. Martha Brewster, *Poems on Divers Subjects* (New London, Conn., 1757), 15.

50. On the origins of this belief, see Robert Bartlett, *Why Can the Dead Do Such Great Things? Saints and Worshippers from the Martyrs to the Reformation* (Princeton, N.J., 2013), 15.

51. Craig M. Koslofsky, *The Reformation of the Dead: Death and Ritual in Early Modern Germany, 1450–1700* (New York, 2000), 40–77.

52. Quoted in Marshall, *Beliefs and the Dead*, 297.

53. John L. Brooke, "'For Honour and Civil Worship to Any Worthy Person': Burial, Baptism, and Community on the Massachusetts Near Frontier, 1730–1790," in *Material Life in America, 1600–1860*, ed. Robert Blair St. George (Boston, 1988), 465–66.

54. Gordon E. Geddes, *Welcome Joy: Death in Puritan New England* (Ann Arbor, 1981), 146.

55. *A Directory for the Publike Worship of God Throughout the Three Kingdoms of Scotland, England, and Ireland* (Edinburgh, 1645), 58.

56. On churchyard crosses, see Margaret Aston, "Puritans and Iconoclasm, 1560–1660," in *The Culture of English Puritanism, 1560–1700*, ed. Christopher Durston and Jacqueline Eales (New York, 1996), 92–121, esp. 97, 103–4.

57. Peter Benes, *The Masks of Orthodoxy: Folk Gravestone Carving in Plymouth County, Massachusetts, 1689–1805* (Amherst, Mass., 1977), 38.

58. James Fitch, *The First Principles of the Doctrine of Christ* (Boston, 1679).

59. Steven C. Bullock and Sheila McIntyre, "The Handsome Tokens of a Funeral: Glove-Giving and the Large Funeral in Eighteenth-Century New England," *William and Mary Quarterly* 69,2 (April 2012): 305–46, esp. 321.

60. Brooke, "'For Honour and Civil Worship,'" 465.

61. Allan I. Ludwig, *Graven Images: New England Stonecarving and Its Symbols, 1650–1815* (Middletown, Conn., 1966); Dickran Tashjian and Ann Tashjian, *Memorials for Children of Change: The Art of Early New England Stonecarving* (Middletown, Conn., 1974); Benes, *Masks of Orthodoxy*; James Blachowicz, *From Slate to Marble: Gravestone Carving Traditions in Eastern Massachusetts, 1770–1870* (Evanston, Ill., 2006).

62. Watters, *"With Bodilie Eyes"*; Diana Hume George and Malcolm A. Nelson, *Epitaph and Icon: A Field Guide to the Old Burying Grounds of Cape Cod, Martha's Vineyard, and Nantucket* (Orleans, Mass., 1983); Lucien L. Agosta, "Speaking Stones: New England Grave Carvings and the Emblematic Tradition," *Markers* 3 (1984): 47–70. On epitaphs in early modern England, see Ralph Houlbrooke, *Death, Religion, and the Family in England, 1480–1750* (Oxford, 1998), 346–55.

63. David E. Stannard, *The Puritan Way of Death: A Study in Religion, Culture, and Social Change* (New York, 1977), 87, 146 ("anxieties"), 146 ("introspective fear"); Blanche Linden-Ward, *Silent City on a Hill: Landscapes of Memory and Boston's Mount Auburn Cemetery* (Columbus, Ohio, 1989), 4 ("ideological dualism").

64. Stannard, *Puritan Way of Death*, 157; Benes, *Masks of Orthodoxy*, 132, 154, 191.

65. James Blachowicz, "The Gravestone Carving Traditions of Plymouth and Cape Cod," *Markers* 15 (1998): 145–46.

66. Ludwig, *Graven Images*, 64 ("engulfed by"); Benes, *Masks of Orthodoxy*, 25 ("salvation" and "less critical"). For an updated view, see Sherene Baugher and Richard F. Veit, "Beyond Death's Heads and Cherubs: Early American Gravemarkers," in *The Archaeology of American Cemeteries and Gravemarkers*, ed. Baugher and Veit (Gainesville, Fla., 2014), 78–124.

67. Benes, *Masks of Orthodoxy*, 54. Likewise, David Watters argues that images of the deceased's face reflect "a belief in some form of contact between saints in heaven and on earth." Watters, *"With Bodilie Eyes,"* 104. Stones outside New England also represented connections between this world and the next. In South Carolina, portrait stones, with carved images of the deceased, helped create a "community that transcended the boundary of death." Jennifer Van Horn, *The Power of Objects in Eighteenth-Century British America* (Chapel Hill, 2017), 156. Also in South Carolina, the typical shape of stones in the first half of the eighteenth century "signified the gate between earth and heaven." Louis P. Nelson, "Word, Shape, and Image: Anglican Constructions of the Sacred," in *American Sanctuary: Understanding Sacred Spaces*, ed. Nelson (Bloomington, Ind., 2006), 157.

68. George and Nelson call this the "commonest epitaph on Cape and Island stones, as on all early American stones." *Epitaph and Icon*, 3. But there is strong evidence that this formulation was almost nonexistent in colonial America before 1750. Caitlin G. D. Hopkins, "Remember Me As You Pass By," February 24, 2010, Vast Public Indifference blog, http://www

.vastpublicindifference.com/2010/02/remember-me-as-you-pass-by.html (accessed December 3, 2017).

69. Lucinda Hallett, 1806, Hyannis Baptist Church Cemetery, Hyannis ("Farewell"); Luther Bassett, 1801, Marstons Mills Cemetery, Barnstable ("O death").

70. Infant Boult, 1808, Hillside Cemetery, Osterville.

71. Sarah Vickery, 1763, Duck Creek Cemetery, Wellfleet.

72. Priscilla Upham, 1785, Old North Cemetery, Truro.

73. A very small number of gravestones feature epitaphs that fall into more than one category. These were coded according to which voice predominates.

74. See, for example, Daniel W. Patterson, *The True Image: Gravestone Art and the Culture of Scotch Irish Settlers in the Pennsylvania and Carolina Backcountry* (Chapel Hill, 2012), ch. 5, which includes dozens of Scotch Irish talking gravestones, 1784–1819; Richard F. Veit and Mark Nonestied, *New Jersey Cemeteries and Tombstones: History in the Landscape* (New Brunswick, N.J., 2008), ch. 3; and countless examples from the Farber Gravestone Collection, http://www.davidrumsey.com/farber/.

75. Cape Cod Gravestones, http://www.capecodgravestones.com/ (accessed May 15, 2018). Created by Robert Carlson, the website includes genealogical data from over 40,000 stones dating from the mid-seventeenth century into the twentieth century, culled from 135 Cape Cod burial grounds. The site also includes detailed records of a subset of stones with what Carlson considers "interesting carved images." Carlson, personal communication, August 28, 2013. The site includes 927 of these; I selected the 810 dating from 1700 to 1849. The gravestones do not, therefore, represent a random cross-section of Cape Cod markers. But because Carlson chose the stones for their images, selection bias should not influence the epitaphs.

76. This relatively small difference is not considered statistically significant at the usual 5 percent confidence threshold (chi-square = 1.546, p = 0.214).

77. Samuel Chapman, 1796, Dennis Village Cemetery, Dennis.

78. For the data comparing the five epitaph types and the five age groups, the chi-square is 78.967 and $p < 0.001$, thus the relationship is statistically significant.

79. Hopkins, "Remember Me As You Pass By."

80. Scholars used to argue that the change from death's heads to winged cherubs represents the more "optimistic" theology of Awakening revivalists. Stannard, *Puritan Way of Death*, 157; Benes, *Masks of Orthodoxy*, 132, 154, 191. Historians now understand that most revivalists were Calvinists, like their seventeenth-century forebears.

81. The lone scholarly treatment of talking gravestones attempts to put them in the context of English emblem books from the 1630s, even though none of the cited epitaphs date from before 1760. Agosta, "Speaking Stones."

82. Sally M. Promey, "Religion, Sensation, and Materiality: An Introduction," in *Sensational Religion*, 7.

83. Patience Hall, 1791, Harwich Cemetery, Harwich. A more common version of the couplet was "Go home my friends dry up your tears / I must lie here till Christ appears." See, for example, Thankful Nye, 1810, Falmouth Cemetery, Falmouth.

84. Olivia Weisser, *Ill Composed: Sickness, Gender, and Belief in Early Modern England* (New Haven, Conn., 2015), ch. 5.

85. Abigail Baker, 1804, South Dennis Cemetery, South Dennis.

86. For example, Alven and Ruben Tobey, 1805, Falmouth Cemetery, Falmouth.

87. Lewis Parker, 1807, Falmouth Cemetery, Falmouth.

88. Mary Collins and Caleb K. Collins, 1817, Truro Cemetery, Truro.

89. Ruth Crowell, 1799, Cobb's Hill Cemetery, Barnstable.

90. Hannah Dunster, 1766, Brewster Cemetery, Brewster.

91. Azubah Handy, 1819, Cotuit Mosswood Cemetery, Barnstable.

92. On the eighteenth century, see Seeman, *Pious Persuasions*, 52–53; on the nineteenth, Margaret Bendroth, "Children of Adam, Children of God: Christian Nurture in Early Nineteenth-Century America," *Theology Today* 56,4 (January 2000): 495–505.

93. Francis Jones, 1811, West Barnstable Cemetery, West Barnstable.

94. Caroline Huckins, 1795, Lothrop Hill Cemetery, Barnstable.

95. Infant Lovell, 1803, Baptist Church Cemetery, Hyannis.

96. Google Books Ngram Viewer, https://books.google.com/ngrams (accessed January 8, 2015): usage of (cemetery + cemeteries) surpassed (churchyard + churchyards) in 1848, with "churchyard" never regaining its primacy. "Burial ground" and "graveyard" were always used much less frequently.

97. Philippe Ariès, *The Hour of Our Death*, trans. Helen Weaver (New York, 1981), ch. 10.

98. Quoted in Linden-Ward, *Silent City on a Hill*, 143, from Irving's *Sketch Book* of 1819.

99. Barbary Weekes, 1798, First Congregational Church Cemetery, Harwich.

100. Seth Hall, 1793, Harwich Cemetery, Harwich.

101. Eric Parisot, "Piety, Poetry, and the Funeral Sermon: Reading Graveyard Poetry in the Eighteenth Century," *English Studies* 92,2 (April 2011): 175.

102. Phebe Gorham, 1775, Lothrop Hill Cemetery, Barnstable. Quotation marks in original epitaph.

103. Edward Young, *The Consolation* (London, 1745), 117.

104. *Dictionary of National Biography*, "Anna Letitia Barbauld," accessed January 11, 2015.

105. Anna Letitia Barbauld, "On the Death of Mrs. Jennings," in *Poems* (London, 1773), 107–9.

106. Maria Otis, 1826, West Barnstable Cemetery, West Barnstable.

107. Quoted in Ramie Targoff, *Posthumous Love: Eros and the Afterlife in Renaissance England* (Chicago, 2014), 13–14.

108. Lorraine Daston, ed., *Things That Talk: Object Lessons from Art and Science* (New York, 2004).

109. Scholars who grant objects agency include Barbara Bolt, "Material Thinking and the Agency of Matter," *Studies in Material Thinking* 1,1 (April 2007): 1–4; and Jim Johnson [Bruno Latour], "Mixing Humans and Nonhumans Together: The Sociology of a Door-Closer," *Social Problems* 35,3 (June 1988): 298–310.

CHAPTER 4

1. *Albany Centinel*, January 26, 1798, 1–2 (democracy), 3 (Morse), 1, 4 (advertisements).

2. Ibid., 3.

3. Peter Gay, *The Enlightenment, an Interpretation: The Rise of Modern Paganism* (London, 1973). See also Owen Chadwick, *The Secularization of the European Mind in the Nineteenth Century* (New York, 1975).

4. Catherine A. Brekus, *Sarah Osborne's World: The Rise of Evangelical Christianity in Early America* (New Haven, Conn., 2013), 9. See also Susan Juster, *Doomsayers: Anglo-American Prophecy in the Age of Revolution* (Philadelphia, 2003); Leigh Eric Schmidt, *Hearing Things: Religion, Illusion, and the American Enlightenment* (Cambridge, Mass., 2000); James Delbourgo, *A Most*

Amazing Scene of Wonders: Electricity and Enlightenment in Early America (Cambridge, Mass., 2006); and Adam Jortner, *Blood from the Sky: Miracles and Politics in the Early American Republic* (Charlottesville, Va., 2017).

5. Jonathan Sheehan, "Enlightenment, Religion, and the Enigma of Secularization: A Review Essay," *American Historical Review* 108,4 (October 2003): 1061–80, quotation at 1075–76.

6. David D. Hall, John Bidwell, and James Raven, "The Atlantic World," in *A History of the Book in America: Volume One: The Colonial Book in the Atlantic World*, ed. Hugh Amory and David D. Hall (New York, 2000), 153.

7. Andie Tucher, "Newspapers and Periodicals," in *An Extensive Republic: Print, Culture, and Society in the New Nation, 1790–1840*, ed. Robert A. Gross and Mary Kelley (Chapel Hill, 2010), 391 (37 in 1776), 393 (238, actually in 1800).

8. Jonathan I. Israel, *Radical Enlightenment: Philosophy and the Making of Modernity, 1650–1750* (New York, 2001), ch. 21.

9. Michael Hunter, "The Decline of Magic: Challenge and Response in Early Enlightenment England," *Historical Journal* 55,2 (June 2012): 399–425, quotation at 403.

10. John Aubrey, *Miscellanies* (London, 1696), iv.

11. Francis Hutchinson, *An Historical Essay Concerning Witchcraft, with Observations upon Matters of Fact* (London, 1718).

12. This paragraph is indebted to Hunter, "Decline of Magic," 417–22. See also Euan Cameron, *Enchanted Europe: Superstition, Reason, and Religion, 1250–1750* (New York, 2010), 291–92.

13. Michael P. Winship, *Seers of God: Puritan Providentialism in the Restoration and Early Enlightenment* (Baltimore, 1996), 148; Conrad Wright, *The Beginnings of Unitarianism in America* (Boston, 1955), 3. Wright's "supernatural rationalism" applies to the second half of the century.

14. Josiah Cotton, "History of the Cotton Family," 1728–1755, HL, ms Am 1165, pp. 214–15. Viewed online http://nrs.harvard.edu/urn-3:FHCL.HOUGH:23518884.

15. Cotton's essay is incisively analyzed in Douglas Winiarski, "'Pale Blewish Lights' and a Dead Man's Groan: Tales of the Supernatural from Eighteenth-Century Plymouth, Massachusetts," *William and Mary Quarterly* 55,4 (October 1998): 497–530.

16. Josiah Cotton, "Some Observations Concerning Witches, Spirits, & Apparitions, Collected from Divers Authors," in Cotton, "History of the Cotton Family," unpaginated essay after p. 444 ("seq. 488" online).

17. Ibid., seq. 489–90.

18. Hutchinson, *Historical Essay Concerning Witchcraft*, xiii–xiv.

19. Quoted in Winiarski, "'Pale Blewish Lights,'" 489, 518–19.

20. Quoted in ibid., 519.

21. Lennard J. Davis, *Factual Fictions: The Origins of the English Novel* (New York, 1983), 8.

22. "The Morning Apparition," *New England Magazine of Knowledge and Pleasure* 1,1 (August 1, 1758): 54.

23. See, for example, "The Apparition," *Philadelphia Minerva*, February 18, 1797; "An Apparition," *Public Ledger* (Philadelphia), July 16, 1839.

24. Smuggler: *State Gazette of South Carolina*, April 17, 1786; lover: *Essex Gazette* (Salem, Mass.), December 18, 1770; slave: "The Ghost," *Weekly Museum* (New York) 10,31 (January 20, 1798): 2; farmer's daughter: "The Ghost, A Tale," *New York Journal*, May 28, 1767; cat: many versions, including "An Apparition," *New York Weekly Magazine* 1,42 (April 20, 1796): 329.

25. "Extract of a Letter from Paris," *Pennsylvania Packet*, November 15, 1783.

26. "The Ventriloquist: A Singular Narration," *Herald of Freedom* (Boston), June 30, 1789. See also "Anecdote," *Weekly Magazine* (Philadelphia) 3,31 (February 9, 1799): 156.

27. Terry Castle, *The Female Thermometer: Eighteenth-Century Culture and the Invention of the Uncanny* (New York, 1995).

28. [Benjamin Rush], "On the Different Species of Phobia," *Weekly Magazine* (Philadelphia) 1,6 (March 10, 1798): 180. This first appeared in the *Edinburgh Magazine* in 1787.

29. "Of Spectres and Apparitions," *Boston Evening Post*, July 30, 1739; originally published in the *London Magazine* in 1732. One of the first to blame nurses was John Locke, *An Essay Concerning Human Understanding*, 9th ed., 2 vols. (London, 1726), 1:368.

30. "Essay on Mental Prejudices," *Pennsylvania Mercury*, February 3, 1786. See also Stephen Duck, "On Poverty," *Pennsylvania Gazette*, February 9, 1731; *Boston Chronicle*, April 12, 1770; [Anna Laetitia Aikin], "On the Pleasure Derived from Objects of Terror," *Independent Gazetteer* (Philadelphia), March 29, 1783; and "An Account of the Conversion of the Reverend Mr. John Thayer," *New Hampshire Gazette*, November 12, 1788.

31. Four dozen editions of Young's *Night Thoughts*, more than two dozen of Hervey's *Meditations*. Eric Parisot, "Piety, Poetry, and the Funeral Sermon: Reading Graveyard Poetry in the Eighteenth Century," *English Studies* 92,2 (April 2011): 175; Parisot, "The Work of Feeling in James Hervey's *Meditations Among the Tombs* (1746)," *Parergon* 31,2 (2014): 122.

32. "Essay on Mental Prejudices."

33. *New England Weekly Journal*, December 1, 1729. See also *American Weekly Mercury* (Philadelphia), February 23, 1725.

34. *Boston Gazette*, June 27, 1737.

35. *American Weekly Mercury* (Philadelphia), July 21, 1737; *New-York Weekly Journal*, July 25, 1737; *Boston Evening Post*, August 1, 1737; *New England Weekly Journal*, August 2, 1737; *Boston News-Letter*, August 4, 1737.

36. Compare the ghost story from the 1790s analyzed in Elaine Forman Crane, *Witches, Wife Beaters, and Whores: Common Law and Common Folk in Early America* (Ithaca, N.Y., 2011), ch. 6, when "money, not murder" caused the aggrieved spirit to return from the dead (10).

37. On the impact of the Cock Lane ghost, see E. J. Clery, *The Rise of Supernatural Fiction, 1762–1800* (New York, 1995), ch. 1; Sasha Handley, *Visions of an Unseen World: Ghost Beliefs and Ghost Stories in Eighteenth-Century England* (London, 2007), 141–48; and Douglas Grant, *The Cock Lane Ghost* (New York, 1965).

38. Handley, *Visions of an Unseen World*, 144.

39. Grant, *Cock Lane Ghost*, 28.

40. Handley, *Visions of an Unseen World*, 144–45.

41. *Boston Evening Post*, May 10, 1762.

42. *Boston News-Letter*, August 19, 1762; *Newport Mercury*, August 31, 1762; *Boston Post Boy*, September 20, 1762; *Boston Evening Post*, May 16, 1763.

43. *New York Gazette*, March 5, 1767.

44. *Virginia Gazette*, May 5, 1768. Originally in the *Pennsylvania Journal*, April 3, 1768. See also "French Sagacity," *Independent Journal* (New York), May 27, 1786; *New London Gazette*, June 30, 1769; *Boston Evening Post*, May 27, 1771; *Pennsylvania Packet*, January 6, 1780; *Daily Advertiser* (New York), July 13, 1786; *New-York Daily Gazette*, March 14, 1789; *Centinel of Freedom* (Newark, N.J.), March 13, 1798; *Time Piece* (New York), August 6, 1798.

45. William G. McLoughlin, ed., *The Diary of Isaac Backus*, 3 vols. (Providence, R.I., 1979), 3:1275. Other evidence of late eighteenth-century belief in the spirit world includes *An Affecting Relation of the Appearance of Thomas Ostrehan's Apparition to His Friend Robert Straker* (Phil-

adelphia, 1767); *Massachusetts Centinel*, June 4, 1785; Franklin Bowditch Dexter, ed., *The Literary Diary of Ezra Stiles*, 3 vols. (New York, 1901), 1:385–86; [Samuel Stearns], *An Account of the Late Wonderful American Vision, Exhibiting the Judgments That Must Shortly Come to Pass* (London, 1791), 10–13; Crane, *Witches, Wife Beaters, and Whores*, ch. 6; Jortner, *Blood from the Sky*, ch. 2; Herbert Leventhal, *In the Shadow of the Enlightenment: Occultism and Renaissance Science in Eighteenth-Century America* (New York, 1976), ch. 3; and Handley, *Visions of an Unseen World*, 148–53.

46. *Pennsylvania Evening Herald*, August 20, 1785. See also ibid., August 24, 1785.

47. *Pennsylvania Packet*, August 31, 1785.

48. "A Ghost," *Springer's Weekly Oracle* (New London), January 13, 1798. The other newspapers that carried the same article, some under the title "A Beautiful Ghost," are, in chronological order: *Gazette of the United States* (Philadelphia), *Porcupine's Gazette* (Philadelphia), *Keene (N.H.) Rising Sun, Centinel of Freedom* (Newark, N.J.), *Albany Centinel, Providence Gazette, Mohawk Monitor, Salem Gazette, Newburyport Herald, Portsmouth Oracle of the Day, Salem (N.Y.) Northern Centinel, Rutland (Vt.) Herald, Charleston City Gazette, Portland (Me.) Oriental Trumpet, Otsego (N.Y.) Herald, Boston Independent Chronicle, Carlisle (Pa.) Gazette, Boston Gazette, Georgia Gazette*, and *Concord (N.H.) Mirrour*. The last article appeared February 27, more than six weeks after the original printing.

49. *Litchfield (Ct.) Monitor*, January 31, 1798.

50. *Centinel of Freedom* (Newark, N.J.), March 13, 1798.

51. *Salem (Mass.) Gazette*, March 20, 1798.

52. M. W., "Notices from the Invisible World," *Worcester Magazine* 3,22 (August 1787): 287–88. For similar examples, see "Extract of a Letter from Dublin," *Vermont Gazette*, April 19, 1784; "An Authentic Account of Lord ——'s Death," *Methodist Magazine* (Philadelphia) 1,10 (October 1797): 463–64; "Remarkable Story of a Ghost," *Philadelphia Repository*, September 26, 1801; and the multiple American reprints of *England's Timely Remembrancer*, including a 1752 Boston edition, a 1770 Newport edition, and a 1791 Boston tenth edition.

53. Samuel Stearns, *The American Oracle, Comprehending an Account of Recent Discoveries in the Arts and Sciences* (New York, 1791), 96–98.

54. See, for example, [Lawrence Price], *A Wonderful Prophesie Declared by Christian James, a Maid of Twenty Two Years of Age* (London, 1656); and *A Miraculous Proof of the Resurrection; or, The Life to Come Demonstrated, Being a Strange But True Relation of What Hapned to Mistriss Anna Atherton* (1669; London, 1680).

55. Douglas L. Winiarski, *Darkness Falls on the Land of Light: Experiencing Religious Awakenings in Eighteenth-Century New England* (Chapel Hill, 2017), 248–66.

56. Ann Kirschner, "'Tending to Edify, Astonish, and Instruct': Published Narratives of Spiritual Dreams and Visions in the Early Republic," *Early American Studies* 1,1 (Spring 2003): 198–229; Juster, *Doomsayers*. For a complete list, see Richard Lyman Bushman, "The Visionary World of Joseph Smith," *Brigham Young University Studies* 37,1 (1997–98): 198–200.

57. On the extent to which the concept of hell "saturated private and public discourse" in this period, see Kathryn Gin Lum, *Damned Nation: Hell in America from the Revolution to Reconstruction* (New York, 2014), 3.

58. *An Account of a Trance or Vision of Sarah Alley* (n.p., 1798), 6–7. See also *A Wonderful Account of a Little Girl of Nine Years Old* (n.p., 1800); and *A True Narrative of a Most Stupendous Trance and Vision, Which Happened at Sharon, in Connecticut, in January, 1789* (n.p., 1793).

59. *The Vision and Wonderful Experience of Jane Cish* (Philadelphia, 1797), 12.

60. *Wonderful Account of a Little Girl*, 3.

61. *A True and Wonderful Account of Mr. Thomas Say, of Philadelphia, While in a Trance, for Upwards of Seven Hours* (n.p., 1792), 6–7.

62. On Swedenborg and "modern heaven," see Colleen McDannell and Bernhard Lang, *Heaven: A History* (New Haven, Conn., 1988), ch. 7. "Gates ajar" refers to Elizabeth Stuart Phelps's popular Spiritualist novel of the same name, first published in 1868.

63. *True Narrative of a Most Stupendous Trance*, 3.

64. Ibid., 4–8.

65. Ibid., 8–12.

66. [Richard Johnson], *False Alarms; or, The Mischievous Doctrine of Ghosts and Apparitions, of Spectres and Hobgoblins, Exploded* (Philadelphia, 1802), 3–6. See also William Frederick Pinchbeck, *Witchcraft: The Art of Fortune-Telling Unveiled* (Boston, 1805); *The Supernatural Magazine, for 1809* (Dublin, 1809); and Robert Bloomfield, *The Fakenham Ghost: A True Tale* (Philadelphia, 1810?).

67. Johnson, *False Alarms*, 6–13. See also Jortner, *Blood from the Sky*, 84.

68. Emma Clery argues that even after Radcliffe's ghosts are explained away, there remains a powerful supernatural component: religion. Clery, *Rise of Supernatural Fiction*, 112–14.

CHAPTER 5

1. L. B. [L. Bleecker], "The Dead Infant; or, The Agonizing Mother," *New-York Weekly Magazine; or, Miscellaneous Repository* 2,53 (July 6, 1796): 3. Eighteen other stories by "L. B." in the *New-York Weekly Magazine* are attributed to "Miss Bleecker" by Edward W. R. Pitcher, *An Anthology of the Short Story in 18th and 19th Century America*, 2 vols. (Lewiston, N.Y., 2000), 2:776–80.

2. Quoted in Andie Tucher, "Newspapers and Periodicals," in *An Extensive Republic: Print, Culture, and Society in the New Nation, 1790–1840*, ed. Robert A. Gross and Mary Kelley (Chapel Hill, 2010), 397. Emphasis in original. On magazines and the literary culture of the 1790s, see also Bryan Waterman, *Republic of Intellect: The Friendly Club of New York City and the Making of American Literature* (Baltimore, 2007), esp. 41–49; and Robb K. Haberman, "Periodical Publics: Magazines and Literary Networks in Post-Revolutionary America" (PhD diss., University of Connecticut, 2009).

3. Tucher, "Newspapers and Periodicals," 397.

4. *New-York Weekly Magazine; or, Miscellaneous Repository* 1,1 (July 1, 1795): 1.

5. Carol Margaret Davison, *History of the Gothic: Gothic Literature, 1764–1824* (Cardiff, Wales, 2009), esp. 43; E. J. Clery, *The Rise of Supernatural Fiction, 1762–1800* (New York, 1995), esp. 2–4. Recent work sees the Gothic employing certain Enlightenment concepts such as the autonomous individual even as it reacts against rationalism. Siân Silyn Roberts, *Gothic Subjects: The Transformation of Individualism in American Fiction, 1790–1861* (Philadelphia, 2014).

6. Paula R. Backscheider, *Elizabeth Singer Rowe and the Development of the English Novel* (Baltimore, 2013), 1.

7. Elizabeth Singer Rowe, *Friendship in Death: In Twenty Letters from the Dead to the Living* (London, 1728), 56–59. On *Friendship in Death* in the context of English apparition literature, see Backscheider, *Elizabeth Singer Rowe*, 60–68.

8. Rowe, *Friendship in Death*, 88–89.

9. Ibid., 29, 35–37.

10. On ministerial efforts to moderate mourners' grief, see Philippe Ariès, *The Hour of Our Death*, trans. Helen Weaver (New York, 1981), 325–27; and Erik R. Seeman, *Pious Persuasions: Laity and Clergy in Eighteenth-Century New England* (Baltimore, 1999), 47–49.

11. Rowe, *Friendship in Death*, 13, 18.

12. Quoted in Martha Tomhave Blauvelt, *The Work of the Heart: Young Women and Emotion, 1780–1830* (Charlottesville, Va., 2007), 30.

13. Ibid., 23.

14. Philaretes, *Letters from the Dead to the Living* (Philadelphia, 1750), iii–iv, 15.

15. Quoted in Susan M. Stabile, *Memory's Daughters: The Material Culture of Remembrance in Eighteenth-Century America* (Ithaca, N.Y., 2004), 221, 274n178.

16. See also the letter Sarah Prince Gill wrote to be opened only after her death, in which she addressed her readers "as from the invisible world." *Devotional Papers, Wrote by the Late Mrs. Sarah Gill, of Boston*, 2nd ed. (Norwich, Conn., 1773), 23.

17. Max Cavitch, *American Elegy: The Poetry of Mourning from the Puritans to Whitman* (Minneapolis, 2007), 16.

18. M. Halsey Thomas, ed., *The Diary of Samuel Sewall, 1674–1729*, 2 vols. (New York, 1973), 2:704.

19. John Danforth, *Honour and Vertue Elegized in a Poem, upon an Honourable, Aged, and Gracious Mother in our Israel, Madam Elizabeth Hutchinson* (Boston, 1713).

20. Cotton Mather, *Monica Americana: A Funeral Sermon, Occasioned by the Death of Mrs. Sarah Leveret* (Boston, 1705), 29–30.

21. In addition to Danforth and Mather: Speaking: Cotton Mather, *Corderius Americanus: An Essay upon the Good Education of Children* (Boston, 1708). Spoken to: Cotton Mather on Abigail Mather, in Gordon E. Geddes, *Welcome Joy: Death in Puritan New England* (Ann Arbor, 1981), 173; John Charmion, *John Charmion's Latin Epitaph from his Ardent Love to Learning and Learned Men, on Mr. Pemberton . . . Translated into English* (Boston, 1717); Thomas Foxcroft, *A Sermon Preach'd at Cambrige, after the Funeral of Mrs. Elizabeth Foxcroft* (Boston, 1721); *An Elegy upon His Excellency William Burnet, Esq.* (Boston, 1729); and *An Elegy Occasioned by the Sudden and Awful Death of Mr. Nathanael Baker of Dedham* (Boston, 1733).

22. John Warren, *A Monody on the Death of the Hon. Thomas Russell, Esq.* (Boston, 1796). See also Samuel S. Smith, *A Funeral Sermon, on the Death of the Hon. Richard Stockton, Esq.* (Trenton, N.J., 1781); Richard Alsop, *A Poem, Sacred to the Memory of George Washington* (Hartford, 1800); and several each by Phillis Wheatley and Annis Boudinot Stockton.

23. *An Elegiac Poem, Sacred to the Memory of the Rev. George Whitefield* (Boston, 1770), 4.

24. On the origins of the "odor of sanctity," see Susan Ashbrook Harvey, *Scenting Salvation: Ancient Christianity and the Olfactory Imagination* (Berkeley, 2006), ch. 6.

25. Robert E. Cray Jr., "Memorialization and Enshrinement: George Whitefield and Popular Religious Culture, 1770–1850," *Journal of the Early Republic* 10,3 (Autumn 1990): 339–61; Christopher Allison, "Relics and the Sacred Body in Early America, 1750–1850" (PhD diss., Harvard University, 2017).

26. Quoted in Patricia C. Willis, "Phillis Wheatley, George Whitefield, and the Countess of Huntingdon in the Beinecke Library," *Yale University Library Gazette* 80,3 (April 2006): 175n9.

27. Julian D. Mason Jr., ed., *The Poems of Phillis Wheatley*, rev. ed. (Chapel Hill, 1989), 55–56; Vincent Carretta, *Phillis Wheatley: Biography of a Genius in Bondage* (Athens, Ga., 2011), 72 ("freedom").

28. Carretta, *Phillis Wheatley*, 48, provides the figure of nineteen elegies. The count of eleven that speak with the dead is my own.

29. Ibid., 108, 156.

30. Wheatley scholars who ignore speaking with the dead include Carretta, *Phillis Wheatley*; Cavitch, *American Elegy*, 184–95 (the topic is mentioned very briefly on 190); Joanna Brooks, "Our Phillis, Ourselves," *American Literature* 82,1 (March 2010): 1–28; Jennifer Lynn Holley, "The Child Elegy" (PhD diss., University of Connecticut, 2012), 71–76; Antonio Bly, "Wheatley's 'On the Death of a Young Lady of Five Years of Age,'" *Explicator* 58,1 (Fall 1999): 10–13; R. Lynn Matson, "Phillis Wheatley—Soul Sister?" *Phylon* 33,3 (1972): 222–30; and Astrid Franke, "Phillis Wheatley, Melancholy Muse," *New England Quarterly* 77,2 (2004): 224–51 (the topic is mentioned briefly on 231).

31. Jennifer Thorn, "Phillis Wheatley's Ghosts: The Racial Melancholy of New England Protestants," *Eighteenth Century* 50,1 (Spring 2009): 73–99, quotation at 91. The most insightful analysis of apostrophizing the dead in elegies examines a later period: Mary Louise Kete, *Sentimental Collaborations: Mourning and Middle-Class Identity in Nineteenth-Century America* (Durham, N.C., 2000), 39–47.

32. Lucia Hodgson is the exception that proves the rule, spending two paragraphs examining Wheatley's use of speaking with the dead. Hodgson, "Infant Muse: Phillis Wheatley and the Revolutionary Rhetoric of Childhood," *Early American Literature* 49,3 (2014): 663–82, esp. 678.

33. Mason, *Poems of Phillis Wheatley*, 97. Emphasis added.

34. Ibid.

35. Ibid., 80–81. Carretta, *Phillis Wheatley*, 7, shows that 22 percent of the slaves on her voyage died.

36. Wendy Raphael Roberts, ed., "'Slavery' and 'To Mrs. Eliot on the Death of Her Child': Two New Manuscript Poems Connected to Phillis Wheatley by the Bostonian Poet Ruth Barrell Andrews," *Early American Literature* 51,3 (2016): 665–81, quotation at 676.

37. Adam Smith, *The Theory of Moral Sentiments* (London, 1759), 10. For historical and literary context, see Janet Todd, *Sensibility: An Introduction* (London, 1986).

38. Steven C. Bullock and Sheila McIntyre, "The Handsome Tokens of a Funeral: Glove-Giving and the Large Funeral in Eighteenth-Century New England," *William and Mary Quarterly* 69,2 (April 2012): 342. On frugal funerals during the Revolution, see T. H. Breen, *The Marketplace of Revolution: How Consumer Politics Shaped American Independence* (New York, 2004), 213–17.

39. On this dynamic in the Philadelphia area, see Stabile, *Memory's Daughters*, ch. 4.

40. Brooks, "Our Phillis, Ourselves," 12. See also Sarah Knott, *Sensibility and the American Revolution* (Chapel Hill, 2009), 17–18, 47–49.

41. Mason, ed., *Poems of Phillis Wheatley*, 57–58, 72.

42. An important exception is Carretta's biography. The dominant approach is represented by Matson, "Phillis Wheatley—Soul Sister?"; William H. Robinson, *Phillis Wheatley in the Black American Beginnings* (Detroit, 1975); Bly, "Wheatley's 'On the Death of a Young Lady of Five Years of Age'"; April C. E. Langley, *The Black Aesthetic Unbound: Theorizing the Dilemma of Eighteenth-Century African American Literature* (Columbus, Ohio, 2008), ch. 2; Cavitch, *American Elegy*, 184–95; and Holley, "The Child Elegy," 71–76.

43. Quotation from Carretta, *Phillis Wheatley*, 51.

44. Carretta, personal communication, July 11, 2016.

45. Kevin J. Hayes, "Poetry in the Time of Revolution," in *The Cambridge History of American Poetry*, ed. Alfred Bendixen and Stephen Burt (New York, 2008), 129–52.

46. Carla Mulford, ed., *Only for the Eye of a Friend: The Poems of Annis Boudinot Stockton* (Charlottesville, Va., 1995), 94. See also *An Elegy Occasion'd by the Death of Major-General Joseph Warren* (Watertown, Mass., 1775); Barnabas Binney, *Lines Sacred to the Memory of the Late Major-General Joseph Warren* (Providence, R.I., 1775?); and St. John Honeywood, *Poems* (New York, 1801), 67. On General Warren as a martyr, see Sarah J. Purcell, *Sealed with Blood: War, Sacrifice, and Memory in Revolutionary America* (Philadelphia, 2002), 18–19.

47. Jerrold E. Hogle, "Elegy and the Gothic: The Common Grounds," in *The Oxford Handbook of the Elegy*, ed. Karen Weisman (New York, 2010), 565–84; Serena Trowbridge, "Past, Present, and Future in the Gothic Graveyard," in *The Gothic and Death*, ed. Carol Margaret Davison (Manchester, Eng., 2017), 21–33.

48. Robert Blair, *The Grave: A Poem*, 4th ed. (1743; London, 1753), 7–8.

49. Edward Young, *The Complaint; or, Night-Thoughts on Life, Death, and Immortality. Night the First* (London, 1742), 10.

50. Eric Parisot, *Graveyard Poetry: Religion, Aesthetics, and the Mid-Eighteenth-Century Poetic Condition* (Farnham, Eng., 2013), 50. See also Evert Jan Van Leeuwen, "Funeral Sermons and Graveyard Poetry: The Ecstasy of Death and Bodily Resurrection," *Journal for Eighteenth-Century Studies* 32,3 (2009): 353–71.

51. John Trumbull, *An Elegy on the Death of Mr. Buckingham St. John* (New Haven, Conn., 1771). See also Joel Barlow, *An Elegy on the Late Honorable Titus Hosmer, Esq.* (Hartford, Conn., 1782), 5–6; and Samuel Austin, *A Funeral Oration, on Mr. David Ripley, of Windham* (New Haven, Conn., 1783), 11–12.

52. David S. Shields asserts that the collection includes "writings by men and women belonging to a New York City salon," but the volume says the poems are mostly by the female author, with a few designated as the work of "a young Gentleman." Shields, *Civil Tongues and Polite Letters in British America* (Chapel Hill, 1997), 311n4; *Effusions of Female Fancy, by a Young Lady, Native of America* (New York, 1784), [4].

53. Clark Sutherland Northrup, *A Bibliography of Thomas Gray* (New Haven, Conn., 1917), 123–44.

54. Quoted in Catherine Robson, *Heart Beats: Everyday Life and the Memorized Poem* (Princeton, N.J., 2012), 134.

55. *Effusions of Female Fancy*, 19, 20.

56. Ibid., 21, 22, 23, 26.

57. "Editors' Address," *New Star: A Republican, Miscellaneous, Literary Paper* 1,1 (April 11, 1797): 1.

58. On the local nature of magazine culture in the 1780s and 1790s, see Haberman, "Periodical Publics."

59. Clery, *Rise of Supernatural Fiction*, 32.

60. Donald A. Ringe, *American Gothic: Imagination and Reason in Nineteenth-Century Fiction* (Lexington, Ky., 1982), 28.

61. See also, for example, Anti-Ghost, "A Receipt for a Modern Romance," *Weekly Magazine* (Philadelphia) 2,22 (June 30, 1798): 278.

62. John Burton, *Lectures on Female Education and Manners*, 3rd ed. (1793; Dublin, 1794), 371–72, 374. See also Joseph Robertson, *An Essay on the Education of Young Ladies* (London, 1798), 42–44.

63. Cathy N. Davidson, *Revolution and the Word: The Rise of the Novel in America* (New York, 1986), 27.

64. Knott, *Sensibility and the American Revolution*, 45.

65. Clery, *Rise of Supernatural Fiction*, 134–35; Davidson, *Revolution and the Word*, vii, ch. 8.

66. *Jemmy and Nancy; or, A Tragical Relation of the Death of Five Persons* (Norwich, Conn., 1775?); "Harriet's Ghost," *Dunlap's Maryland Gazette*, September 26, 1775; [Joseph Brown Ladd], "Lovers Tragedie; or, The Storie of Eldred and Isabel," *Columbian Herald*, December 8, 1785; [Mary Robinson], "Llweyn and Gyneth: An Exotick Poem," *Massachusetts Centinel*, February 8, 1786; "Henry and Selima," *New York Daily Advertiser*, June 13, 1786; "The Ghost of Edwin," *Massachusetts Magazine* 4,1 (January 1792): 49; "Jamie's Dream; or, Mary's Ghost," *Weekly Museum* (New York) 4,194 (January 28, 1792): 2; Julia, "Edward's Ghost," *Weekly Museum* (New York) 5,249 (February 16, 1793): 2; "Mary's Dream; or, Sandy's Ghost," in *The Two Babes in the Wood; or, The Norfolk Gentleman's Last Will and Testament* (New York, 1795?), 7; "The Braes of Yarrow," *New York Magazine or Literary Repository* 7 (August 1796): 442–43; "Amelia, a Fragment," *Rural Magazine* (Newark, N.J.) 1,51 (February 2, 1799): 2-3 (the only prose work in this group); and "Edwin's Ghost," *Weekly Museum* (New York) 11,25 (February 9, 1799): 2.

67. "The Ghost of Edwin," 49.

68. "Jamie's Dream; or, Mary's Ghost," 2. See also [Robinson], "Llweyn and Gyneth."

69. "Harriet's Ghost."

70. "Edwin's Ghost," 2. See also "Amelia, a Fragment," of American authorship, according to Mary Mauritia Redden, *The Gothic Fiction in the American Magazines (1765–1800)* (Washington, D.C., 1939), 127–28.

71. "Henry and Selima."

72. Philander, "Written in a Grave-Yard," *Gentlemen and Ladies' Town and Country Magazine* (Boston) 1,7 (August 1789): 348–49. See also "Meditations, Written in a Church-Yard," *Weekly Museum* (New York) 9,47 (May 13, 1797): 2; and "A Soliloquy: Written in a Country Church-Yard" *South-Carolina Weekly Museum* 1 (May 27, 1797): 662–63.

73. Female Scribbler, "The Church Yard," *Weekly Museum* (New York) 5,256 (April 6, 1793): 2. Attributed to Richard Alsop in Charles W. Everest, *The Poets of Connecticut* (Hartford, Conn., 1844), 104.

74. [Anna Young], "Lines Occasioned by the Writer's Walking One Summer's Evening in the Grave-yard of the Church of Wicacoe," *Universal Asylum and Columbian Magazine* (Philadelphia) 6,8 (August 1791): 121–23. Young wrote this poem in 1777.

75. Evelina, "The Rural Mourner: A Sentimental Fragment," *Massachusetts Magazine; or, Monthly Museum* 3,5 (May 1791): 277.

76. W. D. B., "A Fragment," *Weekly Museum* (New York) 4,205 (April 14, 1792): 2.

77. Ibid.

78. Valentine Rathbun, *An Account of the Matter, Form, and Manner of a New and Strange Religion* (Providence, R.I., 1781), 6.

CHAPTER 6

1. Quoted in Paul B. Moyer, *The Public Universal Friend: Jemima Wilkinson and Religious Enthusiasm in Revolutionary America* (Ithaca, N.Y., 2015), 12.

2. Jon Butler, *Awash in a Sea of Faith: Christianizing the American People* (Cambridge, Mass., 1990), ch. 8.

3. Quoted in Nathan O. Hatch, *The Democratization of American Christianity* (New Haven, Conn., 1989), 64.

4. E. Brooks Holifield, *Theology in America: Christian Thought from the Age of the Puritans to the Civil War* (New Haven, Conn., 2003), 319.

5. To compare with communication between the living and dead among African Americans, see Albert J. Raboteau, *Slave Religion: The "Invisible Institution" in the Antebellum South* (New York, 1978), 30–31; James H. Sweet, *Recreating Africa: Culture, Kinship, and Religion in the African-Portuguese World, 1441–1770* (Chapel Hill, 2003), 140–54; Jason R. Young, *Rituals of Resistance: African Atlantic Religion in Kongo and the Lowcountry South in the Era of Slavery* (Baton Rouge, 2007), 152, 167; and LeRhonda S. Manigault-Bryant, *Talking to the Dead: Religion, Music, and Lived Memory Among Gullah/Geechee Women* (Durham, N.C., 2014); among Amerindians, see Charles Francis Adams Jr., ed., *New English Canaan of Thomas Morton* (New York, 1883), 248; Reuben Gold Thwaites, ed., *The Jesuit Relations and Allied Documents*, 73 vols. (Cleveland, 1896–1901), 8:137–39, 13:151–53; and Geoffrey Symcox and Blair Sullivan, eds., *Christopher Columbus and the Enterprise of the Indies: A Brief History with Documents* (Boston, 2005), 163.

6. These rough estimates are found in William M. Newman and Peter L. Halvorson, *Atlas of American Religion: The Denominational Era, 1776–1990* (Walnut Creek, Calif., 2000), 39.

7. Marguerite Beck Block, *The New Church in the New World: A Study of Swedenborgianism in America* (1932; New York, 1968), 3–8.

8. Peter Gardella, *American Angels: Useful Spirits in the Material World* (Lawrence, Kans., 2007), 61. Medieval Catholic theologians largely agreed that only saints' souls joined the ranks of angels. Some went further and asserted that the souls of all righteous humans became angels. David Keck, *Angels and Angelology in the Middle Ages* (New York, 1998), 26–27; David Luscombe, "Anselm on the Angels," *Rivista di Storia della Filosofia* 48,3 (1993): 545–47.

9. Emanuel Swedenborg, *Heaven and Its Wonders and Hell: From Things Heard and Seen*, trans. John C. Ager (1758; West Chester, Pa., 2009), 494, 311.2. Following convention I cite *Heaven and Hell* by paragraph rather than page number.

10. B. F. Barrett, ed., *The Swedenborg Library: The Author's Memorabilia* (Philadelphia, 1881), 13.

11. Colleen McDannell and Bernhard Lang, *Heaven: A History* (New Haven, Conn., 1988), 181–83.

12. To be fair, McDannell and Lang acknowledge that Swedenborg did not originate the idea of heavenly reunions. But they insist that "prior to the mid-nineteenth century, American ministers schooled in Calvinist theology showed little interest in describing the social relationships of heaven" (*Heaven*, 258). This, however, overlooks the extent to which laypeople—and even ministers such as Cotton Mather—anticipated meeting loved ones in heaven.

13. Block, *New Church in the New World*, 13.

14. Clarke Garrett, *Spirit Possession and Popular Religion: From the Camisards to the Shakers* (Baltimore, 1987), 146–47.

15. Block, *New Church in the New World*, 61–62.

16. *Pennsylvania Gazette*, June 2, 1784.

17. Elizabeth Duché, quoted in Clarke Garrett, "Swedenborg and the Mystical Enlightenment," *Journal of the History of Ideas* 45,1 (January 1984): 70.

18. Block, *New Church in the New World*, 173.

19. Frank Luther Mott, *Golden Multitudes: The Story of Best Sellers in the United States* (New York, 1947), 305–6.

20. "An Account of Infants, or Little Children, in Heaven," *Halcyon Luminary and Theological Repository* (New York) 2,7 (July 1, 1813): 309.

21. Hatch, *Democratization of American Christianity*, 170–79; Holifield, *Theology in America*, 361–69.

22. "Thoughts on the State of Infants in Heaven," *New Jerusalem Magazine* (Boston) 1 (1827–28): 248–49.

23. Catherine L. Albanese, *A Republic of Mind and Spirit: A Cultural History of American Metaphysical Religion* (New Haven, Conn., 2007), 187–88; Ann Braude, *Radical Spirits: Spiritualism and Women's Rights in Nineteenth-Century America*, 2nd ed. (1989; Bloomington, Ind., 2001), 34–35; Robert S. Cox, *Body and Soul: A Sympathetic History of American Spiritualism* (Charlottesville, Va., 2003), 12–16; Leigh Eric Schmidt, *Hearing Things: Religion, Illusion, and the American Enlightenment* (Cambridge, Mass., 2000), 228–30.

24. Swedenborg, *Heaven and Hell*, 249.

25. Schmidt, *Hearing Things*, 201, 222.

26. Robert Hindmarsh, *Rise and Progress of the New Jerusalem Church, in England, America, and Other Parts*, ed. Edward Madeley (London, 1861), 48, 121, 193.

27. "On Seeing Spirits," *New Jerusalem Magazine* (Boston) 1 (1827–28): 216, 218.

28. Ibid., 218.

29. Swedenborg, *Heaven and Hell*, 249.

30. Quoted in Block, *New Church in the New World*, 70.

31. John Clowes, *A Memoir of the Late Rev. John Clowes* (Manchester, 1834), 135.

32. Quoted in Schmidt, *Hearing Things*, 222. See also Block, *New Church in the New World*, 132–33.

33. John Martin, ed., *Diary of the Mission, Spiritual and Earthly, of the Late James Johnston* ([Liverpool], 1881), 4, 134, 131. See also James Johnston, *The Everlasting Church: As "Represented" in the Remarkable Manuscript, Entitled "Intercourse with Angels"* ([New York], 1866).

34. Block, *New Church in the New World*, 133; Schmidt, *Hearing Things*, 224; Richard Silver, "The Spiritual Kingdom in America: The Influence of Emanuel Swedenborg on American Society and Culture, 1815–1860" (PhD diss., Stanford University, 1983), 50–51, 207.

35. "On the Nature of Influx," *Halcyon Luminary and Theological Repository* (New York) 2,5 (May 1, 1813): 204–9, quotations at 207–8.

36. *A True and Wonderful Account of Mr. Thomas Say, of Philadelphia, While in a Trance, for Upwards of Seven Hours* (n.p., 1792); Benjamin Say, *A Short Compilation of the Extraordinary Life and Writings of Thomas Say* (Philadelphia, 1796).

37. "The Vision of Thomas Say," *New Jerusalem Church Repository* (Philadelphia) 1,2 (April 1, 1817): 91–99, quotation at 91. Emphasis in original.

38. "Education of Infants," *New Jerusalem Missionary and Intellectual Repository* (New York) 1,7 (November 1, 1823): 230–31; "A Few Plain Answers to the Question, 'Why Do You Receive the Testimony of Baron Swedenborg?'" *Herald of Truth* (Cincinnati) 1,2 (March 31, 1825): 39–41.

39. Block, *New Church in the New World*, 99; Schmidt, *Hearing Things*, 223–24.

40. Sarah P. Worcester, printed open letter, February 6, 1845, Bridgewater, Massachusetts, p. 1, Samuel Worcester Papers, Alphabetical Files, Academy of the New Church Archives, SwL.

41. Ibid., 1–2.

42. Ibid., 1.

43. "Statements made by Samuel H. Worcester, with regard to himself & the New Era, Sept. 1845," p. 5. Samuel Worcester Papers, SwL.

44. Gary Laderman, *The Sacred Remains: American Attitudes Toward Death, 1799–1883* (New Haven, Conn., 1996), 73.

45. Stephen J. Stein, *The Shaker Experience in America* (New Haven, Conn., 1992), 3–8; Garrett, *Spirit Possession*, ch. 6, quotation at 152.

46. On Shaker celibacy, see Erik R. Seeman, "'It Is Better to Marry than to Burn': Anglo-American Attitudes Toward Celibacy, 1600–1800," *Journal of Family History* 24,4 (October 1999): 397–419, esp. 410–13.

47. Valentine Rathbun, *An Account of the Matter, Form, and Manner of a New and Strange Religion* (Providence, R.I., 1781), 6, 9–10.

48. Amos Taylor, *A Narrative of the Strange Principles, Conduct and Character of the People Known by the Name of Shakers* (Worcester, Mass., 1782), 9.

49. William Plumer to Miss Coombs, February 19, 1783, quoted in Garrett, *Spirit Possession*, 189.

50. "Some Account of the Tenets and Practice of the Religious Society Called Shakers," *American Museum* (Philadelphia) 1,2 (February 1787): 148. See also Jeremy Belknap to Ebenezer Hazard, April 11, 1784, in *Collections of the Massachusetts Historical Society*, 5th ser., vol. 2 (1877): 327–28; and Glendyne R. Wergland, ed., *Visiting the Shakers: Watervliet, Hancock, Tyringham, New Lebanon, 1778–1849* (Clinton, N.Y., 2007), 24. For the period around 1800, see Thomas Brown, *An Account of the People Called Shakers: Their Faith, Doctrines, and Practice* (Troy, N.Y., 1812), 78, 221, 258, 321.

51. *Testimonies of the Life, Character, Revelations and Doctrines of Our Ever Blessed Mother Ann Lee* (Hancock, Mass., 1816), 230, 228.

52. Erik R. Seeman, "Native Spirits, Shaker Visions: Speaking with the Dead in the Early Republic," *Journal of the Early Republic* 35,3 (Fall 2015): 347–73. Quotation from "Containing Letters, & Communications from the Spiritual World, Beginning May 17, 1841," vol. 2, Shaker Collection, VIII.B.207, WRHS, microfilm reel 81, p. 107.

53. For "worldlings," see Rufus Bishop, "A Daily Journal of Passing Events, Begun January the 1st, 1830," Shaker Manuscript Collection, NYPL, August 21, 1836.

54. Esther Bennett, Sodus Society Daily Record, June 21, 1835, Shaker Collection, Box 28, Volume 2, NYSL; Anne Buckingham Diary, February 26 and August 6, 1837, Shaker Collection, Box 5, Volume 1, NYSL.

55. Bishop, "Daily Journal," February 4, 1838 (quotation), February 11, 1838 (too crowded to dance).

56. Wergland, *Visiting the Shakers*, 285. See also, for example, the anonymous 1843 report, "Four Months Among the Shakers," in Wergland, *Visiting the Shakers*, 89.

57. Bishop, "Daily Journal," February 4, 1838.

58. On interest in corpses across cultures and times, see Erik R. Seeman, *Death in the New World: Cross-Cultural Encounters, 1492–1800* (Philadelphia, 2010).

59. Brad S. Gregory, *Salvation at Stake: Christian Martyrdom in Early Modern Europe* (Cambridge, Mass., 1999), 175. Gregory uses the phrase for early modern Protestants, but it can be applied to Shakers as well.

60. Quoted in Stein, *Shaker Experience*, 110–11. On Shaker attitudes toward relics, see Sally M. Promey, *Spiritual Spectacles: Vision and Image in Mid-Nineteenth-Century Shakerism* (Bloomington, Ind., 1993), 119–21.

61. "Holy bones" is my phrase for powerful human remains that are not necessarily Catholic. Erik R. Seeman, *The Huron-Wendat Feast of the Dead: Indian-European Encounters in Early North America* (Baltimore, 2011).

62. Bishop, "Daily Journal," May 9 and 11, 1835.

63. Ibid., May 11, 1835.

64. Stephen C. Taysom, *Shakers, Mormons, and Religious Worlds: Conflicting Visions, Contested Boundaries* (Bloomington, Ind., 2011), 3; Jean M. Humez, "'Ye Are My Epistles': The Construction of Ann Lee Imagery in Early Shaker Sacred Literature," *Journal of Feminist Studies in Religion* 8,1 (Spring 1992): 83–103, esp. 90. Mob attacks on Shakers continued at least through 1830. Adam Jortner, *Blood from the Sky: Miracles and Politics in the Early American Republic* (Charlottesville, Va., 2017), 107–9.

65. Bishop, "Daily Journal," May 11 and 12, 1835.

66. Christopher Allison, "Relics and the Sacred Body in Early America, 1750–1850" (PhD diss., Harvard University, 2017), chs. 1 and 2.

67. Edward Deming Andrews, *The People Called Shakers: A Search for the Perfect Society*, 2nd ed. (New York, 1963), 277.

68. Laderman, *Sacred Remains*, ch. 2.

69. Bishop, "Daily Journal," April 12 and 13, 1838.

70. Ibid., June 3, 1839. See also New Lebanon Ministry to Enfield, New Hampshire, Ministry, March 3, 1839, quoted in Promey, *Spiritual Spectacles*, 138–39.

71. *A Revelation of the Extraordinary Visitation of Departed Spirits of Distinguished Men and Women of All Nations* (Philadelphia, 1869), 19.

72. Bishop, "Daily Journal," December 4, 1839.

73. Jean M. Humez, ed., *Mother's First-Born Daughters: Early Shaker Writings on Women and Religion* (Bloomington, Ind., 1993), 231. See also Wergland, *Visiting the Shakers*, 93.

74. Louis J. Kern, *An Ordered Love: Sex Roles and Sexuality in Victorian Utopias—the Shakers, the Mormons, and the Oneida Community* (Chapel Hill, 1981), 106 (proportion of female visionists). Kern argues that inspired instruments were predominantly female because visions provided them with a "sexual outlet." I am more persuaded by Ann Braude's argument about female "passivity." Braude, *Radical Spirits*, 23–24, 83.

75. Stein, *Shaker Experience*, 132–33.

76. Jean M. Humez, "'Weary of Petticoat Government': The Specter of Female Rule in Early Nineteenth-Century Shaker Politics," *Communal Societies* 11,1 (Spring 1992): 1–17, quotation at 7.

77. Humez, *Mother's First-Born Daughters*, viii–ix.

78. Sarah Markham to Esther Markham, July 26, 1843, LC, Shaker Collection, reel 1, item 13.

79. Ibid.

80. No one has studied the suicide rate among Shakers. Glendyne R. Wergland insists that "suicide was not unusual among the Shakers," but this may be because she wrote a book on Isaac Newton Youngs, whose father and cousin both cut their own throats, and who may himself have committed suicide. Wergland, *One Shaker Life: Isaac Newton Youngs, 1793–1865* (Amherst, Mass., 2006), 189 (quotation), 20 (father), 237n2 (cousin). Six of the 445 recorded burials in the Watervliet cemetery were suicides; it is unclear whether a rate of 1.3 percent is high for the period. Thomas A. Malloy and Brenda Malloy, "The Disappearing Shaker Cemetery," *Markers* 9 (1992): 260.

81. Bishop, "Daily Journal," March 30 and April 8, 1838. Emphasis in original.

82. Richard Bell focuses on polemics against suicide in *We Shall Be No More: Suicide and Self-Government in the Newly United States* (Cambridge, Mass., 2012). My view is that ordinary people became increasingly sympathetic toward self-murderers, based on the long-term trend in Europe and the United States away from convicting suicides as "felons against the self." Michael MacDonald, "The Secularization of Suicide in England, 1660–1800," *Past and Present* 111,1 (May 1986): 50–100.

83. Genealogical data from the Enfield Shaker Cemetery, www.findagrave.com: Rosina [*sic*] Allen (1778–1812), Abner Allen (1776–1855).

84. Rozina Allen to Abner Allen, July 29, 1843, LC, Shaker Collection, reel 1, item 13.

85. Lovicy Wood (1830–42), Anna Granger (1809–92), Enfield Shaker Cemetery, www.findagrave.com.

86. Lovicy Wood to Anna Granger, May 21, 1843, LC, Shaker Collection, reel 1, item 13. On Sarah Harrison, see Stephen J. Paterwic, *Historical Dictionary of the Shakers* (Lanham, Md., 2008), 104.

87. Mark S. Schantz, *Awaiting the Heavenly Country: The Civil War and America's Culture of Death* (Ithaca, N.Y., 2008), 40–45, 68.

88. Elder Nathaniel to Eldress Dana, June 3, 1846; Rozina Allen to Abner Allen, July 29, 1843; Lovicy Wood to Anna Granger, May 21, 1843; Sarah Markham to Esther Markham, July 26, 1843, all in LC, Shaker Collection, reel 1, item 13.

89. McDannell and Lang, *Heaven*, 264–73.

90. On the similarities between Mormon and non-Mormon ideas about death, see M. Guy Bishop, "To Overcome the 'Last Enemy': Early Mormon Perceptions of Death," *Brigham Young University Studies* 26,3 (Summer 1986): 63–79.

91. Samuel Morris Brown, *In Heaven as It Is on Earth: Joseph Smith and the Early Mormon Conquest of Death* (New York, 2012), 5. See also Mary Ann Meyers, "Gates Ajar: Death in Mormon Thought and Practice," in *Death in America*, ed. David E. Stannard (Philadelphia, 1975), 112–33.

92. Brown, *In Heaven as It Is on Earth*, 239–47.

93. *The Doctrine and Covenants of the Church of Jesus Christ of Latter-day Saints*, 137:1–5, https://www.lds.org/scriptures/dc-testament?lang=eng (accessed August 22, 2017).

94. *Elders' Journal* (Kirtland, Ohio) 1,2 (November 1837): 28–29; *Elders' Journal* (Far West, Mo.) 1,3 (July 1838): 43.

95. Ronald O. Barney, ed., "Letters of a Missionary Apostle to His Wife: Brigham Young to Mary Ann Angell Young, 1839–1841," *Brigham Young University Studies* 38,2 (1999): 179–80.

96. Heber C. Kimball to John Taylor, November 9, 1840, Church History Library, Salt Lake City, Utah.

97. Samuel M. Brown, "Early Mormon Adoption Theology and the Mechanics of Salvation," *Journal of Mormon History* 37,3 (Summer 2011): 3–52, quotation at 33.

98. Kimball to Taylor, November 9, 1840. The earliest firsthand source of Smith's new teaching is his letter to the Quorum of the Twelve, December 15, 1840, in Matthew C. Godfrey et al., eds., *The Joseph Smith Papers*, 7 vols. (Salt Lake City, 2008–18), 7:457–72, esp. 469–70. Thanks to Spencer McBride for bringing this letter to my attention.

99. Bernard Mary Foschini, "'Those Who Are Baptized for the Dead,' I Cor. 15:29: An Exegetical Historical Dissertation," *Catholic Biblical Quarterly* 13,3 (July 1951): 283.

100. It is possible that two early Christian groups—Marcionites and Cerinthians—baptized the living in the name of those who accepted Christ but died before receiving

baptism. Jeffrey A. Trumbower, *Rescue for the Dead: The Posthumous Salvation of Non-Christians in Early Christianity* (New York, 2001), 36–39.

101. Julius Friedrich Sachse, *The German Sectarians of Pennsylvania, 1708–1800*, 2 vols. (Philadelphia, 1899), 1:365–66.

102. D. Michael Quinn, *Early Mormonism and the Magic World View* (Salt Lake City, 1987), 193. See also John L. Brooke, *The Refiner's Fire: The Making of Mormon Cosmology, 1644–1844* (New York, 1994), 44, 187, 243.

103. Evan L. Ivie and Douglas C. Heiner, "Deaths in Early Nauvoo, Illinois, 1839–46, and in Winter Quarters, Nebraska, 1846–48," *Religious Educator* 10,3 (2009): 163–74, esp. figure 6.

104. Richard A. Meckel, "Immigration, Mortality, and Population Growth in Boston, 1840–1880," *Journal of Interdisciplinary History* 15,3 (Winter 1985): 401.

105. Alexander L. Baugh, "'For This Ordinance Belongeth to My House': The Practice of Baptism for the Dead Outside the Nauvoo Temple," *Mormon Historical Studies* 3,1 (Spring 2002): 47–58.

106. This is a rough estimate. According to Ivie and Heiner, "Deaths in Early Nauvoo," Nauvoo was home to 5,150 residents in 1841. The median age in the 1840 U.S. census was 17.8. I am assuming that about half of those who lived in Nauvoo were likewise adults.

107. M. Guy Bishop, "'What Has Become of Our Fathers?' Baptism for the Dead at Nauvoo," *Dialogue* 23,2 (Summer 1990): 85–97, esp. 88–91.

108. Joseph Fielding to Brother Robinson, December 28, 1841, in *Times and Seasons* (Nauvoo) 3,5 (January 1, 1842): 649 (hereafter *T&S*).

109. J. H. Johnson, "Baptism for the Dead," *T&S* 2,23 (October 1, 1841): 565.

110. Bishop, "'What Has Become of Our Fathers?'" 93, 96.

111. Scott G. Kenney, ed., *Wilford Woodruff's Journal*, 9 vols. (Midvale, Utah, 1983–85), 2:167 (April 9, 1842) (hereafter *WWJ*).

112. *T&S* 2,24 (October 15, 1841): 577–78.

113. *WWJ*, 2:226 (April 16, 1843). For the very similar account of Willard Richards, see Andrew F. Ehat and Lyndon W. Cook, eds., *The Words of Joseph Smith: The Contemporary Accounts of the Nauvoo Discourses of the Prophet Joseph* (Provo, Utah, 1980), 195–96 (hereafter *WJS*).

114. *WJS*, 199.

115. "Baptism for the Dead," *T&S* 3,12 (April 15, 1842): 760.

116. *WWJ*, 2:388 (April 7, 1844).

117. *WJS*, 352. Report of Thomas Bullock, April 7, 1844.

118. *WWJ*, 2:455 (August 26, 1844), 2:504 (February 6, 1845).

119. On outsiders' criticism of baptism for the dead, see Terryl Givens, *The Viper on the Hearth: Mormons, Myths, and the Construction of Heresy* (New York, 1997), 49; and Patrick Q. Mason, *The Mormon Menace: Violence and Anti-Mormonism in the Postbellum South* (New York, 2011), 118.

120. *WWJ*, 2:414 (June 27, 1844).

121. Quoted in Laurel Thatcher Ulrich, *A House Full of Females: Plural Marriage and Women's Rights in Early Mormonism, 1835–1870* (New York, 2017), 51.

CHAPTER 7

1. All four Jocelyn diaries are held by CHS. "Lines to Isaac Our Little Nephew," Elizabeth Jocelyn Diary, undated entry, 1847 ("beaming," "exquisite").

2. Elizabeth Jocelyn Diary, February 15, 1839 ("reflecting"); Margaret Jocelyn Diary, February 1839 ("father painting").

3. Phoebe Lloyd, "Posthumous Mourning Portraiture," in *A Time to Mourn: Expressions of Grief in Nineteenth-Century America*, ed. Martha V. Pike and Janice Gray Armstrong (Stony Brook, N.Y., 1980), 71–89, esp. 71.

4. Elizabeth Jocelyn Diary, February 15 ("lock of hair"), March 2 ("prayers"), and February 19, 1839 ("almost cruel"); Margaret Jocelyn Diary, March 2, 1839 ("cloth cap").

5. Elizabeth Jocelyn Diary, April 8, 1839; Frances Jocelyn Diary, February 11, 1840; Frances Jocelyn Diary, November 28, 1850, quoted in Toby Maria Chieffo-Reidway, "Nathaniel Jocelyn: In the Service of Art and Abolition" (PhD diss., College of William and Mary, 2005), 182.

6. See, for example, the plaster cast James Gibson Powers created from his dead son's head in 1838. Stacy C. Hollander, *Securing the Shadow: Posthumous Portraiture in America* (New York, 2016), 182–83.

7. For the first half of the nineteenth century, I use "mainstream Protestantism" to refer to denominations from Episcopalians and Unitarians to Baptists and Methodists: basically all except new religious movements such as Shakers, Mormons, and Universalists. Despite the differences among mainstream denominations, they shared many (though not all) ideas about heaven and the soul's fate after death. On the presence of a broad-based "distilled Protestant vernacular," see T. J. Tomlin, *A Divinity for All Persuasions: Almanacs and Early American Religious Life* (New York, 2014), 2. On the unity and power of the "Protestant mainstream," see Elizabeth Hayes Alvarez, *The Valiant Woman: The Virgin Mary in Nineteenth-Century American Culture* (Chapel Hill, 2016), 10. For a contrary view, see R. Laurence Moore, *Religious Outsiders and the Making of Americans* (New York, 1986).

8. A few key titles include Susan E. Klepp, *Revolutionary Conceptions: Women, Fertility, and Family Limitation in America, 1760–1820* (Chapel Hill, 2009); Mary Louise Kete, *Sentimental Collaborations: Mourning and Middle-Class Identity in Nineteenth-Century America* (Durham, N.C., 2000); Mary Kelley, *Learning to Stand and Speak: Women, Education, and Public Life in America's Republic* (Chapel Hill, 2006); David Paul Nord, *Faith in Reading: Religious Publishing and the Birth of Mass Media in America* (New York, 2004); and E. Brooks Holifield, *Theology in America: Christian Thought from the Age of the Puritans to the Civil War* (New Haven, Conn., 2003).

9. *Oxford English Dictionary*, "cult," def. 2.b ("strange"), 2.a ("veneration"). On cults of the dead in other times and places, see, for example, Emily Ahern, *The Cult of the Dead in a Chinese Village* (Stanford, Calif., 1973); F. D. Blackley, "Isabella of France, Queen of England, 1308–1358, and the Late Medieval Cult of the Dead," *Canadian Journal of History* 15,1 (April 1980): 23–47; Åke Hultkrantz, "The Cult of the Dead Among North American Indians," in *Belief and Worship in Native North America*, ed. Hultkrantz (Syracuse, N.Y., 1981), 91–114; Hugo G. Nutini, *Todos Santos in Rural Tlaxcala: A Syncretic, Expressive, and Symbolic Analysis of the Cult of the Dead* (Princeton, N.J., 1988); and Susan-Mary Grant, "Patriot Graves: American National Identity and the Civil War Dead," *American Nineteenth Century History* 5,3 (Fall 2004): 74–100.

10. Robert A. Orsi, *Between Heaven and Earth: The Religious Worlds People Make and the Scholars Who Study Them* (Princeton, N.J., 2005), 2.

11. For a recent application of the concept to an African traditional religion, see Samuel Edukubile Etikpah, "The Kundum Festival in Ghana: Ritual Interaction with the Nonhuman Among the Akan," *Journal of African Religions* 3,4 (2015): 343–96.

12. Robert A. Orsi, *History and Presence* (Cambridge, Mass., 2016), ch. 1; Sally M. Promey, ed., *Sensational Religion: Sensory Cultures in Material Practice* (New Haven, Conn., 2014).

13. Allan I. Ludwig, *Graven Images: New England Stonecarving and Its Symbols, 1650–1815* (Middletown, Conn., 1966); Peter Benes, *The Masks of Orthodoxy: Folk Gravestone Carving in Plymouth County, Massachusetts, 1689–1805* (Amherst, Mass., 1977); James Blachowicz, *From Slate to Marble: Gravestone Carving Traditions in Eastern Massachusetts, 1770–1870* (Evanston, Ill., 2006).

14. Blanche Linden-Ward, *Silent City on a Hill: Landscapes of Memory and Boston's Mount Auburn Cemetery* (Columbus, Ohio, 1989).

15. Gary Laderman, *The Sacred Remains: American Attitudes Toward Death, 1799–1883* (New Haven, Conn., 1996), 50. See also Michael Kammen, *Digging Up the Dead: A History of Notable American Reburials* (Chicago, 2010), 10, 18.

16. Karen Halttunen, *Confidence Men and Painted Women: A Study of Middle-Class Culture in America, 1830–1870* (New Haven, Conn., 1982), 124.

17. Marla R. Miller, *The Needle's Eye: Women and Work in the Age of Revolution* (Amherst, Mass., 2006), 96 (as young as five); Maureen Daly Goggin, "Stitching (in) Death: Eighteenth- and Nineteenth-Century American and English Mourning Samplers," in *Women and the Material Culture of Death*, ed. Goggin and Beth Fowkes Tobin (Farnham, Eng., 2013), 66 ("all classes").

18. Marla R. Miller, *Rebecca Dickinson: Independence for a New England Woman* (Boulder, Colo., 2014), 42.

19. Exceptions include Miller, *The Needle's Eye*; and Laurel Thatcher Ulrich, *The Age of Homespun: Objects and Stories in the Creation of an American Myth* (New York, 2001), chs. 4 and 6.

20. Goggin, "Stitching (in) Death"; Jamie L. Brummitt, "Mary Lyman's Mourning Piece," *Conversations: An Online Journal of the Center for the Study of Material and Visual Cultures of Religion* (2014), http://mavcor.yale.edu/conversations/object-narratives/mary-lyman-s-mourning -piece (accessed July 28, 2016); Catherine E. Kelly, "Mourning Becomes Them: The Death of Children in Nineteenth-Century American Art," *Antiques* 183,4 (July/August 2016): 80–87.

21. A research assistant and I created a database from books, articles, and online collections. We found 225 examples of mourning embroidery, 189 of which fall within this chapter's geographical and chronological parameters.

22. Betty Ring, *Girlhood Embroidery: American Samplers and Pictorial Needlework, 1650– 1850*, 2 vols. (New York, 1993), 1:20.

23. Kelley, *Learning to Stand and Speak*, 67.

24. Ring, *Girlhood Embroidery*, xvii, 24.

25. By comparison, gravestones on Cape Cod almost universally had at least a brief epitaph (only 3.6 percent [20/554] from 1800 to 1849 did not).

26. "Mourning Sampler c. 1815," Art Institute Chicago, Department of Textiles Collection, http://www.artic.edu/aic/collections/artwork/193391?search_no=19&index=160 (accessed July 29, 2016).

27. Mark S. Schantz, *Awaiting the Heavenly Country: The Civil War and America's Culture of Death* (Ithaca, N.Y., 2008), ch. 2, esp. 40–41.

28. National Museum of American History, "American Samplers," http://americanhistory .si.edu/collections/search/object/nmah_1148275 (accessed August 2, 2016).

29. National Society of the Colonial Dames of America, "American Samplers and Pictorial Needlework," http://nscda.org/historical-activities/samplers/ (accessed August 9, 2016).

30. Samuel Taylor Coleridge, *Poems on Various Subjects* (London, 1796), 31.

31. First published in 1817. "Christ, Of All My Hopes the Ground," Hymnary.org, http://www.hymnary.org/text/christ_of_all_my_hopes_the_ground (accessed August 15, 2016). The verses include 1 Cor. 9:24, Acts 20:24, and Phil. 3:14.

32. Margaret Bendroth, "Children of Adam, Children of God: Christian Nurture in Early Nineteenth-Century America," *Theology Today* 56,4 (January 2000): 495–505.

33. Nigel Llewellyn, "Elizabeth Parker's 'Sampler': Memory, Suicide, and the Presence of the Artist," in *Material Memories*, ed. Marius Kwint, Christopher Breward, and Jeremy Aynsley (New York, 1999), 59–71, esp. 63.

34. The sampler's date is uncertain. It states that Caroline "Died June 7th 18" followed by a circle that seems decorative. The likeliest year is 1818.

35. "Come, And Let Us Sweetly Join," Cyberhymnal, http://cyberhymnal.org/htm/c/o/comelusj.htm (accessed August 15, 2016).

36. An exception to the scholarly consensus is Thomas W. Laqueur, *The Work of the Dead: A Cultural History of Mortal Remains* (Princeton, N.J., 2015), 186.

37. To compare with the power of human remains among Africans in the Americas, see J. B. Moreton, *West India Customs and Manners* (London, 1793), 162; J. Stewart, *A View of the Present State of the Island of Jamaica* (London, 1823), 267; Jerome S. Handler and Frederick W. Lange, *Plantation Slavery in Barbados: An Archaeological and Historical Investigation* (Cambridge, Mass., 1978), 185–86; and Vincent Brown, *The Reaper's Garden: Death and Power in the World of Atlantic Slavery* (Cambridge, Mass., 2008). Among Amerindians, see David Beers Quinn, ed., *The Roanoke Voyages, 1584–1590*, 2 vols. (London, 1955), 1:425–27; Peter Gose, *Invaders as Ancestors: On the Intercultural Making and Unmaking of Spanish Colonialism in the Andes* (Toronto, 2008), 139–55; and Erik R. Seeman, *The Huron-Wendat Feast of the Dead: Indian-European Encounters in Early North America* (Baltimore, 2011).

38. Gordon E. Geddes, *Welcome Joy: Death in Puritan New England* (Ann Arbor, 1981), 117–19.

39. Laderman, *Sacred Remains*, 31.

40. *Diary of Sarah Connell Ayer* (Portland, Me., 1910), 341 (entry of November 12, 1832). See also Laura Hadley Moseley, ed., *The Diaries of Julia Cowles: A Connecticut Record, 1797–1803* (New Haven, Conn., 1931), 77 (entry of April 25, 1800); and Nancy Thompson Diary, CHS, October 27, 1821.

41. Mary Ware Allen Johnson Diary, AAS, May 9, 1836.

42. Margaret Jocelyn Diary, February 1839.

43. On beautiful corpses in imaginative literature, see Jessica F. Roberts, "'The little coffin': Anthologies, Conventions, and Dead Children," in *Representations of Death in Nineteenth-Century U.S. Writing and Culture*, ed. Lucy E. Frank (Aldershot, Eng., 2007), 141–54. On the nineteenth century as the "Age of the Beautiful Death," see Philippe Ariès, *The Hour of Our Death*, trans. Helen Weaver (New York, 1981), ch. 10.

44. Mary Ware Allen Johnson Diary, July 29, 1838. See also T. Merritt, ed., *Memoir, Diary, and Letters, of Miss Hannah Syng Bunting, of Philadelphia*, 2 vols. (New York, 1837), 2:100 (letter of November 30, 1827).

45. Edward Wagenknecht, ed., *Mrs. Longfellow: Selected Letters and Journals of Fanny Appleton Longfellow, 1817–1861* (New York, 1956), 141 (entry of September 11, 1848).

46. Elizabeth Pierce Diary, Poor Family Papers, SL, March 30, 1826. Viewed online at http://nrs.harvard.edu/urn-3:RAD.SCHL:29082228 (accessed October 5, 2017).

47. E. Brooks Holifield, "The Religion of the Protestant Child in Early America," *Church History* 76,4 (December 2007): 767.

48. Louisa Jane Trumbull Diary, AAS, February 7, 1833.

49. Benjamin B. Wisner, ed., *Memoirs of the Late Mrs. Susan Huntington, of Boston, Mass.* (Boston, 1826), 226 (entry of March 1820). See also Mary Wilder Tileston, ed., *Caleb and Mary Wilder Foote: Reminiscences and Letters* (Boston, 1918), 55–56 (letter of September 6, 1837), 101–2 (letter of October 3, 1842); and Robert V. Wells, *Facing the "King of Terrors": Death and Society in an American Community, 1750–1990* (New York, 2000), 48 (letter of December 7, 1829).

50. Louisa Adams Park Diary, AAS, May 2, 1801.

51. Ibid.

52. Ibid., May 23 and 24, 1801.

53. *The Diary of William Bentley, D.D.: Pastor of the East Church, Salem, Massachusetts*, 4 vols. (Salem, Mass., 1905–14), 2:372 (entry of May 10, 1801).

54. [Lucius M. Sargent], *Dealings with the Dead, by a Sexton of the Old School*, 2 vols. (Boston, 1856), 1:45–46. See also Theodore Dwight Jr., *The Father's Book; or, Suggestions for the Government and Instruction of Young Children*, 2nd ed. (Springfield, Mass., 1835), 88.

55. Laderman, *Sacred Remains*, 32–34.

56. Joseph S. Buckminster, *A Sermon Preached at the Church in Brattle Street, Boston, December 18th, 1808, the Lord's Day After the Publick Funeral of His Excellency James Sullivan* (Boston, 1809), 36.

57. Peter Holt, *A Sermon Delivered at Deerfield, New-Hampshire, February 25, 1811, at the Funeral of the Reverend Timothy Upham* (Concord, N.H., 1811), 16–17.

58. For example, Josiah Whitney, *A Funeral Sermon, Delivered at Brooklyn, on the 30th Day of November 1789, at the Interment of Mrs. Mehitabel Tyler* (Norwich, Conn., 1790), 15–16; William Miltimore, *A Sermon, Occasioned by the Death of Mrs. Clarissa Webber* (Portland, Me., 1815), 13–14; James Freeman and Samuel Cary, *Funeral Sermons, Preached at Kingschapel, Boston* (Boston, 1820), 44; and Henry Cogswell Knight, *Lectures and Sermons*, 2 vols. (Boston, 1831), 2:12. Ruth Bascom reported hearing a sermon that spoke for the dead. Ruth Henshaw Miles Bascom Diary, AAS, April 7, 1841.

59. Stephen Marini, "Hymnody as History: Early Evangelical Hymns and the Recovery of American Popular Religion," *Church History* 71,2 (June 2002): 273–306; Candy Gunther Brown, *The Word in the World: Evangelical Writing, Publishing, and Reading in America, 1789–1880* (Chapel Hill, 2004), ch. 7.

60. Janis Van Wagoner Diary, NYSL, July 31 and August 2, 1838.

61. Hymnary.org, https://hymnary.org/text/thou_art_gone_to_the_grave_but_we_will_n (accessed October 9, 2017).

62. Agnes Jeffrey Sentiment Album, 1827–1876, UR, undated entry (likely 1830s), p. 183.

63. Hymnary.org.

64. Janis Van Wagoner Diary, September 6 and 7, 1838.

65. Hymnary.org, https://hymnary.org/text/sister_thou_wast_mild_and_lovely (accessed October 9, 2017).

66. Janis Van Wagoner Diary, January 18, 1839.

67. The first two are found in John Wesley and Charles Wesley, *Funeral Hymns* (London, 1746), 2–3, 17–19; the second two at Hymnary.org.

68. Helen Sheumaker, *Love Entwined: The Curious History of Hairwork in America* (Philadelphia, 2007), xiii.

69. Quoted in ibid., 20.

70. Lynne Templeton Brickley, "Sarah Pierce's Litchfield Female Academy, 1792–1833" (PhD diss., Harvard University, 1985), 675n73.

71. Halttunen, *Confidence Men and Painted Women*, 139.

72. Marcia Pointon, "Materializing Mourning: Hair, Jewellery, and the Body," in *Material Memories*, ed. Marius Kwint, Christopher Breward, and Jeremy Aynsley (New York, 1999), 39–57, esp. 42. For a pendant and ring that describe their hair contents as "sacred," see Sarah Nehama, *In Death Lamented: The Tradition of Anglo-American Mourning Jewelry* (Boston, 2012), 47, 81.

73. Wagenknecht, *Mrs. Longfellow*, 142 (entry of September 12, 1848).

74. *Diary of William Bentley*, 3:127 (entry of December 13, 1804).

75. Louisa Jane Trumbull Diary, July 13, 1832.

76. Eliza M. Spencer Diary, typescript, MHS, June 21, 1834.

77. Philippa C. Bush, ed., *Memoir of Anne Gorham Everett, with Extracts from Her Correspondence and Journal* (Boston, 1857), 311 (letter of November 2, 1843). Emphasis added.

78. Wendy M. Schaller, "Children Borne Aloft: Nicolaes Maes's Ganymede Portraiture and the Context of Death and Mourning in the Seventeenth-Century Netherlands" (PhD diss., Ohio State University, 2001), 50; Kathryn Beattie, "Aspects of Acceptance and Denial in Painted Posthumous Portraits and Postmortem Photographs of Nineteenth-Century Children" (MA thesis, Concordia University, 2005), 6.

79. For other examples, see Hollander, *Securing the Shadow*, 119; and Lloyd, "Posthumous Mourning Portraiture," 77.

80. All items made in Great Britain and held by the Victoria and Albert Museum, London. Museum numbers 918-1888 (ring), 920-1888 (brooch), 925-1888 (locket).

81. Charles Beecher, ed., *Autobiography, Correspondence, Etc., of Lyman Beecher, D.D.*, 2 vols. (New York, 1864), 1:178.

82. Shepard Alonzo Mount to William Shepard Mount, May 15, 1868. Quoted in Martha Pike, "In Memory of: Artifacts Relating to Mourning in Nineteenth-Century America," in *American Material Culture: The Shape of Things Around Us*, ed. Edith Mayo (Bowling Green, Ohio, 1984), 55.

83. Jane Minot Sedgwick Diary, NEHGS, November 8, 1841. See also Priscilla Wakefield, *Variety; or, Selections and Essays, Consisting of Anecdotes, Curious Facts, Interesting Narratives, with Occasional Reflections* (Philadelphia, 1809), 159–60.

84. George W. Bethune, *Memoirs of Mrs. Joanna Bethune* (New York, 1863), 189–90 (entry of September 25, 1831).

85. Sarah Brown Ruggles Eaton Diary, RIHS, February 15, 1834.

86. Jay Ruby, *Secure the Shadow: Death and Photography in America* (Cambridge, Mass., 1995); Rachel McBride Lindsey, *A Communion of Shadows: Religion and Photography in Nineteenth-Century America* (Chapel Hill, 2017), ch. 2.

87. See also Hollander, *Securing the Shadow*, 176, 177.

88. Ibid., 197; Geoffrey Batchen, *Forget Me Not: Photography and Remembrance* (New York, 2004), 11, 13.

89. Hollander, *Securing the Shadow*, 217.

90. Batchen, *Forget Me Not*, 65, 66, 70.

91. David Morgan, *The Sacred Gaze: Religious Visual Culture in Theory and Practice* (Berkeley, 2005), 3.

92. Jack Larkin, *The Reshaping of Everyday Life, 1790–1840* (New York, 1988), 104.

93. Blanche Linden-Ward, "Strange but Genteel Pleasure Grounds: Tourist and Leisure Uses of Nineteenth-Century Rural Cemeteries," in *Cemeteries and Gravemarkers: Voices of American Culture*, ed. Richard E. Meyer (Logan, Utah, 1992), 293–328; Linden-Ward, *Silent City on*

a Hill; Thomas Bender, "The 'Rural' Cemetery Movement: Urban Travail and the Appeal of Nature," *New England Quarterly* 47,2 (June 1974): 196–211; Stanley French, "The Cemetery as Cultural Institution: The Establishment of Mount Auburn and the 'Rural Cemetery' Movement," in *Death in America*, ed. David E. Stannard (Philadelphia, 1975), 69–91; David Charles Sloane, *The Last Great Necessity: Cemeteries in American History* (Baltimore, 1991), 53–64; Jeffrey Smith, *The Rural Cemetery Movement: Places of Paradox in Nineteenth-Century America* (Lanham, Md., 2017).

94. Colleen McDannell, *Material Christianity: Religion and Popular Culture in America* (New Haven, Conn., 1995), ch. 4; Dell Upton, *Another City: Urban Life and Urban Spaces in the New American Republic* (New Haven, Conn., 2008), ch. 9.

95. Felicia Hemans, "Dirge of a Child," in *The Poetical Works of Mrs. Felicia Hemans*, 4th American ed., 2 vols. (New York, 1828), 2:82. At least ten editions of this volume were published in the United States before 1850.

96. Azubah Handy, 1819, Cotuit Mosswood Cemetery, Barnstable.

97. Upton, *Another City*, 217–21, quotation at 219; Sloane, *Last Great Necessity*, 29–34.

98. On the "democratic family" in America, see Steven Mintz and Susan Kellogg, *Domestic Revolutions: A Social History of American Family Life* (New York, 1988), ch. 3. On "domestic religion" and the presence of the dead within familial settings across time and space, see Jonathan Z. Smith, "Here, There, and Anywhere," in *Relating Religion: Essays in the Study of Religion*, ed. Smith (Chicago, 2004), 323–39.

99. Many thanks to my Buffalo colleague Neil Coffee for help with the Latin. He points out that *familiares* includes unrelated household members such as servants and slaves, and could even extend to friends. I use it, however, only for blood relations.

100. Sloane, *Last Great Necessity*, 42; Upton, *Another City*, 221–23, quotation at 223.

101. Catherine Henshaw Diary, AAS, April 14, 1805.

102. Merritt, ed., *Memoir, Diary, and Letters, of Miss Hannah Syng Bunting*, 1:117 (entry of April 1827), 2:135 (letter of July 24, 1831).

103. *Diary of Sarah Connell Ayer*, 57–59 (entry of August 29, 1808), 229 (entry of June 21, 1822).

104. "The Village Grave-Yard," *The Club-Room* (Boston) 1,2 (March 1, 1820): 70–77. For a small sampling of similar pieces, see "The Grave-Yard," *Guardian; or, Youth's Religious Instructor* (New Haven) 3,3 (March 1, 1821): 90–92; "The Grave of a Mother," *Religious Miscellany* (Carlisle, Pa.) 1,19 (May 30, 1823): 295–96; and "The Mother's Lament," *Ladies' Magazine* (Boston) 1,1 (January 1828): 16–17.

105. Reprinted or excerpted: "Life," *Ladies' Literary Cabinet* (New York) 2,14 (August 12, 1820): 106–7; *Christian Advocate and Journal and Zion's Herald* (New York) 5,2 (September 10, 1830): 8; "The Village Graveyard," *Youth's Companion* (Boston) 5,17 (September 14, 1831): 67–68. Read to students: Mary Ware Allen Johnson Diary, March 26, 1838.

106. Anna Eliza Heath Commonplace Book, MHS, undated entry, likely early 1820s; Anna Eliza Heath Diary, MHS, March 18, 1825.

107. Linden-Ward, *Silent City on a Hill*, ch. 6; Sloane, *Last Great Necessity*, 34–43.

108. Quoted in Linden-Ward, *Silent City on a Hill*, 168.

109. William M. Story, ed., *Life and Letters of Joseph Story*, 2 vols. (Boston, 1851), 2:65.

110. George Waterman Jr., "My Mother," *Godey's Magazine and Lady's Book* (New York) 28,1 (January 1844): 45.

111. "Untitled," *New-York Mirror* 11,34 (February 22, 1834): 270. See also, for example, J. G. Percival, "Death: (An Extract)," *Knickerbocker; or, New York Monthly Magazine* 7,6 (June 1836):

572; and "Our Parents Sleep There," *Every Youth's Gazette* (New York) 1,27 (December 24, 1842): 398.

112. "Laurel Hill Cemetery," *Episcopal Recorder* (Philadelphia) 24,2 (March 28, 1846): 5.

113. W. Nixon, "Miniature Sketches: Laurel Hill Cemetery, Philadelphia," *Ladies Repository and Gatherings of the West* (Cincinnati) 6,11 (November 1846): 336.

114. Sarah Brown Ruggles Eaton Diary, October 21, 1837. On tourism in Laurel Hill, see Aaron Vickers Wunsch, "Parceling the Picturesque: 'Rural' Cemeteries and Urban Context in Nineteenth-Century Philadelphia" (PhD diss., University of California, Berkeley, 2009), 99, 115–18.

115. Sarah Brown Ruggles Eaton Diary, March 6 and April 13, 1834.

116. Louisa Jane Trumbull Diary, February 9, 1833.

117. Eliza M. Spencer Diary, September 10, 1832.

118. Ibid., August 4, 1833.

119. James Hervey, *Meditations and Contemplations*, 4th ed., 2 vols. (London, 1748), 2:51.

120. Adelia M. Beckley Lamb Diary, typescript, CHS, May 1834.

121. Findagrave.com, https://www.findagrave.com/cgi-bin/fg.cgi?page=gsr&GScid=1993801 (accessed October 30, 2017).

122. Adelia M. Beckley Lamb Diary, July 10, 1836, March 1, 1840, July 1838.

123. Colleen McDannell and Bernhard Lang, *Heaven: A History* (New Haven, Conn., 1988), ch. 7.

124. Orsi, *History and Presence*, 25.

125. For example, Mark A. Peterson, "Puritanism and Refinement in Early New England: Reflections on Communion Silver," *William and Mary Quarterly* 58,2 (April 2001): 307–46; Louis P. Nelson, ed., *American Sanctuary: Understanding Sacred Spaces* (Bloomington, Ind., 2006); David Morgan, *Visual Piety: A History and Theory of Popular Religious Images* (Berkeley, 1998); and Promey, *Sensational Religion*.

126. I infer this from the fact that their father was a deacon there, and the North Church minister presided over all four sisters' marriages. Samuel W. S. Dutton, *The History of the North Church in New Haven* (New Haven, Conn., 1842), 128 (deacon); *Vital Records of New Haven, 1649–1850*, 2 vols. (Hartford, Conn., 1917), 2:939, 984, 1058, 1059 (marriages).

127. Douglas A. Sweeney, *Nathaniel Taylor, New Haven Theology, and the Legacy of Jonathan Edwards* (New York, 2003).

CHAPTER 8

1. *Vital Records of Brookline, Massachusetts, To the End of the Year 1849* (Salem, Mass., 1929), 207.

2. Anna Eliza Heath Diary, MHS, March 18, 1825.

3. Ibid., April 7, 1825.

4. Ibid., April 19, 1825.

5. Samuel Whelpley, *Thoughts on the State of Departed Souls* (Morristown, N.J., 1807), 4.

6. Henry Holcombe, *The Funeral Sermon of Joseph Moulder* (Philadelphia, 1817), 21.

7. Robert A. Orsi, *History and Presence* (Cambridge, Mass., 2016), 4.

8. The returned dead could still be menacing. In addition to belief in ghosts, scattered written and archaeological evidence suggests that some nineteenth-century New Englanders thought that those who died of consumption could return and cause their relatives to waste

away. Paul S. Sledzik and Nicholas Bellantoni, "Bioarcheological and Biocultural Evidence for the New England Vampire Folk Belief," *American Journal of Physical Anthropology* 94,2 (June 1994): 269–74.

9. Renée L. Bergland, *The National Uncanny: Indian Ghosts and American Subjects* (Hanover, N.H., 2000); Nicola Brown, Carolyn Burdett, and Pamela Thurschwell, eds., *The Victorian Supernatural* (New York, 2004); John Lardas Modern, *Secularism in Antebellum America* (Chicago, 2011). An important exception: Judith Richardson, *Possessions: The History and Uses of Haunting in the Hudson Valley* (Cambridge, Mass., 2003).

10. "Appearances of Spectres, or Phantoms Occasioned by Disease," *Western Star* (Stockbridge, Mass.), March 3, 1804.

11. "Power of Conscience," *Farmer's Cabinet* (Amherst, N.H.), September 28, 1838; "Local Affairs," *North American* (Philadelphia), November 25, 1846.

12. "Windsor Apparition," *National Advocate* (New York), January 19, 1813; "Singular Case of Spectral Illusions," *Torch Light* (Hagerstown, Md.), November 17, 1836 (from the *New York Sun*).

13. *Advice to the Fair Sex: In a Series of Letters on Various Subjects* (Philadelphia, 1803), 125; Walley Chamberlain Oulton, *The Wonderful Story-Teller; or, Pocket Library of Agreeable Entertainment* (Brookfield, Mass., 1805), 107.

14. Frederick Henry Quitman, *A Treatise on Magic; or, On the Intercourse Between Spirits and Men* (Albany, 1810), iii; "The Ghost," *Daily National Intelligencer* (Washington, D.C.), September 29, 1824.

15. "The Dread of the Supernatural," *Washington Whig* (Bridgeton, N.J.), October 21, 1822.

16. "The Ghost," *Reservoir and Public Reflector* (Frederick, Md.), July 28, 1829 (from the *Boston Patriot*).

17. The version I use is "Apparition!!!" *Mercantile Advertiser* (New York), September 23, 1803.

18. Elaine Forman Crane, *Witches, Wife Beaters, and Whores: Common Law and Common Folk in Early America* (Ithaca, N.Y., 2011), ch. 6, figures on 200.

19. The version I use is "Remarkable Trial," *Northern Whig* (Hudson, N.Y.), July 25, 1809. For the other reprintings, see Crane, *Witches, Wife Beaters, and Whores*, 257n52.

20. "Ghost or No Ghost," *The American* (New York), August 3, 1831; "Extraordinary—If True," *Watch-Tower* (Cooperstown, N.Y.), August 8, 1831.

21. "Ghost or No Ghost," *The American* (New York), August 3, 1831.

22. Ibid.

23. "Ghost or No Ghost," *Evening Post* (New York), August 3, 1831.

24. "The Mysterious Knocking," *Evening Post* (New York), August 24, 1831.

25. "The Mysterious Knocking at Albany," *National Gazette and Literary Register* (Philadelphia), September 15, 1831.

26. "A Well Authenticated Ghost," *North American* (Philadelphia), July 21, 1842. The clearest version of the deposition is in "Murder Disclosed," *Macon (Ga.) Weekly Telegraph*, August 9, 1842.

27. "A Marvellous Story Spoiled," *Public Ledger* (Philadelphia), July 28, 1842. Emphasis in original.

28. "A Story of a Ghost: Salem Witchcraft Revived," *New-Hampshire Patriot*, August 25, 1842.

29. Susan Thompson, *The Penny Press: The Origins of the Modern News Media, 1833–1861* (Northport, Ala., 2004). Only scattered issues of the *Sun* survive from before 1859.

30. "Singular Affair," *Baltimore Sun*, February 26, 1846. The deposition appeared in "A Genuine Ghost Story," *New Bedford (Mass.) Mercury*, April 24, 1846.

31. "Singular Affair," *Baltimore Sun*, February 26, 1846.

32. David Keck, *Angels and Angelology in the Middle Ages* (New York, 1998), 161–65.

33. Peter Marshall and Alexandra Walsham, "Migrations of Angels in the Early Modern World," in *Angels in the Early Modern World*, ed. Marshall and Walsham (New York, 2006), 10.

34. Anne F. Sutton and Livia Visser-Fuchs, "The Cult of Angels in Late Fifteenth-Century England: An Hours of the Guardian Angel Presented to Queen Elizabeth Woodville," in *Women and the Book: Assessing the Visual Evidence*, ed. Lesley Smith and Jane H. M. Taylor (Oxford, 1997), 252.

35. Peter Marshall, "The Guardian Angel in Protestant England," in *Conversations with Angels: Essays Towards a History of Spiritual Communication, 1100–1700*, ed. Joad Raymond (New York, 2011), 296.

36. John Calvin, *The Institutes of the Christian Religion*, trans. Henry Beveridge, 2 vols. (1536; Edinburgh, 1845), 1:196 (book 1, ch. 14, para. 7).

37. John Bayly, *Two Sermons: The Angell Guardian. The Light Enlightening* (Oxford, 1630); Richard Baxter, *The Protestant Religion Truly Stated and Justified* (London, 1692).

38. Elizabeth Reis, "Otherworldly Visions: Angels, Devils, and Gender in Puritan New England," in *Angels in the Early Modern World*, ed. Marshall and Walsham, 282.

39. Increase Mather, *Angelographia; or, A Discourse Concerning the Nature and Power of the Holy Angels* (Boston, 1696), 40; Joseph Emerson, *Early Piety Encouraged: A Discourse Occasion'd by the Joyful and Triumphant Death of a Young Woman of Malden* (Boston, 1738), 26.

40. See, for example, Mather, *Angelographia*, 103.

41. *Works of Jonathan Edwards Online*, http://edwards.yale.edu/ (accessed December 1, 2017).

42. Marshall and Walsham, "Migrations of Angels," 39n136. Ann Braude mentions in a footnote but does not explore the "popular notion that virtuous people became angels after death." Braude, *Radical Spirits: Spiritualism and Women's Rights in Nineteenth-Century America*, 2nd ed. (1989; Bloomington, Ind., 2001), 43.

43. Theophilus Rowe, ed., *The Miscellaneous Works, in Prose and Verse, of Mrs. Elizabeth Rowe*, 2nd ed., 2 vols. (London, 1749), 2:24. The identification of the letter's recipient is from Paula R. Backscheider, *Elizabeth Singer Rowe and the Development of the English Novel* (Baltimore, 2013), 166.

44. Elizabeth Singer Rowe, *Friendship in Death: In Twenty Letters from the Dead to the Living* (London, 1728), 80. See also 75.

45. "Wrote, on the Annaversay [*sic*] of My Dear Parent's Death (A Day, never to be forgot by me)," Hannah Griffitts Papers, Box 1, Folder 12, February 13, 1759, HSP. See also Griffitts's 1763 elegy to her mother, Box 1, Folder 36.

46. *The History of Clorana, the Beautiful Arcadian; or, Virtue Triumphant* (London, 1737), 119–20. See also *The History of Eliza Warwick*, 2 vols. (London, 1778), 2:248–49; and "On the Death of Miss R——D——," *Pennsylvania Magazine* 1,3 (March 1775): 135.

47. Martha Read, *Monima; or, The Beggar Girl: A Novel* (New York, 1802), 85, 397. Cathy N. Davidson, *Revolution and the Word: The Rise of the Novel in America* (New York, 1986), 361 ("widely read"), citing three book-length editions and numerous pirated and condensed versions. See also Eliza Parsons, *The Girl of the Mountains: A Novel*, 2 vols. (Philadelphia, 1801), 1:66; and Maria Regina Roche, *Nocturnal Visit: A Tale*, 2 vols. (Philadelphia, 1801), 2:66.

48. "Addressed to a Mother, on the Death of Two Infants," *American Register* (Philadelphia) 1 (January 1, 1807): 195–97. See also Sylvia D. Hoffert, "'A Very Peculiar Sorrow': Atti-

tudes Toward Infant Death in the Urban Northeast, 1800–1860," *American Quarterly* 39,4 (Winter 1987): 601–16, esp. 609.

49. A few examples: "The Little Girl's Answer to Her Baby Cousin," *Juvenile Miscellany* (Boston) 2,3 (July 1827): 106; "Lines, on Hearing a Mother Bid Farewell to Her Little Daughter," *New York Evangelist* 7,31 (July 30, 1836): 124; "The Dying Mother's Prayer," *Christian Secretary* (Hartford, Conn.) 23,24 (August 23, 1844): 4.

50. Ann S. Stephens, "The Black Seal," *Ladies' Companion* (New York) 12,1 (November 1839): 18.

51. "The Departed," *Liberator* (Boston) 13,18 (May 5, 1843): 72.

52. For example, "The Widow's Daughter," *Rural Repository* (Hudson, N.Y.) 9,16 (December 29, 1832): 121; and Lydia Huntley Sigourney, *Letters to Mothers* (Hartford, Conn., 1838), 212.

53. Anna Eliza Heath Diary, April 19, 1825; H. Gally Knight, "The Portrait," *Christian Examiner and Theological Review* (Boston) 1,6 (November/December 1824): 452–53.

54. Quoted in Paul C. Rosenblatt, *Bitter, Bitter Tears: Nineteenth-Century Diarists and Twentieth-Century Grief Theories* (Minneapolis, 1983), 18 (entry of March 10, 1844).

55. Clifford Merrill Drury, ed., *First White Women over the Rockies*, 2 vols. (Glendale, Calif., 1963), 2:270 (entry of July 18, 1844). See also *Memoir of Mrs. Mary E. Van Lennep, Only Daughter of the Rev. Joel Hawes*, 6th ed. (Hartford, Conn., 1850), 67 (entry of December 19, 1840).

56. Adelia M. Beckley Lamb Diary, CHS, April 7, 1839. See also April 30, 1837, on her brother's "angel spirit"; and Caroline G. Curtis, ed., *The Cary Letters* (Cambridge, Mass., 1891), 313 (letter of September 28, 1825).

57. Louisa Jane Trumbull Diary, AAS, January 5, 1834. See also *Diary of Sarah Connell Ayer* (Portland, Me., 1910), 56 (entry of August 12, 1808).

58. Mary Wilder Tileston, ed., *Caleb and Mary Wilder Foote: Reminiscences and Letters* (Boston, 1918), 59 (letter of September 20, 1837). See also Elizabeth Jocelyn Diary, CHS, December 20, 1842; and Edward Wagenknecht, ed., *Mrs. Longfellow: Selected Letters and Journals of Fanny Appleton Longfellow, 1817–1861* (New York, 1956), 144 (entry of October 14, 1848).

59. Mary Ware Allen Johnson Diary, AAS, July 2, 1838. See also R. H. Lee, ed., *"Draveil"; or, The Life of Harriet Preble* (Philadelphia, 1876), 196–97 (entry of January 26, 1839); and W. Emerson Wilson, ed., *Phoebe George Bradford Diaries* (Wilmington, Del., 1975), 265 (letter of September 1841).

60. Elisah Andrews, *Sermon, Delivered at the Funeral of Mr. Samuel Phillips* (Worcester, Mass., 1810), 17; Nathan Holman, *A Sermon, Preached After the Death of Roland Green Sweet* (Providence, R.I., 1816); Isaac Tompkins, *A Sermon . . . at the Ordination of the Rev. Moses Welch, as an Evangelist* (Newburyport, Mass., 1819), 23.

61. Louisa Adams Park Diary, AAS, July 10, 1848.

62. Sarah Brown Ruggles Eaton Diary, RIHS, July 19 and August 19, 1833.

63. Sarah Read Hersey Diary, MHS, 1793 (p. 166). Because the diary is out of chronological order, I include the page numbers added by an archivist. I have pieced together Hersey's biography from *Vital Records of Leicester, Massachusetts, to the End of the Year 1849* (Worcester, Mass., 1903), 47, 49, 165, 260; Findagrave.com; the U.S. Census; and her diary.

64. Sarah Read Hersey Diary, December 6, 1826 (51).

65. Lewis Bayly, *The Practice of Pietie: Directing a Christian How to Walke That He May Please God*, 12th ed. (1612; London, 1620), 237–38. See also Cynthia Garrett, "The Rhetoric of

Supplication: Prayer Theory in Seventeenth-Century England," *Renaissance Quarterly* 46,2 (Summer 1993): 328–57.

66. For example, Harvey Newcomb, *The Young Lady's Guide to the Harmonious Development of Christian Character*, 3rd ed. (Boston, 1841), 86; *The Mother's Catechism*, 5th ed. (New York, 1825), 25–27; and *The Book of Private Devotion, a Series of Prayers and Meditations . . . Chiefly from the Writings of Hannah More* (New York, 1836).

67. Gordon Campbell, *Bible: The Story of the King James Version, 1611–2011* (New York, 2010), 74–76 (informal/formal), 74 ("supernatural beings").

68. Julian D. Mason Jr., ed., *The Poems of Phillis Wheatley*, rev. ed. (Chapel Hill, 1989), 89.

69. Sam D. Gill, "Prayer," in *The Encyclopedia of Religion*, ed. Mircea Eliade, 16 vols. (New York, 1987), 2:489. William James's influential definition—that prayer is "every kind of inward communion or conversation with the power recognized as divine"—likewise emphasizes communication but is limited by a Protestant bias toward "inward" interaction with "the" (singular) divine. James, *The Varieties of Religious Experience: A Study in Human Nature* (New York, 1902), 464.

70. John Preston, *The Saints Daily Exercise: A Treatise Concerning the Whole Dutie of Prayer* (London, 1629), 13–14.

71. Isaac Watts, *A Guide to Prayer; or, A Free and Rational Account of the Gift, Grace, and Spirit of Prayer*, 4th ed. (1715; London, 1725), 3–24.

72. Sarah Read Hersey Diary, December 25, 1819 (42–43).

73. Ibid., December 6, 1826 (51).

74. Ibid., August 30, 1825 (55), July 30, 1837 (78).

75. Ibid., July 4, 1826 (58), July 30, 1826 (59).

76. Ibid., July 30, 1828 (60).

77. Susan M. Stabile, *Memory's Daughters: The Material Culture of Remembrance in Eighteenth-Century America* (Ithaca, N.Y., 2004), 178.

78. Jemima Bliss Brewer Diary, CHS, March 8, 1843. When I examined this diary in 2017, it was being deaccessioned and given to MHS. See also Mercy Flynt Morris Diary, CHS, August 17, 1830; Ruth Henshaw Miles Bascom Diary, AAS, April 2, 1842; and Elizabeth Jocelyn Diary, February 12, 1847.

79. Eliza M. Spencer Diary, MHS, June 21, 1835.

80. On the powerful bonds between women and their adult children, see Terri L. Premo, *Winter Friends: Women Growing Old in the New Republic, 1785–1835* (Urbana, Ill., 1990), ch. 2.

81. Sarah Read Hersey Diary, July 30, 1827 (60).

82. *The Life and Letters of Elizabeth Payson Prentiss* (New York, 1882), 106 (letter of March 3, 1847).

83. Alfred Lee, ed., *A Life Hid with Christ in God, Being a Memoir of Susan Allibone, Chiefly Compiled from Her Diaries and Letters* (Philadelphia, 1856), 243 (entry of August 1839). See also Louisa Adams Park Diary, May 26, 1801; Elizabeth Heath Howe Diary, MHS, undated entry, 1826; Janis Van Wagoner Diary, NYSL, January 18, 1839; *Memoirs of Catharine Seely, and Deborah S. Roberts, Late of Darien, Connecticut*, 2nd ed. (New York, 1844), 199 (entry of December 10, 1837); and Adelia M. Beckley Lamb Diary, November 21, 1846.

84. *The Universal Dream-Dictionary; or, Interpreter of Dreams and Visions* (Baltimore, 1804), 33.

85. Sarah Read Hersey Diary, June 27, 1834 (90).

86. University Libraries, University of Colorado Boulder, Manuscript Census for 1830, http://libguides.colorado.edu/c.php?g=483520&p=3306545 (accessed November 20, 2017).

87. Sarah Read Hersey Diary, March 22, 1840 (80).

88. Ibid., January 1, 1835 (133).

89. Findagrave.com, https://www.findagrave.com/memorial/39685414 (accessed November 20, 2017). It is unclear how Hersey got to Rawson Brook. Most likely she moved back to central Massachusetts before her death. It is also possible the marker stands above an empty grave. Least plausible is that her sons sent the corpse from Canada to Leicester.

90. Joanna Bethune, ed., *The Unpublished Letters and Correspondence of Mrs. Isabella Graham* (New York, 1838), 113, 123 (letter of November 1773).

91. Ibid., 123. See also the English Methodist Mary Bosanquet, who communicated with her husband from his death in 1785 until her death in 1815. Anna M. Lawrence, *One Family Under God: Love, Belonging and Authority in Early Transatlantic Methodism* (Philadelphia, 2011), 182–84.

92. Lucia McMahon, "'So Truly Afflicting and Distressing to Me His Sorrowing Mother': Expressions of Maternal Grief in Eighteenth-Century Philadelphia," *Journal of the Early Republic* 32,1 (Spring 2012): 59. See also James Brown Diary, RIHS, May 20, 1798.

93. Rebecca Boylston Clark Diary, NEHGS, November 1, 1804.

94. Charles Francis Adams, ed., *Letters of Mrs. Adams, the Wife of John Adams*, 3rd ed., 2 vols. (Boston, 1841), 2:261 (letter of March 11, 1805).

95. Quoted in Rachel Hope Cleves, *Charity and Sylvia: A Same-Sex Marriage in Early America* (New York, 2014), 55 (entry of April 11, 1821). See also Lucia McMahon and Deborah Schriver, eds., *To Read My Heart: The Journal of Rachel Van Dyke, 1810–1811* (Philadelphia, 2000), 105 (entry of August 10, 1810); Benjamin B. Wisner, ed., *Memoirs of the Late Mrs. Susan Huntington, of Boston, Mass.* (Boston, 1826), 234 (entry of June 22, 1820); Anna Eliza Heath Diary, March 18 and April 19, 1825; Horatio Gray, *Memoirs of Rev. Benjamin C. Cutler, D.D., Late Rector of St. Ann's Church, Brooklyn, N.Y.* (New York, 1865), 164 (entry of October 31, 1836); and Lee, *"Draveil,"* 197.

96. Eliza M. Spencer Diary, December 8, 1836.

97. Louisa Jane Trumbull Diary, May 9, 1835.

98. Sarah Brown Ruggles Eaton Diary, April 4, 1834.

99. "On The Anniversary of That Day . . . in which Providence Depriv'd me of its Greatest and Dearest Blessing, my Beloved Parent, feb^y 13th O.S. [Old Style] 1753," Hannah Griffitts Papers, Box 1, Folder 7, HSP.

100. Sarah Brown Ruggles Eaton Diary, September 17, 1833.

101. Leigh Eric Schmidt, *Hearing Things: Religion, Illusion, and the American Enlightenment* (Cambridge, Mass., 2000), ch. 5.

102. Eighteenth-Century Collections Online, author=Swedenborg, search for "spirit land" and "spirit-land" (accessed November 28, 2017).

103. "The Two Graves," *Episcopal Watchman* (Hartford, Conn.) 1,30 (October 15, 1827): 236.

104. "The Spirit Land," *Liberator* (Boston), January 21, 1832.

105. For example, "Guardian Angels," *Rural Repository* (Hudson, N.Y.) 18,6 (August 28, 1841): 48; "First Death of a Household," *Liberator* (Boston), April 22, 1842; and George Waterman Jr., "My Mother," *Godey's Magazine and Lady's Book* (New York) 28,1 (January 1844): 45.

106. Adelia M. Beckley Lamb Diary, February 25, 1843, October 20, 1844.

107. Mary Ware Allen Johnson Diary, May 11, 1838. The story is "Consumption," in *Lights and Shadows of Scottish Life: A Selection from the Papers of the Late Arthur Austin*, 3rd ed. (Ed-

inburgh, 1823), 355–68. She may have read it in one of its three appearances in American magazines.

108. "Died," *Cleveland Herald*, May 28, 1844.

109. "Died," *Vermont Watchman and State Journal* (Montpelier), November 27, 1845.

110. "Deaths," *Vermont Chronicle* (Bellows Falls), August 26, 1846.

111. Nicholas E. Tawa, *Sweet Songs for Gentle Americans: The Parlor Song in America, 1790–1860* (Bowling Green, Ohio, 1980), 15, 21.

112. Colin B. Atkinson and Jo B. Atkinson, "Changing Attitudes to Death: Nineteenth-Century Parlour Songs as Consolation Literature," *Canadian Review of American Studies* 23,2 (Winter 1993): 79–100.

113. *Alone* (New York, 1848).

114. *Leila Grey: A Ballad* (Boston, 1845); *When Stars Are in the Quiet Skies* (Baltimore, 1845); *The Burial of Mrs. Judson at St. Helena, Sep. 1, 1845* (Boston, 1846); *To Mary in Heaven* (Boston, 1846).

115. *The Willow Song; or, Voices from the Spirit Land* (Boston, 1847); *Voices from the Spirit Land* (Philadelphia, 1848).

116. S. R. Brown, *The Sister's Call: A Sacred Song*, 2nd ed. (New York, 1839).

117. Google Ngram Viewer, "Swedenborg," 1800–1850 (accessed November 29, 2017).

118. Robert Darnton, *Mesmerism and the End of the Enlightenment in France* (New York, 1970), 3–8; Eric T. Carlson, "Charles Poyen Brings Mesmerism to America," *Journal of the History of Medicine* 15,2 (April 1960): 121–32; Catherine L. Albanese, *A Republic of Mind and Spirit: A Cultural History of American Metaphysical Religion* (New Haven, Conn., 2007), 190–93; Emily Ogden, *Credulity: A Cultural History of U.S. Mesmerism* (Chicago, 2018), 90–99.

119. *St. Louis Magnet* 2 (1846).

120. Ernest Joseph Isaacs, "A History of Nineteenth-Century American Spiritualism as a Religious and Social Movement" (PhD diss., University of Wisconsin, 1975), 24.

121. R. H. Collyer, "Public Exhibitions" and "Introduction," *Mesmeric Magazine; or, Journal of Animal Magnetism* (Boston) 1,1 (July 1842): 14–15, 2. See also J. Stanley Grimes, *Etherology, and the Phreno-Philosophy of Mesmerism and Magic Eloquence*, rev. ed. (1845; Boston, 1850), ch. 15.

122. Isaacs, "History of Nineteenth-Century American Spiritualism," 55.

123. Andrew Jackson Davis, *The Principles of Nature, Her Divine Revelations, and a Voice to Mankind* (Boston, 1847), 43, 660. See also Albanese, *Republic of Mind and Spirit*, 209–14.

124. John C. Spurlock, *Free Love: Marriage and Middle-Class Radicalism in America, 1825–1860* (New York, 1988), 94.

125. Ann S. Stephens, "The Black Seal," *Ladies' Companion* (New York) 12,1 (November 1839): 18.

126. Edward Everett to Rev. C. W. Upham, Edward Everett Letters, MHS, July 22, 1838.

127. Edward Everett Diary, MHS, January 1, 1837, January 7, 1838.

128. On male expressions of grief in sentimental literature, see Mary Louise Kete, *Sentimental Collaborations: Mourning and Middle-Class Identity in Nineteenth-Century America* (Durham, N.C., 2000), 70; Jessica F. Roberts, "'The little coffin': Anthologies, Conventions, and Dead Children," in *Representations of Death in Nineteenth-Century U.S. Writing and Culture*, ed. Lucy E. Frank (Aldershot, Eng., 2007), 141–54.

129. One measure of men's lesser investment in mourning culture is the topic's near absence from histories of nineteenth-century fatherhood. Stephen M. Frank, *Life with Father: Parenthood and Masculinity in the Nineteenth-Century American North* (Baltimore, 1998), has

one paragraph on illness and death (79–80); Shawn Johansen, *Family Men: Middle-Class Fatherhood in Early Industrializing America* (New York, 2001), has a few pages (79–82).

130. Mary P. Ryan, *Cradle of the Middle Class: The Family in Oneida County, New York, 1790–1865* (New York, 1981), 77 (70 percent), 257 (63 percent is my calculation based on figures in Table C.2).

CONCLUSION

1. *Biography of Mrs. J. H. Conant, the World's Medium of the Nineteenth Century*, 2nd ed. (Boston, 1873), 18–19.

2. Ibid., 27.

3. Ann Braude, *Radical Spirits: Spiritualism and Women's Rights in Nineteenth-Century America*, 2nd ed. (1989; Bloomington, Ind., 2001), 25.

4. J. H. Crawford to Achsa Sprague, February 24, 1859. Quoted in ibid., 19.

5. *Oxford English Dictionary*, "séance," def. 2.

6. A stunning ethnography of one group of spiritists is Piers Vitebsky, *Living Without the Dead: Loss and Redemption in a Jungle Cosmos* (Chicago, 2017).

7. On the movement's anti-organizational tendencies, see Braude, *Radical Spirits*, ch. 7.

8. Letter to the editor, *Banner of Light*, September 15, 1860. Quoted in Molly McGarry, *Ghosts of Futures Past: Spiritualism and the Cultural Politics of Nineteenth-Century America* (Berkeley, 2008), 38.

9. The 750,000 figure, based on extrapolations from the U.S. census, is higher than the previous estimate of 620,000. J. David Hacker, "A Census-Based Count of the Civil War Dead," *Civil War History* 57,4 (December 2011): 307–48.

10. Drew Gilpin Faust, *This Republic of Suffering: Death and the American Civil War* (New York, 2008), 185.

11. Elizabeth Stuart Phelps, *The Gates Ajar* (1868; Boston, 1869), 9, 10, 15.

12. Ibid., 84–88.

13. See, for example, Nina Baym, ed., *Three Spiritualist Novels by Elizabeth Stuart Phelps* (Urbana, Ill., 2000); and Lisa A. Long, "'The Corporeity of Heaven': Rehabilitating the Civil War Body in *The Gates Ajar*," *American Literature* 69,4 (December 1997): 781–811, esp. 792–93.

14. Phelps, *Gates Ajar*, 89. Emphasis in original.

15. Sigmund Freud, *Totem and Taboo: Resemblances Between the Psychic Lives of Savages and Neurotics*, trans. A. A. Brill (1913; New York, 1918), 110.

16. Sigmund Freud, "Mourning and Melancholia," in *The Standard Edition of the Complete Psychological Works of Sigmund Freud*, trans. James Strachey, 24 vols. (London, 1953), 14:244 ("dejection," "libido"), 250 ("pathological").

17. Philippe Ariès, *The Hour of Our Death*, trans. Helen Weaver (New York, 1981), ch. 12 ("denial"). On continuing bonds, see Dennis Klass and Robert Goss, "Spiritual Bonds to the Dead in Cross-Cultural and Historical Perspective: Comparative Religion and Modern Grief," *Death Studies* 23,6 (September 1999): 548; and Catherine Seigal, *Bereaved Parents and Their Continuing Bonds: Love After Death* (London, 2017).

18. Dennis Klass, "Solace and Immortality: Bereaved Parents' Continuing Bond with Their Children," *Death Studies* 17,4 (July 1993): 345 ("presence"), 352 ("linking objects").

19. Ibid., 353.

20. Melissa D. Irwin, "Mourning 2.0: Continuing Bonds Between the Living and Dead on Facebook," *Omega: Journal of Death and Dying* 72,2 (December 2015): 119–50. See also Erin Willis and Patrick Ferrucci, "Mourning and Grief on Facebook: An Examination of Motivations for Interacting with the Deceased," *Omega: Journal of Death and Dying* 76,2 (December 2017): 122–40.

21. Irwin, "Mourning 2.0," 138, 137, 133, 136.

22. Pew Research Center, "Many Americans Mix Multiple Faiths," http://www.pewforum .org/2009/12/09/many-americans-mix-multiple-faiths (accessed December 15, 2017).

23. The Futon Critic, "Week of September 9, 2012," http://www.thefutoncritic.com/ratings /2012/09/11/sundays-cable-ratings-kardashians-long-island-medium-top-demos-viewers -529014/cable_20120909 (accessed December 15, 2017).

24. "Teenage Daughter Takes Responsibility for Her Death," *Long Island Medium*, November 5, 2017, https://www.youtube.com/watch?v=Iy6KXzx8fNs (accessed December 16, 2017).

INDEX

Adams, Abigail, 251–52
African Americans, 5, 53, 126, 139–46, 172, 274 n.11
Africans, 193, 210
Albany, New York, 104–7, 171, 235
Allen, Mary Ware, 243, 244, 256
All Hallows' Eve, 36
All Saints Day, 16
Amerindians, 5, 53, 57, 172, 193, 210, 274 n.11
Andrews, Ruth Barrell, 143
angels, 22–23, 82, 191, 212, 239, 252, 313 n.42; communication with, 108; at deathbeds, 155; in fiction, 222; as guides to heaven, 84, 136; visions of, 125–27, 159, 161–72, 181, 263–65. *See also* guardian angels; Moroni
Anglican Church. *See* Church of England
animal magnetism, 259
apostrophe, 46–50, 132, 254; in elegies, 49–50, 54, 62–63, 147, 248; in epitaphs, 74, 96, 100; in hymns, 208–9; in parlor songs, 257–58
apparitions. *See* ghosts
astral spirits, 27, 38, 132
atheism, 20, 22, 27, 110, 185. *See also* sadducism
Athenian Mercury, 36
Aubrey, John, 108
Augur, Hezekiah, 190–91
Ave Maria, 254
Ayer, Sarah Connell, 221–22

Backus, Isaac, 120
Bacon, Francis, 20, 111
Baconian methodology, 12, 20–21, 24–25, 112
ballads, 12, 25, 38, 150, 152
Baptists, 120, 159–60, 180, 208, 227, 230; in the cult of the dead, 216, 254. *See also* Freewill Baptists

baptizing the dead. *See* proxy baptism
Barbauld, Anna Letitia, 100–102
Barrow, Henry, 86
Baxter, Richard, 35–36, 81, 111, 123, 238
Beacon, Joseph, 29–32, 33–34, 123
beatific vision, 15, 68–69, 74, 80–81, 92, 97, 133, 162, 180
Beecher, Lyman, 215, 218
Beissel, Conrad, 183
Bekker, Balthasar, 26, 109
Bentley, William, 206, 210–11
Bible, 68, 84, 94, 201, 219, 250, 269; language of, 84, 245–46, 251; in the Protestant Reformation, 13, 238; use of in elegies, 145, 199, 201. *See also* King James Bible
Bishop, Rufus, 173, 175–76
Blair, Robert, 147
Bodin, Jean, 22
Book of Mormon, 181, 183
Booth, Ann, 181–82
Bosanquet, Mary, 316 n.91
Bradford, William, 70–71
Bradstreet, Anne, 62–64, 200, 284 n.73
Brewster, Martha, 84–85
broadsides, 146; and ballads, 25, 38, 150; and elegies, 9, 42–43, 53, 57–60, 65–69, 136, 147, 199; and visions, 5
Brothers, Richard, 166
Buell, Samuel, 80
Bunting, Hannah Syng, 221
Bunyan, John, 250
burial *ad familiares*, 186, 220, 222, 226–27, 247, 249–50
burial *ad sanctos*, 85–86, 220
burial grounds. *See* cemeteries
Burned-Over District, 180
Burroughs, George, 37–38
Byrd, William, II, 77

ACKNOWLEDGMENTS

I am deeply grateful to many individuals and institutions for giving me the intellectual and financial support that allowed me to write this book. I owe a debt of gratitude to my long-time employer, the University at Buffalo (UB), and its College of Arts and Sciences. Two sabbatical semesters—one at the start of the project, one toward the end—facilitated research and then writing. The university's history librarians, Charlie D'Aniello and Mike Kicey, purchased crucial databases and monographs; the Interlibrary Loan staff brought me microfilm and books from near and far. When I was director of UB's Humanities Institute, Dean Bruce Pitman supported my scholarship with a research fund. In my time at the Humanities Institute I learned more than I could have imagined from my amazing executive directors, Carrie Bramen and Libby Otto, and five cohorts of brilliant scholars. This book's endnotes are sprinkled with citations to works I learned about from anthropologists, literary scholars, and art historians.

In the project's early stages, three outstanding graduate student research assistants—Elisabeth Davis, Austin Mitchell, and Paul Zwirecki—gathered a vast array of sources. UB history Ph.D. Jake Newsome and Professor of Classics Neil Coffee helped with translations from German and Latin, respectively. Archivists in England and America—too many to name—helped me track down the primary sources that form the book's backbone. They also helped me find the illustrations that enliven my arguments. In particular I thank Andreane Balconi at the American Folk Art Museum in New York, who went out of her way to secure permission to use images of two objects in private collections; thanks as well to the objects' owners, David A. Schorsch and Amelia J. Zoler. Further aiding my research, treasured colleagues Adrian Weimer and Doug Winiarski sent me sources any time they ran across someone speaking with the dead. At a crucial stage, Adrian and Doug, along with Rick Pointer, read a draft book proposal. Rick's comments were particularly valuable in helping me see what the book was really about. Warm thanks to all three.

Once I started writing I benefited from the critical perspectives of numerous scholars. Sam Brown, Vin Carretta, Peter Marshall, Spencer McBride, Bob Orsi, Rich Veit, and Alex Walsham read chapters and offered valuable comments. Four workshops provided forums for receiving constructive suggestions. In Buffalo I presented two chapters to the Early Modern Research Workshop. Thanks to all my faculty and graduate student colleagues in that lively group. I will mention two for special recognition: Bob Daly, for his unmatched knowledge of puritan poetry, and Hal Langfur, who is about the best intellectual companion a person could hope for. I likewise presented two chapters to Rochester U.S. Historians (RUSH). I'm grateful to all participants, especially Paul Moyer, who gave one chapter the closest reading ever, and Alison Parker, the group's tireless organizer. I likewise thank the Omohundro Institute and the Early Modern Studies Institute for selecting me to participate in a *WMQ*-EMSI workshop at the Huntington Library titled "Religion in the Early Americas," where participants and audience members provided valuable suggestions for revision. Finally, at a late stage, friends and colleagues at the Massachusetts Historical Society's Boston Area Early American History Seminar, especially the commentator, Ken Minkema, pushed me to clarify my ideas about the cult of the dead. Many thanks to all for their time and expertise.

When I began to publish my findings, I benefited from the wisdom of scholars I wish I could thank directly: anonymous evaluators for journals. Some of my efforts resulted in publication and some did not, but the book is better for the input I received from all the editors and readers. I am grateful to the University of Pennsylvania Press for permission to reuse several paragraphs that first appeared in "Native Spirits, Shaker Visions: Speaking with the Dead in the Early Republic," *Journal of the Early Republic* (Fall 2015), and to Cambridge University Press for permission to republish material that appeared in "The Presence of the Dead Among U.S. Protestants, 1800–1848," *Church History* (June 2019).

At Penn Press I had the pleasure of working with Bob Lockhart for the second time. Bob is the ideal editor, willing to read chapters and offer suggestions with an eye toward clarity and the big picture. He also found two outside readers who offered incredibly helpful suggestions: Doug Winiarski and an anonymous scholar. The book owes its present form to their thoughtful, thorough readings of an overly long manuscript. They have my deep gratitude.

Two funerals while I was writing reminded me that powerful bonds of family shape all that I do. Those funerals, for my maternal grandparents, got me to think about speaking with the dead in new ways and allowed me to re-connect with relatives I hadn't seen in far too long. Extra warm thanks to Katie Rose Barany for sending me the audio file with my grandfather's voice and for allowing me to quote from her eulogy. Spending time during the funerals with my parents and brother in the place I grew up illuminated the crucial role they played and continue to play in my life. I owe them more than they could know. But I am most indebted to my daughters, for the gift of laughter, and my wife, Victoria Wolcott: best friend and historical fellow traveler.